Melvin M. Tumin

SOCIAL STRATIFICATION

the forms and functions of inequality

second edition

D1173392

PRENTICE-HALL FOUNDATIONS OF MODERN SOCIOLOGY SERIES

The
Lawrence Lee Pelletier
Library

Allegheny College

PRENTICE-HALL
FOUNDATIONS OF MODERN SOCIOLOGY SERIES
Alex Inkeles, Editor

WITHDRAWN

INDUSTRIAL SOCIOLOGY
Ivar Berg

INTRODUCTION TO SOCIAL RESEARCH, Second Edition
Ann Bonar Blalock/Hubert M. Blalock, Jr.

RACE AND ETHNIC RELATIONS
Hubert M. Blalock, Jr.

DEVIANCE AND CONTROL
Albert K. Cohen

MODERN ORGANIZATIONS
Amitai Etzioni

SOCIAL PROBLEMS
Amitai Etzioni

LAW AND SOCIETY: An Introduction
Lawrence M. Friedman

THE FAMILY, Second Edition
William J. Goode

SOCIETY AND POPULATION, Second Edition
David M. Heer

WHAT IS SOCIOLOGY? An Introduction to the Discipline and Profession
Alex Inkeles

GENDER ROLES AND POWER
Jean Lipman-Blumen

THE SOCIOLOGY OF SMALL GROUPS, Second Edition
Theodore M. Mills

SOCIAL CHANGE, Second Edition
Wilbert E. Moore

THE SOCIOLOGY OF RELIGION, Second Edition
Thomas F. O'Dea/Janet Aviad

THE EVOLUTION OF SOCIETIES
Talcott Parsons

FOUNDATIONS OF MODERN SOCIOLOGY, Fourth Edition
Metta Spencer/Alex Inkeles

SOCIAL STRATIFICATON: The Forms and Functions of Inequality, Second Edition
Melvin M. Tumin

WITHDRAWN

305
T831sa

second edition

SOCIAL STRATIFICATION
The forms and functions of inequality

MELVIN M. TUMIN
Department of Sociology
Princeton University

Prentice-Hall, Inc., Englewood Cliffs, New Jersey 07632

Library of Congress Cataloging in Publication Data

TUMIN, MELVIN MARVIN, 1919—
  Social stratification.
  (Prentice-Hall foundations of modern sociology series)

  Includes bibliographies and index.
  1. Social classes.   2. Equality.   I. Title.
II. Series.
HT609.T8 1985   305   84-17772
ISBN 0-13-818659-6

For Sylvia, Jonathan, and Zachary

Editorial/production supervision: Sylvia Moore
Manufacturing buyer: John Hall

© 1985, 1967 by Prentice-Hall, Inc., Englewood Cliffs, New Jersey 07632

All rights reserved. No part of this book may be
reproduced, in any form or by any means,
without permission in writing from the publisher.

Printed in the United States of America

10 9 8 7 6 5 4 3 2 1

ISBN 0-13-818659-6 01

Prentice-Hall International, Inc., *London*
Prentice-Hall of Australia Pty. Limited, *Sydney*
Editora Prentice-Hall do Brasil, Ltda., *Rio de Janeiro*
Prentice-Hall Canada Inc., *Toronto*
Prentice-Hall of India Private Limited, *New Delhi*
Prentice-Hall of Japan, Inc., *Tokyo*
Prentice-Hall of Southeast Asia Pte. Ltd., *Singapore*
Whitehall Books Limited, *Wellington, New Zealand*

CONTENTS

PREFACE   ix

CHAPTER   1
SOCIAL STRATIFICATION: FIVE BASIC CHARACTERISTICS   1

The Antiquity of Social Stratification   1
The Ubiquity of Stratification   2
The Social Patterning of Stratification   3
The Diversity of Form and Amount of Stratification   5
The Consequences of Stratification   6

CHAPTER   2
HISTORICAL AND CONTEMPORARY THOUGHT AND THEORY   8

From Plato to Marx   8   Karl Marx   11
Max Weber   12   Recent Americans   14

CHAPTER   3
HOW SOCIETIES GENERATE STRATIFICATION: DIFFERENTIATION AND RANKING OF STATUSES   19

CHAPTER   4
HOW SOCIETIES GENERATE STRATIFICATION: ASSESSING THE SOCIAL IMPORTANCE OF STATUSES   25

ALLEGHENY COLLEGE LIBRARY

86-8399

v

CHAPTER 5
**HOW SOCIETIES GENERATE STRATIFICATION: DIFFERENTIAL
REWARDING OF STATUSES   29**

CHAPTER 6
**BASIC ELEMENTS AND PROCESSES: VARIATIONS
IN SYSTEMS OF STRATIFICATION   36**

The Depth of Stratification   **36**
The Span of Stratification   **37**
Modes of Acquisition of Statuses   **37**
Emphasized Institutional Area   **39**
The Criteria That Determine Reward Level   **40**
Mobility   **41**   Types of Strata Formed   **42**
Distinctiveness of Strata   **42**
Class Consciousness and Solidarity   **43**
Summary: The Open Versus the Closed Society   **44**

CHAPTER 7
**PROPERTY: CONCEPTS, MEASUREMENTS,
AND PROBLEMS   48**

Measurements and Comparisons of Property   **50**
Property and Subjective Perceptions   **50**
Property and Reference Groups and Standards   **51**
Other Problems in Measuring Income   **52**
Measuring Inequality   **53**

CHAPTER 8
**PRESTIGE AND HONOR: CONCEPTS, MEASUREMENTS,
AND PROBLEMS   58**

Preferability and Popularity   **60**
Honor and Income   **61**
Honor, Power, and Deference   **61**
Congruence/Incongruence Among Income, Honor, and Power   **62**
The Social Patterning of Evaluation   **63**
Three Types of Evaluation of Statuses   **64**
The Universal Quest for Honor   **65**
Honor, Reference Groups, and Reference Standards   **65**
Reactions to Degradation   **66**   Self-Ghettoization   **66**
Convivialism and Connubialism: Tests of Equality of Honor   **66**
Honor and Life Style   **68**
Conspicuous Consumption and Status Seeking   **68**

CHAPTER 9

POWER: CONCEPTS, MEASUREMENTS, AND PROBLEMS 71

Five Sources of Power 71
Legitimate and Illegitimate Sources and Uses 72
Four Main Contexts of Power 72
The Patterning of Power: Equality and Inequality 74
Origins and Persistence of Inequality in Power 75
The Measurement of Power 75   Is There a Power Elite? 77
The Enjoyment of Power for its Own Sake: Power as a Reward 78
Variations in Power Distributions 80

CHAPTER 10

THE DEPTH OF INEQUALITY IN PROPERTY, PRESTIGE, POWER, AND EDUCATION 83

The Depth of Income Differences 84
The Depth of Prestige Differences 87
The Depth of Educational Differences 91

CHAPTER 11

THE SPAN OF CONSEQUENCES: LIFE CHANGES AND INSTITUTIONAL PATTERNS 96

Analyzing Causal Connections: Independent, Intervening,
    and Dependent Variables 96
Life Chances 100   Institutional Patterns 105

CHAPTER 12

THE SPAN OF CONSEQUENCES: LIFE STYLES AND BELIEFS, IDEOLOGIES, AND ATTITUDES 110

Life Styles 110
Beliefs, Ideologies, Values 113

CHAPTER 13

THE SHAPE OF STRATIFICATION SYSTEMS: FROM AGGREGATES TO CLASSES 119

Marx and Weber on Classes and Status Groups 120
Continuous Versus Discrete Variables 120
Combined SES Index 121
How Many Levels Should Be Distinguished? 122
Objective Versus Subjective Criteria 123

The Reputational Approach   124
Are There Classes in the United States?   125
From Statistical Aggregates to Solidary Classes   126
Mobility and ''False Consciousness''   126
Classes as Imperatively Coordinated Associations   127
The Absence of Marxist-Type Classes   128
The Shape of the System: Today and Tomorrow   129

CHAPTER   14
SOCIOECONOMIC MOBILITY: CONCEPTS, MEASURES,
TRENDS   132

What Kind of Mobility Should Be Studied?   134
Problems in Studying Mobility   135
Calculating Mobility   139
Other Uses of Mobility Tables   143
Some Generalizations About Mobility   144
Race and Mobility   145
Sex and Mobility   146
International Comparisons   148

CHAPTER   15
SOME THEORETICAL PROBLEMS   151

Is Stratification Inevitable?   153
Is Stratification Efficient? For Whom? For What?   154
Consequences of Inequality in Property for a Society   158
Why is Stratification So Widespread?   159

INDEX   163

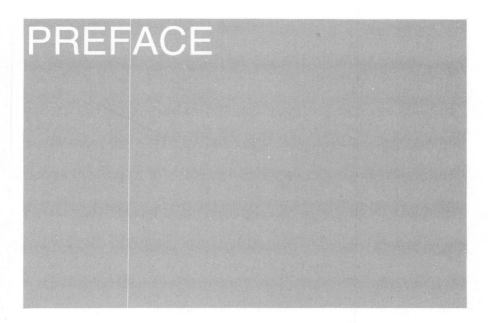

PREFACE

Some form and amount of inequality in property, prestige and power are found in all societies of the world today, and, as far as we can tell, such inequality has been characteristic of all past societies as well. Much if not most of the inequality in any society is socially patterned; that is, it is governed by laws and norms. The amount and type of inequality is also consequential, both for whole societies and for the individual members of those societies. People who are unequal in property, power, and prestige also differ in their life chances, their institutional patterns of conduct, their life styles or culture patterns, and in their attitudes, ideologies, and beliefs.

The antiquity and universality of patterned inequality, or social stratification, suggest that there are common features in all societies that generate and sustain it. At the same time, societies differ considerably in the depth, span, and shape of their systems of stratification. Today's societies range, for instance, from extreme inequality, such as is found in the caste systems of South Africa and India, to something approaching total equality, as in the case of the socialist kibbutzim, or agricultural communes, in the state of Israel. The modern welfare states in the Western capitalist democracies lie somewhere between those two extremes.

The fact that social stratification is ancient, universal, patterned, diverse, and consequential makes it a matter of great interest to sociologists. They are concerned with exploring the origins, forms, and consequences of such inequality and with the processes that tend to sustain and those that tend to produce changes in systems of stratification.

Nothing that sociologists can reveal about these aspects of patterned inequality can prove that they are per se good or bad, helpful or harmful. Such judgments are in the realm of "values," and, as such, they fall outside the area where facts can be decisive. But policy makers and others concerned with the well-being of societies and their people can be materially aided in their judgments by an understanding of how inequalities arise, how they are sustained, how they change over time, and what are their consequences for a range of social and personal goals. It is the aim of this book to contribute to such an understanding.

The present volume is a greatly revised version of the original book which appeared in 1967. New concepts have been introduced; significant changes in emphasis have been effected; the empirical data have been brought up to date insofar as the available research has made it possible; and relevant theoretical literature that has appeared since 1967 has been taken into account.

In preparing this revision I have been assisted by a number of people. Professor Meng Chee Lee, now of the University of Singapore, prepared a very useful critical evaluation of the first edition and brought my attention to new data. Michelle Gambone, doctoral candidate at Princeton, has helped greatly in compiling new empirical materials and she is also responsible for the index. Michael Simpson and David Woolwine, doctoral candidates at Princeton, have also helped considerably in bringing empirical findings up to date. Blanche Anderson has been wonderfully adept at translating my manuscript into legible final copy. Cindy Gibson has contributed in many important ways to the production of the manuscript. I am grateful to all these people.

CHAPTER 1
SOCIAL STRATIFICATION
Five Basic Characteristics

Three of the good things in life that are everywhere both scarce and desired are property, or rights over goods and services; power, or the ability to secure one's way in life even against opposition; and prestige, or social honor. In all societies in the past and in all societies today, people at different levels receive unequal amounts of these three classes of good things. In effect, in all societies there is a hierarchy of positions, or groups of positions, called strata (singular, stratum) that are set off from each other by the amount of property, power, and honor they command. To that condition, where societies are arranged into hierarchies of positions or strata that command unequal amounts of property, power, and honor, we give the term stratification.

There are, of course, other good things in life that are distributed unequally among the people of a society. One might think of a miscellaneous class of things called *psychic gratifications,* including love, security, peace of mind, optimism about the future, sense of self-worth, and that vague thing called happiness. Inequalities in these matters are rightfully included in the study of stratification if it can be shown that they, too, are scarce and desired and that they result from inequalities in property, power, and prestige.

The phenomenon of stratification properly commands much attention from sociologists because of five important characteristics it exhibits. It is (1) ancient; (2) ubiquitous; (3) socially patterned; (4) diverse; and (5) it has far-reaching consequences. Each of these features now deserves further comment.

THE ANTIQUITY OF SOCIAL STRATIFICATION

According to historical and archaeological records, stratification was present even in the small wandering bands that characterized society in the earliest days of man. In such primitive conditions both age and sex, in combination with physical strength, must have been important criteria of stratification. *Women and children last* was probably the dominant rule of order.

Reliable written historical records date from several thousand years ago. Such records tell us, whether we speak of the ancient Babylonians, Persians, Hebrews, or Greeks, that *nobility* of descent was a matter of great consequence; that there were rich and poor, powerful and humble, freemen and slaves; and that such hierarchical arrangements were the natural order of things, particularly, of course, to those at the top of the hierarchies.

So, too, in the better documented periods, starting about two thousand years ago, when the idea was widespread that a social hierarchy was a natural and unavoidable feature of social life. This was true in China, India, and Africa, as well as in Europe and in the New World. Similarly, among the ancient American Indian kingdoms there were nobles and commoners—a few who had many of the world's goods and many who had few of these goods. The poor and powerless deferred to, obeyed, and served the few who were powerful and rich and were believed to be of superior origin.

Such arrangements and rearrangements by which certain selected portions of a population come to enjoy disproportionate amounts of property, power, and prestige have always characterized human history.

THE UBIQUITY OF STRATIFICATION

Today, serious expressions of discontent with the prevailing modes of distributing goods and services mark the entire world. The discontent is, of course, eloquent testimony to its presence. On one level the nations of the world constitute a worldwide system of stratification: the "haves" versus the "have-nots." And *within* every nation, including all the so-called socialist countries, stratification is also to be found.

Stratification is also present in nonliterate societies, whose traditions are largely oral and for whom the technological features of a civilization based on writing, science, and discovery are, as yet, only of tangential importance. For instance, among the Bushmen, who hunt, gather their food, and live in bands of from fifty to one hundred people, each of which is self-governing, stratification is present though in very rudimentary forms; hence, no strata in the ordinary sense are found. There are, however, socially prescribed inequalities between men and women and between adults and children. Although it is important to differentiate between systems where stratification is based primarily on age and sex and those which depend on other criteria, it is equally important to note the universality of some form of socially structured and sanctioned inequality of power, property, and prestige.

THE SOCIAL PATTERNING OF STRATIFICATION

The Significance of Social Definitions

Although differences in such factors as strength, intelligence, age, and sex can serve as bases on which positions are distinguished, such differences are never by themselves sufficient to explain why some receive more power, property, and prestige than others. Biological traits do not become relevant in patterns of social superiority and inferiority until they are socially recognized and given importance by being incorporated into the beliefs, attitudes, and values of the human beings involved. The old and physically weak but wise man of noble descent is, therefore, as likely to be chief as the young, strong warrior of less noble descent. So, too, the manager of an industrial plant normally attains this dominant position, not by physically fighting his way to the top, but by having the socially defined right kind and amount of education, training, skills, personality, character, and the like. The determination of who is the fittest and who is the most entitled to enjoy larger amounts of property and power is always part of a complex social and cultural pattern, often having little to do with biological traits per se.

The Significance of Norms and Sanctions

The social-pattern aspect of stratification also suggests that the distribution of rewards in any community is governed by norms, that is, conventional rules. At any given moment the norms are likely to reflect the interests of those who have enough power to enforce the rules they deem best. In virtually every community one finds that most persons conform to such rules, even though they are at the lowest rungs of the ladder of stratification and are deprived of all but the most meager portion of the good things of life. Such acceptance of the way of life by even the most demeaned and deprived segments of a population testifies to the strength and durability of the norms once they are established and once the ruling groups are believed to have control over the sanctions required to enforce the rules.

The Need to Socialize Each Generation

A third implication of the social aspect of stratification concerns the way in which the norms of the community are carried down from generation to generation. There is no evidence that any kind of mentality—slave, ruling, or otherwise—is biologically inherited. To the contrary, all the evidence indicates that every child has to be taught the rules of his group. The adults, for their part, obey and conform because they fear earthly or divine punishment, or have a simple belief in the rightness of things as they are, or are incapable of imagining that things could be different. In turn children learn to obey partly because they are required to believe in the rightness of their parents' views and they fear punishment or desire rewards from their parents, or because they themselves cannot see or imagine alternatives. In short, social transmission or socialization into the norms from one generation to the next is indispensable to the continuity of these norms. Every society must be recreated anew at the birth of each child. No set of social patterns has any greater permanence than that given to it by the patterns of transmission from adult to child, which are technically called the processes of socialization.

The Inherent Instability of Social Arrangements

If norms have stability and continuity because of the socialization process and the sanctions that ensure conformity, they are also unstable and discontinuous partly because that process and those sanctions never work perfectly. They are always uneven in their effectiveness from one family to the next and from one generation to the next. For this reason, among others, every system of stratification is continuously changing.

A second source of inherent instability in systems of stratification results from the differences in the birth rates of various strata. If members of the ruling class fail to have enough competent children to fill adequately the traditional ruling roles, then some of the sons and daughters of nonelite origins will probably be recruited for these positions. This failure to produce enough adequate substitutes becomes especially acute when a society is growing and expanding.

The Connections of Stratification with Other Institutions

To say that stratification is *social* also implies that the system of stratification is always connected with other aspects of a society. We speak of such connections as institutional interdependencies or institutional interrelationships, and we mean that the existing stratification arrangements are affected by and have effects upon such other matters as politics, kinship, marriage and the family, economics, education, and religion.

An example of the connections of stratification with politics is the phenomenon of the inheritance of power, by which the sons of the ruling elite succeed their parents at the socially defined appropriate time.

The connections of stratification with economics are illustrated by the fact that the decisions as to what goods will be manufactured, what services will be provided, what salaries or wages will be paid, and what work conditions will be are often made by those who either control the capital required to implement these decisions (as in the United States) or command the political power controlling these decisions (as in the Soviet Union) or both. By such linkages the structure and function of the economy are closely interwoven with the system of stratification.

In sum, we say stratification is socially patterned because

1. The makeup of any system of stratification is dependent upon conventionally ascribed meanings and socially defined criteria and prescriptions.
2. Norms and sanctions are key ingredients in the shaping and maintenance of the system.
3. The norms have to be taught anew to each generation.
4. Any system is likely to be unstable, at least to some degree, because socialization is never identical throughout the society and because of other disturbing factors, such as differential rates of birth for different strata.
5. Any system of stratification is intimately connected, both as affector and affected, with other systems in the society, such as political, familial, religious, economic, and educational institutions.

Such social patterning leads to the practice of adding the adjective *social* to the noun *stratification* so that the phenomenon most often gets called *social stratification*. It should be understood, however, that by that term we refer to economic inequalities in goods and services; political inequalities in terms of power; and that special part of social inequality called prestige or honor.

THE DIVERSITY OF FORM AND AMOUNT OF STRATIFICATION

We have previously alluded to the diversity in both the forms and amount of stratification. So far as amount is concerned, the theoretical possibilities stretch from one extreme, where all statuses would be considered entitled to equal amounts of power, property, and prestige, to the other extreme, where each and every status would be assigned unequal amounts. No society has existed at either of these theoretical extremes, though a society such as traditional India, with its more than five thousand subcastes, approaches the extreme of total inequality; and the agricultural communal cooperatives in Israel, the *kibbutzim,* approach the extreme of total equality.

The diversity in amount of stratification found in societies of the past and present is matched by diversity in *form.* Here too, such terms as *class, caste,* and *estate* are useful to express the different ways in which strata can be arranged, degrees of sharpness of distinction among strata, chances to change one's stratum, and degrees of legal recognition of strata as entities.

Class, caste, and estate are very general terms. Although all systems of the world could be classified under them, we need many other terms to distinguish more adequately the varying forms of class and caste systems that exist in the world today. Thus, while the relations between Blacks and Whites in the United States have some rather castelike characteristics, it is also true that many class elements are present. The same observation about the mixture of types would have to be made regarding modern India. And still other terms would be required to characterize adequately the kinds of stratification systems we find in the Soviet and East European societies or the complex social arrangements found in Latin American countries, with their mixtures of primitive, peasant, and industrial life and their confluences of traditional and modern criteria of stratification.

THE CONSEQUENCES OF STRATIFICATION

The consequences that flow from inequalities in property, power, and prestige can be classified under four general headings: (1) Life Chances; (2) Institutional Patterns of Conduct; (3) Life Styles; and (4) Values, Attitudes, and Ideologies.

Life Chances

Life chances refer to the probabilities that one will enjoy (or fail to enjoy) a range of opportunities, achievements, and satisfying experiences during the course of one's life. These include such things as infant survival; having good physical and mental health; the opportunity to go to school for the number of years one's talents permit; acquiring socially valued and well-paid skills; having a chance at a range of desirable occupations; earning a decent income; being able to exert a respectable amount of influence over the political affairs of one's community and nation; having a satisfying degree of control over the course of one's own life; enjoying social honor; experiencing improvement in one's material well-being; and living to advanced years. Life chances, then, refer to the most important opportunities, achievements, and experiences in life.

Institutional Patterns of Conduct

The term *institutional patterns of conduct* refers to the patterns of behavior of everyday life in all the basic institutions of society: the economy, the political system, the educational network, the family, and religion, among others. Sociologists are interested in how inequalities in property, power, and honor influence these patterns of conduct. Do people in different income groups raise their children differently? If they do, why do they do so? Do they resolve their family quarrels in different ways? Or monitor their children's education differently? Institutional patterns, therefore, refer to the most fundamental affairs of daily life throughout the course of one's life.

Life Styles

The term *life style* refers to the ways in which people use their disposable energy, time, and resources to lay claim to certain levels of honor that they believe are due them and that they consider desirable and acceptable. How do they dress and do their hair? What kinds of autos do they purchase? How do they decorate their homes? What is their style of visiting and entertainment? What forms of recreation and leisure activities do they pursue? What are their special modes of address and greeting? What media do they read, listen to, or watch? To what organizations do they belong? What are their patterns of speech and gesture? These are the kinds of activities that comprise life style and that often help to distinguish people at different levels of social acceptability and honor.

Values, Attitudes, and Ideologies

The terms *values, attitudes,* and *ideologies* refer to sets of beliefs about, and orientations to, such questions as the following: What defines a good society? What are the ingredients of a good personal life? What is the proper relationship between the individual and society? How much freedom and what kind should people have? How much, if anything, does the system owe to those who do not prosper on their own? Can one trust others? Can one expect others to come to one's aid in times of need? Is it worthwhile to bring children into the world today?

Answers to some of these questions are among the most fundamental belief systems; they refer to crucial issues of public policy and personal conduct.

To the extent that people in different stratified positions enjoy different life chances, engage in different forms of institutional conduct, exhibit different life styles, and affirm different values, attitudes, and ideologies, the system of stratification is obviously a most consequential feature of a society.

CHAPTER 2
HISTORICAL AND CONTEMPORARY THOUGHT AND THEORY

Since ancient times social philosophers have been deeply concerned with economic, social, and political inequalities. They have theorized about the naturalness, permanence, and inevitability of such inequalities and have also asked whether they were good for any social purpose. These are still leading questions of students of social stratification today. It will pay, therefore, to survey briefly what thinkers through the ages have had to say about these and related matters.[1]

FROM PLATO TO MARX

For Plato a new society involved not only the implementation of justice but also the provision for social stability and internal discipline. It was with these features in mind that he dreamed of a society ruled by philosopher kings. The society that Plato envisioned was explicitly meant to be class-structured, so that all citizens would belong to one of three classes: the Guardians, the Auxiliaries, or the Workers. The Guardians were to be subdivided into ruling and nonruling groups. To each of these major strata, separate and definite functions were assigned.

Plato sensed that those most suited for ruling—the role of the Guardian class—might be born to parents of the two other classes. Accordingly, he eliminated any possibility of inheritance of class status and provided for perfect equality of opportunity for all children regardless of birth, so that each would have an equal chance to manifest natural qualities and be trained to fulfill his or her proper role in life. If such a selection and training process could be made to work perfectly, then, according to Plato, there would be justification for giving the Guardians absolute power. Mindful too of the possibly corrupting influence of family sentiments, Plato proposed the abolition of the family within the Guardian group and insisted that its members ''must not possess any private property beyond the barest necessities,'' so that they would not be tempted to institute policies protecting their property interests and instead would be able to focus on communal welfare.

Plato has obviously proposed a highly stratified society in which, however, total equality of opportunity, total elimination of private property, and single-minded concern for the common welfare are the distinguishing features of the ruling class.

Aristotle's *Politics* is no less significant a document in the history of ideas about social inequality.

> Now in all states there are three elements: one class is very rich, another very poor, and a third is a mean. It is admitted that moderation and the mean are best, and therefore it will clearly be best to possess the gifts of fortune in moderation; for in that condition of life men are most ready to follow rational principle. But he who greatly excels in beauty, strength, birth, or wealth, or on the other hand is very poor, or very weak, or very much disgraced, finds it difficult to follow rational principle. Of these two the one sort grow into violent and great criminals, the others into rogues and petty rascals.[2]

Aristotle was clearly concerned with the consequences of inequality in birth, strength, and wealth for the maintenance of decent government and the constitution of a wise and moderate population. Modern inquiries into the relationship of social stratification to politics, such as studies of the voting behavior of different classes, are concerned with similar problems.

St. Thomas and St. Augustine were equally intent on prescribing the proper mode of arranging men in hierarchical orders and also in understanding why human society *everywhere* was characterized by such distinct gradations in power, property, and prestige. In *The City of God,* Augustine wrote of the miserable and the poor as follows:

> Inasmuch as they are deservedly and justly miserable, they are by their very misery connected with order. . . . They would . . . be more wretched if they had not that peace which arises from being in harmony with the natural order of things.[3]

Nearly two thousand years separate Aristotle and Machiavelli, but the range of concerns expressed by the former remain central in the thinking of the Italian Renaissance genius. Machiavelli asked *who* is fit to rule, and what *form* of rule will produce order, happiness, prosperity, and strength. He saw tension between the elite and the masses as a constant feature of organized society; such tension is accompanied by fear of the masses among the elite, and envy and fear of tyranny among the masses. But Machiavelli saw more virtue in democratic rule than did many previous philosophers, since he believed that the collective decisions of the people are likely to display more wisdom than the decision of princes. He said in his *Discourses*:

> As to the people's capacity of judging things, it is exceedingly rare that, when they hear two orators of equal talents advocate different measures, they do not decide in favor of the best of the two; which proves their ability to discern the truth of what they hear. And if occasionally they are misled in matters involving questions of courage or seeming utility, so is a prince also many times misled by his own passions, which are much greater than those of the people.[4]

Machiavelli also had numerous doubts about the rationality of the masses and believed that they tend to behave emotionally and need long training in popular rule: Selection for ruling positions is most effective if those most naturally suited for such positions have equal opportunity to be discovered, recruited, and trained. Here, in short, Machiavelli announced a notion of an "open society," commonly advocated today, one in which inequality in *situation* is legitimate and desirable so long as there has been equality of *opportunity* to become unequal. Without such equality of opportunity most of the available talent in any generation will be lost.

With Thomas Hobbes a whole new vision of humanity entered into the realm of political discourse. For Hobbes, more than any of his predecessors, was persuaded that there was a fundamental equality among all. The natural implication, as Hobbes saw it, is that equality must take the place of inequality in power and privilege. Hobbes saw all men as equally interested in acquiring power and privilege and equally insatiable in their desires for the good things of life. Their simultaneous striving for power and privilege must surely lead to a chaotic condition, unless there is a set of rules by which they agree to abide. These rules constitute a "social contract" under whose terms the people unanimously and willingly turn over their right to rule to one man who embodies their collective desires and will. In turn, the sovereign is restricted in his role by a body of laws deriving from the Natural Law and, of course, from the consent of the governed. If a minority refuse to engage in such a contract with their sovereign, they are nevertheless, according to Hobbes, bound by the will of the majority.

In this "ideal" society, no privileged classes are allowed, since they will corrupt the equality of rule provided by the sovereign. And the sovereign may be removed if he fails to govern so as to protect equally the safety of all.

Later social philosophers—including Locke, Burke, and Bentham among the English, Rousseau among the French, and Hegel among the Germans—were all aware that the emergence of social classes or strata, based either on inherent differences, acquired differences, or some combination of both, may present urgent problems. Each had his own notion as to what structure of government would deal most efficaciously with such difficulties.

By the turn of the nineteenth century, popular revolutions had begun. The old order of aristocratic rule was crumbling everywhere in Europe, and the new American Republic was demonstrating an unexpected capacity for growth and development. Theories about the natural rights of oligarchs were everywhere being challenged by competing theories about the natural rights of all men to an equal share in the good things in life. The industrialization of society in Western Europe was, moreover, proceeding rapidly. With it there emerged the kinds of social classes, based on wealth and power, that resemble those of today.

KARL MARX

No one in the history of social thought has made the struggle between competing social and economic classes so central a feature of society and so dominant a source of social change as did Karl Marx. And no set of ideas has had such an enduring effect as those advanced by Marx more than one hundred years ago.

"The history of all hitherto existing societies," Marx declared with great vigor in the opening of his famous *Communist Manifesto*," is the history of class struggles."

How do classes arise? According to Marx, classes develop on the basis of the different positions or roles which individuals fulfill in the productive scheme of a society. The key concepts for Marx are the modes of production—such as agriculture, handicraft, or industrialism—and the relations of production—the major status roles and their relationships in the economic enterprise. In an agricultural world the principal statuses are landowner and serf, or tenant and slave; in a handicraft economy, guildmaster and apprentice, or entrepreneur and home worker; in an industrial situation, the capitalist owner of the factories is pitted against the nonowning worker.

A crucial term in these relationships is that of "versus" or "against." As Marx saw it, men in different relations to the means of production naturally have opposed interests. In bourgeois capitalist society, those who own the factories have a vested interest in maximizing profit and seek to keep for themselves the surplus or profit which has been created by the worker. Naturally the worker resents this "exploitation." But the capitalist class, by virtue of its economic power, is able to control the power of the state and to use it to block any effective expression of discontent by the workers.

The capitalist owners secure even more effective control over the economy and its products when the workers are fragmented and disorganized, or when they are unaware of the sources of their debased situation, so that they do not actively seek to remove the causes of their distress.

A key notion here is that workers constitute a class without necessarily being aware that they do so, or without necessarily taking any collective action on the basis of their common membership in the class. But they do constitute a class, according to Marx, on two *objective* grounds: (1) their common economic situation vis-a-vis the instruments of production, and (2) their relatively uniform powerlessness in the face of state power that is used to frustrate their expressions of discontent. This notion of the *objectivity* of class existence is a distinguishing feature of the Marxist approach to the study of stratification. The Marxist approach is also distinctive in its emphasis on the power of the economic factor—the ability of the relations of production to shape and determine the total social situation. Though acknowledging the contributions of ideology and style of life, Marx insisted that property is the fundamental determinant or *substructure*, while the status of *superstructure* or "derivative" is assigned to ideologies, cultural modes, forms of family life, educational processes, and other such factors that may, and often do, reinforce the differences initially generated by differences in property.

Three other terms are important in the Marxist approach to the study of stratification: class consciousness, class solidarity, and class coflict.

Class consciousness refers to the recognition by a class, such as workers, of the role its members play in the productive process, and of their relations to the owning class. Consciousness also involves an awareness of the extent to which the owning class exploits the working class by depriving the workers of a fair share of the "surplus value" created by their work. A final stage of consciousness is reached when the working class understands that only by unified action to overthrow the capitalist owners can the workers hope to achieve their due.

Class solidarity refers to the extent to which workers act together to achieve political and economic aims.

Class conflict has two aspects: (1) the unconscious struggle between workers and capitalists for shares in the productive output at a time when class consciousness is not well developed, and (2) the conscious and deliberate struggle between the two classes that occurs when the workers become aware of their historic role and act collectively to improve their situation, and ultimately, to take over ownership of the instruments of production.

For Marx it was inevitable that under the "proper" circumstances, i.e., when workers did not feel hopeless or were not beguiled by religious promises of a rich afterlife, they would develop an awareness of their situation and would act collectively upon it. But because Marx perceived that workers frequently did not achieve the requisite awareness, he advanced the notion of "false consciousness," which led workers to act as though they did not have to overthrow capitalism to achieve their "due." Any form of accommodation to and acceptance of capitalism by workers Marx called "false consciousness."

MAX WEBER

Most of modern sociological research and writing about stratification combines some aspects of Marxist thought with some of the ideas of Max Weber, a distinguished German social historian, economist, and sociologist, whose major work was done in the first quarter of the twentieth century.

Weber agreed with certain fundamental features of Marxist thought, particularly with the crucial significance of the economic aspects of stratification. For Weber, as for Marx, control over property was a basic fact in the determination of the life-chances of an individual or a class. In contrast to Marx, however, Weber added to the economic dimension of stratification two other dimensions, *power* and *prestige*. Weber saw property, power, and prestige as three separate though inter-acting bases on which hierarchies are created in any society. Property differences generate *classes*; power differences generate *political parties*; and prestige differences generate *status groupings* or *strata*.

Marx and Weber differ on the question of how likely it is that members of the same economic class will constitute members of a "community"—a group of persons united by common purposes which they seek to achieve through united effort. Weber also differs from Marx about the probability that workers will "rise" to such "true" class consciousness and unite for common class struggle against the system that exploits them. This action will take place, Weber said, when the contrast in life chances is *not* accepted by the worker as inevitable, and when he sees the contrast as a result of the distribution of property and the economic structure of society.

Weber recognized that many kinds of class actions are possible, only some of which seek to change the basic forms of the prevailing system of property relations. Marx, too, showed this awareness when he spoke of workers acting with false consciousness, and acting in ways that fall short of trying to overthrow the existing system of property ownership.

Weber is the more sophisticated sociologist by modern standards in the extent to which he recognized the conditions necessary for the formation of communities. He says quite explicitly that while economic classes do not normally constitute communities, status groups do. Status groups are formed on the basis of common amounts of socially ascribed prestige or honor. And whereas differences in property can constitute the basis for differences in honor or prestige, other factors are often just as important, if not more so. Usually, Weber says, status stands in sharp opposition to the pretensions of property. Both the propertied and the propertyless can, and frequently do, belong to the same status group.

As distinguished from the consequences of property differences for life chances, status differences, according to Weber, lead to differences in *life styles* which form an important element in the social exclusiveness of various status groups. Status groups acquire honor primarily by usurpation. They claim certain rewards and act out their claims in terms of certain manners and styles of behavior and certain socially exclusive activities. And while status groups do not usually rest on any legal basis in modern societies, corresponding legal privileges are not long in developing once the status groups stabilize their positions by securing economic power. In short, along with Marx, Weber recognized the essential significance of property differences in the formation of status groups and in the ultimate hardening of the lines of distinction and privilege among them. He differed from Marx in the importance that he ascribed to status groups and in the lesser likelihood that he assigned to the development by members of an economic class of a sense of community and a commonly felt need for concerted action against the system.

The third form of association to which Weber gave prominence is the party. Though economic classes, status groups, and political parties are all "phenomena of the distribution of power within a community," according to Weber, parties differ from classes and status groups in several crucial ways. While the central significance of classes is economic, and that of status groups is honor, "'parties' live in a house of 'power.'" Parties are only possible within communities that have some rational order and "a staff of persons who are ready to enforce it. For parties aim precisely at influencing this staff, and, if possible, to recruit it from party followers."[5]

Weber saw an intimate relationship between classes, status groups, and parties. He described it as follows:

> . . . parties may represent interests determined through "class situation" or "status situation" and they may recruit their following, respectively, from one or the other. But they need be neither purely "class" nor purely "status" parties, and frequently they are neither.[6]

In sum, what we have in Weber's approach is a view of society containing three kinds of social aggregations, differing in degree of self-conscious unity and commonality of purpose, and differing in the particular aspect of social reward or resource with which they are primarily concerned. Thus we have the economic focus of classes, the honor basis of status groups, and the power center for parties. These often have overlapping memberships, and sometimes under special circumstances, the economic class is virtually identical with the status group and the political party. But this is only one of many possibilities.

RECENT AMERICANS

One can easily see the impact of Marx and Weber on the thinking and writing of some of the outstanding students of stratification in American sociological ranks. Perhaps the most prominent early name in this field is Robert Lynd. Lynd's *Middletown*, published in 1930, is the first major work in American sociology to analyze a "typical" American community in terms of the impact of economic power on the political, social, educational, and religious insitutions of the community. There are generous admixtures of both Marxian and Weberian thought in Lynd's approach.

Another outstanding American student of stratification is W. Lloyd Warner, whose "Yankee City" series of studies launched the empirical study of stratification in American sociology. Warner follows the Weberian emphasis on honor or status groups and attempts to understand American communities in terms of the ways in which the various segments of the community associate with each other, primarily on the basis of real or assumed equality of social standing. He and his students have devoted considerable effort to discovering how Americans of differing social and economic situations view each other; on what basis they rank each other; on what criteria they associate or refrain from associating with each other.

More than anyone else, Warner has been responsible for the emphasis in American studies of stratification on reputation and prestige. He sought to develop an Index of Status Characteristics, based on such criteria as occupation, residence, income, and house style, which he believed Americans use to estimate each other's social worthiness and by which, accordingly, they guide themselves in choosing who will be their friends and with whom they will permit their children to associate.

In sharp contrast to Marx, Warner relied more on "subjective" criteria of stratification, i.e., how the members of a community view their situations, than on the "objective" differences between them, such as income. This greater reliance on subjective factors recalls the Weberian doctrine that status groups are not coterminous or identical with economic classes.

Warner's influence, aside from the spread of the methods of research in which he pioneered, has chiefly been to convey a view of American society as stratified by classes that consist of persons who enjoy the same prestige rating. Because he believed that classes are formed on these estimates of prestige, Warner postulated the existence of a six-class structure in America, as against the more common two-class or three-class system, so that, in the typical Warnerian study, we find reference to the upper-upper and the lower-upper classes, the upper-middle and the lower-middle classes, and the upper-lower and the lower-lower classes.

A third major influence on American studies of stratification has been C. Wright Mills. In *The Power Elite* Mills argued that *power* is the key concept in social relations, and effective power, at least in American society, derives from advantageous economic positions. The economic elite, Mills asserted, joins with the military elite (the military high command) to form a power elite that views itself as a privileged group and that sees interests as paramount to and as distinct from those not of the elite. American social, economic, and political policy tends to reflect, said Mills, the joint decisions of these three elites, who form various combinations, with varying degrees of influence distributed among them, depending on the issue at stake.

The close connection between economic and political power, it will be recalled, was claimed by both Marx and Weber and was elaborated and analyzed in a particular community by Lynd. With the further impetus given by Mills' writings, this has come to be an approach to stratification that often stands in sharp opposition to Warner's "reputational" approach. Yet almost no student of stratification today relies alone on such objective indices as income and education, or on such subjective indices as imputed honor or prestige. Most empirical studies of stratification employ some elements of both objective and subjective measures. There is no consensus among American sociologists that the social strata or classes in America consist of strictly economic interest groups, or of status groups, or of political interest groups.

In the mainstream of thinking and theorizing about stratification is the work of Talcott Parsons, one of the leading interpreters of Max Weber and an influential theorist in his own right. Parsons believes the essence of stratification in any society to be the relative moral evaluation enjoyed by different social units. As for the

ALLEGHENY COLLEGE LIBRARY

criteria by which this evaluation is determined, Parsons leans heavily in the Warnerian direction and he takes subjective judgments by others as the basis of the formation of strata of social units or statuses. He follows Warner in arguing that property is only one of the many possible bases of evaluation. He also develops Weber's implicit notions about the imperativeness of stratification by noting that moral judgment and evaluation of all action is a *sine qua non* of all societies, since societies are by definition organizations of activities around common purposes and values; hence a distinction must always be made between that which is better and that which is worse, in terms of the agreed-upon ends and values of the society. Thus those members of the society who exemplify the most valued qualities or perform the most valued functions are likely to receive the highest ranking. Parsons then develops a classification of the conditions under which one set of qualities or performances is likely to be valued more highly than others. These conditions are put in terms of the main "thrust" of a given society—whether the society focuses on achieving desired ends, or emphasizes the need for cohesion and integration. The kind and degree of stratification is thus explained by Parsons in terms of other major features of the society, and hence represents a series of hypotheses of the most general and most widely applicable kind.

Equilibrium versus Conflict Theories

Parsons may be said to be the progenitor of the school of thought called "functionalism," sometimes also called the "equilibrium school." Starting with the famous article by Kingsley Davis and Wilbert Moore, called "Some Principles of Stratification,"[7] the members of this school of thought have tried to explain how stratification gets developed and endures by specifying the "functions" that stratification, or patterned inequality, plays in any society. They see such inequality as inevitably arising out of the requirement that societies decide what tasks they consider most important. Given this decision, it follows, say these theorists, that those persons who possess the scarce talents needed for effective performance of these most valued functions must be given unequal amounts of property, power, and honor to induce them to take on the training required for those tasks, and to motivate them to perform them conscientiously. Inequality is thus seen as both rational and efficient.

This line of thought has evoked much criticism, particularly from those who believe that the shape of any society is determined primarily by those who have the power—economic, social, and political—to decide which tasks shall be emphasized and how the rewards the society has to offer shall be distributed. Advocates of this view also point to the way in which the inequalities in any one generation are passed on, through family inheritance, to the following generation, without much regard to the "rationality" or "effectiveness" of such transmitted inequality. The system of social stratification is thus seen as one which is put and kept in place by the exercise of power, and which generates conflict and instability rather than equilibrium and stability. The unequal distribution of the good things—

property, power, and prestige—is seen as constituting a set of privileges enjoyed by a small elite who make it difficult if not impossible for many others to enjoy a fair share of the good things.

Perhaps the most frequently discussed subject in the current literature is that of mobility, i.e., the movement of people, both within and between generations, up and down the ladders of property, power, and prestige. Starting with the very important book, *The American Occupational Structure*, by Peter Blau and Otis Dudley Duncan,[8] in 1967, much effort has been expended in attempting to measure how much movement actually takes place. There have been significant refinements in the methodology required to achieve precision in these measurements. The basic question to which most studies address themselves is that of "opportunity," i.e., how much chance is there for a person who starts from humble origins to move up. Put in other terms, this is the much-discussed question of whether the United States is still the land of opportunity. While most earlier studies focused almost entirely on white males, there is a new tendency to include Blacks and women in the populations studied.

Of great interest, too, are the increasingly frequent studies which try to compare the amounts and forms of inequality and mobility among various nations. Here the central issues are the connections, if any, between inequality and mobility, on the one hand, and such other national features as public versus private ownership of industries, economic productivity, the amount of democracy and freedom, and the shape and size of welfare systems through which income is redistributed. Such studies make modern sociology very relevant to the great political struggles between opposing superpowers in the world today and to the dominant problems of newly modernizing nations.

Clearly, then, the study of stratification has assumed a central place in modern sociology. Hundreds if not thousands of studies have been carried out, here and abroad, in the last four decades. Moreover, virtually every study of social phenomena such as crime, divorce, population growth, religious involvement, voting patterns, and educational careers, gives a prominent place to the factor called "socioeconomic standing," as measured by some combination of occupational prestige, income, and educational level. Such interest in the influence of socioeconomic inequalities will most probably continue as long as those inequalities persist and prove to be consequential for the life chances and the institutional patterns of the different strata that make up modern societies.

NOTES

1. See Andrew Hacker, *Political Theory* (New York: Macmillan, 1961) for an excellent survey.

2. Aristotle, *Politics* (New York: Modern Library, 1943), p. 190.

3. St. Augustine, *The City of God* (New York: Modern Library, 1950), p. 690.

4. Niccolo Machiavelli, *The Prince and the Discourses* (New York: Modern Library, 1940), p. 163.

5. H. Gerth and C. W. Mills, *From Max Weber* (New York: Oxford University Press, 1958), p. 194.

6. *Ibid.*, p. 94.

7. *American Sociological Review*, X, No. 2, (April 1945), 242-49.

8. New York: John Wiley and Sons, 1967.

CHAPTER 3
HOW SOCIETIES GENERATE STRATIFICATION
Differentiation and Ranking of Statuses

Because systems of stratification are integral parts of the societies in which they operate, we have to understand how all societies are built, shaped, and maintained, so that we can then see how stratification systems fit into them.

A minimal definition of a society states that it consists of a number of people who share a common territory and government, affirm the same ideal values that define the good life, interact with each other as they go about performing the requirements of everyday life, and participate in a set of common styles and modes of conduct, called the culture pattern. Some students would add other factors such as a common language, and a pervasive "we-feeling." Other students might subtract some of the elements listed. But the definition as given above will do for our purposes here.

Now we can state what any society, as defined above, must do if it is to endure more than one generation. We deliberately say "if," since societies do not have to survive and many don't. If, then, a society is to endure, it must perform the following six tasks, or functions, at some reasonable level of effectiveness:

1. Recruit new members through biological reproduction, immigration, adoption, capture, or some combination of those.

2. Convert new members into functioning adults by socializing them into norms and values, educating them in necessary skills and abilities, and enculturating or absorbing them into the culture patterns.

3. Produce, distribute, and exchange goods and services; this is the economic function.

4. Maintain internal and external order; this is the political function.

5. Maintain them in reasonable states of physical and mental health.

6. See to it that they acquire an acceptable sense of the meaning and purpose of life and feel motivated to carry on the tasks of daily life.

Any one of these tasks or functions can be performed by a variety of different structures. For example, in today's society, schools, families, churches, and peer groups all serve to socialize, educate, and enculturate young people. Additionally, any one structure can help perform several if not all of the basic tasks. Thus the family acts to recruit new members, socialize and enculturate them, produce and distribute goods and services, maintain order, look to the health of the new members, and see to it that they acquire meaning, purpose, and motivation. The fact that any function can be served by numerous structures and any structure can serve numerous functions makes great diversity possible in how societies are built and operate, and makes them open to change.

In the long run, all of these functions are required for societal endurance. That is why they are called the functional prerequisites. At the same time, it is possible for a society to act as if it cared about one of these functions more than about the others, and, in fact, most societies do act that way. Modern western democratic societies appear to care most about producing and distributing wealth, and secondarily about maintaining internal and external order. Modern totalitarian societies, by contrast, act as if they cared most about internal and external order, and only secondarily about producing and distributing wealth. Other societies seem most deeply concerned about meaning and purpose, and they emphasize their religious institutions accordingly. Such specialization in one or two functions is called "institutional emphasis," and it is found in virtually all societies.

FOUR BASIC PROCESSES REQUIRED TO GET BASIC TASKS PERFORMED

To ensure, as they must, that all the functional prerequisites are performed to some satisfactory degree, all societies engage in four basic processes: (1) They identify and *differentiate* positions, or *statuses,* such as father and mother, to which various *roles,* i.e., responsibilities and rights, are assigned; (2) they specify and *rank,* or measure, the skills these roles require along with the personal qualities of the people who are to perform them; (3) they *assess* the relative importance of the various roles for the well-being of the society; and (4) they *assign rewards* in the form of property, prestige, and power to the status-roles and, in turn, to the people who perform them.

We shall refer to these four processes by the key word in each: differentiation, ranking, assessment, and rewarding. And we shall use the terms "status," "role," and "status role" interchangeably. Now we can explore each of these four processes in more detail.

DIFFERENTIATION OF STATUSES

The activities of the members of any society, as they go about meeting the requirements of survival, must be sufficiently coordinated to form standard patterns.

People must know where to go, when, by what means; what to do, for how long, in what relationships with others; when to finish; how to depart—and so on through the routines of daily life. This patterning and predictability can result only if societies have decided what work is to be done, who is to do it, by what means, with what resources, and with what expectations of reward.

The fact that most people in the world get up when they are supposed to, dress in acceptable ways, eat customary foods, go to work on time, and perform their work routines, domestic or other, with reasonable efficiency, may seem so ordinary as to be unworthy of comment. In fact, the amount of order and coordination found in most societies represents an extraordinary achievement. All the people involved have had to be trained to behave in those ways, often against their own impulses and often in the face of the unsatisfactoriness of everyday life. The achievement and maintenance of so much order and predictability is truly remarkable.

The underlying mechanism for accomplishing this orderly patterning of everyday life requires, first, the creation and standardization of positions or statuses such as parent and child, husband and wife, teacher and pupil, and employer and employee. These statuses are distinguished from each other by assigning to each of them distinctive roles, that is, sets of (1) obligations or duties; (2) resources needed to meet those obligations; and (3) rights that may be exercised in the discharge of the responsibilities. Statuses and roles thus constitute the building blocks of every society.

It is crucial that responsibilities, resources, and rights be assigned to statuses, not to particular individuals. For only by doing so can societies establish general and uniform rules, or norms, that will apply to the many and diverse individuals who are to occupy the same statuses, for example, all the different women and men who will play the role of parent.

The role responsibility of a parent, for example, is to provide for the well-being of the children and the household in general. The role resources the parent needs to discharge this responsibility include command over the goods and services that the family produces and over how its members use time, space, and energy. The role rights the parent enjoys include respect, obedience, and deference from children, support from the spouse, and freedom from interference by outsiders.

In turn, the role responsibilities of people in the status of children include learning their lessons, developing required attitudes and skills, and behaving obediently in the household. The role resources they require and to which they are entitled may include the availability of time and energy to do these tasks, freedom from interference by other members of the family, and the availability of schools and other media of instruction. The role rights the children enjoy, in their status as children, include support, protection, guidance, affection, and nourishment from their parents.

It can be seen, then, that when statuses, such as parent and child, are intertwined in a network of obligations and rights, as they always are, the rights of one are the obligations of the other and vice versa. Parents have the right to command; children have the obligation to obey. Children have the right to support; parents have the obligation to provide the support. (Though we are obviously talking of one special kind of family system, the general features of status and attached role responsibilities, resources, and rights, apply to all family systems.)

The same process of status differentiation, through specification of the attached roles, applies to all the functional prerequisites. Consider, for example, the network of statuses and roles in an industrial bureaucracy or in such other bureaucracies as an army, a university, or a city administration. If these very complex arrangements are to work with even the least bit of efficiency, statuses must be clearly differentiated with regard to their role responsibilites, resources, and rights, so that the personnel involved know what they are expected to do, have what they need to get their tasks done, and are able to exercise the rights they are due as they go about discharging their responsibilities.

To the complex pattern of statuses and roles, as well as the relationships among them, that are involved in meeting the functional prerequisites, we give the name *social institution*. We can thus speak about the social institutions of any society as those patterned sets of positions, relations, and activities involved in biological reproduction, socialization and enculturation, production and distribution of goods and services, and the maintenance of order. The total network of all the social institutions and the connections among them constitutes the core social structure or social organization of the society.

SPECIFYING AND RANKING THE ESSENTIAL CHARACTERISTICS OF STATUSES

Once the roles attached to statuses have been adequately differentiated, it is next required to recruit, train, and place the kinds of people who are believed capable of performing the role responsibilities. To make that judgment, one must consider a number of relevant and important criteria. These might include the following: Is the task difficult or simple? Clean or dirty? Safe or unsafe? Does it require speed or can slow people do it? How much intelligence is needed? How much of what kind of education may be required? Can people of all ages and sexes perform the role equally well? Does it matter whether people are short or tall? Good looking or unattractive by local standards? Aggressive or passive? These criteria fall into three groups:

1. general qualities of the tasks, for example, difficulty, cleanliness, danger, and so forth
2. the skills and abilities that are believed necessary for adequate role performance such as surgical, numerical or linguistic skills
3. personal characteristics that people are thought to need if they are to learn and perform the roles effectively, such as intelligence, aggressiveness, politeness, and speed

Once roles have been so specified, the next task is to identify the people who possess the abilities and characteristics considered important and then to try to recruit them, train them, and place them in the appropriate roles.

Efficiency in performance of the functional prerequisites, we see, depends on the accuracy of the specification of roles and people and on the adequacy of the mechanisms for locating, recruiting, and training and placing them in the appropriate tasks.

In small, nonindustrial, and usually nonliterate societies, these requirements are met in simple, straightforward ways because the dominant assumption is that any normal adult can deal with all the adult task requirements. The only differentiations that are made are between the sexes and various age groups, since in most such societies there are firm notions as to which roles are best performed by males versus females and equally firm notions about when young people are considered ready for adult roles and when adults are considered too old for normal adult performance.

Other distinctions may also arise when tasks become specialized and differences in abilities among adults become recognized as relevant and important. Some may be deemed more suited than others to lead fishing expeditions or hunting parties. Others may be considered more suited for the position of chief or headman. Special recognition may also be paid to such important other roles as priest or magician. Usually, however, these specialties are few in number, and there is nothing like the complex division of labor in modern societies.

As societies become more populous, their requirements become more complex to meet, and the number of different status roles must be increased proportionately. The task of finding the right people, recruiting them, training them, and placing them appropriately becomes even more difficult. Elaborate systems of formal education, training, and placement are developed to meet these new needs. Consider the fact that in the United States today there are about sixty million young people in school at any one time, more than one hundred million people in the labor force and approximately twenty thousand different occupations (according to the *Dictionary of Occupations*) into which these people have to be fitted. Most of that is achieved with relatively little central planning and coordination. There is obviously, therefore, an enormous amount of inefficiency in any such society, if only because the dimensions of the tasks are staggeringly great and the mechanisms needed for effective planning and coordination are so relatively inadequate.

Everyone is familiar, for example, with the problems that arise when one tries to determine which young people are suited for various levels of higher education. Recent controversies over aptitude and intelligence tests are eloquent evidence of the problems here. The task of estimating the suitability of people for various jobs is at least as complicated and perhaps even more so.

We stress the underlying fact that some effort must always be made to characterize jobs and people sufficiently well to feel confident about assigning people to their most fit places so that the tasks of the society can best be achieved; and that unavoidably involves ranking of the tasks and personnel on the criteria considered relevant. Such ranking is, at first, nonevaluative. That is, jobs are rated as harder or easier, cleaner or dirtier, safer or more dangerous; and people are judged slower, smarter, or more skillful than others without implying that some are socially more important and others less so because of these characteristics. Doctors and garbagemen are both required at all times to deal with dirty and often dangerous things; and historical scholarship and composing sonatas are easily as difficult in their own ways as lifting heavy objects or digging trenches. These illustrations show that the assessment of the social importance of an occupation is not based alone on its ease or difficulty, cleanliness or dirt, safety or danger, or other such ranked characteristics. While social evaluation, as we shall see, incorporates certain ranked characteristics of jobs, the ranking itself is and must be, at first, nonevaluative, since its main purpose is to ensure that the right people get into their appropriate places.

CHAPTER 4
HOW SOCIETIES GENERATE STRATIFICATION
Assessing the Social Importance of Statuses

Once status roles have been differentiated and their required skills and characteristics identified and ranked, it is next required, if a society is to be effective about meeting its functional prerequisite tasks, that it assess the importance of the various tasks so that it can then give priority of attention and resources to those it deems most important. The range of possibilities here goes from one extreme, at which all tasks and status-roles are considered equally important, to the other pole, where each task has a different priority value.

While some attention must be paid to all the functional prerequisites, any society can, and most do, devote special attention and concern to a selected number of the problems that face it, leaving the others to fend for themselves with little or no public intervention.

For example, in medieval Europe, where religion dominated virtually all aspects of life, closest attention was paid to the identification and recruitment of people considered fit to serve roles of religious leadership. If nepotism and chicanery were also rife in these systems, as they were, that was due largely to the importance and profitability of religious power.

In modern totalitarian societies, where the maintenance of internal and external order enjoys the highest priority, the greatest attention is paid to the fitness of prospective candidates for leadership roles in political institutions.

In modern, capitalist societies such as our own, where the good life is defined primarily in terms of material wealth, the most diligent attention is paid to the task of finding, recruiting, training, and placing the right people in the appropriate roles involved in the production and distribution of goods and services.

By contrast, though good family life is also considered fundamental to a good society, little public attention is paid to the competence of people for marriage and parenthood. For here, as in smaller societies, it is assumed that few skills are involved and that any normal adult can, without any real formal training, perform satisfactorily as spouse and parent. The task of raising even two children to adequate, healthy adulthood is, of course, as complex and difficult a problem as any person ever has to meet. Yet this is not widely believed, and the result is that virtually all adults—as defined alone by age and sanity—are permitted to marry, procreate, and rear children, as they best see fit, with virtually minimal interference from any authorities.

The common belief that little intelligence and skill are required to teach children is evident, too, in the relatively modest requirements for becoming certified as a teacher and in the relatively low honor and rewards that teachers receive. Similar observations apply to such other tasks as social work, nursing, and other "helping" professions, particularly those in which women make up most of the labor force. The traditional belief has been that if women can do the work, it can't be very difficult or very important, except, again, in the abstract. Though obviously such beliefs are undergoing rapid and extensive change, they still enjoy a good deal of currency and support.

In any event, it is evident that societies most often choose only some areas of requirements to emphasize, and they attune their efforts at role recruitment and training accordingly.

Why any society selects some institutional tasks over others for special emphasis can be answered only by examinining its cultural and social history to see how, over time, it came to settle on the emphasis it adopted. Historical studies are now available to make clear how, for example, national honor and military might came to be of greatest concern to some European nations and how, at the same time, the concern among church leaders for religious piety and conformity emerged as a correlated emphasis, often sharing dominance, but sometimes competing for dominance, with the secular nobility.

There are also abundant historical studies that reveal how the concern among non-noble, secular merchants for a greater share of wealth, power, and honor translated itself into the bourgeois revolutions which reshaped most European societies from the seventeenth and eighteenth centuries to today. Those studies show, too, how the failures of some of those revolutions, particularly the failure to democratize state power, resulted in the emergence of modern totalitarian societies with their great emphasis on internal and external order and on the careful selection of political elites to administer and manage such order.

Anthropological scholarship in the twentieth century has also helped make clear how various nonwestern societies developed special emphasis on kinship systems, or on political rule, or on military dominance of their areas. In any event, it is to these kinds of studies we must turn to understand how institutional emphases develop and how and why societies come to resemble or differ from each other in these matters.

From time to time, too, societies get very narrow in their institutional emphases so that they seem to concentrate quite disproportionate amounts of attention and resources on one small set of tasks within one particular institution. An example in point is the development in the United States more than two decades ago of a great, almost overwhelming, concern for its leadership in science and mathematics, particularly as these studies bore on the development of military and space technology. Because the Soviet Union had sent the first satellite into space, it was feared that the United States would lag far behind the USSR in these matters. As a result, we developed extravagant crash programs of education in science and mathematics aimed at turning out many more young people who would specialize in these fields. Extraordinary amounts of money, time, and energy were devoted for some ten years to this program, whose results, one fears, hardly justify the expenditures.

A great deal is at stake in such decisions, for much of the shape of the society is formed by the actions which follow. Those decisions influence, among other things, the views of life and its possiblities that are held by the youth of the society, whose ambitions and aspirations are attuned to possibilities, as are the goals of institutions, such as schools, that are dedicated to training for adult life. Success and failure in life depend importantly on the degree of proficiency and skill one acquires in the roles in the more highly assessed institutions.

We shall soon see, too, how one's shares of property, power, and prestige are largely determined by the institutional sector in which one works and the level of skill and proficiency one can bring to that work.

Equally important are the impacts that special societal emphases have upon the general configuration of the society and of its culture. If most emphasis is placed upon military prowess and national honor, less of the society's scarce resources will be available to spend on programs of social welfare, or on the development of the arts and sciences, or on family problems and those that afflict the aged.

While some trade-offs seem unavoidable, it is always a matter of debate as to whether the kinds of emphases the society has decided upon can be justified, given the harm caused to unemphasized or neglected areas of societal problems. That decisions about institutional emphases are at bottom matters of value judgment does not negate their importance, but only points to the unavoidability of such value judgments in the most important decisions we ever make.

It is obviously crucial, then, who makes the decisions about importance and priority. When we say a society "decides" we are using a metaphor that leaves much unclear. It would probably be more accurate to say that such decisions are made by those who have the power, formal or other, to command the resources necessary to implement it. With rare exceptions, and those mostly only since the emergence of democratic government, the basic decisions about what is socially more and less important have been made by self-perpetuating elites. These elites may be in power because of their positions in the religious structure; or they may be hereditary kings and nobles; they may be the owners and managers of industry, the leaders of the military forces, the elders of the clan or the rulers of the dominant political party.

Often, too, several elites combine to determine the dominant emphasis of the society. The classical alliances of church and crown, of political and military juntas, and of industrial and political leaders are examples in point. President Eisenhower's warnings about the danger of the concentration of power in the hands of the military-industrial complex is a recent version of the case.

It stands to reason that if special elites have the power to determine the importance of different tasks, they are most likely to assign the greatest importance, and hence the greater share of society's resources, to the functions from which they stand most to benefit. Their judgments about the best interests of society may not coincide at all with the judgments of other people. But their judgments will prevail if they have the requisite power to implement them. The society will therefore take shape in accordance with their special interests and their views of the good life and the good society.

Elite decisions have dominated societies throughout the world until the relatively recent emergence of democratic government. However imperfect the democracy may be in modern democratic societies, the power to decide what the societies will care about most has now been spread more than ever before to a wider sample of the population. The unending debate in modern congresses and parliaments regarding societal priorities is evidence of the new sharing of power in the decisions about such matters.

Must societies emphasize some tasks and missions, and the associated status roles, more than others? Could they not express equal concern about all the major institutional requirements? Could they not make the judgment that all the functional prerequisites are of equal importance and hence deserve equal shares of the resources?

The possibilities, as we have noted, lie on a continuum that ranges from one exteme, where all institutional requirements are judged equally important, to the other extreme, where one small set of tasks from only one institution, for example, training of clergy, scientists, or soldiers, is assigned the only importance, and the resources are allocated exclusively to that one set. In between these two extremes we find all the societies of the world, with their differing and shared judgments about what constitutes the good life, which tasks are most important, which status roles are to be most cared about, and where the scarce resources are to be spent. The actual societies of the world provide examples of that whole range.

It is not possible to say which of the many different positions along this continuum of possibilities is more natural, or more efficient, or better for the well-being of the society. At least it is not possible to make such judgments without first bringing forth the standards we will use. Those standards will unavoidably reflect our own values about society—how we think it ought to function, what we think most important, how we think scarce resources ought to be allocated. Societies have flourished—by some standards—both under conditions of very heavy emphases on only one institutional task and under conditions of relatively equal concern for all major institutions. It all depends, of course, on what one considers a proper definition of flourish, which is simply another way of talking about one's version of the good life and the good society. There can be no debate about the crucial role in the shaping and maintenance of societies of those concepts of the good society and the good life.

CHAPTER 5
HOW SOCIETIES GENERATE STRATIFICATION
Differential Rewarding of Statuses

Once statuses have been differentiated, characterized and ranked, and assessed for their importance, some way must be found to identify, recruit, train, and place the "right" people in the "right" slots.

Many societies, the totalitarian ones in particular, do this coercively. The ruling group identifies which tasks it deems most important; it sets up a series of schools for training young people; it decrees who can and will go to the various kinds of schools; it supervises their education and training carefully; and when it is satisfied that the young people are ready for adult tasks, this ruling group assigns individuals to those tasks, monitors their performance, and allocates income, honor, and power to them in accordance with its views on these matters.

In the more democratic societies, however, the amount of central state control and coercion is much less. While a ruling elite makes most of the decisions about education and training, it is an elected elite subject to recall. Moreover, its decisions are often strongly influenced by the pressures from representatives of industries, teachers, professional organizations, and even parent groups. In any event, school systems are established, some of them more centrally controlled, as in Europe, than others, as in the United States, where there are 14,000 local school districts, each with considerable autonomy.

Where equal opportunity is the ideal, even if not the actual, norm, as is true in most democratic societies, young people in collaboration with their parents, peers, and advisers fashion their own notions about future life careers and the education they will need to realize their ambitions. In selecting the kind of life careers they intend to pursue, and hence the kind of school and the duration of their education, young people and their parents are influenced by such knowledge as they have about the kind of work various jobs entail, the availability or scarcity of jobs, the anticipated incomes from the jobs, and the amount of social honor that various occupations receive. These decisions, as we shall see later, are likely to be differentiated, sometimes sharply, by the socioeconomic status of the parents. People from different socioeconomic levels tend, on the average, to have somewhat different notions of what jobs are desirable and available; and they have, accordingly, different views about how much formal education is worthwhile securing. These ideas change over time, to be sure, but differences in these matters persist still today.

The differences in the incomes and honor quotients of the available jobs arise, in free societies, from a number of sources: the age of the industry; the scarcity (genuine or artificial) of suitable personnel; the economic soundness of the industry or activity; the condition of the world market for various goods and services; the pressures of trade unions and professional organization; and bodies of legislation governing such things as minimum wages, working conditions, tenure, security, and other associated features. Sometimes, too, the international political scene may play a significant role in influencing the demand for certain kinds of skills and aptitudes, for example, military-related matters. Moreover, new developments in technology may generate whole new industries, as today in the computer area. In any event, in capitalist democratic societies, an array of jobs at all different levels of income and honor is available for consideration. These differences in income and honor may have little or much to do with what is believed to be the most important goods and services the society ought to be producing. The interest of venture capitalists in maximizing income may have much more influence in determining wage levels and occupational prestige.

Once young people have acquired the training they believe needed for the kinds of jobs and careers they mean to pursue, they proceed to work and receive incomes and associated job prestige. It is at that point that stratification enters into the process. For now the new generation becomes internally divided into echelons of people working at jobs that receive different amounts of income and honor. In short, if the rewards people receive for their work are different, then the previously stratified society becomes restratified at the turn of the generations. New kinds of people, that is, people from humble origins, may come to occupy high prestige and income posts, but so long as the property and honor rewards are different, stratification is in motion.

There are, however, quite sizable differences in the amount of inequality in wages and honor among similar western societies. Some western societies, (for example, Denmark and Sweden) regulate the wages so that while the ratio of the wages of the best-paid to those of the worst-paid workers, before taxes and transfer payments, may be as high as 10 to 1, that ratio declines to 6 or 7 to 1 after taxes and transfer payments. The state of Israel's ratio is closer to 5 or 4 to 1. Other western societies, such as France and the United States, practice or permit much more inequality, so that their ratios are 15 or 20 to 1 before taxes and transfers and perhaps 10 or 11 to 1 after taxes and transfers. We put the numbers this tentatively because the data are not comparably good for all the nations, who often change their guidelines from one election to another. In any event, a quite substantial difference is present, even between societies that are very much alike, in how much inequality exists.

The range of possibilities stretches from one imaginary extreme of total equality of wages for all to the other imaginary extreme of total inequality. All actual societies of the world fall in between these two extremes. None is totally equal and none is totally unequal. Of this range of possibilities, we now know that no one version, that is, no amount of inequality or equality, is any more natural or logical than any other. These are matters for human decision, not of following some eternal and unavoidable principles that determine what is best.

We also know that any one version of equality or inequality is as easy or difficult to establish as any other, assuming the proper conditions. At any given time, of course, some scheme may prove extremely difficult to implement, as, for instance, if one were to introduce very great inequalities in wages in a society that has had a tradition of near-equality in such matters or vice versa.

Since human children are born without any innate sense of what is fair or just and do not have any instinctive needs or pressures for equality or inequality, it must be presumed that, with proper training and education and appropriate social controls, any form and amount of equality or inequality could be instituted and maintained. If children grow up in a situation where their adults share equally whatever good things are available, these children are likely to find such sharing quite natural and easy to practice when they get to be adults. If by contrast they grow up under circumstances where everyone seeks to get the maximum share possible for himself, then the children are likely to find that mode of conduct relatively easy to learn and to adopt as their own as adults. Nothing about human nature makes one of these lessons and experiences easier or more attractive than the others. Neither selfishness nor altruism, neither cooperation nor competition, is built into human nature. We have no genes that determine which of these patterns we will adopt.

Why, then, is inequality or reward so widely practiced and accepted? The first part of the answer is that the historical societies out of which modern European or western societies have emerged were characterized by a great deal of inequality. Slave states, feudal societies, serfdoms, and people with massive land holdings in total command of the lives and labor of many others—these were characteristic of earlier societies. It is no accident, therefore, that today's societies, which are direct heirs of those historical societies, exhibit a good deal of inequality in their distribution of rewards as well.

There is also a deeply ingrained set of philosophical notions about the fairness and efficiency of rewarding people unequally in proportion to their contributions to the total wealth of a nation. Adam Smith, in his *Wealth of Nations,* argued that nations would grow wealthy in proportion to the extent to which everyone, under conditions of rationality and freedom, would do the kind of work for which they were best suited and were then rewarded in accordance with their contribution to total wealth. Moreover, Smith claimed, as the material wealth of a nation increased, social and spiritual wealth would increase as well. In short, unequal rewards for unequal work would yield maximum material wealth and with it, maximum social and spiritual wealth too. That set of notions has dominated western European societies, including the United States, in the past and is still widely favored.

A third reason for the persistence of the ideology and practice of unequal rewarding is the degree to which such inequality suits and serves the interests of the best-paid and most powerful people. The unequal rewards in income serve their interests in material well-being quite well, while unequal amounts of honor that different occupations and incomes receive serve the ego needs of the most advantaged people quite handsomely as well. They have every good reason, therefore, to seek to maintain the ideology and practice of unequal rewarding, and they often have enough power to do so, albeit within limits.

A fourth reason for today's inequality is the fact that no effective challenge has been mounted in modern western societies against the basic principles of unequal rewarding. Only Marxism, with its emphasis on the fairness and justice of equal material rewards for unequal work and equal honor for all work, stands as a possible alternative. Though a number of European societies have strong communist parties and though a number of them are run by prime ministers and parties that call themselves socialist, the general rule everywhere is still that there will be unequal incomes and honor for various kinds of labor. Perhaps it is most important in this regard that Marxism is mostly identified with systems such as the Soviet Union, which are neither wealthy nor free, so that no actual examples of successful socialism can be pointed to. The coincidence of wealth and freedom in capitalist democracies is therefore taken by many as evidence that capitalism, with its emphasis on unequal rewarding, is somehow indispensable to wealth and freedom. This gives the general support to the refined intellectual rationale for capitalist inequality advanced by some sociologists, to the effect that unequal rewards are required to get the best people into the most important positions.

One of the outstanding features of modern societies, however, is the disparity, often severe, between the assessed importance of various roles and the rewards received by their occupants.

The most spectacular examples of that disparity are the salaries paid to athletes and entertainers, as compared to those paid to positions such as Supreme Court justices, U.S. senators, and even the President of the United States. One might try to make out a case that people who provide mass entertainment and diversion are thereby providing very important public services. But if such entertainment functions were seriously to be judged as more socially important than those performed by high-level political and judicial posts, all sense would be depleted from the term social importance.

Another example of the disparity between importance and reward is the case of relatively high wages paid to certain elite craft union members as compared to the wages received by people in such professions as nursing, teaching, and social work. No sensible appeal to differences in importance could be used to justify that discrepancy.

A third example is that of the much greater average incomes received by doctors and dentists, than those earned by college professors, orchestra members, and various artists.

A fourth disparity is that between the incomes of top level bankers and brokers, who have control over investment capital, and those received by high-level civil servants, who play crucial roles in government.

Each of these four examples illustrates a different type of factor that operates to reduce, if not distort, the expected correlation between assessed social importance and rewards.

The case of athletes and entertainers illustrates the power of people who can earn large sums of money for their employers to command large incomes in return. Popularity and mass appeal are the key words here, and these have little or no discernible connection to social importance.

The case of the higher incomes of craftsmen illustrates the power of organizations to secure higher incomes for their members through threats to withdraw their services and through restriction of the numbers who may enter their crafts.

The case of the doctors and dentists illustrates the power of organized elites to make their services scarce by restricting the numbers permitted to enter their ranks, thereby ensuring higher incomes for those who have been admitted. Their power to command high fees also results from their ability through their organizations to prevent the government and the public from influencing the level of fees.

The case of the bankers and brokers illustrates how control over investment capital and the income that capital can earn, without any significant concern for how the capital is used, is often an influential determinant of one's level of income.

In none of these cases is there any serious attempt to justify the differences in incomes by reference to differences in social importance. Instead, the most frequent explanations typically include "what the market will bear," or "one must look out for number one," or "that's the way the cookie crumbles," or "all of life is unfair." Neither fairness nor justice nor equity enters into these rationales.

In a recent analysis (*New York Times,* August 29, 1983) of the very high incomes earned by the best tennis players, the author writes:

> At the heart of the dispute is the right of tennis players to make as much money as they can . . . . They feel they have a right to be paid cash inducements because they are putting fans in the seats the same way their names are expected to increase sales for the products they endorse . . . . The feeling among the top players is that promoters and sponsors would not be paying these inducements unless they could afford them and were themselves making money. Thus, the catch phrase in tennis today is "maximizing one's income."

One outstanding female player adds: "It's free enterprise and we should never take away the human *incentive* to make money!"

Whatever else one may think of the claims of tennis players to "the right to maximize their incomes," they at least have the virtue of not pretending to any noble motives or to the greater social importance of skills in tennis over less well-paid occupations. One would have to devise a curious equation to attach social importance to the enjoyment provided by tennis players. In the last analysis, the justification of such very high earned incomes has to be put in terms of their market value to the people who decide to employ and pay them. Market value and social importance may be connected in some ways, but it is not clear how.

Attention must also be paid to the amount of income which is received by people as *unearned income,* as the tax law defines it, in the form of interest and dividends on various kinds of savings and investments, along with the *capital gains* people make by buying and selling properties. We do not know how much of the total amount of income in the society is secured that way. Nor do we know how much of the income-earning capital was secured by its owners through inheritance or theft. Crude and unverifiable estimates put the sum of inheritance somewhere between 10 percent and 25 percent of all income. Even if it is the lower figure, that much adds a substantial amount to the inequality in the society, especially since it is almost surely concentrated among the people who are already the wealthiest. One may wish to defend the right to inheritance of money on other grounds, but one could not sensibly evoke any justification in terms of the contribution to important social goals and values. Nor will the history of how such inherited money was first acquired support any notions about contributions by their acquirers to important social purposes.

These observations show that even though some of the inequality in incomes in today's societies can be shown to be linked to inequalities in social importance, other quite different factors play very large roles in determining some of the shape of the income distribution.

Crucial throughout is the power to make the decisions. Those who control property and are in charge of its utilization can and do act, within certain legal limits, as they best see fit; most often they are guided almost entirely by their desire to maximize their wealth. They will, therefore, usually try to pay their employees as little as they can. In this context they may be constrained by the power of their employees, who can cause them losses through strikes and withholding of effort; by the need to compete effectively with other employers; and, occasionally, by government regulations and requirements. In the last analysis, therefore, it is the power to force one's views on one's opponents that determines how much one will receive.

These observations apply most strongly to the private sectors in modern capitalist societies. For there the dominant principle is maximization of income with no reference to social well-being. In the public sectors of such societies, however, the aim of maximizing income is not central. Standards of wages and salaries are set by legislation and administrative rulings, which reflect to some extent the amount of force that employees can bring to bear to secure favorable legislation, as well as the supply and demand for appropriately trained and skilled employees. Inequalities in the incomes of government employees reflect years of service more than any other principle. Wages tend to be uniform throughout all government departments, regardless of the type of service performed, and standardized guides, based on years of service, determine who will get how much and when. In recent years, the organization of government employees into effective unions has introduced still another power element into the determination of income distribution.

In state-controlled, totalitarian societies, such as the Soviet Union and China, where the private sector is of relatively trivial or no importance, the determination of income differentials is largely a matter of fiat or decree by the ruling cadres of party officials. Such decrees govern the incomes of virutally all members of the labor force since they all work for state enterprises. Political leaders, ballerinas, generals, and film directors may thus secure relatively very high incomes and honor if the commissars decide that these occupations are important to collective well-being and hence deserve unequal rewards.

The paradox is heightened by the fact that in such state-controlled societies almost all *legitimate* income is received in the form of wages, since, in principle, there is no unearned income. The disproportionate material well-being that high political leaders and others around them enjoy in the Soviet Union is a function not of unearned income but of "earned" income that they have decided to award themselves on the grounds of their importance to the society.

In any event, we see now the intimate connections between the processes in which all societies engage as they go about fulfilling the prerequisites of survival and the emergence of systems of stratification. Differentiation, ranking, assessment of importance, and rewarding status-roles are indispensable to the fulfillment of survival prerequisites. When and if the rewarding is unequal, whatever the forces that determine this matter, the system of stratification has been brought into existence. For *stratification,* it will be recalled, is *patterned inequality in property, power, and prestige assigned to various status-roles.*

To the inequality that arises out of differential wages and salaries must be added whatever other amounts are contributed by the unearned income of which we have spoken. Those unequal incomes tend to be accompanied by somewhat matching amounts of unequal honor, at least occupational honor, and such unequal power as unequal honor and income can yield.

All questions of equal or unequal rewards aside, it makes perfectly good sense for any society to ask itself which of its many tasks it feels most urgent to attend to at any given moment and to which, therefore, it might wish to devote larger shares of its collective resources, even if only for the moment. Such decisions represent moral and political responses to changing needs as they are perceived by the society. If self-selected and self-perpetuating elites have the greatest power to make such decisions in today's societies, as they have had in the past, that does not detract from the wisdom of thinking and worrying about priorities and urgencies. For in principle the decisions about priorities can be made by larger numbers of people, speaking more representatively for the wider constituencies that make up the society. In the same vein, the decisions about how to reward status-roles can also be decided far more democratically than has been true in the past. Whether such more democratic decisions will result in the same, more, or less inequality in income remains to be seen. All three are possibilities, and nothing in human nature or the basic needs of society sets lower or upper limits on these matters or decrees which is the best arrangement to put into practice.

CHAPTER 6
BASIC ELEMENTS AND PROCESSES
Variations in Systems of Stratification

Though all systems of stratification are generated and kept in motion by the same four processes—status differentiation, ranking, assessment, and rewarding—there are numerous and important differences among them. This can best be understood, first, as statistically expectable differences, which arise simply because there are so many elements and processes that together compose any stratification system, and there are quite numerous forms which all those elements and processes can assume. Later in this chapter we will present a table that discloses some thirty different elements, some version of which is found in every stratification system; and that table could be enlarged to include quite a few more ingredients of stratification. For the moment we will select only some of those thirty for special consideration.

THE DEPTH OF STRATIFICATION

The term *depth of stratification* is used to refer to the amount of inequality—in property, prestige, or power—that is found in a society. It is also sometimes referred to as the range of stratification. However called, it focuses on how one or more of the good things are distributed. In Chapter 9 we will examine the depth of inequality in various western countries, with special emphasis on the case of the United States. For the moment let it suffice to say that the depth of inequality can vary greatly, from almost no differences among the best and worst off to a situation where there is massive inequality represented by the few having possession of giant shares while the vast majority have little of anything. The societies of the world today vary greatly in this regard. They occupy spots widely distributed along the possible continuum and therefore exhibit what we call varying depths of stratification.

THE SPAN OF STRATIFICATION

Sometimes the terms *scope* is used instead of *span*. In any event, the reference here is to the extent to which inequality is found throughout the good things of life or is confined to only one of them; and it refers also to the extent to which people who are unequal in one or more of the basic good things are also unequal in four other classes of things: (1) life chances, or the chance to enjoy favorable versions of the important events, experiences, and situations in the normal course of a life (2) institutional patterns, or the ways in which the basic requirements of everyday life, such as work and family, are conducted (3) life styles, or the ways in which people use their disposable energy, income, and time to consume goods and services and are identified, by those styles, as belonging to certain levels of income and honor (4) attitudes, values, ideologies, and beliefs about the good society, the good life, how societies ought to be run, how children ought to be raised, how criminals ought to be treated, and similar important issues.

One of the leading hypotheses in sociology is that such differences as are found in any of these four classes of things are most probably closely connected to the differences among people in their quotients of property, power, and prestige. As such, they are seen as the consequences of stratification. In Chapter 10 we will examine some details about the span of stratification, particularly in the United States.

MODES OF ACQUISITION OF STATUSES

A crucial element in all systems of stratification is the mode by which people acquire the statuses in which they receive their shares of income, and honor, and perhaps power.

The most general distinction is between acquiring a status through achievement as against through ascription. The former refers to the process by which one acquires a status because one is judged to have the abilities, skills, and other relevant qualities that enable one to fulfill the role. One earns one's way into the status, so to speak. One gets one's position on merit.

Status-by-ascription, by contrast, refers to the process by which one acquires a status because one has some special, favored characteristics that may have little or nothing to do with one's ability to perform the role. If males are given preference in jobs over females, or Whites over Blacks, or Christians over Jews, those are examples of status-by-ascription. Maleness, whiteness, and Christianity are ascribed, not achieved, characteristics. One is born into them or inherits them, and they may have little or nothing to do with one's ability to perform the role for which one has been chosen.

A special form of status-by-ascription is *status-by-inheritance.* The classic case is that of the prince who inherits the status of king on the death of his father. He has earlier acquired the status of prince simply because he is the son of the king. A similar case is one in which the son of the owner of a company is placed into an executive position because he is the son of the owner, even though he may be much less qualified than others who are not related to the owner. This kind of favoritism for relatives is also called *nepotism.*

Statuses are also sometimes acquired by *influence* or *patronage.* Friends or relatives who have positions to award may give special consideration to each other's children; or people who have worked to help elect a candidate to office may then be rewarded with positions without much regard to their abilities or the possibly greater qualifications of others who desire the positions.

Other factors that operate to determine who will get positions include luck, personal charm and persuasiveness, and sometimes coercion; for example, politicos may order people who are beholden to them to give jobs to people whom the politicos desire to favor.

Also worthy of mention are the instances where positions are acquired through fawning and flattery; or through exchange of valued goods and services, as when a position is secured by granting sexual favors; or where bribes may enable an individual to be given advantaged consideration over others for available positons.

Still other factors that influence status acquisition and that have little or nothing to do with suitability for the position are various eligibility rules, such as those which require job applicants or candidates for school admission to be natives or residents of a given area—local, state, or national. Age eligibility rules are of the same order.

In modern societies, status-by-achievement or merit is said to be the dominant and governing principle, while favoritism for veterans and handicapped and special considerations for women and minorities are considered to be necessary supplements to make the competitive situation more fair than it would otherwise be.

Yet even in societies where the rule of status-by-achievement is dominant, ascribed and inherited characteristics and other nonachievement factors often play a significant role. When, for example, children of wealthier and better-educated parents get a head start in life because of their family situations, inheritance, luck, and a host of ascriptive factors are helping determine who lands where. Such advantaged youth may then go on to acquire the skills necessary for efficient role performance, and in that sense they come to earn their positions. But they have had a head start over others that has nothing to do with their own merit.

Yet ascriptive and inherited advantages of the kinds just described may or may not be decisive. Children of advantaged families may go to better schools and have a better chance, for that reason, to be admitted to top-rate medical or law schools. But they must earn their way into those advantageous slots. They must, in short, validate themselves on the basis of merit. So, too, the son of the owner of a firm who has been made an executive is likely to be required to validate himself by effective performance or lose the position. Even the prince who becomes king may be required to validate his position as king by at least a modicum of adequate performance or else run the risk of being deposed. Such validation of one's right to a position is required to some degree virtually everywhere, though it is least important in the cases of wholly inherited statuses.

The processes by which statuses are acquired are important because they help determine how efficient people will be at their roles and, in turn, how productive of valued goods and services the whole system will be; how fair the system will be considered; how open it is to new ideas and talents; how much opportunity is present for people to move from one status situation to another; how much voluntary assent people are likely to give to the rules of the system and, in turn, how much political solidarity they will tend to express.

EMPHASIZED INSTITUTIONAL AREA

A second major feature of any system of stratification is the institutional area in which the most highly rewarded statuses are located. The institutional areas include the economic, political, religious, familial, and educational sectors of the society. Societies often give the highest rewards to those who play important roles in those institutions on whose activities the societies place the highest value and whose achievements are considered to be most important for overall well-being.

When religion is the dominant institution—as in medieval, church-dominated states and in modern fundamentalist states such as Iran—the highest rewards, including power and prestige, as well as property, are likely to be awarded to the chief religious specialists, such as bishops, cardinals, caliphs, and imams. By contrast, in modern secular societies, with their emphasis on material productivity and wealth, those who occupy key positions in the economic sector, such as executives of large corporations, their lawyers, and their accountants, receive relatively great amounts of income and often enjoy much power and prestige. In other societies, such as the Soviet Union, where political purity and power and military might are dominant concerns, the positions in the political and military hierarchies are awarded the highest amounts of property, honor, and power. In all these cases it is evident that those who have the capital and power to decide these matters are likely to designate themselves as those most entitled to high rewards.

Evidence that an institution and its roles are dominant is to be found in the following indicators, among others:

1. the degree of publicly expressed concern about the institutional activities, as brought forth in major speeches by political leaders, especially on important public holidays or holy days
2. the amount of formal governmental attention devoted to the oversight of the institutional activity, as when cabinet posts or special administrative agencies are created for such supervision

3. the efforts devoted to keeping good records and getting good measures of the output of the institutional area, as in the case of the Gross National Product in the United States and other western societies that are concerned mostly with their economic productivity

4. the number of laws that are passed to insure that the institutional activities in question are conducted in accordance with dominant ideas about how to do those things most effectively

5. the corollary amount of public attention to, and prosecution of, malfeasances in the conduct of the emphasized activities

6. the degree of attention paid in schools and training academies to the preparation of young people for careers in the emphasized activities.

Any institutional area that is marked by several of these indicators can be expected to be one in which the highest rewards of the society will be offered.

THE CRITERIA THAT DETERMINE REWARD LEVEL

The foregoing observations make societies sound quite rational, since they appear to do many of the things required to serve their most important values most effectively. In fact, however, every society shows major departures from this rational scheme in two ways: (1) roles in other than dominant institutions often command very high rewards and (2) various nonrational criteria influence the level of reward that roles will receive.

To the already cited examples of athletes and entertainers, we can add money-handlers, lawyers, and newscasters, not to mention those who inherit great wealth and those who live very well off the proceeds of illegal or semilegal operations, such as gambling casinos. In each of these cases, some principle other than skilled contribution to dominant values explains the ability of the people involved to command high incomes. Those principles include the ability to make others wealthy, as in the case of popular athletes, entertainers, and newscasters; the ability to protect or increase the wealth of others, as do lawyers, accountants, and money-handlers; the operation of luck, as in the case of heirs to fortunes; the power to coerce others, as with gangsters; and the power and acumen to cash in on high consumer demand, as in the case of casino operators.

In general, the same kinds of nonachievement factors that determine who gets into various statuses also determine levels of reward. Luck, connections, inheritance of privileged place, personal appearance and charm, the ability to flatter the appropriate people, the support of a patron, and the exchange of intimate favors often enter into the final determination of reward levels. In addition, ascriptive factors, such as age, sex, race, and religion, may shape the reward structure through the operation of stereotypes and discrimination.

Modern societies, then, show a mix of status-by-achievement and reward according to meritorious performance, on the one hand, and a range of quite different, much less rational factors on the other. The existence of the latter does not mean that the former are not operative, any more than does the official affirmation of the former ensure that irrational factors will be absent. Those who are inclined to indict a society for its corruption or lack of fairness will naturally stress the non-merit, nonachievemental factors at work, while those who are inclined to applaud the society will see those discrepancies as unfortunate, exceptional slippages in a system that is otherwise reasonably principled and fair in its conduct.

However much societies today may strain toward principled and fair conduct in their allocation of statuses and rewards, a very strong force often runs directly counter to those themes. It is the fact that property, power, and prestige tend to reinforce themselves and to be self-cumulating and augmenting. Wealth breeds wealth, power generates more power, and honor helps greatly to generate more of itself. Some version of those processes seems everywhere to be at work in the determination of the amount and kind of inequality in the society. That means that the shape of the stratification system at any given time is likely to reflect the ability of already advantaged people to secure and increase the advantages, along with their role skills and their contributions to important social goals.

The extent to which this is the case can be determined only by close examination of the evidence. The well-documented persistence of elites who are intimately connected with previous generations of elites strongly suggests that privilege does maintain itself, and, in that way, the principles of status by achievement and reward for meritorious performance in dominantly valued areas are undermined. We shall see some statistical evidence about the inheritance of advantage in a later chapter devoted to mobility.

MOBILITY

Though mobility will later be treated at some length, it is important to speak of it here, if only briefly, since it is a major dimension on which systems of stratification vary. The central question about mobility is the extent to which it is possible for people to move up and down (vertical mobility) on the ladders of property, power, and prestige, either within their own lifetimes (intragenerational) or over generations (intergenerational). The son of a blue collar worker who becomes a professional (lawyer, or doctor, and the like) is an example of inter-generational upward mobility. The young person who starts out as a blue-collar worker and through education and effort qualifies for higher-ranking, better-paid, white-collar tasks is an example of intragenerational upward mobility. The son of a professional who, for various reasons, qualifies only for semi-skilled, blue-collar work is an instance of intergenerational downward mobility; and the person who starts out as a skilled, white-collar employee but, for various reasons, "skids" into semi-skilled or unskilled, blue-collar work, is an example of intragenerational downward mobility.

A system of stratification is said to be open and mobile, or, oppositely, closed and rigid, in proportion to the extent to which people move up or down the various ladders of reward, either during their own lifetimes or over generational time. Every system of stratification can be characterized by its types and degrees of mobility.

TYPES OF STRATA FORMED

We now have most of the terms we need to consider another important variation in systems of stratification, namely, the types of strata that are formed. A stratum (singular of strata), we recall, consists of a set of statuses which are sufficiently alike in their characteristic amounts of property, prestige, and power to be treated as a unit. The presence of two or more such strata, differentiated by their average quotients of reward and interacting in the total society, constitutes a system of stratification.

Once strata are distinguished by their average rewards we can examine them for other differences. Perhaps the most embracing distinction made in today's societies is between systems in which there are classes as against those in which there are castes. The principal difference is between the mobility or openness of the class system as against the immobility, closedness, or rigidity of the caste system.

DISTINCTIVENESS OF STRATA

The distinctiveness of strata is a crucial matter in this context. For if members of the various strata can easily be distinguished from each other it is eminently easier, in turn, for the dominant stratum to keep the strata apart where they so desire and to enforce the rules of separation. One also expects that where the strata are easily distinguishable, mobility between them will be less and the political relations will be more hierarchical and authoritarian. The classic case in a modern society today is that of the black and white castes in South Africa. The term *caste* may also be applied, but to a considerably lesser degree, to the relations between Blacks and Whites in the United States.

Strata become distinct from each other as each of the following factors becomes different:

Objective Factors

1. the average level of education and jobs
2. the average amount of property, prestige, and power
3. life chances, for example, health and longevity
4. institutional patterns of conduct, for example, modes of rearing children, marital relations, and political participation
5. life styles, or cultural patterns, for example, modes of dressing, eating, entertaining, and decorating homes; media consumed
6. physical features, such as skin color, eye color, general cast of face, and stature

These are called objective factors because one can verify their presence or absence without asking people what they think or feel about these matters.

Subjective Factors

1. values, attitudes, ideologies, and beliefs about important social issues
2. consciousness of kind; mutual awareness of each other as being in the same objective conditions that differ from those of other strata
3. acceptance of membership in the stratum: the admission that one is of a given stratum and the acceptance of that designation as proper
4. sense of common fate: the belief that all people who belong to a stratum have a common fate
5. stratum solidarity: the sense that the only way to improve their fates is through collective effort as a stratum, along with an agreement about who are the enemies or forces that must be overcome if the stratum's fate is to be altered.

CLASS CONSCIOUSNESS AND SOLIDARITY

When these five subjective factors are brought into being, one has a stratum *for itself,* that is, a united group of people with common objective characteristics, a common sense of fate, and a common determination to act collectively to improve their situations. At that point we have reached the fullness of what Karl Marx called *class consciousness* and *solidarity.*

Among the factors that help bring on stratum or class consciousness and solidarity are the harshness of rule by the dominant class; continuous economic and social suffering; unfair standards of justice; steady denial of political rights; and rigidity, immobility, or lack of opportunities to improve one's conditions or those of one's children.

Among the factors that work to diminish class consciousness and solidarity are the following: the presence of other important nonclass identities, such as religion and race, that members of the stratum hold and to which they feel loyalty; the influence of a common transstratum system of values that urges commonality of interests among all strata: the presence of opportunity for mobility and the encouragement to identify with persons in higher positions; the lack of distinct political programs and parties in which to express distinct class interests; and the increasing ability over time to use existing educational and political instruments to improve life chances.

In an open class system, the opportunities for people to improve their fates by individual effort are likely to be sufficiently successful to prevent the development of class consciousness and solidarity. Marx's prediction that the classes in western European societies would develop into solidary, that is, consciously political, united groups, was based on the assumption that the conditions of the working class would worsen over time, and individual mobility would be virtually impossible. It would then become apparent to the members of the working class that it was illusory to hope for any improvement through individual effort and that only class struggle against common class enemies would produce any results.

The actual developments in western societies do not bear out Marx's predictions, since class struggle and class warfare seem not to have replaced individual effort, individual mobility, and trade union activities as the mechanisms of improvement of fate. Instead, there has been a significant increase in what is called *embourgeoisement,* by which it is meant that the working classes have beome increasingly indistinguishable from the bourgeoisie, or middle classes, in their life chances, life styles, institutional patterns of conduct, and attitudes toward the system of stratification and its possibilities.

SUMMARY: THE OPEN VERSUS THE CLOSED SOCIETY

We have examined, albeit briefly, nine elements that can and do vary among different systems of stratification:

1.   the depth of stratification
2.   the span of stratification
3.   modes of acquisition of statuses
4.   institutional areas emphasized
5.   criteria that determine reward level
6.   mobility
7.   types of strata formed
8.   distinctiveness of strata
9.   stratum consciousness and solidarity

These are, as we noted earlier, only some of the elements and processes that are found in stratification systems. To present a concise view of other factors that vary, we shall suppose that we are distinguishing between an open and a closed society and specify the ways in which the elements and processes vary as between these two forms of society.

Table 6–1 presents in summary form some thirty such features, including those already discussed in this chapter. All thirty features listed in the table are different in the open as opposed to the closed or in the class versus the caste system. But they are not all equally important; and they do not all differ in the same degree in the two types of system. Yet we expect some differences on all these elements. Taken together they comprise the specifications of an open versus a closed or class versus caste type of stratification system. The word *type* is important. We mean to suggest that the types we specified by the thirty characteristics are *imaginary* in their fullness, and that actual systems of stratification approximate these typical features only more or less. Thus, while two systems may both be sufficiently open to be called class systems, they may differ a good deal in their degrees of openness, and in other features as well. Thus, both the United States and British systems are class-type systems; but there is more mobility in the United States, and the classes in Britain are more distinctive and differentiated. So, too, with caste-type systems. Both the Indian and South African systems of stratification fall into the caste type as judged by lack of mobility among strata. But the Indian system is substantially less closed, or more open, than is the South African; and because of sharp color distinctions in South Africa, its castes are far more easily distinguishable.

The different forms that these thirty elements take are matters of considerable importance. For they may be greatly influential in determining how many people will enjoy decent shares of the good things of life; how much control over their own destinies and fates they will be able to wield; how many patterns of basic conduct they share; how optimistic they feel about their futures and those of their children; how much of a sense of stake in the system they feel; how politically active they will be and in behalf of what causes. In effect, this says that a range of features associated with degrees of equality and mobility have a great deal to do with the total shape of the society, its social, material, and spiritual productivity, and its conduct as a collective entity.

TABLE 6-1   Open Versus Closed Systems of Stratification

Characteristics of System of strata	Open-system version	Closed-system version
1. Unit of evaluation and reward	Usually an occupational status modified by specific identity traits and resource levels; family as main carrier of evaluation and reward	Families and castes evaluated and rewarded as units
2. Mode of acquiring membership	Achievement and continuing validation	Ascription, primarily by inheritance
3. Evaluation criteria	Some personal qualities but most often skills and abilities relevant to occupation and other valued task achievements	Holiness, purity, proper ancestry
4. Rules for distributing evaluation and reward	Required to be explicit, formal, "fair" to all; subject to change by bargaining	Often implicit; traditionally based on holy books and sayings, without any consideration of "fairness"; unchanging
5. Bases of strata formation	Temporary aggregations based on common rewards	Permanent aggregations based on common hereditary traits and family linkages
6. Educational levels	Quite different, but relatively high average population; universal literacy	Extremely different; few people remain at advanced levels; very low average level, massive illiteracy
7. Income and property differences	Often substantial, but inequality considered earned, temporary, and subject to change; some emphasis on desirability of equality	Marked differences; inequality considered to be right and permanent

TABLE 6-1 *Continued*

Characteristics of System of strata	Open-system version	Closed-system version
8. Prestige differences	Same as for property	Major emphasis of system is honor through purity and holiness
9. Power differences	Same as for property and prestige	Marked differences considered to be right and permanent
10. Degree of congruence among levels of property, prestige, and power	Some effort toward congruence, but significant incongruence often present; uncertain dominance by any of the three over others	Perfect congruence among all rewards; honor through purity as the major determinant of overall ranking
11. Life chance differences	Correspond to property differences but softened by redistributive mechanisms (for example, taxation and welfare)	Marked, durable, consequential differences; life chances most affected by prestige or honor
12. Institutional patterns	Modest differences that are temporary and quickly reduced by influence of mass media	Sharp and significant differences
13. Life style differences	Temporary differences in styles, often rapidly diminished by sharing visibility through mass media and by mass production of cheap versions of elite styles	Distinctive and durable differences associated closely with undiminished differences, especially in sacred purity
14. Values, ideologies, beliefs, and attitudes	Only modestly differentiated; generally diffuse and shared throughout the society; openly debated	Sharply different; hostile and conflicting views; no public debate; no transstratum agreements
15. Stratum consciousness of kind (fellow members)	Little or none, with much mobility aspiration; upper strata used as reference groups	Intense consciousness and constant mutual recognition; acknowledgment of common stratum membership
16. Degree of stratum membership acceptance	Membership seen as accidental and temporary, with no need to resign or accept fate and with much pressure to attempt to alter fate	Great resignation and acceptance of fate as ordained and permanent
17. Sense of common stratum fate	Little or none; fate seen individually, and mobility based on individual accomplishments	Belief in joined and inescapable collective fate of stratum with little or no possibility of individual mobility or escape
18. Degree of stratum solidarity	Little or none	Intense, persistent, and mutually enforced

TABLE 6-1 *Continued*

Characteristics of System of strata	Open-system version	Closed-system version
19. Frequency and consequences of contact between strata	Informal; much mixture in public institutions, no harmful consequences	Contact minimized, except in exchange of services; anything more seen as degrading and contaminating
20. Social intimacy between strata	Approved, attempted, desired; not often achieved	Disapproved, not attempted, not desired; punished when visible
21. Visibility of stratum membership	Blurred and mixed	Clear and distinct
22. Legal and religious restrictions on occupational roles	Few or none; temporary at best	Strong, numerous, forceful
23. Justification of strata distinctions	Purely secular; considered alterable and believed to be temporary, if not accidental	Believed to be divinely sanctioned; natural, inevitable, permanent
24. Sanctions employed to maintain stratum unit	Few or none; at most, some ridicule, ostracism, or social discrimination	Very severe sanctions; death penalty possible for violating caste taboos
25. Enactment of sanctions to restrain deviation from stratum rules	No official agents; no legitimacy for any such sanctions, either from within or without strata	Acceptance of legitimacy of sanctions by any higher outside caste member, as well as by own caste peers
26. Rewards for conformity to stratum regulations	None of importance except acceptance within stratum and freedom from ridicule for mobility-striving	Promise of great improvement of fate in afterlife
27. Durability of strata	Considered temporary and shifting	Considered permanent and unalterable
28. Other restraints on interstratum mobility	Few or none, except inadequacy of required resources and incapacity to obliterate marks of previous stratum membership	Durability of imprint of stratum characteristics, including subtle features of bearing and life style of stratum
29. Mobility among strata	Approved, possible, desired	Disapproved, impossible, not desired
30. Unit of mobility	Families or, more often, an individual who acquires new criteria	Whole castes or subcastes

CHAPTER 7
PROPERTY
Concepts, Measurements, and Problems

Of the three major good things in a society, property is the easiest to define. The most general definition holds that property refers to rights over goods and services of all kinds. Those goods and services can be tangible or intangible; durable or temporary; personal or public, that is, held alone or shared with others, or owned by the state.

In all societies people are allowed at least some personal rights over goods and services, even if these are relatively trivial compared to those held in common with others. In the Israeli socialist kibbutzim, for instance, people are allowed a minimum of personal household goods, but all property beyond that is considered commonly owned by the commune itself. In other societies, such as the Soviet Union, most people can and do own personal property, but most of the property required to produce and distribute basic goods and services is owned by the state, presumably on behalf of everyone. In still other societies, such as the United States, the largest share of all property is privately owned, even if jointly by stockholders.

The distribution of property is a crucial matter because of the numerous and important uses which property can serve. Seven such uses can be identified.

Property is necessary, first, at all levels of well-being, simply to ensure physical survival. We all require food, shelter, and clothing.

Second, property serves to provide comfort and sometimes luxury. As peoples' wants increase, many of the things formerly called luxuries become redefined as necessities. It has been said that the poor of the United States are among the world's wealthy people because certain items, such as refrigerators, indoor plumbing, flush toilets, heating, and electric power, that elsewhere are seen as luxuries, are here considered minimal necessities.

Property serves, third, to provide security against the possible hazards and costs of illness, unemployment, infirmity, or old age. Only a minority of people in the world have anything resembling such security, but the desire for and the validity of providing for such security is a well-developed theme in modern societies, particularly in the most developed welfare states such as Sweden and Denmark. Such security can be funded and administered by the state, using compulsory universal contributions; or it can be managed individually, as in private pension plans; or there may be some combination of both public funds, such as social security and private pension schemes.

The fourth use of property is to acquire still more property. The income derived from savings and investments is the example in point. It is well recognized that it requires a good deal of money in order to make a good deal of money. These conditions apply only to a minority of people in the richest countries. But the theme of income from investment has become a standard feature of western life. The growth of the number and percent of people who buy shares in companies or invest in "money funds" testifies to the increasing salience of the idea of using money to make money.

The fifth function property serves is as a source of honor. Sometimes the mere possession of a good deal of money is sufficient to garner honor from others. More often, as we shall see in the next chapter, wealth can produce honor when it is used to purchase and consume the appropriate, honorific life style.

Sixth, property is a major source of power. Those who have sufficient property can command the services of others; they can influence the shape of legislation; they can purchase advantageous life chances and achieve more control over their own destinies than those with less property. The command over the labor of slaves and serfs is an extreme example of this use of property.

A seventh and quite disapproved function of property is to provide ego gratification from its sheer possession. The pathological version of this use of money is seen in the miser who takes pleasure out of mere ownership, often to the point of living poorly in order to maintain his funds.

Since inequalities in property result in these other important inequalities, the ways in which property is distributed is a crucial concern in all societies. The result is that in all known societies there are codes and norms that govern the ownership and distribution of property. And in developed societies some of these are embodied in law. In capitalist, rich societies, the codes of law relevant to property and its uses have themselves become enormously complex. Very great incomes can be earned by those such as accountants, corporate lawyers, tax lawyers, and investment counselors, who become proficient in property law and who can help others either to gain more property and/or to protect property already secured.

Another result of the perceived importance of property is that great efforts are made, especially in developed societies, to keep track of the growth and flow of property. Such measures as the Gross National Product, which specifies the amount of all goods and services produced in a given year, are used to estimate national wealth, and much of the sense of national well-being or the lack thereof is made to rest on the changes in the GNP from one year to the next.

Still another result is the development of governmental agencies to oversee a number of those uses. Examples in point include the Federal Trade Commission, the Securities and Exchange Commission, public utility commissions, environmental protection agencies, and the various bureaus that monitor the quality of consumer goods and services. Still other government bureaus, such as the Occupational Safety and Health Administration, serve to protect the health and safety of employees while the Civil Service Commission functions to insure fair play in the hiring and firing of personnel. The presence of such agencies testifies to the awareness of the great power that control over property can give to its owners and the need, therefore, to give some balancing power to those who do not have that power and to protect those who cannot protect themselves.

MEASUREMENTS AND COMPARISONS OF PROPERTY

The amount of property any person or group possesses is easier to measure and to compare than their amount of honor or power. This is simply due to the agreement to accept a common medium of exchange, called money, and to express all amounts of property in terms of units of the money. While many smaller and isolated societies still conduct their exchanges of property on the basis of barter, for example, a dozen eggs may be worth a pound of apricots, nearly everyone in the world is to some important degree attuned to some form of money. Once a standard form of money is accepted, it can be used to measure the value of such otherwise incomparable items as cars, homes, furs, diamonds, and string beans. In turn, that means it can be used to estimate the total amount of property that any individual or group possesses and to investigate and describe the patterns of distribution of wealth and income.

PROPERTY AND SUBJECTIVE PERCEPTIONS

It is a commonplace to speak, sometimes even with a reverent tone, of things on which no money value can be placed, for example, love, happiness, and peace of mind. Of greater social importance in modern societies is the problem of translating certain "social goods," such as security, safety, and health, into money terms so that the cost-benefit ratios of trade-offs, such as between productivity and safety or clean air, can then be more effectively estimated. This is a much-favored pursuit, especially in those circles where economists dominate. But there is much resistance to this effort to assign values to social hazards or benefits on the grounds that the meaning and import of those hazards and benefits is thereby impoverished. Nevertheless, the efforts to reduce all matters of interest to common money units continue to flourish.

Other problems in the measurement of social goods and benefits arise out of the range of subjective meanings that the same things can have for different people. The possession of a new automobile may be a matter of great pride and ego gratification for some, yet considered in much less emotional terms by others. Does the automobile have the same *value* for both kinds of people?

Similar problems arise because of the different implications of losses and gains in property for people at different levels of well-being. A 10 percent reduction in income for people who are already rather poor is certain to have far greater implications for their general well-being than a 10 percent reduction for those who are very well-to-do. In the same vein, a 10 percent gain for the poorer ones may mean far more for their lives than a 10 percent gain for the wealthier ones.

PROPERTY AND REFERENCE GROUPS AND STANDARDS

The same sum of money can also have different meanings for people at the same income level, depending on their *reference standards,* that is, the people and the criteria against which they compare their own well-being and in terms of which they formulate their desires. To be able to afford membership in an exclusive country club may thus be a matter of great meaning and value for some but be utterly without significance for other equally well-off people.

Such variations in the subjective meanings of various amounts of money suggest that interpretations of the distribution of wealth and income must always be hedged to some degree. To say one person or class of people earns twice as much as another may be minimally correct and yet not justify the conclusion that those who have twice as much are twice as well-off, not if we wish to take subjective perceptions of well-being into account in making such judgments.

While those are necessary cautions in estimating and interpreting distributions of property, we nevertheless achieve considerable understanding of the role of property and the significance of its distributions by using money estimates. In doing so, we confine ourselves to two main components: income and wealth.

Income refers to the money gained as salaries and wages; or as the result of entrepreneurial activities, for example, by storekeepers; or as interest and dividends on investments. The first two are called *earned income;* the last is called *unearned.*

Wealth, by contrast, includes all income, earned or unearned, plus the value of such things as homes, automobiles, insurance policies, pension rights, jewelry, furs, clothing, books, and furniture, as well as anything else that costs someone money to secure and that in principle has a determinable value on the "market," that is, what a willing buyer would pay to a willing seller, or what an insurance company will pay as compensation for loss, or what it would cost to replace the item.

In estimating the amount of property people have, we are mostly confined to their earned incomes, simply because these are the sums on which we have the most reliable information. While some concealment of income is practiced everywhere, the least occurs in regard to wages and salaries. This is due to the well-developed systems of compulsory reporting in western societies. The major concealments here involve those payments in cash or kind for goods and services that proprietors do not report and individuals' earnings that do not go through the bookkeeping of companies or institutions even though they are required by law to report all such payments. Some estimate this black-market economy at 25 percent of all earned income.

In the United States, for example, the ratio of reported income to actual income is about 98 percent of wages and salaries, 91 percent of entrepreneurial income, and 45 percent of property income. By contrast, in France, comparable ratios are 89, 34, and 35 percent, indicating that around two-thirds of all entrepreneurial and property income in France is concealed. Apparently the least concealment occurs in the United Kingdom and West Germany.[1]

The concealment of property income constitutes a very serious loss in income estimates and, of course, in taxes. Most of such concealment goes on among the most wealthy of people. In 1966, for example, those who reported taxable incomes of over $100,000 a year derived only 15.2 percent of their incomes from wages and salaries, 13.3 percent from small businesses and 66.8 percent from *capitalist* sources, that is, investments in stocks, bonds, and real estate.

Looked at another way, the wealthiest 5 percent of the population control 50 percent of all wealth, including 83 percent of all corporate stocks, and, more extremely yet, the wealthiest 1 percent control 31 percent of all wealth, including 61 percent of all corporate stocks.[2]

These figures indicate that our estimates of how much income and wealth people possess are only approximations, sometimes quite inadequate ones. Since these inadequacies are most pronounced among the wealthiest people who acquire the largest share of unearned and unreported income, these figures also show that the disparities between the richer and poorer people are probably far greater than the official reports reveal.

OTHER PROBLEMS IN MEASURING INCOME

A number of other problems confront students of income distributions.

First is the question of whether to count the incomes of individuals, of families, or of households. All three yield different results. Households may include unrelated people living in a common home and sharing income and expenses, and, of course, they may be of quite different sizes.

A second problem has to do with estimating the value of *income-in-kind*, that is, products grown or made at home. This problem is most relevant in the incomes of farming people.

A third question concerns the value of domestic services, for example, cooking, cleaning, and caring for children. Where these services are provided by paid domestic help, their value enters into income figures through the reports of the income of the domestic help, and some of it may also enter in as a legitimate deduction for certain classes of working wives. Otherwise, domestic services are not counted as part of income. Needless to say, the person who works at domestic duties instead of going out onto the job market sacrifices income that might have been earned.

A fourth problem is presented by perquisites, known as "perks," that is, certain special goods and services that employees, usually executives, receive. Free automobiles, chauffeurs, memberships in social clubs, use of corporate health and recreational facilities, counselling programs, tuition aid to children—those and many other items actually enhance the material and psychic well-being of the recipients, but only some of these are tallied as income. At the top of the list of profitable perks are stock options, which permit the recipient to purchase company stock at advantageous prices while the gains from any subsequent sale are taxed as capital gains and hence at lower tax levels than regular income.

Finally, mention should be made of the problems created by "shelters," or various ways, permitted by law, or sometimes overlooked and hence not forbidden, by which people defer income earned in a given year until a later date in the hope that the taxes that will later be owed will be smaller than those owed at the time the income was earned. Though such shelters are available in one form or another for virtually all income earners in the society, the largest gains in sheltering are made by people at the top of the income ladder. No one really knows how much income goes unreported because of the provisions for sheltering.

The income tax officials are, of course, well aware of all these problematic matters, and their decisions, which change from year to year, are embodied in the Internal Revenue codes. The variable treatment of these matters results in different and discrepant estimates of income. Notwithstanding these difficulties, income, as reported to the census bureaus of the western countries, remains the most reliable approximation we have of total income, and it is on the basis of reported income that the census calculates the distribution and shares.

MEASURING INEQUALITY

Assuming the reliability of income data, the next problem is how best to calculate the amount of inequality in the distributions. Reliable estimates of inequality are needed to investigate the possible relationships between amounts of inequality, on the one hand, and such other things as productivity or wealth, political freedom, political solidarity, and rates of various pathologies, such as illness and crime. Measures of inequality also alert a society to the existence of a condition that it may define as unacceptable, as when it appears that new and larger percentages of the population are living at what are considered substandard incomes, while the higher earners are remaining as well-off as or better than before.

The most common method for estimating and reporting inequality involves arraying all incomes so that one can calculate what percent of the total income is earned by different portions of the population, ranging from the highest to the lowest earners. These arrays can be in deciles, that is tenths, or quintiles, fifths, or any other division one wishes to make, including the top and bottom 50 percent of income earners. The most useful figures are those reported in deciles, for then one can reduce these to quintiles if one wishes, or to 50 percent groups.

Once the data are arrayed, one can calculate the ratios of the share of income of one segment to that of another, for example, the share of total income earned by the top tenth or fifth of income earners to that earned by the bottom tenth or fifth. Since the bottom and top tenths are more extreme groups, the ratio of their incomes to each other will, of course, show a higher amount of inequality than when we compare fifths.

For example: In 1972 in the United States the top 10 percent of income earners received 28.4 percent of all reported income, while the bottom 10 percent received 1.2 percent. The ratio of 28.4 percent to 1.2 percent is 23.4 to 1. That is, the share of the 10 percent of top earners was 23.4 times greater than the share of the bottom 10 percent.

If, however, we use quintiles, or the top and bottom 20 percentiles, we get a quite different picture. For the top 20 percent earned 44.8 percent of all reported income while the bottom 20 percent earned 3.4 percent, and the ratio of 44.8 to 3.4 is just over 13 to 1, which is considerably smaller and less unequal (or more equal) than 23.4 to 1.

It obviously matters a good deal, therefore, which divisions in the income ladder one uses and compares. Both the decile and quintile ratios are correct, as it would be, too, if we compared the top and bottom 5 percent or 1 percent groups. But they obviously give very different pictures of how much inequality is present. There is no way of saying that one is a more accurate or more ample or more reliable estimate of inequality than the other.

Another problem arises in regard to which income figure one uses: income before taxes and transfer payments, income after taxes but before transfers, or income after taxes and transfers. Significant changes occur, especially in the developed welfare states, between taxed and untaxed income, and before and after receipt of transfer payments. (The latter include welfare benefits, unemployment insurance, veterans' pensions, and all other forms of transfer of income from the original recipients to others who are considered entitled.)

For example: In 1972 the income figures reported above, which were pretax figures, changed after taxes so that the ratio of the top 10 percent to the bottom 10 percent, after taxes, was 17.7 to 1 (as compared to the pretax figure of 23.4 to 1), and the ratio of the top 20 percent to the bottom 20 percent changed to just under 9.1 to 1, again a sharp reduction in inequality from the pretax figure of 13 to 1.

To show the impact of transfer payments we must use another and somewhat different report of income for the year 1972 in the United States simply because we do not have the information about transfer payments for the figures reported above.

Table 7-1 illustrates the changes that occur in shares and ratios before taxes and transfers, after taxes, and after taxes and transfers combined. We report here only for the top and bottom quintiles (information in deciles is not available). Note the following ratios of the shares of the top to the bottom quintiles of income earners:

1. Before taxes and transfers (column B): 53.1 to 1.7 or 31.2 to 1
2. After taxes, before transfers (column D): 51.9 to 1.8 or 28.8 to 1
3. After taxes and transfers (column F): 47.1 to 6.3 or 7.48 to 1.

Clearly there is a very significant decrease in the measured inequality between pretax and transfer income and after taxes and transfers.

TABLE 7-1   Combined Effects of Federal Individual Income and Payroll Taxes and Transfer Payments on the Distribution of Income, United States: 1972 Quintile Shares in Percentages.[3]

A	B	C	D	E	F
Population Category and Income Quintile	Total Income before taxes and transfers	Total Individual Income and Payroll taxes paid	Total Income after Income and Payroll taxes	Cash Transfers Received[a]	Total Income after taxes and Transfers
Total Population					
Lowest 20 percent	1.7	1.1	1.8	40.2	6.3
Top 20 percent	53.1	57.9	51.9	9.6	47.1

[a]Includes old-age, survivors, and disability insurance, unemployment and workmen's compensation, public and general assistance (welfare), veterans' benefits, and military retirement pay.

The table shows other interesting information. First, the reduction in the inequality ratio to 7.48 to 1 from 31.2 to 1 was achieved without great loss to the top 20 percent. Their share of income, before and after taxes and transfers, went from 53.1 percent of all income earned to 47.1 percent, that is, approximately an 11 percent loss in their *relative* well-being. But since these figures do not include other sources of income usually available only to higher income groups, such as income from stocks, bonds, and property, it is probably true that the top 20 percent actually retained or even increased their relative advantage after taxes and transfers.

The figures for the second, third, and fourth quintiles (not shown in the table) reveal that they did not contribute disproportionately to the taxes and transfers or that they suffered significant losses along ths way. For instance, the next to the top fifth, that is those in the 60 percent to 80 percent brackets, earned 24.1 percent of all income before taxes and transfers and 22.8 percent after taxes and transfers, a 5.3 percent reduction in relative well-being. But this was not due to disproportionate taxes, since their share of income after taxes was 24.4. percent, which is .3 percent higher than their share before taxes. The difference in their *relative* standing at the end is due to a somewhat less proportionate share of the transfers received.

The *relative* improvement in the shares of the bottom 20 percent is due, as the table shows, to the fact that they received 40.2 percent (column E) of all the transfers made. It is this transfer that raises their share from 1.7 percent to 6.3 percent of total imcome.

Note, finally, that though much greater equality has been achieved through taxes and transfers, the bottom 20 percent still earn less than one-third the share (20 percent) they would earn if there were equality, while the top 20 percent earn 47.1 percent or over twice as much as they would earn (20 percent) under equality.

It is evident that estimating incomes and inequalities in the fashion just shown makes some very interesting and useful information available. But it does not express the amount of inequality with a single figure. Instead, one has to proceed item by item and step by step through the income distribution to convey the sense of the inequality.

Various complex methods have been devised to try to express the amount of inequality as a single number. The most commonly used is one called the Gini Coefficient, which is a measure of the amount of difference between a country's actual income distribution and what it would be if there were total equality, that is, when every decile of income earners earned 10 percent of the income. With the Gini Coefficient, countries can be ranked relative to each other, or the inequality at one period can be compared with that of another period for the same country. But there are as many, if not more, problems involved in using the Gini Coefficient to represent the amount of inequality as in using comparisons and ratios between the shares of various deciles or quintiles.[4]

In Chapter 10 we will examine the range or depth of inequality at some greater length, and in Chapter 15 we will attend to the question of the claimed necessity and positive value of inequality. In the interim it will suffice to speak only to the questions of how much is a lot or a little inequality and how much is acceptable.

The answers can, of course, only be put in terms of "it all depends." Leaving aside questions of the positive or negative impact of various amounts of inequality on other features of a society, the decision as to whether a country exhibits too much, just the right amount, or too little inequality is obviously a matter of one's own sense of what ought to be found in a society. The judgment of how much equality is acceptable is a moral judgment. It may be predicated, in part, on the estimates of the influence of inequality on other desired outcomes. But, in the end, given all that information about consequences, one has to judge for oneself whether the amount of inequality is desirable.

The same kinds of consideration apply to the acceptability of the desire for high levels of living and of the expectation that those levels ought to improve every year. There is clearly no *inherent* virtue or vice either in wealth or poverty. Our judgments of these matters depend on what else we want out of our lives and our societies, how much effort we believe ought to be devoted to procuring wealth, and what other values may be sacrificed en route. All other considerations aside, it is clear that living well is to be preferred to living poorly. The desire to live well has become a dominant theme in western society and is perhaps the most contagious cultural orientation ever invented.[5]

NOTES

1. Malcolm Sawyer, "Income Distribution in OECD Countries," in OECD, *Occasional Studies,* July 1976, p. 13, Table 2.

2. Frank Ackerman, et al., "The Extent of Income Inequality in the United States," in *The Capitalist System,* Richard C. Edwards et al., eds., (Englewood Cliffs, N.J.: Prentice-Hall, Inc., 1972). The data are for 1966 and are derived from Internal Revenue Service reports for that year. Though these figures are nearly twenty years old, there is no good ground to suppose that there has been a significant change in these matters. The distribution of incomes (and presumably of wealth) seems to have been remarkably stable over the past twenty years.

3. B.A. Okner and A.M. Rivlin, in *Education, Inequality and Life Chances,* Vol. 2, (Paris: organization for Economic Cooperation and Development, 1975) Adaptation of table used with permission, "Income Distribution Policy in the U.S.," p. 205, Table 12.

4. See Sawyer, *Occasional Studies,* for an examination of the estimates of inequalities that arise when different methods are used.

5. See Arthur Okun, *Equality and Efficiency: The Big Tradeoff* (Washington, D.C.: The Brookings Institution, 1975), for a very serious and important discussion of the pros and cons of more or less equality and more or less national wealth.

CHAPTER 8
PRESTIGE AND HONOR
Concepts, Measurements, and Problems

The terms *prestige* and *honor*, which we use interchangeably here, are extremely hard to define. They are probably best understood from the sense that one cumulates from the synonyms offered for them. Roget's *Thesaurus* lists over a hundred, including notability, high repute, fame and renown, respect, regard, reverence, esteem, veneration, looking up to, admiration, and having a high opinion of. All these are versions of what sociologists call *positive evaluation.*

Evaluation, itself, refers to the special kind of judgment that ascribes to a status a certain amount of value, on a hierarchy of more or less value. That means that some statuses enjoy higher honor or prestige than others. Used that way, those terms differ from the sociological usage of the terms *esteem*, which refers to the good opinion that a person may receive from his peers and colleagues for the excellence with which he discharges his duties. People at the same occupation can enjoy different amounts of esteem, while the occupation itself receives a certain amount of honor compared with other occupations.

The honor accorded a status must also be distinguished from the honor accorded to selected people for excellence, such as military valor, or brilliant science, or drama. That is different from the variable amounts of honor or prestige given to occupations for the importance of the social service that people in them perform or for the skills and education required to perform them. While such honor is less rich in its connotations than that given for outstanding performances, it is unavoidable that richness be surrendered if we are to construct a measure of honor on which many statuses, occupational or other, can be scored and arrayed.

In full awareness of the unavoidability of that trade-off between richness of meaning and measurability, the first large-scale study of honor focused on occupations. The two sociological investigators studied a nationwide sample of people from all levels of society to determine how the respondents would evaluate ninety occupations selected from the more than 20,000 listed in the *Dictionary of Occupational Titles*.[1] Though this is considered the first major study of occupational prestige, that term itself was not used in securing judgments about various occupations. Instead, people were asked to "Please pick out the statement that best gives your own personal opinion of the general *standing* that such a job has: (1) excellent standing; (2) good standing; (3) average standing; (4) somewhat below average standing; (5) poor standing; or (6) I don't know where to place that one."

The responses were then converted into numerical scores—the higher the rating the higher the score. In that way, the researchers were able to establish a rank order of the ninety occupations, from high to low, or from the most to the least prestigious, that is, from those which were most often said to have *excellent standing* to those most often thought to have *poor standing*."

Confidence in this technique and in the reliability of the scores is enhanced by the fact that in 1963 the study was replicated (done over) employing the same questions, the same ninety job titles, and the same sampling techniques for obtaining respondents (but not the same respondents). The outcomes for 1947 and 1963 were remarkably alike, though several occupations gained and others lost prestige.

A selected sample of the ninety occupations, with their prestige scores and ranks, is displayed in Table 8–1. We take these scores from the 1963 study that replicated the 1947 study and got essentially the same results.

TABLE 8-1

Occupation	Prestige Score	Rank among 90 Occupations
Supreme Court Judge	94	1
Physician	93	2
Scientist	92	3.5
College Professor	90	8
Lawyer	89	11
Minister	87	17.5
Airline Pilot	86	21.5
Sociologist	83	26
Public School Teacher	81	29.5
Artist (Painter)	78	34.5
Economist	78	34.5
Trained Machinist	75	41.5
Policeman	72	47
Insurance Agent	69	51.5
Mail Carrier	66	57
Automobile Repairman	64	60
Truck Driver	59	67
Singer in a Nightclub	54	74
Taxi Driver	49	80.5
Garbage Collector	39	88
Shoe Shiner	34	90

Our confidence in these ratings is strengthened even more by two studies of occupational prestige in various countries. One[2] compared six countries, and the other[3] compared twenty-two countries with the United States. The overall conclusion, with certain qualifications, was that there is a "striking uniformity of occupational prestige from country to country." Such dissimilarities as were found seem most probably connected to levels of economic development.

We do not know with any certainty what the respondents had in mind when they assigned different amounts of standing to them. When they were asked to state the one main thing "about such jobs that gives this standing," 18 percent said, "It pays well"; 16 percent cited "service to humanity"; 14 percent said "social prestige"; another 14 percent cited "education, hard work, and money"; 9 percent said "moral honesty and responsibility"; another 9 percent said "intelligence and ability"; and the remainder of the judgments are distributed among a variety of other categories. Those are the percentages for the whole population studied.

When the population's answers are then analyzed by special subgroupings, such as the education of the respondent, interesting and important variations appear. Thus only 7 percent of college-educated people cited the fact that a job pays well as against the 24 percent of those with eighth grade education or less who picked out this criterion. By contrast, 24 percent of those with some college cited "service to humanity" while that criterion was chosen by only 11 percent of those with eighth grade education or less. There are comparable differences when the people are divided by their owm occupations. (The smallest differences, trivial in all cases, were found between males and females.)

Various other studies[4] have tried to learn more about the elements that go into judgments of the honor of occupations. The criteria that emerge most often, though with variable strength, include the amount of education and skill required to perform the job, the amount of public power the jobholder wields, the amount of income received at the work, and the importance to the society of the work. Underlying these judgments seems to be a realization that there are relatively few people who can perform highly skilled work that requires a good deal of education and relatively many who can perform less-skilled, less "important" jobs.

PREFERABILITY AND POPULARITY

Two other dimensions of public attitudes toward various occupations and performances should be noted. The first, *preferability,* refers to the judgments people make about the jobs they would prefer for themselves or their children when they take realistic possibilities into account. People can and do give high honor to some jobs while expressing their own preferences for other jobs with lower honor.

The second dimension is the popularity of a position, such as that enjoyed by some entertainers and athletes. Outstanding performers of this kind are probably better known than anyone else in the society; many of them get wages, salaries, and bonuses that bear no relationship to anything except their ability to draw crowds and thus make money for their employers.

Such performers may also secure honor of the kind given to supreme court justices, doctors, and professors if and when they become involved in performing good public deeds, such as fund raising for cancer research. They are often recruited for such purposes. But the honor they get for those actions is not attached to their regular occupations, nor does it normally alter the general public opinion about how much honor their regular occupations deserve.

Mention should be made, too, of the term *fame*. The most common understanding is that fame refers to the condition of being very highly reputed and very well known. Fame can be attributed, therefore, both to people with high honor and to people with great popularity. Albert Einstein and Mohammed Ali are both famous—one for science, the other for prize fighting.

HONOR AND INCOME

Excluding such exceptional cases as those of highly paid entertainers and athletes, there is a high correlation between the prestige of an occupation and its average income.[5] This is determined by putting all occupations into a rank order first on the basis of their prestige scores and then on the basis of their incomes. Then, through simple statistical techniques, the *correlation* or match between the two rank orders is analyzed. Numerous studies of this kind have demonstrated that there is a significant correlation, so that if you know the rank on prestige of an occupation you can make a reasonably good estimate of its probable rank on income, and vice versa. It is not possible to say, however, whether prestige determines income or income determines prestige. It is sure that other factors, such as education and scarcity, also play a role.

HONOR, POWER, AND DEFERENCE

We cannot speak of a measured correlation between honor and power since there are no standard units with which to measure the power of an occupation. Nevertheless, common sense suggests there is a correlation between honor and power, such that those with highly rated occupations (and correspondingly high incomes) are also likely to have more power—both personal and social—than that enjoyed by people in lower-rated, lower-paid jobs.

Yet it also seems true that today it is no longer possible, or at least much less possible than before, for people with high honor jobs and high incomes to command deference and obedience from others, except where they have direct control over the well-being of such others, and even then the power to command is limited. More than ever before, especially in the service sectors of society, commanding has given way to requesting. Employees may no longer be treated as servants. Salespeople, waitresses and waiters, bus drivers, ticket takers and train conductors, counter people, and governmental bureau employees who serve the public no longer act deferentially and often have no hesitancy about exerting the power that their role gives them to make their clients and customers wait on their pleasure. If power means the ability to command and receive deference and obedience, then it is clear that the possession of high honor and income yields much less power than formerly.

These changes from an older pattern have arisen mainly out of a combination of three factors:

1. the increased interdependence of people in urban environments, so that people with lower honor and income may be in charge of goods and services that people with higher honor require
2. the increased legitimacy of the notion of the equal worth of all people, regardless of their different honor quotients and incomes
3. the absence of effective sanctions with which people of high honor and income might command deference and obedience from others

CONGRUENCE-INCONGRUENCE AMONG INCOME, HONOR, AND POWER

Though most studies show fairly close correlations between property and honor, the correlation is by no means perfect. The result is that some, if not many, people are higher on one of the ladders than on the other.

To that kind of disparity between the positions on the ladders of income and honor the term *status incongruence* (versus congruence) is applied. Sometimes other terms are used, such as status crystallization, or the lack thereof, and status consonance or dissonance.

Status incongruence is an old phenomenon. In traditional England a person in trade might become quite wealthy but would be denied honor because he was "in trade," which was held in low repute since no "gentleman" ever engaged in trade. In general, status incongruence occurs when improved economic conditions make it possible for people to earn higher incomes than before, but not to command a matching amount of honor because of their occupations. Or they may be members of a demeaned race or religion, so that though they occupy the same nominal occupations as others, their membership in the demeaned groups detracts from the honor their occupation would normally receive. Such has been the experience in this country of Jews and Catholics as they moved into the professions and of Blacks as they secured education and higher-rated occupations.

A reverse kind of status dissonance is seen in the case of the college professor whose occupational honor quotient is significantly higher on the honor scale than is his income on the income scale.

Since the possibilities of status dissonance are numerous in mobile societies, it is no accident that status dissonance is fairly widespread today and that it has become a matter of some interest to sociologists. The basic assumption is that status dissonance creates a situation of tension, which the person experiencing that tension will feel impelled to resolve.

One earlier study offered the following hypotheses about the influence of status incongruence on behavior:

1. The greater the incongruence (between honor and income, for example) the more uncertain is the overall honor rating.
2. In the face of incongruence, efforts will be made to increase the lower-ranking item.
3. If an individual cannot raise the lower-ranking item, he will tend to avoid those people who react negatively to his lower rank.
4. If an individual cannot raise the lower-ranking item, he will tend to reject the system of evaluation which causes him to be humiliated.
5. People who enjoy congruence at a high level, for example, high income and high prestige, will exhibit less need to prove their standing.
6. There will be fewer mutual friendships and less trust among people with incongruent rankings than among those with congruent rankings.[6]

Sociologists are interested not alone in the impact on individuals or groups of various kinds of status incongruence, but of the consequences for the society at large as well. One wants to know, for example, whether in societies where status incongruence is widespread there are also higher rates of disorders and pathologies than those found in societies with lower frequencies of incongruence. Or, is there more or less social conflict in the two kinds of societies? Is there a higher quotient of scientific and literary creativity in one rather than in the other? Such societywide consequences, as well as more personal ones such as the political and interracial attitudes of congruent versus incongruent people, have been studied over the past twenty years. The results, however, are too diverse to be able to report any consensus about either the personal or social consequences. But the topic remains both interesting and important. If people care much about both income and honor, as they do in societies such as the United States, then the lack of one or the other most probably will have some notable influence on the conduct of people and of groups and, in turn, on the society at large.[7]

THE SOCIAL PATTERNING OF EVALUATION

The ways in which societies distribute honor are as varied as the ways in which they distribute property. The result is a continuum ranging from one extreme of great equality to the other of great inequality. The Israeli *kibbutz* is an outstanding example of the attempt to reach near total equality, while the traditional Indian caste system is near the extreme of total inequality. In the latter, there is a steep pyramid of honor, based originally on religious purity, but now including education, occupations, and incomes, so that a large majority occupy very lowly evaluated positions, virtually devoid of any honor, while only a relatively small and mostly hereditary elite occupies the topmost positions. There is even an underclass, called the untouchables, which can rightfully be said to have negative honor.

Such variations show that it is possible for societies to endure under very different arrangements. Nor is very much known about the relationship between the distribution of honor and the productive efficiency of a society, except to reiterate that the more equal societies also seem to be more well developed and wealthier.

In all events, some amount of inequality in honor is found everywhere.

THREE TYPES OF EVALUATION OF STATUSES

Why should that be so? We know there are no instincts in humans that cause them to seek more honor than others; and we cannot therefore account for societal patterns of honor on instinctual grounds. Instead we must search for the sources of inequality in the character of societies and their requirements.

To do so, it is first necessary to distinguish three different levels or types of evaluations that all societies practice.

The first is a judgment about the normative acceptability of the status role. Are the position and its role legal? Acceptable? Tolerable? That is a minimal kind of judgment to which all status roles *must* be submitted. For no society can afford to be indifferent to this question except at peril to its own order and safety.

The second judgment asks whether status roles are being performed at the expected level of conscientiousness and effectiveness. Are people doing what they are supposed to do in the ways they are supposed to be doing them? The concern here is mostly with that large number of roles that virtually everyone plays, such as parent, spouse, neighbor, citizen, breadwinner, and housekeeper, which every normal adult can presumably discharge without special training.

Every society must concern itself, at least to some extent, with these roles, for their successful performance is indispensable to the smooth flow of daily life. Most societies are quite permissive about these roles; they permit many differences in how they are perfromed, and they refrain from exercising any serious scrutiny of their performance. Consider, in this regard, how loosely governed in our society is the role of parent, how little interference there is, and how many different styles and modes of playing the role of parent are permitted. Yet everyone, everywhere, is subject to the judgment as to whether they perform these roles of daily life sufficiently well to be entitled to the normal rewards of daily life, including acceptance in the community and freedom from official interference.

A third judgment made in all societies has to do with whether some status roles are more important than others or are more to be cherished or valued, for any one of a number of reasons, such as their contribution to religious purity, economic abundance, military might, aesthetic attractiveness, or whatever.

In principle, it is possible for a society to deem all its institutional tasks to be equally important or equally to be cherished and valued. In fact, however, virtually all set aside one or two for special attention and special honor. They do so partly because it is easier to care about one or two than about four or five tasks. Such special treatment and honor tends to become a deeply ingrained habit, especially when the society measures its well-being by how well it is doing on the selected tasks. In any event, when tasks are selected for special attention and honor, stratification of honor has entered into the system. Inequality in honor thus springs from the same sources and enters at the same point into a society's structure as inequality in income.

THE UNIVERSAL QUEST FOR HONOR

These social traditions regarding the allocation of honor are supported everywhere by the crucial role which honor plays in the survival and well-being of every individual. When we are dependent children—no matter in what society—, others must think well enough of us to permit us to survive and help us to do so, or else we cannot do so. So, too, as we grow, unless others think well enough of us to grant us opportunity to develop, we cannot do so. Further, unless others think well enough of us to inform us we are commendable and worthy, we cannot think well enough of ourselves; we cannot achieve the sense of self-esteem that seems indispensable to healthy survival.

Basic theories in sociology and social psychology tell us that we require such self-esteem to keep our sanity and that we have only the opinions of others about us from which to derive that sense of self-esteem. One does not need the good opinion of *everybody* in order to function. But one cannot function at all if one does not have the good opinion of those who have the power to shape our destinies. All of us are dependent upon the good opinion of some such people at every stage in our lives.

The quest for honor takes on a special character when we learn to care about being better thought of than others, that is, about being more honored than others. We do not have to be taught to care about that, nor do we need to be "better thought of" to survive. But once involved in caring about distinctive honor, the failure to command it can cause serious upset, and the ability to command it can bring a sense of well-being for which nothing can substitute.

HONOR, REFERENCE GROUPS, AND REFERENCE STANDARDS

Where the quest for honor is the operative theme in a society, some will have much and many will have less or little honor. But if possessing honor is considered important by everyone, it becomes important that those who get the least honor find some way to deal with such degradation.

REACTIONS TO DEGRADATION

The most widely employed technique to avoid degradation involves choosing the right groups with whom to compare oneself and the right standards or criteria by which to judge oneself. Those groups to which we refer ourselves for comparison are called *reference groups* (sometimes called *reference others*), and the standards of criteria are called *reference standards* or *reference criteria*.

In his 1941 study of the distribution of honor in a pseudonymous northeastern city called "Yankee City"[8] W. Lloyd Warner, an anthropologist, discovered that a large number of people, who could not claim much honor on the criteria of prestigious occupation, income, residence, and family origin, rejected these criteria and substituted, instead, such things as decency, morality, and good citizenship, of which they could, of course, claim an abundance, and in terms of which they could therefore feel equal, if not superior, in honor to those who rated above them on other criteria, such as wealth. In short, they shifted their reference criteria to secure the amount of honor they desired.

SELF-GHETTOIZATION

To make this effective, they had to confine their personal relationships to people who were equally low rated on the standard criteria. In that way they were able to claim and receive an acceptable amount of honor from their peers. They reinforced these favorable self-estimates by casting aspersions on the more highly rated people, attributing their apparent success in life to luck, immoral conduct, or unfair inherited advantages.

Such techniques for managing degradation are practiced wherever the unequal distribution of honor imposes the threat or actuality of degradation on some. It is not always possible to engage successfully in these honor-saving techniques, but they are found everywhere. In extreme cases, such as that of the Indian untouchables, the groups isolate themselves or are forcibly isolated from any intimate contact with more highly rated people. The presence of religious, racial, and ethnic ghettos everywhere is evidence of the practice of isolation, forced or voluntary or both. The degraded group itself often exercises restraint on its own members to prevent them from mingling with others. Such in-group restraint is achieved through social shaming, scolding, ostracism, or even physical force where necessary. The avoidance of unhappy experiences with others and the comforts of moving comfortably among one's own people serve as additional forces to keep ghetto walls intact.

CONVIVIALISM AND CONNUBIALISM: TESTS OF EQUALITY OF HONOR

The honor attached to occupations, we see, is but one element, albeit an important one, in the total amount of honor that individuals or groups seek and receive. Religious, ethnic, and racial affiliations, family origins, area of residence, and even personal character and conduct can and often do enter into the judgments others make as to how much honor to accord us. Given so many and diverse possible criteria, the determination of who is equal may be a very difficult task.

The most trustworthy index of equality in traditional societies, and still to some extent in modern societies, is with whom one shares or is permitted to share convivialism, that is, participate with others in those situations in which one can choose one's partners. This is expressed in whom one invites home or by whom one is invited; with whom one dines (commensalism); with whom one goes on vacations or to concerts, games, and celebrations. The greatest intimacy and hence the surest test of equality is found in whom one marries. Connubialism, as marrying is called, is everywhere viewed as something that only people who are equal in honor can and should do.

In traditional societies, formal laws and informal customs operate to govern convivialism and connubialism. While most such laws have been eliminated in modern societies, the practice of sharing intimacy only with those considered equal in general honor is widespread.

On the other hand, social and economic mobility have increased so greatly that it becomes ever more common for people from quite different social and economic backgrounds to enjoy a new equality of achieved honor, based on their own educational and occupational accomplishments. Some of the results of this new equality are to be seen in the marriage announcements in newspapers, which clearly reveal that people of quite different origins are now marrying as equals. The new equality is seen operating, too, in the roster of the freshmen classes of prestigious schools, where young people of the most diverse ethnic, religious, racial, and socioeconomic backgrounds are brought together as nominal, if not actual, social equals from then on. Attendance at and graduation from such universities increasingly serves to erase all previous inequality of honor.

Such new equalizations do not, however, eliminate the significance of honor from modern life. For though distinctive degrees of honor based on ascriptive criteria may have been sharply reduced, they have been amply supplanted by equally distinctive degrees of achieved honor. Graduation from a prestigious school may erase all stigma of low origins, but by the same token, it creates a new group of unequally honored people.

The rule of reserving convivialism and connubialism for one's honor-peers does not seem to have lost its force in the new environment. Honorific credentials, albeit newly achieved, must be vouchsafed, even if access to these credentials is now much more open and generous than before. Those credentials are crucial as validations of one's eligibility for club memberships, participation in prestigious charities, easy acceptance at various churches and synagogues and election to their governing boards, welcome admission to a neighborhood, and, of course, access to potential marriage partners. Though one can often break into exclusive circles if one has enough money, considerations of honor still remain important.

HONOR AND LIFE STYLE[9]

One validates one's claim to a stated level of honor by the style of life that one leads. Included in style are the kinds of homes one buys, the neighborhoods in which one lives, the cars driven, the clothes worn, the parties given, the schools to which children are sent, and, of course, the voluntary associations to which one belongs: churches, clubs, charities, and the like. Social acceptance as an equal by those from whom one seeks such acceptance depends greatly on being able to exhibit the appropriate life style. The guiding principles here are likely to vary among communities and among income levels.

CONSPICUOUS CONSUMPTION AND STATUS-SEEKING

In his classic book, *The Theory of the Leisure Class,* Thorstein Veblen[10] long ago noted that the "idle rich" engaged in the conspicuous consumption of leisure and luxury and in conspicuous waste of costly goods and services to prove that they did not have to work for a living and that they had enviable amounts of wealth.

While modern societies have come to place great emphasis on achievement and have come to honor wealth gained through achievement as much as that gained through inheritance, the themes of conspicuous consumption of leisure, luxury, and waste remain salient. In modern journalistic parlance, this is called *status-seeking,* or the pursuit of distinction through leading a conspicuously luxurious style of life. Luxury and leisure are sought, not only as ends in themselves, but as means to public honor.

Such status-seeking is perhaps more frantic today than it ever has been, most particularly though not exclusively, among those whose new wealth enables them to engage in the consumption of leisure and luxury, but who do not know well enough how and what to do with their money to validate their claims to honor. Whole new professions specialize in providing assistance to these beleagured status-seekers. Advertising of luxurious goods and services is clearly aimed at them; the purchasing of honor is an explicit theme of such advertising. Certain news media cater to *status anxiety* as a regular feature[11] and books on these methods have become quite popular.[12]

The explanation of status anxiety may lie in three factors:

1.   the traditional criteria of honor, such as distinguished family and old wealth, are available only to a few
2.   a substantial number of people enjoy relatively equal occupational honor and the honor of high incomes
3.   few can claim any genuine honor for excellence in enterprises of public significance

In the absence of these possible sources of dinstinctive honor, all that seems left to those who care about such distinctiveness is to conspicuously consume the right goods and services somewhat more stylishly than others.

The more general concern about honor, which is found among everyone, remains, for the reasons stated, a very active impulse in modern society and makes the distribution of honor a vital social pattern.

NOTES

1. Cecil C. North and Paul K. Hatt, "Jobs and Occupations: A Popular Evaluation," *Opinion News,* September, 1947, pp. 3–13. For a description of the procedures and an evaluation of the reliability of the technique, see Delbert C. Miller, *Handbook of Research Design and Social Measurement* (New York: McKay, 1970). For additional analysis and replication and revisions of the North-Hatt study, see Albert J. Reiss, Jr. *et al., Occupations and Social Status* (New York: The Free Press, 1961).
  In the Reiss book one will find a very serious critique of the North-Hatt study, one which raises important questions about the validity of the concept of job prestige, the soundness of the methods employed, and the usefulness of the scale devised. These are well known; but the kind of analysis done by North and Hatt is the one that most people employ still today, albeit with certain modest revisions, especially when they compare prestige ratings in various nations.

2. Alex Inkeles and Peter H. Rossi, "National Comparisons of Occupational Prestige," *American Journal of Sociology,* 61 (January 1956), 329–39.

3. Robert W. Hodge, Donald J. Treiman, and Peter H. Rossi, "A Comparative Study of Occupational Prestige," in *Class, Status and Power,* 2nd ed., eds. Reinhard Bendix and Seymour Martin Lipset (New York: The Free Press, 1966), pp. 309–34.

4. Joseph Gusfield and Michael Schwartz, "The Meanings of Occupational Prestige of the NORC Scale," *American Sociological Review,* 28, 265–71 and Richard L. Simpson and Ida H. Simpson, "Correlates and Estimates of Occupational Prestige," *American Journal of Sociology,* 66 (September 1960), No. 2, 135–49.

5. The standard reference here is the analysis by Otis Dudley Duncan on the correlation, in the United States, of the prestige, median income, and median educational attainment of all occupations. See his "A Socio-Economic Index for All Occupations," in Reiss, *Occupations,* especially pp. 84–85 and 121–24.

6. These hypotheses are my own paraphrased versions of some of the formulations of Andrzej Malewski in his "The Degree of Status Incongruence and Its Effects," *The Polish Sociological Bulletin,* No. I, (7), 1963. The possible number of incongruent combinations would grow if we were to add power to income and honor in estimating congruence.

7. There is by now a very substantial body of literature covering various aspects of status crystallization or congruence. We cite a few below to indicate the range of problems considered.

   a. J.H. Abramson, "Emotional Disorder, Status Inconsistency and Migration," *Milbank Memorial Fund Quarterly,* 44 (January, 1966), 23–48.

   b. Hubert M. Blalock, Jr., "The Identification Problem and Theory Building: The Case of Status Inconsistency," *American Sociological Review,* 31 (February 1966), 52–61.

   c. Leonard Broom and F. Lancaster Jones, "Status Consistency and Political Preference: The Australian Case," *American Sociological Review,* 35 (December 1970), 989–1001.

   d. Joseph S. Fauman, "Status Crystallization and Interracial Attitudes," *Social Forces,* 47 (October 1968), 53–60.

   e. Gerhardt E. Lenski, "Status Crystallization: A Non-Vertical Dimension of Social Status," *American Sociological Review,* 19 (August 1954), 405–13.

   f. David Segal *et. al.,* "Status Inconsistency and Self-Evaluation," *Sociometry,* 33 (September 1970), 347–57.

g.   Melvin Tumin *et. al.,* "Status Mobility and Anomie: A Study in Readiness for Desegregation," *British Journal of Sociology,* 3 (September 1959), 253–76.

8.   See W. Lloyd Warner and Paul S. Lunt, *The Social Life of a Modern Community* (New Haven: Yale University Press, 1941). Also see the summary volume called *Social Class in America* (Chicago: Science Research Associates, Inc., 1949).

9.   Max Weber, the distinguished German sociologist, is responsible for introducing the term *life style* into the lexicon of sociology. He used the term to refer to the actions employed to claim and validate a certain degree of honor. He says, "...the style of life required by status groups makes them prefer special kinds of property or gainful pursuits and reject others." He also uses the term *status groups* to refer to those groups which are formed among people with common degrees of honor. In doing so, he distinguished that kind of honor group from others, called *classes,* which are formed mostly on the basis of common levels of income, though, of course, as Weber puts it, social honor is determined most of the time by the average class, that is, economic situation, of these status-group members. Weber here is using *status* to mean honor, while we have used the term simply to refer to any position, without regard to its degree of honor. For elaboration of these ideas see Max Weber, "The Development of Caste" from his *Religion of India*trans. and ed. Hans G. Gerth and Don Martindale (Glencoe, Illinois: The Free Press, 1958); see also, *Max Weber: Essays in Sociology,* trans. Hans Gerth and C. Wright Mills (New York: Oxford University Press, 1946).

10.   Thorstein Veblen, *The Theory of the Leisure Class* (New York: The Modern Library, Random House, Inc., 1934).

11.   *New York Magazine,* September 15, 1983.

12.   See, for example, Joan Kron, *Home Psychology: The Social Psychology of Home and Decoration* (New York: Clarkson N. Potter, 1983).

CHAPTER 9
POWER
Concepts,
Measurements,
and Problems

The most general meaning of power is the ability to secure one's own ends or desires, even against the opposition of others. So defined, power may be acquired from a number of sources.

FIVE SOURCES OF POWER

First is positional or role power, which derives from the authority given to people by virtue of their positions. The president of an organization has the authority or power of his office; so do judges, police, employers, teachers, and anyone in a formal relationship in which one partner has the legal or customary right to command some or all aspects of the relationship. Positional authority, then, may be thought of as legitimate role-specific power. It stretches as far as the limits of the formal relationship but no farther. It is specific to the status relationships to which it is attached.

A second source of power lies in the possession of goods and services that enable the possessors to purchase what they want.

A third source of power is found in skills and abilities that enable people to provide services that others desire. Craft skills, military acumen, economic expertise, medical knowledge, and literary artistry are among the skills that give their possessors a certain amount of power over those who desire the benefits of their skills.

A fourth source of power lies in personal qualities, such as beauty, guile, charm, or charisma, that enable some to persuade others to do their bidding or to seek their favor.

Power is derived, fifth, from the force, psychological, social, or physical, that one commands and with which one can threaten others and cause them to do their bidding, out of fear for their bodies, their freedom, or their property.

Power, in sum, derives from role-specific authority, the possession of goods and services, skills, personal qualities, and coercive force. Some students identify all nonrole power as influence, so that power is equal to the sum of authority and influence.

LEGITIMATE AND ILLEGITIMATE SOURCES AND USES

Legitimate and acceptable powers must be distinguished from those that are deemed illegitimate and unacceptable. Yet all illegitimate powers rest on the same bases as those which yield legitimate power. Gangsters, thieves, terrorists, prostitutes, gamblers, and others in the illegitimate world are able to exert power because of their role-specific authorities in that world, or because of their material resources, skills, personal qualities, and psychological and physical coerciveness. Moreover, those who secure resources from the illegitimate world, that is, money from stealing, gambling, or drug peddling, can use such illegally acquired assets as a source of power in both the legitimate and illegitimate world. Money secured in legitimate ways, such as through work, can be used for either legitimate or illegitimate ends, such as to purchase illegal drugs or to gamble illegally, or to secure a position or contract through bribery. In the same vein, a person with superior role authority can use the power of his position, such as the ability to fire another person, to coerce the subordinate, illegally, into desired forms of behavior. Though the crossovers between the legitimate and illegitimate worlds are fairly frequent and important, we eliminate any consideration of them in the discussion that follows because we desire to focus alone on the system of legitimate norms and patterns of distribution of power.

FOUR MAIN CONTEXTS OF POWER

Power can be exercised in four major contexts.

Political Affairs

First is the shaping of the affairs and conduct of organized political communities, such as towns, cities, states, the nation at large, and the international community. Here it is relevant to speak of the power of both individuals and groups, including associations, firms, political parties, and whole communities. Such collectivities derive their power from most of the same sources as do individuals: from their positional roles, for example, the greater powers of the federal over local governments by virtue of constitutional provisions; or from their resources, such as the hydroelectric power they can build and on which they collect tolls, the votes in the electoral college to which they are entitled, or their membership in the Security Council of the United Nations. Groups also derive power from the skills and abilities of their members, as in the instance of lobbyists for professional associations and trade unions, or from their ability to exert coercive force, as in the case of highly armed nations. The only source of power that is available to individuals but is not often relevant to groups or collectivities is the power that comes from personal qualities, such as charm, beauty, or charisma.

Institutional Patterning

A second context in which power is relevant is in the interplay of roles in the basic institutions, such as the economy, the polity, the family, the educational system, and the church. Examples include relations between employers and employees, teachers and pupils. Since we each occupy some position in each of the basic institutions that govern daily life, we are always involved in such relationships in which the balance of power, as well as patterns of dominance and submission, are important elements in determining the pattern of conduct. Role-specific authority is probably most important here.

Ensuring Life Chances

A third context in which power operates is in the competition for a share of valued life chances, such as surviving the first year of life, maintaining good health, securing good opportunities for schooling and jobs, and living through a reasonable span of years. These add up to the ability to control one's destiny.

Personal Relations

The fourth and final context in which power is important is the network of personal relations outside the institutional roles. These include encounters with others in stores, on the street, or in buses, subways, and planes; in friendships and love relationships; at ballparks and stadiums; in neighborhoods and all other such places in which most of the people are not formally bound to us, nor we to them, but with whom we must coordinate interests, desires, and movements. A high-priced ticket gives us room and privacy in an athletic arena, at a theater, or on a train or plane; quotas of personal charm and beauty determine how many will seek one out as companion and how many one will be able to induce to become companions; physical size or the appearance of possible danger commands a certain degree of deference.

It is clear that not all the kinds of power are equally relevant, or even relevant at all, in all the four contexts of power just specified. But one or more of those types of power is crucially relevant in all the four contexts.

There is no necessary relationship among the amounts of power of an individual or group in one of these contexts and their power in the others. One may be very

powerful in national affairs and yet be relatively powerless in personal relationships and in such role-relationships as marriage and parenthood. Or, one may
be quite dominant in the intimacy of one's home and yet be subject to the will of
virtually everyone outside the home. Or, one may be powerful in an institutional
role, such as at work, and have little or no power in national affairs or personal
relationships.

THE PATTERNING OF POWER: EQUALITY AND INEQUALITY

All four contexts of power—political, institutional, life chances, and personal
relations—are socially patterned to some degree. There are visible and legitimate
norms that help determine who will have how much power. Laws and customs
govern our community relations; jobs and laws of property and contract govern our
resources; patterned systems of education and training shape our skills and abilities;
formal political controls and economic resources determine our levels of coercive
power; and prevailing criteria of beauty and charm determine which of us will be
deemed to possess those desirable qualities.

In many if not most contexts power is distributed unequally. One or more of
the participants is able or entitled to exert more power than the others. The obvious
exceptions are impersonal momentary encounters, as with people who are shopping
in the same stores or waiting on the same lines for service, in which, at least in
democratic societies, one is nominally equal and equally entitled. No one may claim
or attempt to secure any special privileges or preferences without incurring the
resistance or counterforce of others. Outside of these egalitarian situations, power is
most often distributed unequally.

Even in intimate personal situations such as marriages, where the law and
customs may command equality between the partners and where equality is
viewed as the ideal to be striven for, it often proves impossible to divide power
equally. The result is that either one partner emerges as the dominant one in most
decisions, or the partners divide areas of decisions, or they take turns at being
dominant. The husband may have more power over the disposal of family income,
while the wife has most to say about how the house will be run and how the
children will be reared, or vice versa. This pattern is best seen as one of divided
powers and serial inequality rather than equality of power. The persistence of such
serial inequality in a society that calls for equality may be seen as a carry-over
from earlier customs and laws where the spouses were assigned, by law and
custom, different sets of powers over different aspects of the marriage and family
relationship.

In general, then, power is distributed unequally far more often than equally,
and it is a crucial feature of virtually all relationships everywhere.

ORIGINS AND PERSISTENCE OF INEQUALITY IN POWER

The same explanations as were earlier offered for the inequalities in property and honor apply as well to the case of power. Today's societies are the heirs of older societies in which the traditions and laws called for the dominance of certain kinds and classes of people over others: nobles over serfs; males over females; older people over younger people; holy men over laics; owners of property over the landless.

Those traditions and laws must originally have derived mostly from the sheer play of physical power, which then rapidly became reinforced by attaching to those unequal powers the sanction of divinities and using forceful punishment to quell disobedient subordinates. Powerful people seized land and other material resources and thereby were able to command the deference and obedience of those who needed those resources. With those resources, those powerful people could purchase arms and retainers and thereby strengthen their hold on power. So, too, people who were thought to command divine interventions were able to coerce others to obey their wills by the threat of divine punishments. In those and other ways echelons and strata of unequal people were developed. Their relationships became deeply institutionalized over time, so that inequality in power seemed natural and inevitable. Whatever other accounts may be offered for the onset of inequality of power, the factors just listed must be given prominent place.

THE MEASUREMENT OF POWER

Though we can almost always judge, at least impressionistically, who has more and who has less power in a relationship, it is extremely difficult to measure such power precisely or even as imprecisely as we measure property and prestige. There are no standard scales or indicators, such as exist in the cases of property and prestige. We do not even have a good verbal conceptualization of what "one unit" of power might be. Instead, we are confined to talking in gross terms about situations and encounters in which various people are more or less able to impose their views and wishes on others.

Even if we had reliable ways in which to measure power in one situation, we would still be quite perplexed about how to calculate a sum total of the power that individuals or groups possess over a number of situations. For, to do so, we would need a common unit which was additive and in which, therefore, one unit in one situation could be considered the equivalent of one unit in a different situation, for example, one unit of power to shape a piece of legislation as against one unit of power to secure a favorable life chance, such as adequate health care. We lack such units and such arithmetical procedures, and the result is that we can speak only quite imprecisely about the sum total amount of power people possess.

This difficulty plagues students of power even when they restrict themselves to measuring power in only one area, such as the power to shape the decisions of a political community, whether on the local, state, or national level. Though it is often possible to identify who seems to have most influence over a given bill, or even a series of bills in a particular area, such as pollution control or coal leases, it is beyond our abilities at the moment to aggregate the various amounts of power of an individual or group over a whole series of bills and issues into a meaningful sum total of power. Is the power to shape a bill concerned with interest rates the equivalent of the power to shape a bill regarding pollution control? We do not know how to answer this question except in quite impressionistic and imprecise terms.

Interesting but imprecise methods have been devised for measuring local community power. Most prominent among these is the technique of compiling lists of powerful people suggested by informed observers, and these lists are then scrutinized to see which names appear most often over a range of interests. In that way a roster of "influentials" or "movers and shakers" can be compiled, which will specify those who, in general, are thought to be most influential in a given community.[1] But these are multiple elites in the sense that any good politician knows not only whose support has to be secured in a given issue, but also that he must seek support from quite different people on different issues. Given the difficulties in these matters, we probably have to be satisfied with a list of people, most of whom are influential in one or two areas of policy at most, while only a very small number enjoy power over a broad range of issues.

We are unavoidably required, too, to be quite impressionistic in assessing power in intimate personal relations. Even where these occur within the framework of role-specific rights and duties, as between husband and wife or parent and child, the formal rules are often so very general that there is considerable room for the play of personality and temperament and even physical strength in determining who will rule.

We achieve the greatest precision in measuring power over life chances. Many of these, such as frequency and cost of illness, longevity, and years of school, are formulated in common numerical terms, so that it is possible to compare the amounts of these that different people seem able to command.

Yet there are difficulties here, too. For example, are two illnesses of a given kind only twice as much illness as one illness of the kind in question? Is twelve years of education only three-fourths of sixteen years? Or does completing college mean so very much more than high school that we must weigh the four years very heavily in our calculations?

Such problems require us to be very cautious about comparing amounts of life chances. Yet in these matters we can more sensibly assign numbers to the things that resource power makes possible and thereby come closer than in any other area of power to sound comparisons of the different amounts of power people have over life chances.

The difficulties encountered in measuring power in each of the four contexts means that very little precision is possible in any estimate of the total power possessed over all four areas. While some may command significant power in all four areas, most people surely have variable amounts of power in each of these; and it becomes therefore virtually impossible to calculate a sensible total sum of power that would reflect that variability.

Yet the distribution of power is a crucial matter in any society and in any relationship. For though power is not distributed as a reward for performance, it is intimately connected to the income and honor that are distributed partly in accordance with performance. Often enough, too, the power that derives from the possession of wealth and honor can be and is used to insure that one will continue to enjoy high levels of wealth and honor. In that way, the three inequalities can and often do reinforce each other.

But because we cannot readily measure the amount of power that is possessed by various statuses (as we do in the case of income and honor), we cannot calculate correlations among the property, honor, and power of a number of statuses.

The closest we come to such an overall measure of the amount of the three good things that various positions command takes the form of a composite socioeconomic index or socioeconomic scale (SES), a tool that many investigators use in studying inequality. Such measures as SES, as it is most popularly known, include some measure of income, occupational honor, and educational level, but not of power. Yet it may be supposed, at least from what we know of what kinds of positions and resources yield power, that the higher one's position on an SES scale, the greater is the amount of power that one can exert in social, political, economic, and personal relationships.

There are, of course, exceptions to this statement. There are people, for example, distinguished poets or painters, who are high on prestige but very poor in material resources and devoid of any power. So, too, there are people who are very rich and very powerful but who claim little or no honor, since they secured their money illegally. And, though wealthy people most certainly command high amounts of valued life chances, many of them may have little or nothing to say about the shape of political affairs.

But these exceptions do not occur so frequently, as far as we can tell, to make us doubt seriously that there is a substantial correlation among property, power, and prestige.

IS THERE A POWER ELITE?

When Max Weber asserted that power is one of the three bases (property and honor are the other two) on which aggregates of people are formed, he was referring among other things to the political parties which have become characteristic features of western democracies. People form political parties and others join them in order to aggregate power so that they may have a chance to implement their ideas about how societies ought to be run.

But there is another important way in which power serves as a basis of aggregation. That sense is implicit in the term *power elite* and refers to sets of people who by reason of their official positions, or wealth, or family connections enjoy dominant power in those contexts in which they operate. One may speak, for instance, of a military-industrial-political elite, which consists of those people who exercise governing power in the three sectors indicated.

To speak of them as a collective elite, however, is to suggest that they self-consciously unite to bring the weight of their respective powers to bear as a unified force. This notion is widely discussed in the literature of sociology and political science. Do these power leaders from various areas actually unite? On all issues? On only some? Do they disagree and quarrel as often as they agree? Do they all share the same ideology and values about how a society ought to be run, or are they quite variable in these matters? Do they constitute an effective ruling class, or are they too disunited to justify that term? The disputes on these issues are very strong.

One may reasonably suppose, however, that those who are in top positions and enjoy greatest influence in the major institutional areas are likely to think alike about the existing distributions of power. Though there may be significant exceptions to this rule, one may expect that those in command of any enterprise are likely to be against any proposals for changes that would displace them from their powerful positions and that, at most, they would favor some modest redistribution of power. At least that is what most students of these matters would agree upon.

The answer, then, to the question of whether there is a power elite is "Yes, no, and maybe." An elite of most powerful people can be identified; and they do commonly seek to maintain themselves in power. But there are often sharp differences of opinion and policy among them, so that, for example, top political officials are often very divided on economic and military policies. From the point of view of those who do not have much power in any institutional area, the existence of a powerful elite and the frequent signs of unity among elites from different areas are likely to be seen as evidence that such elites exist, think alike, and constitute an active cabal, if not conspiracy, designed to protect their own interests and prevent any significant change.

Table 9-1 (p. 79) summarizes two opposing views on the question of whether there is a power elite in the United States and whether it constitutes a unified force.[2] The affirmative position is represented here by a composite portrait of the views of C. Wright Mills,[3] and the opposing position summarizes the viewpoint of David Reisman.[4]

THE ENJOYMENT OF POWER FOR ITS OWN SAKE: POWER AS A REWARD

We stated earlier that power is not allocated as a reward, but rather is a derivative from position, property, and prestige and personal characteristics. Now we must enrich that statement by noting how significant the enjoyment of power for its own sake appears to be. Such enjoyment of power is a theme found expressed frequently in novels, plays, essays, and even in modern journalism. But it is not a new or modern theme. For it has everywhere and at all times been true that power,

TABLE 9-1 Two Portraits of the American Power Structure

Power structure	Mills	Riesman
Levels	unified power elite diversified and balanced plurality of interest groups mass of unorganized people who have no power over elite	no dominant power elite diversified and balanced plurality of interest groups mass of unorganized people who have some power over interest groups
Changes	increasing concentration of power	increasing dispersion of power
Operation	one group determines all major policies manipulation of people at the bottom by group at the top	who determines policy shifts with the issue monopolistic competition among organized groups
Bases	coincidence of interests among major institutions (economic, military, governmental) social similarities and psychological affinities among those who direct major institutions	diversity of interests among major organized groups sense of weakness and dependence among those in higher as well as lower status
Consequences	enhancement of interests of corporations, armed forces, and executive branch of government decline of politics as public debate decline of responsible and accountable power—loss of democracy	no one group or class is favored significantly over others decline of politics as duty and self-interest decline of effective leadership

like honor, has been enjoyed for its own sake and that its possession is viewed by those who are fortunate enough to have it as a very valuable thing in life.

These observations apply to all four contexts in which power is exercised: political affairs, institutional patterns, life chances, and personal relationships. A sense of good fortune and well-being seems to accrue to those who enjoy such powers, and probably this sense seems to mount in proportion both to the depth of power in any one area and to the spread of power over several areas. To be able to give orders and not to have to take orders from anyone is seen as a great good. The power to shape one's life as one sees fit, summed up in the word *autonomy*, is seen by many as the most treasured of all human conditions, even when it does not involve control over others.

These remarks suggest then that though much power may be role-specific, that is, assigned to one's status in order to permit one to discharge one's role-obligations, the possession of such role-specific power is very often viewed as a good in itself, over and above its relevance for role-obligations. As such it must be viewed as a reward that people receive, even if it is not intended as such and even if it is often considered immoral, if not pathological, to desire power for its own sake and to relish the ability to exercise it. The enjoyability of power for its own sake serves importantly to make power one of the three main good things in life.

VARIATIONS IN POWER DISTRIBUTIONS

In the western democratic societies, including the United States, as well as Australia, New Zealand, the Scandinavian countries, Israel, Costa Rica, et al., formal political power is more equally shared than in any of the other major countries of the world, present or past. For in most of the rest of the world, political power is monopolized by one or more small elites, including military juntas, religious mullahs, economic barons, political oligarchs, tribal chieftains, and social caste hierarchs. If we add hereditary nobilities, we encompass virtually all the political systems of the world for the last thousand years. In many of these systems power is shared between several of the elites, as in the Soviet Union, where the political and military dictators together govern; or in Brazil, where the military and economic oligarchs exercise power; or in Iran, where religious and military tyrants govern without any democratic controls. In all of them, a few rule and the vast majority are required under severe threat to obey.

The western democracies are characterized, among other ways, by constitutional and traditional requirements that civil authorities shall rule over military officials, that state affairs shall be separated from church affairs, and that transitions from one set of leaders to the next shall be accomplished through peaceful, free elections, in which all citizens are entitled to participate. It is these peaceful transitions through free elections that are taken as the hallmark of western democracy. Only Italy and Germany, among today's democracies, have in the past exhibited a fundamental instability as revealed by their adoption of totalitarian dictatorships as their modes of government. Yet even these two countries have emerged since World War II into political democracies with free elections and have exhibited stable democratic operations since then.

Still, western democracies comprise only a minority of the societies and people of the world, and they achieved their form of power distribution only relatively recently, as historical time is counted. In virtually every case, moreover, some kind of violent revolution or civil war was required to establish a democratic government. Oligarchs and tyrants have not relinquished their dictatorial powers easily and do not do so today.

However much more democratic the western systems may be, a substantial amount of political inequality still characterizes them. This is due mainly to two causes. First, significant economic inequality enables wealthy people and large economic organizations to influence political decisions more than others; second, poorer and less well educated people participate less actively in the political process, and this itself is due in large part to the consequences of economic inequality.

Some students of these matters argue that no real movement toward greater political equality can be achieved without first achieving greater economic equality. Others, however, insist that it is possible for political power to become more equally shared without much alteration in the distribution of income and property.

However that argument may be decided, there is demonstrably greater equality of political power in the western democracies. Moreover, virtually every change in these systems in the past four or five decades has been in the direction of even greater power-sharing and even greater participation in the political process than ever before by groups of people, such as ethnic and racial minorities, women, and poor people, who have participated little if at all in the past.

It is indisputable, too, that the western societies, which are among the wealthiest in the world, exhibit the greatest equality in their distributions of income, and their people enjoy more freedoms—of the press, speech, election, and movement—than anywhere else.

Along with the greater democratization of power and equalization of incomes, has come a new surge of insistence on greater equality in role-relationships in the major institutions. We noted earlier that every important formal relationship—in the schools, in families, in the church, in factories and offices, in health facilities—has undergone change in the past decades so that people who were formerly very unequal now are more equal in their rights than ever before.

Against this movement toward greater equality of power, one must place the inequalities that persist in the four major contexts. It is, therefore, probably fairest to say that in modern democratic societies there is a continuing conflict between the forces of equality and inequality, and there is a continuously changing balance between them.

NOTES

1. The first major study of power in an American community was conducted by Robert and Helen Lynd in 1929. Entitled *Middletown* (New York: Harcourt Brace, Jovanovich, Inc. 1929), it sought by various means to document the depth and range of power in Middletown that was exercised by a small elite of wealthy people. An attempt at greater precision in the measurement of power in a community is to be found in the classic study by Floyd Hunter, *Community Power Structure: A Study of Decision Makers* (Chapel Hill, N.C.: University of North Carolina Press, 1953). Hunter's study uses the *reputational approach,* that is, powerful people are identified by asking others who has power.

A contrasting approach studies who the people were who appeared to influence a number of decisions. An example is found in Robert Dahl's book *Who Governs? Democracy and Power in an American City* (New Haven: Yale University Press, 1961). Still another variant is sometimes called the *positional approach,* in which the people who occupy high formal positions and who wield much informal power are identified as the community power structure. A comparison of these various approaches is found in Linton Freeman et al., "Locating Leaders in Local Communities: A Comparison of Some Alternative Approaches," *American Sociological Review,* 28 (OCTOBER 1963), 79–98. Many sociologists and political scientists have made their contributions to this field of study. While the interest in community power structures is not as great today as it formerly was, studies continue to be made and published.

2.   Reprinted with permission of Macmillan, Inc. from *Culture and Social Character,* Seymour Martin Lipset and Leo Lowenthal, eds., (Glencoe, Ill.: The Free Press, 1961). Copyright © 1961 by the Free Press of Glencoe, Inc.

3.   See C. Wright Mills, *The Power Elite* (New York: Oxford University Press, 1956).

4.   David Reisman et. al., *The Lonely Crowd* (New Haven: Yale University Press, 1950).

CHAPTER 10
THE DEPTH
OF INEQUALITY
IN PROPERTY,
PRESTIGE, POWER,
AND EDUCATION

A major difference among systems of stratification is in the range or depth of the inequalities in property, prestige, and power. The major questions here concern the ways in which the available good things are divided. Do a few have most and the majority have little? Or are the extremes close to each other so that well-being is shared more equally?

These questions are easiest to answer in regard to property, since most property can be translated into money units and, with reservations, it makes sense to say that two dollars is twice one dollar, and that people in the top 10 percent of income earners earn ten times as much as people in the bottom 10 percent.

Comparing amounts of prestige, however, is much more difficult, even if we limit the term to the evaluation given to occupations. For though prestige scores can be calculated, as we saw in Chapter 8, the way the scores are constructed does not permit us to say such a thing as that the prestige of doctors is twice that of plumbers, even if the numbers are eighty-four and forty-two respectively. Even if such comparisons were possible, what would a statement like that mean? We cannot say. It does make sense, however, to state that one occupation is high and another low on the range; or that there is bunching of many occupations at the middle or the bottom; or that all the white-collar occupations have higher scores than the blue-collar ones. These are informative statements, even if they are not as precise or meaningful as we should like.

Comparing amounts of power, either of statuses or people, is even more difficult, since we don't have power scores or scales for various statuses. All our comparisons of amounts of power must therefore be impressionistic, though sometimes we can be quite sure they are accurate, for instance, if we were to say that a U.S. senator has much more political power than an ordinary citizen.

We can also be reasonably sure of the truth of statements such as that in a totalitarian society power is concentrated in the hands of a small, ruling clique, and that no one else has any real power in the shaping of public events except as the rulers permit people to have it. That would be true of any totalitarian society, whether the rulers are military, religious, or political. Such systems obviously have more extreme power distributions than democratic societies, which have structured mechanisms for common participation in decision making.

Both the totalitarian and democratic versions of power distribution differ from those in which, though there are no democratic processes, power is divided among numerous power centers or blocs in the society, including economic magnates, religious leaders, military commanders, secular political authorities, and radical or revolutionary groups and parties, all contesting for power over various aspects of the conduct of the society. Comparisons among such diverse societies are quite common, and they are useful and important to be able to make. They tell a good deal about the distribution of power.

The measurement of power attaching to statuses, however, eludes even that kind of gross measurement, except in one regard. Recall that power over life chances is secured mostly through income and education, particularly in modern, developed societies. We are shortly going to specify the depth of income inequality. It will be helpful, therefore, if we also examine the depth of inequality in education, as that is measured by the differences in numbers of years of school completed.

Because educational achievement is so powerful in shaping life chances, including the chance to secure positions which typically yield power, honor, and income, it makes sense to treat education as a major feature of modern systems of stratification and we shall do so.

THE DEPTH OF INCOME DIFFERENCES

Table 10–1 (p. 85) shows the distribution of family income in the United States in 1982. (The Census defines a family as a "Group of two or more persons related by blood, marriage or adoption and residing together in a household. A family includes among its members the person or couple who maintains the household.")

The first row, labeled "under $2,500" reaches below zero into negative income, that is, those whose net income was less than zero. The top category "over $50,000" stretches to include the few who earn millions of dollars a year. The term *median income* refers to the figure above and below which 50 percent of the population are located, while *mean income* is a weighted average which takes account of the number and percent who earn each of the various levels of income.

The findings in this table can be summed up in various ways. One might point to the fact, for instance, that nearly a third of the families earn less than $15,000 a year; and since these low-earning families typically have the largest number of

TABLE 10-1   Family Income (Total Money Income) by Race of Head of Household

Total Money Income	% All Households	% White Households	% Non-White Households (includes Blacks and Hispanics)
under $2,500	2.3	1.9	4.9
2,500-4,999	3.7	2.7	10.2
5,000-7,499	5.2	4.4	10.8
7,500-9,999	5.4	4.9	8.8
10,000-12,499	6.5	6.2	8.7
12,500-14,999	5.9	5.9	6.2
15,000-19,999	12.1	12.3	11.1
20,000-24,999	12.3	12.6	10.7
25,000-34,999	19.5	20.3	14.5
35,000-49,999	16.0	16.9	9.6
50,000 and over	10.9	11.9	4.6
median income	23,433	24,603	15,211
mean income	27,391	28,603	19,282

Source: U.S. Bureau of Census, *Current Population Reports*, Series P–60, no. 140, 1982, Table 2.

members per family, it would appear that considerably more than a third of all people in the United States live in families that earn less than $15,000 a year. By contrast, about 27 percent (the two highest categories joined) of the families earn over $35,000 a year. Other data about the income of unrelated individuals shows approximately the same kind of distribution.

Table 10–1 also reveals the differences between White and non-White households, the latter including Blacks and Hispanics. The differences are highlighted in the median and mean incomes. White median income is nearly $10,000 more than that of non-Whites; the mean incomes differ by over $9,000.

Another way to look at the income distribution is to examine the shares of total income earned by various portions of the population. Table 10–2 shows the percent of income received in 1982 by each fifth of the families and each fifth of

TABLE 10-2   Percent Distribution of Aggregate Income in 1982 Received by Each Fifth and Top 5% of Families and Related Individuals

	Families	Unrelated Individuals
Lowest fifth	4.7%	3.8%
Second Fifth	11.2%	9.0%
Third Fifth	17.1%	15.2%
Fourth Fifth	24.3%	24.3%
Highest Fifth	42.7%	47.7%
Top 5%	16.0%	19.0%

Source: U.S. Bureau of Census, *Current Population Reports*, Series P-60, no. 140, "Money, Income and Poverty Status of Families and Persons in the U.S., 1982," Table 4.

unrelated individuals and also includes the figure for the percent earned by the top 5 percent of income earners. (These figures differ from those recited in Chapter 7, since the latter were for 1972, while these are for 1982.)

Focusing on family income, we see that the families earning the highest fifth of income earned 42.7 percent of all income, over two times what their share would be if there were total equality (that is, if each fifth earned a fifth of the income), while the bottom fifth earned less than 25 percent of what their share would be if there were full equality. Put another way, the highest fifth secured 9.1 times as much income as the bottom fifth (42.7 versus 4.74).

Nor have these matters changed much at all over the past 35 years. Table 10–3 shows the distributions for five different years, starting with 1947. Looking at the ratios of top to bottom fifths (the last row), we see that those ratios have remained relatively constant over the years since 1947. In 1967 the ratio was lowest; but in 1982 the ratio was highest of all five time points, with the lowest fifth earning an even smaller share of total income in 1982 than it did in 1947.

We saw in Chapter 7 how these shares get altered after taking account of the redistribution of income through taxes and transfer payments. Recall that in 1972, the ratio of income earned by the top fifth of earners to that of the bottom fifth was 31.2 to 1, while after taxes and transfers, that ratio was sharply reduced to 7.48 to 1. That, in effect, is the best estimator of the range of inequality among fifths of the population. The differences would, of course, be larger if we compared bottom and top tenths; and the differences would be even greater if these figures included investment income, which is predominantly earned by the top fifth, and much of which is either not taxed or taxed at considerably lower rates than earned income.

TABLE 10-3   Percent Distribution of Aggregate Income Received by Each 5th and Top 5% of Families, 1947-1982, Selected Years

Percent	1947	1957	1967	1977	1982
Lowest Fifth	5.0	5.1	5.5	5.2	4.7
Second Fifth	11.9	12.7	12.4	11.6	11.2
Third Fifth	17.0	18.1	17.9	17.5	17.1
Fourth Fifth	23.1	23.6	23.9	24.2	24.3
Highest Fifth	43.0	40.4	40.4	41.5	42.7
Top 5%	17.5	15.6	15.2	15.7	16.0
Ratio of Highest Fifth to Lowest Fifth	8.6	7.9	7.3	8.0	9.1

Source: U.S. Bureau of the Census, *Current Population Reports*, Series P-60, no. 140, "Money, Income and Poverty Status of Families and Persons in the U.S., 1982," Table 4, and Series P-60, no. 137, "Money, Income of Household, Families and Persons in the U.S., 1981," Table 17.

(In 1971 the upper 10 percent of income earners received 71.6 percent of all dividends reported.)

Some additional meaning can now be given to these figures by asking how much money a family has to earn to meet minimum standards of food, clothing, shelter, and health. That standard is known as the poverty line. A simpler version of that line is based on the minimal food requirements for a family. But these, of course, are calculated against what it is thought a family must also have available to spend on clothing, shelter, and health. In any event, the *official* poverty index, used by the U.S. government, was first developed by the Social Security Administration in 1964; and it specifies a variable amount of money income, depending on size of family, sex and age of family head, number of children under eighteen, and farm versus nonfarm residence.

For a family of four residing in a metroplitan area, the poverty line in 1982 was just below $10,000 a year. Using that round number for convenience, we can see from Table 10–1 that over 16 percent (2.3 plus 3.7 plus 5.2 plus 5.4) of the households in the United States were living in what was officially designated as poverty in 1982. By comparison, nearly 11 percent of the households earned over $50,000 a year, and nearly 27 percent (10.9 plus 16.0) earned over $35,000. The comparisons become even more stark when we look at the figures for non-White households. For them nearly 35 percent of all households lived below the poverty line, while only 14 percent of non-White households earned over $35,000.

These are the kinds of figures that constitute the substance of the phrase "poverty in the midst of plenty." That is also a dramatic way of calling attention to the depth of income inequality in the United States. Various other features of the income distribution could be selected for notice. But perhaps those just provided will give an approximate and useful idea of that distribution.

We shall later compare some aspects of the distribution in the United States with distributions in other countries. For now we leave income to examine inequalities in occupational prestige.

THE DEPTH OF PRESTIGE DIFFERENCES

The ways in which occupational prestige scores are calculated have been described at some length in Chapter 8. We also saw there a sample of occupations and the scores they received from a national sample of respondents in 1963.

To get a fuller picture of the distribution of occupational prestige, one should scan various tabulations which list more occupations and their prestige scores. A very useful enriched tabulation was compiled in 1967.[1]

In such fuller lists there are some surprises, but not many. For instance, surveyors, who have a highly skilled occupation, fall in the score interval of 50–54 (out of 100), while stock and bond salesmen score in the range 70–74; automobile mechanics score 15–19; and radio and television repairmen and policemen and firemen all fall in the 35–39 range. Whether these are surprising differences probably depends on one's very special sense of these matters. In any event, most of the occupations on the list stand about where one would expect if one takes the average education and skill required to perform the function, the average income earned, and the importance the job is believed to have for the society at large.

A number of efforts have been made to enrich the concept of occupational prestige by joining it, in a combined index, with the standing of occupations on the income and educational ladders. The most elaborate of those efforts was attempted in 1960 when Otis. D. Duncan[2] constructed a socioeconomic index for all occupations.

While this is a more complex and sophisticated ranking than the original set of scores, the author of this combined index has said that it is "remarkable, nevertheless, that the NORC results (the original rankings), particularly with appropriate weighting, conformed so closely to those obtained for all occupations."[3]

Whether one uses the simpler NORC ratings or the more complex socioeconomic index just described to rank occupations, it is clear that there is substantial inequality in the estimates people make of the goodness or excellence of occupations and that this is as close as we can come to an estimate of the differences in prestige or honor in general. Additionally we now know that there are relatively high correlations among income, education, and prestige ratings of occupations, such that, in general, the higher one is on any one of three ranking ladders, the higher is one also likely to be on the other two.

Table 10–4 (p. 89) groups the many occupations listed in the Census into ten major categories and specifies the number and percent of employed people in the labor force in 1979 who were in those occupational categories. Since many occupations are grouped together to form the ten categories, there are some substantial deviations from the rank orders of occupations that are revealed when the occupations are listed separately; but this is a rough approximation of the rank ordering of occupations, so that we may say that the table represents the number and percent of employed people in the labor force in 1979 who were at various levels of occupational prestige.

Worthy of note on this table is the relatively large percent in the upper two categories (27 percent), compared to the relatively smaller percent in the bottom four categories (19 percent), and the bunching of about 50 percent of the labor force in categories four, five, and six. The changing nature of American occupations is revealed here, particularly the shift of the majority of people into white-collar occupations and the percent of people who are achieving increased levels of education and skill.

Special features of occupational honor are shown in Table 10–5 (p. 89), where we see the distribution of the labor force by sex and race. (There are fewer categories here than in the previous table, because a number of categories have been grouped together here under the heading "other blue-collar workers.")

TABLE 10-4   Occupational Distribution of Employed Workers, 1979

Occupation	Number (Thousands)	Percent
Professional, Technical, and Kindred	10,260	16%
Managers and Administrators	7,556	11%
Sales Workers	3,407	5%
Clerical Workers	12,251	19%
Craft and Kindred Workers	10,462	16%
Operatives, except transport	9,624	15%
Transport Equipment Operatives	2,698	4%
Nonfarm Laborers	2,480	4%
Service Workers	6,802	10%
Farm Workers	422	1%

Source: U.S. Bureau of the Census, *Current Population Reports*, "Wage and Salary Data From the Income Survey Development Program: 1979," Special Studies Series, P-23, no. 118, Table B.

TABLE 10-5   Occupational Distribution of Employed Workers by Sex and Race, 1979

	Sex		Race	
	Males	Females	White	Black and Other Races
Occupation	%	%	%	%
Professional and Technical Workers	14.7	15.6	15.5	11.7
Managerial and Administrative Workers	14.0	6.1	11.4	4.8
Sales Workers	5.9	6.9	6.7	2.8
Clerical Workers	6.2	34.6	18.0	16.9
Craft Workers	21.1	1.8	13.7	8.8
Other Blue-collar Workers	25.3	13.0	19.2	28.4
Service Workers	8.7	20.7	12.3	12.4
Farm Workers	4.1	1.3	3.0	2.4

Source: U.S. Bureau of the Census, *Social Indicators III*, Table 7.12, 1980.

Note that men are disproportionately represented in the upper categories of jobs, while women and Blacks are disproportionately represented in the lower groups. Only 13 percent of males are in the lowest two categories compared to 22 percent of women; so, too, only 15 percent of Whites are in those bottom two groups, as compared to nearly 27 percent of Blacks. These data show that the share of inequality alters considerably when one takes account of the sex and race of the work force. The spread from top to bottom is much more stretched out in that case.

Still another and more recent view is shown in Table 10–6, which reveals the median income of occupations for year-round, full-time workers in 1982. The occupation groups are listed roughly in order of their typical prestige scores. In general, a step down in prestige is accompanied by a step down in median income. The deviations from this general pattern are due to the variety of occupations included in the large categories.

TABLE 10-6   Median Income of Occupations, 1982 Year-Round Full-Time Workers, Male and Female

	Males	Females
Occupation Group	*Median Income*	*Median Income*
Executive, Administrative, Managerial	28,820	17,326
Professional Speciality	27,940	18,423
Technical and Related Support	22,260	15,546
Sales	21,901	11,002
Administrative Support Including Clerical	20,508	12,693
Precision Production, Craft and Repair	20,913	13,591
Machine Operators, Assemblers, and Inspectors	17,826	10,876
Transportation and Material Moving	18,508	12,990
Handlers, Equipment Cleaners, Helpers, and Laborers	14,279	11,369
Service Workers	14,459	8,565
Farming, Forestry, Fishing	9,093	5,348

Source: U.S. Bureau of Census, *Current Population Reports*, Series P-60, no. 140, "Money, Income, and Poverty Status of Families and Persons in the U.S., 1982," Table 7.

While this and other problems remain to be solved, one can justifiably conclude that occupations can be ranked and, in fact, are ranked by the general public in an order of higher and lower prestige and that the differences in occupational prestige are accompanied by fairly closely matching differences in the income and educational requirements of the jobs.

The differences between men and women are also revealed rather clearly here. At virtually every job level, men are paid much more income than women. In all cases, men earn at least $7,000 more than women at the same occupational level. Another interesting difference lies in the fact that women, more often than men, earn more at jobs that are lower rated than at those with higher ratings. Such findings require us to be cautious about treating the occupational categories as though they were also in every case categories of unequal job prestige.

The foregoing are selected samples of the best kinds of information available about occupations and their prestige scores. We know, of course, that there is more to honor in general than whatever the occupational prestige scores measure. But we cannot get at that *more* in satisfactory ways, and we must settle for the moment, therefore, with these indicators of honor and with these methods of revealing the depth of inequality in occupational honor. We know, too, that because of the correlations among income, education, and occupational prestige, the measures of the prestige of occupations are also to some important degree measures of the broader range of honor that incomes and educational levels yield to their possessors.

THE DEPTH OF EDUCATIONAL DIFFERENCES

Education is clearly an element in the honor assigned to occupations; it is often treated as a source of honor in itself; it plays a major role in determining what occupation one will achieve and hence, in turn, the probable level of one's income; and, in general, the more education one has, the better equipped is one to deal with problems of everyday life, and the more control will one have over one's destiny.

Additional support for these contentions is found in the fact that the most widely followed model for explaining a son's occupational achievements is one which gives both the fathers' and the sons' educational levels very prominent places. That model is shown in Figure 10–1 in the form of a so-called *path diagram.*[4]

The straight lines with arrows at the end that connect father's education and father's occupation to son's education are meant to indicate that both those variables affect the son's education; then the straight line with the arrow that connects the respondent's education to son's first job is meant to indicate a flow of influence between those two variables. So, both the father's education and the son's education bear importantly on the first job the son gets, and that first job, in combination with

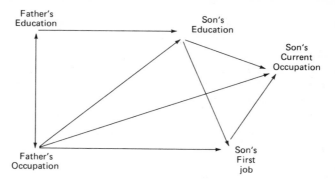

the son's educational level, shapes the destination of the son on the occupational ladder.

It should not be assumed, however, that the variables just cited satisfactorily account for all the variance, that is, for all the distribution of the sons on the occupational ladder. Indeed, as the best study of these matters shows, less than 50 percent of the variation in son's occupation is accounted for by the combined force of father's occupation, son's education, and son's first job. That leaves more than 50 percent of the variance to be accounted for. This sum stands "for all other influences on the variable in question, including causes not recognized or measured, errors of measurement, and departures of the true relationships from additivity and linearity...."[5] So, though the variables measured offer some account for the outcome and though the correlations among income, education, and occupation are high, most of the variance in the outcome, son's occupation, remains unexplained.

Yet, as the authors who constructed this path diagram note, "the size of the *residual* .... (for example, the size of the unexplained variance) is no guide whatever to the validity of a causal interpretation" (p. 175). They argue that the basic model as presented probably is valid and that other factors that might be added "may amount to an enrichment or extension of the basic model rather than an invalidation of it" (p. 175). In short, they believe this is a solid beginning at explaining a very complex process.

Among the unexamined variables that might also be contributing to the outcome are son's measured intelligence, quality of schools attended and quality of their teachers, degree of monitoring and scrutiny in the home, motivational level of the son, influence of peer groups, family connections in the job market, prestige of schools attended, and level of college grades. All of those have been looked at in a number of studies to try to discover how much they may contribute to the determination of the son's occupational level.

The authors further point out that from the point of view of equality of opportunity, it is a salutary finding that so much of the determination of where a son lands is left unexplained by the influence of his father's education and occupation.

For that means that there is more openness in the system, such that some significant portion of the son's destiny is shaped by his own activities rather than by inherited advantages or disadvantages.

Turning now to the actual distributions of education in the United States, we present Table 10-7 (p. 94), which shows the years of school completed by persons twenty-five years of age and over, by age, sex, and race for 1980.

Some of the more important implications of this distribution can be found in the figures that report college graduation. Note that 17.8 percent of Whites finish four years or more of college compared to 7.9 percent of Blacks and Hispanics. Males also outscore females among the Whites (22 percent versus 14 percent) and among Hispanics (9.7 percent versus 6.2 percent), while Black females outscore Black males on this count (8.1 percent versus 7.6 percent). While these figures show severe inequality at the upper end of the scale, the rapid equalization of education in the United States is revealed by the figures that show that the median years of school completed (median = 50 percent above and 50 percent below) by Whites was 12.5 years, by Blacks 12.0 years and by Hispanics 10.9 years. In short, 50 percent of both Whites and Blacks and almost 50 percent of Hispanics had completed high school in 1980, whereas in 1960, or just twenty years before, the medians were 10.9 for Whites and 8.0 for Blacks. (No figures are given for Hispanics in 1960.) The gain by Blacks in twnety years is extraordinary by any measure. Equally extraordinary is the gain in Black college graduates who comprised 3.1 percent of the Black population over twenty-five in 1960, but doubled to 7.9 percent by 1980.

The table, then, shows both severe inequalities at the upper end of the scale and a very substantial equalization at most other levels of educational accomplishment.

The significance of these educational differences can be traced by examining the differences in the incomes earned by people at various educational levels. Table 10-8 (p. 95) shows the mean income, by education and race, for year-round, full-time, male workers in 1981.

Note, from Table 10-8, that in the total population college graduates earn just about twice the sum earned by grammar school graduates and about 50 percent more than high school graduates. These same ratios hold for Whites alone, but there is a smaller difference in the income-payoff for various years of education for Blacks.

From still other reports, we find the following things about the impact of different years of schooling: (1) In 1977, nearly 60 percent of those families earning over $15,000 had dependents enrolled in college, compared with 34 percent for those earning between $5,000 and $10,000 a year. While this is considerable inequality, the fact that 22.6 percent of families earning under $5,000 a year had dependents enrolled in college advises us that opportunities to go to college are by no means totally denied to low-income families. (2) College graduates can expect to earn about $1,400,000 during their lifetimes, which is $350,000 more than the

TABLE 10-7   Years of School Completed, By Race, Sex, and Spanish Origin: 1960 to 1980*

PERCENT OF POPULATION COMPLETING—

YEAR, RACE, AND SEX	Popula-tion (1,000)	Elementary school			High school		College		Median School years completed
		0-4 years	5-7 years	8 years	1-3 years	4 years	1-3 years	4 years or more	
1960, all races	99,438	8.3	13.8	17.5	19.2	24.6	8.8	7.7	10.6
White	89,581	6.7	12.8	18.1	19.3	25.8	9.3	8.1	10.9
Male	43,259	7.4	13.7	18.7	18.9	22.2	9.1	10.3	10.7
Female	46,322	6.0	11.9	17.8	19.6	29.2	9.5	6.0	11.2
Black	9,054	23.8	24.2	12.9	19.0	12.9	4.1	3.1	8.0
Male	4,240	28.3	23.9	12.3	17.3	11.3	4.1	2.8	7.7
Female	4,814	19.8	24.5	13.4	20.5	14.3	4.1	3.3	8.6
1970, all races	109,310	5.3	9.1	13.4	17.1	34.0	10.2	11.0	12.2
White	98,112	4.2	8.3	13.6	16.5	35.2	10.7	11.6	12.2
Male	46,606	4.5	8.8	13.9	15.6	30.9	11.3	15.0	12.2
Female	51,506	3.9	7.8	13.4	17.3	39.0	10.1	8.6	12.2
Black	10,069	15.1	16.7	11.2	23.3	23.4	6.9	4.5	9.9
Male	4,619	18.6	16.0	11.1	21.9	22.2	6.7	4.6	9.6
Female	5,470	12.1	17.3	11.3	24.5	24.4	6.0	4.4	10.2
1975, all races	116,897	4.2	7.4	10.3	15.6	36.2	12.4	13.9	12.3
White	104,065	3.3	6.6	10.6	15.0	37.3	12.8	14.5	12.4
Male	49,259	3.6	6.8	10.6	14.0	33.1	13.6	18.4	12.5
Female	54,806	3.0	6.4	10.6	15.9	41.1	12.1	11.0	12.3
Black	11,096	12.3	14.3	8.5	22.3	27.1	9.0	6.4	10.9
Male	4,925	15.3	14.7	8.1	20.2	25.2	9.7	6.7	10.7
Female	6,171	9.8	14.0	8.9	24.0	28.6	8.5	6.2	11.1
Spanish origin	4,762	18.5	17.9	10.3	15.3	23.0	8.7	6.4	9.6
Male	2,258	18.2	17.1	10.0	15.3	21.1	10.1	8.3	9.8
Female	2,504	18.8	18.7	10.6	15.3	24.7	7.4	4.6	9.3
1980, all races	127,882	3.4	5.9	8.2	13.9	36.8	14.8	17.0	12.5
White	112,899	2.6	5.3	8.4	13.2	37.7	15.1	17.8	12.5
Male	53,556	2.7	5.5	8.3	12.5	33.2	15.8	22.0	12.6
Female	59,343	2.5	5.2	8.4	13.7	41.7	14.4	14.0	12.5
Black	12,613	9.2	11.0	7.2	21.2	30.9	12.5	7.9	12.0
Male	5,585	11.5	10.6	7.1	19.7	30.0	13.4	7.6	12.0
Female	7,027	7.4	11.4	7.3	22.5	31.6	11.8	8.1	12.0
Spanish origin	5,896	15.4	15.7	8.7	15.0	26.8	10.5	7.9	10.9
Male	2,893	15.5	14.7	8.4	14.9	24.4	12.3	9.7	11.2
Female	3,004	15.2	16.6	9.0	15.0	29.2	8.7	6.2	10.6

Source: U.S. Bureau of the Census, *U.S. Census of Population: 1960*, vol. I, and *Current Population Reports*, series P-20, nos. 207, 295; 356, and unpublished data.

*Persons 25 years old and over. Persons of Spanish origin may be of any race. For definition of median, see Guide to Tabular Presentation. See headnote, table 229. See also *Historical Statistics Colonial Times to 1970*, series H 602-617.

TABLE 10-8   Mean Income, by Education and Race, for Males, 1981 (Year-Round, Full-Time Workers)

Educational Attainment	All Races	White	Black
Elementary	15,646	16,023	13,129
High School	20,855	21,429	15,848
College: 1–3 years	24,244	24,876	18,496
College: 4 or more years	32,811	33,361	21,652

Source: U.S. Bureau of Census, Current Population Reports, Series P-60, no. 137, "Money, Income of Household, Families and Persons in the U.S., 1981," Table 47.

expected sum for those who stopped after high school graduation and about $250,000 more than those who started but did not finish college. The differences among females are considerably smaller, and at every educational level the expected lifetime earnings of females are much smaller than those of males. (3) Over 40 percent of those with no education lived at the level of poverty in 1982, compared with 20 percent for those with less than high school graduation and only 4.8 percent for those with one or more years of college.

Such data help clarify the question of how deep is the equality in education in the United States. While no single statement can be made that will neatly summarize all of these findings, one summary statement can be made: Former great differences in educational levels have been sharply reduced over the past twenty to thirty years, and there is every indication that the inequality will be reduced even more in the proximate future, though perhaps at a slower pace.

NOTES

I.   Peter M. Blau and Otis Dudley Duncan, The American Occupational Structure (New York: John Wiley & Sons, Inc. 1967), pp. 122–23, Table 4.1.

2.   Otis D. Duncan, "A Socio Economic Index for all Occupations," in Occupations and Social Status, Albert J. Reiss, Jr. (New York: The Free Press, 1961), pp. 122–23.

3.   Ibid., p. 156.

4.   Adapted from Figure 5.1, Blau and Duncan, Occupational Structure, p. 170. Reprinted with permission of The Free Press, a division of Macmillan, Inc., Copyright © 1967 by Peter M. Blau and Otis Dudley Duncan.

5.   Ibid., p. 171.

CHAPTER 11
THE SPAN OF CONSEQUENCES
Life Chances and Institutional Patterns

To possess unequal amounts of property, prestige, power, and education is to possess unequal resources with which to secure the good things of life that are commonly desired, such as physical and mental health, a good education for one's children, and good job opportunities for them. Unequal resources also mean unequal knowledge about how the world works, unequal information about the facilities of the society; unequal wisdom about managing the development and careers of children. Unequal resources may also lead to differences in the way institutional roles are filled: different patterns of work, family, worship, recreation, and political involvement. So, too, people at different resource levels may adopt quite different styles and fashions and different ideas about the nature of the world, of society, and of human relations. In short, a wide span of inequalties and differences is likely to arise on the basis of the differences in property, power, prestige, and education. It is these consequences we refer to when we speak of the span or scope of stratification. A proper understanding of how any system of stratification works must examine that span of consequences to see how widely and in what ways the inequalities in basic resources exert their influence.

ANALYZING CAUSAL CONNECTIONS: INDEPENDENT, INTERVENING, AND DEPENDENT VARIABLES

The problem here is that one must go beyond the descriptive materials, in which the size and direction of relationships are indicated, to the level of causal and explanatory analysis, where one must attempt to make it clear in what ways and by what intervening forces do different amounts of income (or education or whatever) exert different effects on other behavior patterns. What is it about income that makes the difference? And what is it about education level or occupational prestige that exerts influences on other outcomes? Most studies of stratification remain content with presenting data that describe the extent and direction of relationship among variables, and then they go on to speculate, or simply guess about, how the variables are related.

The simplest set of connecting links can most often be traced in studies of populations divided by income, especially when the outcomes to be explained are different patterns of consumption, such as appliances, autos, the services of lawyers and doctors, or homes in various neighborhoods. If one can assume that the things are purchasable and that they will be consumed in proportion to purchasing power, it makes sense to divide the population by income.

But even here there are problems. The assumption that differences in purchasing power explain the differences in consumption is often quite shaky; it often happens that people at the same level of income differ considerably in their purchasing habits, and people at different income levels resemble each other strongly in those habits. When this is the finding, it is clear that more than simple purchasing power is at work in shaping behavior. One may be satisfied to be able to predict how 60 percent or 75 percent of the people at an income level are likely to behave and not worry about why the remaining 40 percent or 25 percent do not behave in the expected way. That may be enough for marketing people. But it is not enough for sociologists.

We may surmise, for instance, that such a factor as reference group orientation, that is, whom one is trying to look like or keep up with, is influentially at work. Thus, those who purchase beyond their means may be doing so because they are trying to keep up with people who are richer; those who purchase according to their means care mostly about people who are like them in income; and those who consume below their expected levels may be attempting deliberately to avoid the appearance of economic well-being. Or a factor such as attitude-toward-savings may influence consumption behavior, so that those who are very concerned about savings will purchase significantly less than those at the same income level who care less about savings or who have a negative attitude toward savings.

Few studies, however, go on to test whether the assumed connecting link, such as reference group orientation, is the real connecting link. For to do so involves inserting measures of such links into the study from the outset and securing adequate empirical data on how much and in what way they seem to be exerting their influences. To do that requires more time, money, and effort than most sociologists have available. Every new variable added into the study adds costs, if for no other reason than that larger samples have to be drawn to make sure that there are enough representatives from each of the subtypes to permit proper statistical analysis.

For example, if we are dealing with three income levels and if we want to see whether people at the same income level will behave differently in some regard if they have a positive rather than a negative orientation to savings, we must construct six subtypes, that is, positive and negative attitudes toward savings at each of the three income levels. We must be sure, therefore, to get statistically adequate numbers of people into each of the six subtypes. Once we have those numbers, we can test whether people at the same income level will behave differently, depending on their orientation toward savings; or whether people with the same attitude toward savings will behave the same regardless of their income levels; or whether attitudes toward savings will exert a similar but graded influence at all income levels, for example, causing attenuation or increase in the behavior patterns we are trying to understand.

We deliberately used income levels in the previous illustration since the meaning of income as a resource seems reasonably clear. The matter becomes much more complicated, however, when one tries to explain behavior patterns in accordance with different levels of education. For now one must be able to say what it is about such educational differences that leads to differences in behaviors such as child-rearing, voting preferences, mortality rates, and consumption patterns. What is the meaning of the educational level? Does it specify a level of knowledge that is necessary to some forms of behavior and not to others? Or does it indicate an orientation to the future and to careers that may be exercising its effects? Or is it best understood as a set of exposures to various peer groups which differ in their average values? Educational level has been interpreted in all those and other ways in various studies. But again few students have built these possible connecting links into their studies so that they can analyze their possible influences. Most of the time, therefore, we are left to speculate why it is that more years of school are connected with certain patterns of behavior while fewer years seem to lead to other patterns.

The general reasoning here can be illustrated by the following model.

A	B	C
Causal or Independent Variables	Connecting Links or Intervening Variables	Behavioral Outcomes or Dependent Variables
Income and/or Education and/or Prestige	Resource power, or reference group orientation, or attitudes toward savings, or knowledge and skill, and so forth	Size of family, or voting behavior, or consumption habits, and so forth

The variables in Column A are presumed to be causal forces that lead to the outcomes specified in Column C. The causal variables are called *independent*. The outcomes are called *dependent*. The independent variables produce the dependent outcomes either by their direct force, such as sheer size of income, or through the effects of intervening variables (Column B) that mediate and distribute the causal force of the independent variables and thereby produce the outcomes. Any study of the influence of resource differences (Column A) on other behavior (Column C) must attempt to think out the possible linkages beforehand, so that information about those linking or intervening variables can be secured during the course of the study. Otherwise, if at the end of a study we know only the size and direction of the relationships between the independent and dependent variables, we are forced to speculate about why the outcomes are as they are revealed in the study.

With these cautions in mind, we can now turn to examine various consequences of inequalities. These can be grouped under four headings: life chances; institutional patterns; life styles; and ideologies, beliefs, and attitudes.

By *life chances* we refer to such things as the chance to survive the first year of life; to stay healthy, both physically and mentally; to get a good education; to find a proper occupation; to live a normal span of years. These are, in general, the occurrences and experiences in life, the favorable versions of which we enjoy if we are fortunate and the undesirable versions of which we suffer if unfortunate.

Institutional patterns are the ways in which people perform their major institutional roles: how they work, relate as spouses, raise their children, and participate in political and religious affairs.

Life styles refer to those patterns of conduct over which people have options or choices, even if at the same level of resources. These include modes of dressing, eating, using leisure time, decorating the home, spending vacations, and joining groups.

Ideologies, beliefs, and attitudes refer to both general and specific ideas about such things as whether the society is fair, whether people can be trusted, whether welfare benefits are justified, and whether politics is worth participating in.

In general, we expect greatest differences in those areas of daily life where material differences are of greatest and most direct importance and proportionately smaller differences, or none, where those resources do not enrich or limit the options people have. For that reason, we expect that life chances will show the most differences, followed by institutional patterns, life styles, and ideologies and attitudes. We would not be surprised to find many similarities in ideologies among people from all resource levels.

In examining these consequences of stratification here we must confine ourselves to selected samples. The reader must be advised, too, that the data on these matters come from a variety of sources and time periods, and the studies are unequally reliable. Other irregularities occur because some students compare income groups, while others divide populations by education, occupational prestige, or a combined SES score.

In some cases, we will use Black and White as surrogates for poor and rich or high and low education. Because there is much overlap among Blacks and Whites in these matters, however, such findings must be used with caution, and we use them only where no better data are available.

Finally, we must note that in most of the studies reported in these next pages we do not report, since there is little or no evidence, on the factors (intervening variables) that mediate or transmit the influence of the inequalities (the independent variables) onto the various outcomes (the dependent variables). Sometimes we suggest what such mediating or intervening factors might be; other times we do not. These are obviously matters that need further study.

In each case, too, there are possible problems about the direction of causation. For example, does having large families help to produce poverty or do the influences of poverty lead to large families? Or do the influences flow in both directions? Though we most often present the data in a way that suggests that the inequalities in income and education are the responsible, causal factors, it is always worthwhile to raise questions about the possibility that all the factors involved may be reinforcing each other in circular, reciprocal ways.

LIFE CHANCES

Education, Income, and Occupation

While these three have already been examined, it is relevant to cite them again as consequences of stratification that are most visible and consequential. In short, one must treat each of these as both a source of other differences and as something that is itself affected by the other two.

In Chapter 10 we saw that children who come from families where the father is well educated and has a good occupation and income have the best chance to get a good education themselves and to land in occupations that are prestigious and pay relatively well. These patterns illustrate how the chances of fortunate outcome in any one of these three resources are seriously affected by the resource levels in the others.

Various studies reveal how advantage piles on advantage in life careers, so that those who start out fortunate have a much better chance to command fortunate situations in their own lives.

One study,[1] done in 1975, examined the extent to which the social backgrounds and academic abilities of students had an influence on the quality of the colleges they attended. As Table 11–1 (p. 101) shows, even after controlling for academic ability, the socioeconomic status of the students exerted much influence on whether they went to an elite or non-elite institution.

Note that all the figures refer to high-ability students. Of those who were in the lowest socioeconomic bracket, only 6.9 percent went to elite schools, while 33 percent of those at the highest socioeconomic level, went to elite schools. Moreover, of the 2,841 high-ability students covered in the study, 11.1 percent came from the lowest socioeconomic origins while 38.7 percent came from the highest level. In short, socioeconomic level and proportion of high-ability students are related.

Various other studies have shown that the quality of the college has an important bearing on the level of occupation and income after college. In one study done in 1966,[2] for example, it was found that the number of graduates of high-ranking colleges who earned high incomes was about four times greater than the number of graduates of low-ranking colleges. These findings, combined with those

TABLE 11-1   Proportion of High-ability Students Attending Elite Colleges by Socio-economic Status

COLLEGE RANK	SOCIOECONOMIC STATUS (QUINTILES)						
	Low	Lower Middle	Middle	Upper Middle	High	Total	
Nonelite	93.1%	91.2%	86.9%	80.3%	67.0%	79.1%	(N = 1,487)
Elite	6.9%	8.8%	13.1%	19.7%	33.0%	20.9%	(N = 1,354)
Proportion of High-ability Students in each SES Quintile	11.1%	13.7%	15.7%	20.7%	38.7%	100.0%	(N = 2,841)

from Table 11–1, show that the socioeconomic status of one generation exerts a substantial influence on the socioeconomic outcomes of the next generation, even though the connecting linkages are not specified.

Birth Rates

The well-being of any family depends in substantial part on the ratio of the number of members of the family who have to share its total income. The hardships of those who earn lower incomes are worsened by the fact that they typically have more members per family.

Table 11–2 (p. 102) shows the number of children ever born to wives aged thirty-five to forty-four, by socioeconomic status. Every increase in the years of education of the women is accompanied by a decrease in the number of children ever born. Women with zero to eight years of education give birth to nearly twice as many children as women with four years of college. The differences may be due to lack of knowledge of contraception; indifference to planning family size; lack of accessibility of abortions; different conceptions of the role of women; or those and other factors combined. Whatever the reasons, it is clear that the lives of women with low levels of education (who are presumably married to men of lesser education) are made more difficult by the greater number of children to whom they give birth.

The same general patterns are shown in the sections of the table that match birth rates with the income of the families and the occupations of husbands. Every increase in income level is accompanied by a decrease in number of children born; and the same applies to every increase in the prestige of the occupation.

Infant and Maternal Mortality

Using Whites versus Blacks as an indicator of more versus less income and education, we find, too, from Census reports, that the less-advantaged families experience higher rates of infant mortality. That rate has decreased significantly for

TABLE 11-2 Average number of children ever born to wives aged 35 to 44 in married-couple families by socioeconomic status and race/ethnicity

SOCIOECONOMIC STATUS MEASURE	AVERAGE NUMBER OF CHILDREN
Years of School Completed	
Elementary: 0-7 years	4.0
8 years	3.5
High School: 1-3 years	3.3
4 years	2.8
College: 1-3 years	2.6
4 years	2.3
5 years or more	2.0
Family Income	
Under $5,000	3.6
$5,000-$7,499	3.7
$7,500-$9,999	3.4
$10,000-$14,999	3.0
$15,000 and over	2.7
Occupation of Husband	
Professional, technical, and kindred workers	2.5
Managers and administrators, except farm	2.6
Sales Workers	2.6
Clerical and kindred workers	2.7
Craft and kindred workers	3.0
Operatives, including transport	3.1
Service workers, including private household	3.0
Laborers, except farm	3.3
Farm workers	3.4

Source: U.S. Bureau of the Census, "Fertility of American Women, 1979," Current Population Reports, Series P–20, no. 358, Tables 8 and 12, as reported in C.B. Nam and S.G. Philliber, *Population*, 2nd ed. (Prentice–Hall, Inc.: Englewood Cliffs, N.J., 1984), p. 134.

both groups from 1970 to 1977, but the decline in infant mortality in the poorer group is less than that of the wealthier group.

There are also significant differences in the maternal death rate for Blacks and Whites. In 1979, Black mothers died at the rate of 25.1 per 100,000 live births, while White women had a much lower rate of 6.4 per 100,000 live births.

Life Expectancy

Using Black and White once again as an indirect indication of incomes, we find that those inequalities have consequences for the length of life of people from the various groups. But the difference between females and males overrides the income differences. While the life expectancy for Whites, both sexes combines is

73.8 as compared with the Black figure of 68.8, Black women can expect to live longer (73.1 years) than White men (70.0 years). For both Whites and Blacks, life expectancy has increased significantly over the past decades. In 1950 the White life expectancy was 69.1 (male and female combined) compared to the 73.8 in 1977, while the combined Black figure was 60.8 in 1950 compared to the 1977 figure of 68.8.

Unemployment

Of all of life's problems, unemployment is one of the most vexing. Even with unemployment insurance and even if one spouse remains at work while the other is unemployed, the period of unemployment is experienced as a disturbing event, especially for those people whose incomes do not permit them to save enough to tide them over such crises.

Table 11–3 shows the percentage unemployed by years of school completed, and the pattern is quite different from others shown so far. For here unemployment hits harder at those with high school education than at those with less than high school; and those with one to three years of college also have a relatively higher rate than people with less than high school and with four or more years of college.

TABLE 11-3   Percent Unemployed by Years of School Completed: (March 1980)

	YEARS OF SCHOOL COMPLETED							
	Elementary School			Completed High School		College		
	0–4	5–7	8	1–3	4	1–3	4	5 or more
Percent Unemployed	1.6	4.3	6.2	29.5	39.6	13.1	3.7	2.0

Source: Adapted from *Statistical Abstract of the United States*, U.S. Department of Commerce, Bureau of the Census, 1983, page 385, Table 644.

Prevalence of Chronic Diseases

Comparable to loss of work and school in their impact on the course of life are the physical disorders people suffer, even though they may not result in days lost. Data from the Department of Health show that the incidence of diseases is matched rather closely to the distribution of income. People in the lowest income brackets are 3.5 times more likely to contract diabetes and heart disease and 2.7 times more likely to suffer from anemia and arthritis than people in the highest income brackets. The distribution of these disorders through the income ladder follows the expected pattern of an inverse correlation.

Mental Illness and Suicide

A pioneer study in 1967, called *Social Class and Mental Illness,*[3] found a general pattern of inverse relationship, such as that just reported for physical diseases, namely, the higher the socioeconomic standing of the people, the lower the rate of mental illness.

A subsequent study bears out this finding. William Rushing[4] reports an inverse relationship between occupational prestige rankings and hospitalization for mental disorders. The rate of hospitalization was twenty-one per 100,000 for the top-rated occupations as compared to 270 per 100,000 for the lowest occupational level.

Another recent study reports that

> "The lowest social stratum is almost always reported to have a higher rate of disorder than the highest class. In U.S. studies alone, only one out of six studies failed to show this finding. In the 15 non-U.S. studies providing the relevant data, this relationship appeared in all but two. Across all studies, psychopathology in general was found to be at least two and one-half times more prevalent in the lowest class than in the highest class.[5]

This patterning by socioeconomic level is not borne out, however, in regard to suicide. For both male and female Whites have significantly higher rates of suicide than male and female Blacks. White males exceed Black males by about two to one, and White females exceed Black females by nearly three to one. Both White and Black females have much lower rates than their male counterparts.

Crime Commission

Because people commit the crimes for which they have the opportunity, most white-collar crimes, such as embezzlement and fraud, which involve large sums of money, are committed by educated White males to whom others have entrusted their money. By contrast, the bulk of street crimes, such as robbery and assault, are committed by less well educated blue-collar people, and these are disproportionately young. Black youth are very disproportionately represented in this group.[6]

The following statement, written in 1969, apparently applies with equal force today:

> Combine poverty, deteriorated and inadequate housing, lack of good employment opportunities, economic dependency, poor education and anonymous living with population density, social and spatial mobility, ethnic and class heterogeneity, reduced family functions, and broken homes—and an interrelated complex of powerful criminogenic forces is produced by the ghetto environment.... The urban ghetto produces a subculture within the dominant American middle class culture in which aggressive violence is accepted as normative and natural in everyday life, not necessarily illicit.... To be young, poor, male, and Negro; to want what the open society claims is available, but mostly to others; to see illegitimate and often violent

methods of obtaining material success; and to observe others using these means successfully and with impunity—is to be burdened with an enormous set of influences that pull many toward crime and delinquency.[7]

Crime Victimization

Available studies do not, however, show clear-cut class differences in who gets victimized. Thus, the Gallup Report (no. 2200) for May 1982 shows virtually no class patterning at all for total households victimized, nor for such separate categories of crimes suffered as home broken into; money or property stolen; car stolen; home, car, or property vandalized; money or property taken by force or threat of force; and being personally mugged or physically assaulted.

Marriage

Even the chance of getting married seems not to be exempt from the influence of socioeconomic differences. A 1970 study, based on Census data,[8] shows that there is a direct relationship between social class, as measured by income, and the chance for males of being married; the higher the income, the higher the likelihood of marriage.

Marital Stability

Divorce represents a crucial discontinuity in the conduct of life. As such it must be considered one of the more important life chances. The general concurrence among various studies is that the higher the socioeconomic standing, the lower the rate of divorce.[9] But the relationship is not strong, and it is quite irregular.

Summary of Socioeconomic Status and Life Chances

The studies just presented show that the relationship between socioeconomic levels and life chances is variably strong, though sometimes quite irregular, as in the case of unemployment. Overall, however, the most common pattern is that the higher the socioeconomic level the greater the chances for enjoying valued things and experiences, such as health, education, and long life. This generalization holds whether we compare people by incomes, educational levels, or levels of occupational prestige. There seems also to be a regular pattern of Black-White differences such that Whites have substantially more favorable life chances.

INSTITUTIONAL PATTERNS

The second set of consequences that flow from differences in income, education, power, and prestige involve patterns of behavior in the major social institutions: family life, religion, and political behavior, among other things. Here, too, as in life chances, data are quite uneven in their quality; different size and kinds of populations are involved; in the various studies, methods of inquiry vary; and the dates of the reports may be as much as ten or more years apart. But the reports will serve to illustrate how unequal amounts of basic resources may influence institutional patterns of behavior.

Child Rearing

The document most often cited on this subject is a long review and summary of a number of studies published by Urie Bronfenbrenner in 1958.[10] The findings include the following:

1. Mothers at all class levels had become inclined (over the previous twenty-five years) to feed children on demand, wean them later from the bottle, and to begin and complete both bowel and bladder training at a later date. Middle-class mothers were likely to be more permissive in these matters.
2. Shifts in patterns of child rearing occurred more often in middle-class families who had access to and were apparently influenced by government pediatric manuals and other sources of expert opinion.
3. Middle-class mothers tended to be more permissive in regard to children's delinquency, sex, aggressiveness of movement, and freedom outside the home.
4. Middle-class parents had higher expectations for their children and expected them to go further in school and to accept more responsibility inside the home at an earlier date.
5. Middle-class parents were more egalitarian with their children and tended to rely on appeals, reasoning, and the like instead of on physical punishment.

A later analysis of patterns of reproach and punishment done in 1974[11] suggested that while there were some but not great differences between working and middle-class mothers in the frequency of physical punishment of their children, virtually no one, in either middle- or working-class families, neither men nor women, refrained from physical punishment entirely. Between 50 and 75 percent spanked their children sometimes. The highest incidence of spanking occurred among working-class Black men and women. And in general men, both Black and White, spanked their children somewhat more often than women.

Political Behavior

In an earlier review[12] of electoral politics in a number of western-type countries, S.M. Lipset found the class-related pattern to be the most frequent of all. He writes "...most of the structural factors which determine party choice in modern society can be viewed as aspects of the stratification system..." But then he hastens to add that "There are clearly many other social variables which interact with class and politics."

Perhaps the most steady of all patterns is the correlation between socio-economic level and the percent of people who register to vote and who actually vote. Table ll–4 shows this clearly. Every increase in education or income is accompanied by an increase in the percentage of people who register and vote. The people who have gone to four or more years of college register and vote almost twice as often as the people with less than high school education, and the same ratio holds approximately for those who earn $25,000 or more versus those who earn under $5,000.

TABLE 11-4   Voting Age Population Reporting Registering or Voting By Education, November 1980 and By Income, November 1980

Education	Percent Registered	Percent Voting
0-8 years	53.0	42.6
High school: 1-3 years	54.6	45.6
High school: 4 years	66.4	58.9
College: 1-3 years	74.4	67.2
College: 4 or more years	84.3	79.9
Family Income		
Under $5,000	50.4	39.4
5,000-9,999	58.4	48.8
10,000-14,999	63.6	54.8
15,000-19,999	66.8	60.3
20,000-24,999	73.5	67.2
25,000 and over	79.2	73.8

Source: U.S. Bureau of the Census, Current Population Reports, Population Characteristics Series, P-20, no. 381, *Voting and Registration in the Election of November, 1980*, Table B.

A modest contrary finding on social class and political participation[13] is based on national surveys of Americans, Britons, West Germans, Italians, and Mexicans. The author found that socioeconomic factors were important only insofar as they affected the extent of the individual's participation in social networks, for example, trade unions, voluntary associations, and professional groups. The two best predictors of political involvement were the degree of exposure to mass media and participation in formal and informal organizations.

Other studies report that socioeconomic standing sometimes bears importantly on party preference. Thus Knoke[14] found that while the strongest effect on party preference was the parental party affiliation, both occupation and social class identification had direct and significant influences.

Religious Patterns

The Gallup Organization conducted a study on religion in America in 1977–78, and the following are some of its more interesting and important findings:

1.   In the country at large, the expressed religious preferences are as follows: Protestant, 60 percent; Roman Catholic, 28 percent; Jews, 2 percent; all others, 4 percent; and no preference, 6 percent.

2.   For those with college education, the preferences were Protestant, 55 percent; Roman Catholic, 27 percent; Jewish, 4 percent; all others 4 percent; and no preference, 10 percent. Evidently, among college people, Jews and people with no preference are significantly overrepresented, Roman Catholics are proportionately represented, and Protestants fall somewhat short of their national figures.

3.   When preferences are tabulated by income, the respective figures are 55, 31, 5, 3, and 6 percent. Virtually the same patterns show up when the groups are tabulated by occupations.

4.   There are small and inconsequential differences in church attendance among different socioeconomic groups, except for significantly low rates of attendance for the very lowest income group.

Another study[15] of socioeconomic standing and religious preference shows quite different results from the Gallup study because it separates various Protestant denominations, so that, for instance, Episcopalians and Congregationalists rank very high on SES (Jews rank highest) while Lutherans and Baptists rank relatively low.

These findings suggest that there is very little patterning of religious behavior by socioeconomic level, at least so far as denominational preference and attendance are concerned. Perhaps other aspects of religious behavior, such as intensity of emotional expression or joint family attendance at services, might show a relationship to income and education, but the data are not available. It seems, then, that religious patterns are different from family and political patterns in their relationship to socioeconomic levels.

The few studies we have reported are a very small sample of a much larger body of material we might have represented. They will suffice, however, as indicators of the extent to which institutional patterns relate to resource levels. We expected and found that such patterns are less closely dependent upon, or influenced by, resource levels than life chances were shown to be.

NOTES

1.   Reprinted with permission from Jerome Karabel and Alexander W. Astin, "Social Class, Academic Ability and College 'Quality,' *Social Forces,* 53 (March 1975), 381–98. Copyright © The University of North Carolina Press.

2.   Irving Krauss, *Stratification, Class, and Conflict,* (Glencoe, Ill.: The Free Press, 1976), p. 144.

3.   A.B. Hollingshead and F.C. Redlich, *Social Class and Mental Illness* (New York: John Wiley & Sons, Inc., 1967).

4.   William Rushing, "Two Patterns in the Relationship Between Social Class and Mental Hospitalization," *American Sociological Review,* 34 (August 1969), 533–41.

5.   Richard Neugebauer et al., "Formulation of Hypotheses About the True Prevalence of Functional Psychiatric Disorders Among Adults in the United States," in *Mental Illness in the United States: Epidemiological Estimates,* Bruce P. Dohrenwend, et. al., (New York: Praeger Publishers, 1980), p. 56.

6.   See the classic study, Marvin Wolfgang, *Delinquency in a Birth Cohort* (Chicago: University of Chicago Press, 1972).

7.   D. Mulvihill and M. Tumin, *Crimes of Violence* (Washington, D.C.: U.S. Government Printing Office, 1969), pp. xxxiii—xxxv.

8.   Phillip Cutright, "Income and Family Events: Getting Married," *Journal of Marriage and the Family,* 32 (November 1970), 628–37.

9.   An important earlier study of divorce is William J. Goode, *After Divorce* (Glencoe, Illinois: The Free Press, 1956). A more recent treatment is that by Paul C. Glick and A.J. Norton, "Frequency, Duration and Probability of Marriage and Divorce," *Journal of Marriage and the Family,* vol. 33 (1971).

10.   Urie Bronfenbrenner, "Socialization and Social Class Through Time and Space," in E.E. Maccoby et. al., *Readings in Social Psychology,* 3rd ed. (New York: Henry Holt and Co., 1958).

11.   Howard S. Erlanger, "Social Class and Corporal Punishment in Child Rearing: A Re-Assessment," *American Sociological Review,* 39 (February 1974), 68–85.

12.   S.M. Lipset, "Elections: The Expression of the Democratic Class Struggle," in *Class, Status, and Power,* R. Bendix and S.M. Lipset, 2nd ed., (New York: The Free Press, 1966), 428.

13.   Paul Burstein, "Social Structure and Individual Political Participation in Five Countries," *American Journal of Sociology,* 77 (1972), 1087–10.

14.   David Knoke, "A Causal Model for the Political Party Preferences of American Men," *American Sociological Review,* (1972), pp. 679–89.

15.   Galen L. Glockel, "Income and Religious Affiliation," *American Journal of Sociology,* 74 (May 1969), 632–47.

CHAPTER 12
THE SPAN OF CONSEQUENCES
Life Styles and Beliefs, Ideologies, and Attitudes

LIFE STYLES

Do people at different levels of income, prestige, power, and education use their discretionary time, money, and other resources in different ways? Do they buy different kinds and amounts of consumer goods and services? Are their friendships different? Do they participate differently in voluntary organizations? These are all questions about life styles.

As with the previous materials on life chances and institutional patterns, we shall present only a limited number of findings, intended mainly as illustrations of the ways and extents to which life styles are connected to levels of resources and honor. Once again, too, the studies are variously good, their samples variously large and representative, and the span of years from which they are drawn rather large. Nevertheless, some decent sense of how resource levels connect to life styles can be garnered from them.

Voluntary Association Memberships

A study[1] was made in 1958 of a national sample of 5,000 people to assess the relationship of social standing to voluntary group memberships and participation.

The authors found that whichever index of socioeconomic standing was used—income, education, occupation, home ownership, or interviewer's subjective rating—an appreciably greater percentage of people from higher SES brackets belonged to voluntary organizations. While 48 percent of the highest income respondents did not belong to any voluntary organization, as many as

76 percent of the lowest income respondents did not belong.

Another study[2] of 1,000 families in Puerto Rico, done somewhat earlier, showed that every increase in educational level was accompanied by an increase in the percentage of people who were members of an organization, ranging from the 31 percent of those with no schooling at all to just under 75 percent of those with thirteen years of school or more.

Another student, Arnold Rose, writes: "Especially among lower-class people, shyness and lack of self-confidence are also important reasons for lack of participation. Those with less education may not understand how voluntary association activity could affect community policies which have a bearing on their lives."[3] Rose is here relating voluntary association membership and activity to the wielding of influence and power, but the remarks remain apposite. Indeed, there seems to be a close similarity between political participation and voluntary group participation both in their frequencies and in the reasons for the differences in those frequencies between various socioeconomic segments.

Participation in Adult Education Programs

Some of the same results are found in the patterns of participation in adult education programs. The Census[4] reports that in 1981, 26.1 percent of those with four years of college participated in some program, as compared with only 11.1 percent of those with four years of high school and 2.2 percent of those with eight years of school or less. The differences between income groups are somewhat smaller: 18.3 percent of those earning between $25,000 and $50,000 participated as compared with 6.3 percent of those earning under $7,500. The differences within the White group are matched somewhat by the same order of differences within the Black group, though, in general, higher percents of Whites than Blacks, at the same educational and income levels, participated in programs. Females exceeded males at every level. Finally, the critical point seems to be attending college, since there are very sharp increases in the percents who participated as between high school graduates and those with one year of college or more.

Audiences for Performing Arts

Even more differentiated are the audiences for performing arts. The National Endowment for the Arts reported that a series of 270 studies showed that in 1976, 65 percent of the audience at performing arts programs had college degrees or more, 59 percent were in professional occupations, and their median income was $20,000. This clearly identifies the audience as dominantly upper level in socioeconomic characteristics.[5]

From those same 270 studies the Endowment made a more detailed calculation of the occupational distribution of the audiences and found a strong influence of socioeconomic standing on participation in performing arts audiences.

Consumption Patterns

Census reports[6] tell about the percents of households at different income levels who owned various numbers of cars, black-and-white TV sets, color TV sets, washing machines, clothes dryers, refrigerators, freezers, dishwashers, and air conditioners.

Though the percentages from the lowest income groups (from less than $3,000 to $7,500 a year) are expectably lowest on all these items, there is a substantial similarity in all income brackets from $7,500 upwards on most items. The greatest similarities are in ownership of one car, a black-and-white TV set, and a refrigerator. The greatest differences are in ownership of color TV, two or more cars, clothes dryer, freezer, dishwasher, and air conditioner. These data give us some idea of what even the poorest people consider necessities and which items represent genuinely discretionary buying, attuned to one's income. For instance, only 1.9 percent of the poorest people own a dishwasher compared to 74.8 percent of the wealthiest group.

Watching Television

People at different educational and income levels differ considerably in their predilections for watching television. A Gallup Organization study[7] showed that while 43 percent of those with grade school education reported TV viewing as their favorite evening pastime, this figure reduces to 33 percent for those with high school education and sinks to 18 percent for those with college education. When groups are divided by income, comparable differences appear, ranging from 42 percent of those at the lowest income levels to 22 percent of those who earned over $20,000 a year.

Language Patterns

The patterns of our speech, including grammar, accents, and vocabularies, are not so much matters of resources or of discretionary activity as do they reflect from whom we learned to speak, and that means people of definable socioeconomic characteristics from different ethnic groups and regions of the country or world. As such, it may seem strange to consider differences in language patterns as differences in life styles.

Yet since language patterns do reflect the training and exposure we have had to others at various socioeconomic levels, they can and often are used to identify our origins and to serve as a basis for the ascription of the degrees of social honor attached to those origins. Everyone is familiar with the influence on social standing in England of the possession of an accent known as Oxbridge, which is taken to reflect a background of attendance at prestigious private (called public) schools and universities.

British novelists and playwrights, such as Dickens and Shaw, have drawn heavily on the class-related character of speech. Richard Hoggart[8] and Basil Bernstein,[9] among others, have analyzed the role of class-identified speech patterns in the shaping of careers. The ongoing disputes in the United States about Black English, Hispanic English, and standard English, testify to the salience of styles of speech as cards of identity and as influences on life chances. These observations suggest that patterns of behavior often have such rich mixtures of both resources (life chances) and honor (life styles) that is is difficult to place a behavior pattern unequivocally under one rather than the other heading. Suppose, for example, a college is both academically excellent and highly prestigious and that its graduates have a genuine advantage in gaining admission to the better graduate and professional schools. Is sending one's children to such a college a matter of life chance or life style? It is obviously both.

The same considerations apply even to such things as family size. The well-to-do have more access to education, knowledge, and all the other things relevant to family planning than do the poor. But stylistic matters are also involved. Poorer people often look on having large families as the right thing to do; men believe they prove masculinity by having many children; women feel that by the standards of their class they validate themselves with large families and fail to do so without them. So, are differences in family size more due to life chances or to life styles?

The same goes for patterns of marriage and divorce, child rearing, choice of residence, and choice of vacation spots—whatever. It must be expected, then, that except in extreme cases some elements of resources (life chances) and some of honor (life styles) will be found in nearly all the behavior patterns examined. Therefore, when research findings are reported under the heading of life chances and others under life styles, it should be understood that these are distinctions of more and less rather than unambiguous differences.

BELIEFS, IDEOLOGIES, VALUES

College Education and Success

The last set of consequences of inequality we explore is the distribution of ideologies, beliefs, and attitudes.

We will not be surprised if these prove to be somewhat, if not much more, alike among socioeconomic segments if only because they are often phrased so abstractly that they can have nearly universal appeal and thereby transcend the influences of differences in property, education, and honor.

One of the earliest studies[10] of these matters was particularly concerned with what different classes believed a successful life included. The author found significant differences in beliefs about the importance of college education for success, the amount of opportunity available to achieve success, whether the future held good chances for achievement, whether diligence and proficiency paid off in achievement. In each of these matters the higher socioeconomic levels were more strongly positive than lower ones, and it did not matter whether level was measured by education, income, or other indicators.

A more recent study, however, suggests that those differences may have largely vanished. Table 12–1 shows the outcomes.

TABLE 12-1   Importance of a College Education by Income Level of Respondent, 1978*

Income Level	% Very Important	% Fairly Important	% Not Too Important	% Don't Know
under $7,000	45	39	13	3
7,000-9,999	37	48	15	—
10,000-14,999	33	40	26	1
15,000-19,999	31	53	14	2
over 20,000	33	49	16	2

Source: Phi Delta Kappa, Inc., "The Tenth Annual Gallup Poll of the Public Attitudes Towards the Public Schools," *Phi Delta Kappan*, 1978, in *Social Indicators III*, U.S. Bureau of the Census, 1980, Table 6–3.
* Question was: How important is a college education today?

The most surprising finding is that higher percentages of the people in the lowest income groups said a college education was very important. That unexpected outcome may be due to a certain cynicism on the part of higher income people about the less-than-expected payoff of their college educations. Or it may be a result of the way the question was put and tabulated. Thus, if we combine the percents saying "very important" with those saying "fairly important" the differences become trivial. Note that the combined percentages, from low to high income, are 84, 85, 73, 84, and 82 percent. Except for the score of seventy-three for the middle group, the differences are inconsequential. The middle group may contain—though we do not know this for sure—a disproportionate percent of people at highly paid crafts and skills for which college education is not required.

In any event, these outcomes suggest that the different socioeconomic levels are becoming much more alike in their affirmed beliefs about the importance of college education. We know, however, from previously shown data, that income levels do distinguish, often sharply, the actual numbers of years of school achieved, both by self and children. The disparity between affirmed belief and actual practice is just what one should expect, since significant, valued additional resources are required to put those beliefs into practice.

Work Ethic and Work Values

Over the past decades various investigators have tried to discover the extent to which differential rates of success of youth from various classes can be explained by different attitudes toward work and success among those people. Gerhard Lenski[11] examined this matter in 1963 and discovered differences between Catholics and Protestants in a range of attitudes that seemed to bear on career success. These tended to favor the Protestant group, and since there were also substantial socioeconomic differences between the two religious groups, the findings suggested that perhaps Catholic, lower-class fatalism helped generate and support a lower horizon of career possibilities among Catholic youth, while a Protestant middle-class work ethic helped generate and support higher possibilities among their youth.

A number of other studies of this question in the last twenty years have failed to find the patterns Lenski reported, and indeed most suggest that though there may be differences between socioeconomic segments, these no longer correspond with the Protestant-Catholic distinction.

On the matter of class differences themselves another investigator, Melvin Kohn,[12] suggests that the conditions of work that are typically found in upper- and lower-class jobs are quite different, particularly in regard to the amount of complexity, initiative, and variety found in them. These job experiences of fathers lead them, Kohn believes, to place a great deal of stress on self-direction and autonomy in the training of their children; such training, in turn, probably has consequences for the kinds of jobs the young people seek and their success at jobs that require such emphases.

Virtually all investigators of attitudes toward work are agreed that early training in attitudes toward work, effort, diligence, complexity, and initiative probably have significant influences on the school careers of the youth, the years they complete, and the jos they seek and secure. It is also widely believed, though not decisively demonstrable, that there are significant differences in these orientations to school and work between members of different socioeconomic levels.[13] Oscar Lewis'study[14] of the culture of poverty is an eloquent document about these matters at the very lowest rung of the socioeconomic ladder.

Attitudes toward Society, Morals, and Customs

From the Gallup Report of February 1982 (no. 197) we can extract a number of interesting results about the beliefs and values of a national sample of people drawn from different income and educational levels. Except where otherwise noted, the general direction and size of differences for income levels are about the same as those for educational levels.

1. The lower classes tend to exceed richer people, but not by much, in the percents who would welcome it if religious beliefs were to play a greater role in peoples' lives (77 percent versus 69 percent).

2. Forty percent of the people in the income bracket ''$25,000 and over'' favor considering homosexuality as an alternative, acceptable life style as compared with 31 percent of those earning between $5,000 and $10,000 and 22 percent of those earning less than $5,000.

3. Around 80 percent of the people in the upper income bracket ($20,000 or more) would welcome less emphasis on money in the future as compared with around 60 percent of the lower income people who say this.

4.　There are modest but noticeable differences in the percents who would welcome more acceptance of sexual freedom. Twenty-nine percent of those in the highest bracket would, as compared to 22 percent and 19 percent of the two lowest brackets.

5.　All income levels are virtually identical (ranging between 90 percent and 94 percent) in their assertion that they would welcome more emphasis on traditional family ties.

6.　The same similarity is found in the percentages (between 88 percent and 92 percent) who would welcome more respect for authority in the future.

7.　Twenty-three percent of the wealthier people would welcome less emphasis on working hard compared to 39 percent of the poorest people and 30 percent of those who earned between $5,000 and $10,000.

8.　The wealthier people also more strongly favor (18 percent versus 10 percent) more acceptance of marijuana usage, but all classes are dominantly against that acceptance (75 percent of the wealthiest and 87 percent of the poorest people).

9.　Among the greatest differences is that between the 90 percent of the wealthiest people versus 65 percent of the poorest who report themselves as generally satisfied with the way things are going in their personal lives.

10.　Small differences are found in the percentages who report themselves satisfied with the way things were going in the U.S. at the time of the interview. Thirty-two percent of the top group versus 23 percent of the bottom group affirmed their satisfactions. Perhaps the more significant finding is that 62 percent of the wealthiest and 72 percent of the poorest report themselves dissatisfied. All groups seem more satisfied with their personal lives than with the affairs of the society.

11.　Fifty-one percent of the wealthiest group versus 37 percent of the poorest group reported themselves as very happy. If we combine the ''very happy'' with the ''fairly happy'' responses, then 98 percent of the wealthiest group and 86 percent of the poorest say they are happy—whatever that may mean.

From another source[15] we learn that only a relatively small percentage of people from all income levels think that life in the United States is getting better, while between 40 percent and 52 percent of all levels believe life is staying the same, and about a third of each group believes life is getting worse. The results are virtually identical when the sample studied is divided by years of school completed.

Alex Inkeles, who has studied national variations on the question of personal happiness, has a somewhat different view. He reports that on the whole

> happiness is much more commonly reported by the advantaged strata of society, while sadness and despair are more standard in the manual and depressed classes. . . . In all cases [however] the central tendency is toward some mixture of happiness and pain. . . . [Still,] those who are economically well off, those with more education, whose jobs require more training and skill, more often report themselves happy, joyous, laughing, free of sorrow, satisfied with life's progress.[16]

Political Values

Avery M. Guest[17] attempted to test the hypothesis that people's political values reflect the interests of their socioeconomic level. He reasoned that if this were so, people who thought about whether they belonged to the working class should support supposedly working-class interests more strongly than those who are working class but do not think about it, and that the same should be true for middle-class persons with regard to middle-class interests.

The main findings may be stated as follows:

1. All four groups favor government aid in medical problems, while much smaller percentages of all four groups favor such government aid in regard to employment and education.

2. The *aware working-class* group gives more support than the other group to government aid in employment, but the differences are not great at all.

3. The *aware middle class* somewhat more strongly favored government aid than the unaware middle class, and even outscored them in regard to government aid to education.

4. The hypothesized continuum from aware working to aware middle class does not hold up. Neither *class* by itself, nor class awareness, seems to matter on the three issues presented.

The most recent study of differences among socioeconomic segments on various political issues shows both some similar and some different results. Mary Jackman and Robert Jackman[18] report on their findings about a national sample of 1,914 respondents in forty-eight states all of whom were eighteen and over. The people in the sample were divided into four groups: *poor, working class, middle,* and *upper middle.*

The Jackmans found that the poor respondents far more strongly favored the statement that the government should do a lot more or some more about job guarantees and about guaranteeing minimum incomes; the working and middle classes were quite close to each other in these matters; and only on the issue of government support of minimum income did a majority of any group (50.8 percent) express favor.

The Jackmans also explored the opinions of the sample on the questions of how much income inequality they thought proper; what reasons they offered in support of their views about inequality; and finally how the respondents explained actual differences in the class situations of people in the United States.

They found the following:

1. Substantial majorities of all four groups favor some amount of income inequality, the lowest figure being the 72 percent of the poor and the highest being the 91.3 percent of the upper-middle class.

2. Nearly two-thirds or more of all four classes agree that differential achievement deserves differential incomes and that this is the main justification for inequality.

3. As we go from poor- to upper-middle-class groups the percent who believe that differences in opportunities explain differences in income diminishes, but between 70 percent and nearly 90 percent of all groups agree that most of the explanation for differences in income is to be found in some combination of differential opportunities and home environments.

In sum, while one's own class position has some modest effects on how one views inequality, a substantial majority of all groups endorses some amount of income inequality, justifying it on the basis mostly of achievement, and account for it mostly in terms of the combined effects of opportunity and home rearing.

This suggests the existence of a common value system regarding inequality in income, its justification, and the reasons for its occurrence. That value system seems to transcend most of the differences that socioeconomic positions might generate. Such differences seem to operate, instead, as minor differentiations within the common culture of endorsement of inequality and its sources.

NOTES

1.   Charles Wright and Herbert Hyman, "Voluntary Association Memberships of American Adults," *American Sociological Review,* 23 (June 1958), 284–94; and Herbert Hyman and Charles Wright, "Trends in Voluntary Association Memberships of American Adults: Replication Based on Secondary Analysis of National Sample Surveys," *American Sociological Review,* 36, 2 (April 1971), 191–206. The authors found a "small but noteworthy increase in the percentage of American adults who belong to voluntary associations" from 1955 to 1962. Another change was a growth in memberships among lower status groups, and possibly on the part of Negroes.

2.   Melvin Tumin, *Social Class and Social Change in Puerto Rico* (Princeton, N.J.: Princeton University Press, 1961).

3.   Arnold Rose, *The Power Structure* (New York: Oxford University Press, 1967), p. 227.

4.   *Statistical Abstract of the United States,* 1983–84.

5.   *Social Indicators,* III, 1980, Table 11–5.

6.   *Statistical Abstract of the United States,* 1974, Table 646.

7.   Gallup Opinion Index, Report no. 1974, as reported in *Social Indicators,* II, 1980.

8.   Richard Hoggart, *The Uses of Literacy* (London: Chattu and Windus, 1957).

9.   Basil Bernstein, *Class, Codes and Control,* (London: Routledge and Kegan Paul, 1973).

10.   Herbert Hyman, "The Value Systems of Different Classes," in *Class, Status and Power,* R. Bendix and S.M. Lipset, eds. (New York: The Free Press, 1966).

11.   Gerhard Lenski, *The Religious Factor* (New York: Anchor Press, 1963).

12.   Melvin Kohn, *Class and Conformity* (Homewood, Ill.: The Dorsey Press, 1969).

13.   David Featherman reports: "Contrary to current emphasis in the social psychology of religio-ethnic achievement, achievement-related work values and motivations of adults are neither key intervening variables nor do they influence the process of stratification to a substantial degree. The most important variable in explaining the differential socioeconomic achievement of the religio-ethnic subgroups is education, after the variation owing to the handicaps and benefits of social origins has been removed statistically." Featherman, "The Socioeconomic Achievement of White Religio-Ethnic Subgroups: Social and Psychological Explanations," *American Sociological Review,* 36, 2 (April 1971), 207–22.

14.   Oscar Lewis, *La Vida* (New York: Random House, Inc., 1966).

15.   Angus Campbell et. al., *The Quality of American Life* (New York: The Russell Sage Foundation, 1976).

16.   Alex Inkeles, "Industrial Man: The Relation of Status to Experience, Perception and Value," *The American Journal of Sociology,* 66, 1 (July 1960).

17.   A.M. Guest, "Class Consciousness and American Political Attitudes," *Social Forces,* 52, 4 (June 1974).

18.   Mary Jackman, and Robert Jackman, *Class Awareness in the United States* (Berkeley and Los Angeles: University of California Press, 1983).

CHAPTER 13
THE SHAPE
OF STRATIFICATION
SYSTEMS
From Aggregates
to Classes

In considering the span of consequences of inequality we have relied mostly on studies in which the population was first divided into a number of socioeconomic levels; these were then examined to see their similarities and differences in life chances, institutional patterns, life styles, and ideologies and beliefs.

The studies used different methods of dividing the population. Some contrasted educational groups; others compared income levels; still others used occupational prestige levels; some combined several of these; and in a small minority, people were assigned to levels on the basis of their responses to questions about which class they thought they belonged to.

Many of these studies also differed in the number of levels they distinguished. Some contrasted blue- versus white-collar levels; others, rich versus poor; still others compared three, four, or five levels of education or income; some compared Black and White as surrogates for poor and rich. In our versions of these materials, we have not always reported the distinctions in the ways the authors of the studies presented them. Most often we condensed the reports into tables or summaries that presented information about three levels of income or education.

All this raises the questions of how many different socioeconomic levels or strata there are in the United States? How does one decide? Is it best to divide populations by income alone? Or education? Or occupational prestige? Or some combination of all of them? Are there natural breaking points so that the strata can be easily distinguished? Or are the distributions continuous so that any set of distinctions we make is arbitrary? How do we justify the kinds of distinctions we impose on continuous distributions, such as taking the whole span of incomes and dividing it into thirds?

MARX AND WEBER ON CLASSES AND STATUS GROUPS

The guidelines for these questions are chiefly set out in the ideas of Karl Marx and Max Weber.[1] The following versions of their very complex bodies of thought are necessarily highly simplified and touch only on the points that interest us here.

Briefly, Marx saw classes as being formed according to the relationships of the people to the productive system, or the *relations of production,* as he called them.

According to Marx, capitalist societies are composed of two classes: those who own the instruments of production (the bourgeois, or capitalists) and those employed by them (the proletariat, or workers). Numerous other groups stand between owners and workers (clerks, middlemen, professionals, service people), but these are not the decisive political groups in the struggle for fundamental social change. Because, according to Marx, the middle classes lack the independent vision of society necessary to a political ideology, they cannot be decisive forces.

Weber, a keen student of Marx, made a threefold distinction. He called *classes* those aggregates formed by people who had a common economic situation, including the life chances related to them. To those aggregates, however, which were marked by distinctive life styles, with their variable degrees of prestige or honor, Weber gave the name *status groups*. Those aggregates made up of people with common political interests Weber called *parties*. Such parties are marked by consciousness of kind, solidarity, and common action. In short, Weber used the three criteria of property, prestige, and power. Weber in effect said that members of a *class* are not necessarily members of the same *status group* or of the same *party*. There may be significant overlap but not uniform coincidence. When they do coincide, however, the system of stratification is fully developed because then economic, honor, and political identities and interests are joined.

Marx, however, saw economic interests as primary forces. He believed that if men share economic interests, they will also come to see that their respective fates are joined, and they will then develop the solidarity necessary to unified political action. Marx firmly expected that the capitalists would do the same thing and that class war would result. Under the right circumstances the outcome would be the victory of the working class, or proletariat, who would then create a new and classless society.

Both men agreed that economic conditions are likely to be dominant over other considerations, notwithstanding their disagreement over the inevitability of coincidence among economic, honor, and political interests.

CONTINUOUS VERSUS DISCRETE VARIABLES

American and European sociologists are themselves quite divided in the methods they employ to give a shape to the stratification system. They often combine elements from both the Marxist and the Weberian approach insofar as they use both income and occupational prestige as dividers, and many add some version of educational level. But virtually none attempts to divide populations by power, simply because that is virtually impossible to do.

Sociologists differ further in whether they divide the population into distinct classes or levels or whether they measure the correlations between the total distributions of income, occupation, and education.

While such correlational techniques provide a fuller and often more precise measure of the relationship between variables, they are not easily translatable into statements that are commonly comprehensible. Moreover, real problems arise when one tries to analyze the relationship between continous variables such as income and discrete variables such as voting differences or styles of family relations, in which there are only two or three scores or values; for example, one votes for either Republicans or Democrats, or one prefers Catholic to Protestant church affiliation. Many of the outcomes of inequality in which we are interested are presented in such discrete categories.

To deal with these problems sociologists pursue two strategies: (1) They use correlational techniques to analyze the relationships among continuous variables, such as income, education, and occupation; and (2) They cut the populations into discrete classes when analyzing the relationship between any of those continuous variables and other outcomes, such as voting preference, for which there are only two or three values.

Once one has decided to cut a population into discrete segments, one must next decide which of the basic differentiators to employ. Shall we divide the population by income? Or education? Or occupational prestige? Or some combination of those?

No answer here is self-evidently better than any other. This is a matter for empirical exploration. Do income differences seem to match more neatly with voting preferences or mortality rates than do educational or occupational differences? The only way to answer this is to examine all the relationships. When one does so, one sometimes finds that each of the differentiators—income, education, and occupation—shows about the same patterns of outcome. But sometimes, too, the outcomes are different from one differentiator to another. Both sets of results are expectable, since while income, education, and occupational prestige are all fairly strongly correlated, they are by no means perfectly correlated. Therefore, when diverse results emerge, one can only leave the matter at that, reporting that the outcomes seem more closely related to one set of differentiators than to another, for example, income differences match voting preferences, but educational differences do not.

COMBINED SES INDEX

An alternative strategy is to combine two or three of the differentiators into a combined index to see if the differences in the outcomes are more fully accounted for in that way.

But the construction of a combined index is a complex matter. The best index available in the literature at the moment is the socioeconomic index for all occupations constructed in 1961 by Otis Dudley Duncan.[2] It combines income, education, and occupational prestige into one number, based on previously analyzed relationships among these three variables. The score, known as the SES index, can then be used in place of an occupational title, with its known prestige score, to stand for the general socioeconomic standing of a given occupation, based on its income, educational, and prestige level components. Once those scores are arrayed into a distribution, one can then divide that array into separate segments, for example, high, medium, and low SES scores, and use those as the differentiating factors in studying outcomes of inequality; or one can use the full array in further correlational analysis.

Duncan is fully aware of the problems involved in such an index and is particularly sensitive to the fact that as the income levels, educational requirements, and perhaps prestige scores of different occupations shift over time, the index is likely to suffer obsolescence. Withal, it is the best measurement of socioeconomic status available, if by SES we mean the combined influences of income, education, and occupational prestige.

HOW MANY LEVELS SHOULD BE DISTINGUISHED?

The second problem is that of deciding how many different segments to distinguish. Should the population be divided into only high and low on income or education, or high, medium, and low? Or should one make four distinctions? Or five?

The answer has to be put in terms of the existing state of our theory about causal relationships. At the moment, sociologists have enough difficulty in understanding why a given population divides into two groups on a given outcome, such as those who vote Republican or Democratic or those who favor government intervention or are against it. The difficulties increase greatly when one tries to make sense out of three distinctions, such as high, medium, and low mortality rates, or high, medium, and low advocacy of permissiveness in child-rearing; and, of course, the difficulty increases commensurately if one goes beyond three distinctions. Our present understanding of such relationships is simply not strong enough or deep enough to say clearly why a medium level of income should differ from both a high and low level in its effect on various degrees of approval of government intervention or degrees of religiosity.

As to the decision about how many segments or levels to distinguish, the majority of sociologists divide populations into three levels, most often by income, sometimes by a combination of income and education, or income and occupation. There is no rhyme or reason to that practice except perhaps that it falls in line with some adapted version of the Marxist distinction between capitalists and workers, with a middle class inserted for the middle range of values.

Perhaps, too, our traditional way of thinking about the universe as being divided into upper, middle, and lower, or top, middle, and bottom on virtually everything we see contributes to the perpetuation of this tradition. One can avoid at least some of these problems by dealing only with variables that show a continuous distribution so that correlational analysis can be performed. Modern computer technology now makes complicated analyses fairly simple by providing standard, packaged programs so that complex sets of data can be analyzed in a variety of ways.

OBJECTIVE VERSUS SUBJECTIVE CRITERIA

A third problem facing students of stratification involves the terms *objective* versus *subjective* criteria of stratification. The question here is whether populations ought to be divided into strata on the basis of objective criteria, such as income, education, and occupation, or whether one ought to employ subjective criteria, such as the classes people say they belong to when asked, or whether we ought to combine some objective data along with some subjective judgments.

The objective criteria are called objective because one doesn't have to ask people their opinions or judgments to get the needed information. While this is not quite true about occupational prestige, since it is a judgmental scale, the judgments about the prestige of various occupations have now been retested so often and have shown themselves to be so stable over time and place that one can treat prestige scores as objective data. By contrast, asking people where they place themselves in a class structure is subject to all kinds of distortions and anomalies. For example, while many people say they have never thought of themselves as belonging to any class, they are not reluctant to choose some class into which they place themselves when they are requested to do so.

Other problems arise when numbers of people from all places on the occupational and income ladders designate themselves as middle class, rather than selecting working or upper class as their category. They do so, it is assumed, because of the well-known tendency for respondents to avoid extremes in such questions. Perhaps, however, they seek to avoid the boasting implied by the term *upper class* or the stigma involved in designating oneself as a member of the working class or lower class.

Sociologists who employ this self-assigning approach find they must also secure data on the objective facts of education, income, and occupation so that they can see how many and what kinds of anomalies and misidentifications are involved. Then one has to figure out how to deal with objectively high-level people who call themselves *middle* versus objectively lower-level people who call themselves *middle* or *upper*. The combinations of objective and subjective class that result are most often too numerous and confusing to be worth the effort. An example of the problems that arise in using self-identification is seen in Table 13–1 (p. 124) taken from the most recent study[3] of these matters.

TABLE 13-1   Class Identification by Head of Household's Census Occupational Categories, for Nonfarm, Civilian Occupations

CLASS IDENTIFICATION

Occupation	Poor	Working	Middle	Upper-Middle	Upper	Total	N	Working and Poor
Professionals	0.7%	17.3	61.6	19.7	0.7	100%	289	18.0%
Managers	0.9%	20.2	58.8	18.0	2.1	100%	233	21.1%
Sales	3.3%	22.0	61.5	12.1	1.1	100%	91	25.3%
Clerical	6.6%	42.9	41.2	9.3	0.0	100%	182	49.5%
Craftsmen	4.5%	53.0	39.3	2.9	0.3	100%	313	57.5%
Operatives	9.9%	53.0	35.0	0.7	1.4	100%	283	62.9%
Service	21.9%	45.9	29.5	2.2	0.5	100%	183	67.8%
Laborers	17.1%	51.3	30.3	1.3	0.0	100%	76	68.4%
Total	6.9%	38.4	45.2	8.7	0.8	100%	1,650	45.3%

If one wants to take comfort from the results, one can do so, as the authors do, by pointing to the fact that "laborers are over three times as likely to think of themselves as working class or poor as are professionals and managers. Similarly, managers and professionals are approximately ten times more likely than service workers or laborers to identify with the upper middle class."[4] But if one wants to be seriously discomfitted by the outcomes, one can point to the facts that almost identical percentages of professionals, managers, and salespeople call themselves middle class and that nearly 20 percent of people in those occupations call themselves working class. What is one to make of those findings? How much can we rely on self-assignment as an accurate index of place in the stratification system? Apparently self-identification works reasonably well at the extremes of the distributions, but even there it fails to make important distinctions, such as those among professionals, managers, and salespeople. Moreover, as the Jackmans report elsewhere, not very much explanatory power is added to objective distinctions by combining them with various modes of self-identification.

THE REPUTATIONAL APPROACH

Still another approach is called *reputational* and is best illustrated by the well-known studies of "Yankee City" made by W. Lloyd Warner and various associates over thirty-five years ago.[5]

The reputational approach involves using a combination of objective characteristics, such as occupation, education, and area of residence, with judgments by the sociological analysts as to the class into which they would put the respondents. Two measures are constructed; one is called the Evaluated Participation (E.P.) and the other the Index of Status Characteristics (I.S.C.). The former represents the judgments by the observer of the prestige level of the social network, that is, friendships, club, and so forth, of the respondents; the latter uses objective socioeconomic data. Assignments of people into classes are made on the basis of a combination of E.P. and I.S.C. scores.

Most often a class system is constructed that consists of five or sometimes six levels, including an upper and lower section for each of an upper, middle, and lower class. Very often, however, there are not enough people in the upper-upper segment to deal with, and often there are comparably small numbers as well in the lower-lower segment. Moreover, there is almost never enough theory available to explain five levels of differences in conduct. The investigators are therefore often required to collapse the six segments into four or sometimes three in order to make any sense out of the findings. One has to wonder, therefore, whether it was worthwhile imposing a five- or six-class model on the data in the first place.

Warner and his associates used these procedures because they were mainly interested in levels of honorific and invidious distinctions and the consequent social groupings of people at common levels of honor. They thought that in Yankee City they detected enough levels of such distinctiveness and enough separate sets of social groupings to warrant their model of six classes. However, it is certain that if they had pursued the matter further, they would have found even more segmentation; they might just as well have formulated a nine- or twelve-class system, but to equally no avail. In any event, while the interest in social aggregates based on honor is quite justified and follows nicely the ideas about honor provided by Max Weber, few students of stratification now employ any version of the Warnerian approach.

ARE THERE CLASSES IN THE UNITED STATES?

In some senses all the previous problems lead up to the question which has been most hotly debated and for the longest time. It is "Are there classes in the United States and if so, how many?" This is different from asking how many divisions should one make in the distributions of income and education as one tries to understand other outcomes. There the answer depends, as we have seen, on one's purposes and on the strength of the explanatory theory available. Here, however, the question is about the existence of classes; that is, do classes exist in the United States (or elsewhere), and, if so, how many are there and of whom are they composed?

Such a question could easily be answered in societies of medieval Europe where the separate socieconomic segments were recognized by law, marked by different legal rights and obligations, and identified by different customs, occupations, and residences. Everyone knew how many estates there were and to which estate one belonged. So, too, the question of the number of distinct castes is not the least perplexing in South Africa today, where the castes are legally defined, their rights distinguished, their identities clearly symbolized by skin color among other things, and their memberships testified to by the required identity cards.

But in the mobile, albeit unequal, societies of the United States and Western Europe (and in Canada, Australia, and elsewhere) the question of whether classes exist is indeed perplexing and finally can only be solved by first agreeing upon the definitions of the term *class*.

FROM STATISTICAL AGGREGATES TO SOLIDARY CLASSES

In considering these matters in Chapter 6, we noted that there is a significant difference between an aggregate of people who are alike only in that they have a common level of income or education, as against a group of such people who have become aware of each other and of the common fate they share, who feel joined by their common positions and fates, who share a sense of why they are in their circumstances and what they must do if they are to alter their lives and fates, and who band together, self-consciously, as a political group or party, aimed at changing the social order and the distribution of the valued things of the society.

If one insists that a class cannot be said to exist until those conditions of fully developed class consciousness and solidarity are fulfilled, then the socioeconomic segments we have been examining in the past several chapters cannot properly be called classes. For there is no evidence that they are conscious of their common situations, or that they are agreed on the causes of their fates, or that they are joined into self-conscious, political groups aimed at changing their situations. Even the fact that many at the same level may agree on whether they are to be called working or middle class does not testify to the presence among them of any important degree of consciousness, political awareness, or political solidarity. Their common socioeconomic situations may make them "classes in themselves," as Marx puts it, but they are not visibly "classes for themselves" that require common awareness, solidarity, and concerted political action.

MOBILITY AND FALSE CONSCIOUSNESS

The Marxist view of these matters is that the common situation of people who work at but do not own the instruments of production will generate, under proper leadership and education, the consciousness, group cohesion, and united action needed to make them a distinctive "class for itself." But that situation has not come to pass in western-type societies. Numerous factors have occurred which have led to what Marxists call *false consciousness,* that is, workers thinking of themselves as middle-class people with a real chance, through their own efforts or sometimes through trade unions, to improve their conditions of life.

If nothing else, the amount of socioeconomic mobility in western societies, however unchanging it may have been over the past fity years, is apparently sufficient to keep alive the notions of the possibility of rising on the class ladder and of the chance that one's children will move considerably higher on the ladders of socioeconomic distinction than their parents were able to. While there is probably more inheritance of position, that is, sons in the same occupations as fathers, than mobility out of the father's position, there is enough of the latter to refreshen the idea of America and countries like it as lands of opportunity.

CLASSES AS IMPERATIVELY COORDINATED ASSOCIATIONS

One student of these matters, Rolf Dahrendorf, has written

> Thus, what has happened since Marx are in fact changes in the factors that contributed to the intensity and violence of the conflicts of his time. Patterns of conflict regulation emerged in both industry and the state. More and more, the democratic process of decision-making gave both parties a chance to realize their goals. The violence of class conflict was thereby effectively reduced. The institutionalization of social mobility made for a certain degree of openness in both classes. Absolute deprivation on the scales of social stratification gave way, for the proletariat, to relative deprivation, and later, for some, to comparative gratification. Finally, the associations of industry and the state were dissociated to some extent. All these changes served to reduce both the intensity and the violence of class conflict in post-capitalist society, and to make sudden and radical structure changes increasingly improbable. New patterns of class conflict emerge, to which we shall turn presently.[6]

When Dahrendorf speaks of "both classes," he is referring at first to the Marxist conception involving those who own the instruments of production versus those who work at them or capital versus labor. But he means something more and different as well. For in considering the question as to whether there are still such classes, he says

> "social classes and class conflict are present whenever authority is distributed unequally over social positions. It may seem trivial to state that such unequal distribution exists in associations of post-capitalist society, but this assertion nevertheless establishes both the applicability of class theory and the radical difference from all attempts to describe contemporary society as classless."[7]

What Dahrendorf means is that in modern society there are many interest groups, such as capital and labor, or officers and enlisted men, or professors and students who are engaged in joint enterprises in which one is dominant because it has superior authority over the other and uses that authority to serve its own interests, which always prove to be different to some important degree from the interests of the subordinate group. He is calling that situation of unequal authority or "imperatively coordinated associations" among parties with differing interests a class situation or relationship; and he identifies the parties involved as classes and their conflicts as class conflicts. He generalizes further by saying that to the extent that it can be shown that relationships of unequal authority are required by social structures, "the universal existence of classes is postulated by the same token." In effect, Dahrendorf is making the term *class* apply far more broadly than the Marxists do in order, as he puts it, to "discover the changed patterns and conditions of class formation and class conflict"[8].

THE ABSENCE OF MARXIST-TYPE CLASSES

That broad application of the term *class* may be useful for some purposes. But it does little to respond to the persisting query as to whether there are distinct socioeconomic classes of the traditional kind in the United States and other countries like it. In that view, a class is defined as a commonly located socioeconomic segment whose members are aware of their common positions and fates and have joined together in united political activity to alter their fates. By that definition, classes do not exist in the United States or in European countries.

This is not to deny that there are serious disputes and sometimes violent conflicts between segments of the laboring group and segments of capitalist owners and their management agents. Nor is it to deny that the perceived interests of these various groups are often strongly in conflict and that the members of the opposed groups exert as much power as they can to protect and further their own interests, often at the cost of the interests of the others. Sometimes, too, the Democratic and Republican Parties here and the Labor and Conservative Parties in Europe differ enough in their expressed concern for the less-well-off people to give the appearance of class-oriented parties. But it is also true that when the Labor or Socialist Parties gain control of the state and government, as they have recently in a number of European countries (France, Spain, Italy, Greece, and Portugal), their programs often resemble those of their Conservative opponents far more than could be expected from the differences in their names or their nominal programs. Economic crises have forced such governments to engage in austerity measures to the detriment of working classes, perhaps even more than their Conservative predecessors would have dared.

It is also true, however, that when the governments are controlled by self-admitted representatives of the wealthier people, as they are periodically in western European countries, they almost always preserve virtually all the social-welfare measures instituted by previous Labor governments, and they are sometimes forced, by political pressures, to extend these welfare measures.

Every European country and the United States can rightfully be called welfare states in that they all reduce inequality in earned income by redistributing wealth collected through taxes. Much inequality remains, as we have seen in the data about the depth of inequality. But taxation and redistribution do visibly reapportion wealth and well-being.

It is in those senses, among others, that, to the great consternation of orthodox Marxists, modern states no longer can be viewed simply as the arms of the ruling class. Most such states are subject to fierce attacks from both labor and capital. The presence of democratic institutions ensures, to some degree, that the state will act more often as mediator between conflicting class interests than as a one-sided representative of the interests of the capitalist class.

We would conclude that there are no Marxist-style classes in the United States or western Europe. Nor are there societywide, politically joined, groups of people at different socioeconomic levels. Most industrial conflicts are relatively limited in scope and are far more concerned with wages and hours than with larger political goals. Revolutionary parties are wholly inconsequential. Significant amounts of socioeconomic mobility continue to alter the composition of the different socioeconomic levels. Capitalists often fight against each other quite bitterly (importers versus exporters, for example). Traditional class consciousness seems not to be increasing, even though inequality in all good things remains the dominant pattern. Numerous groups form and become politically active, even if only temporarily, to secure larger shares of the good things of life; but those groups do not coalesce into nationwide, enduring organizations of the disadvantaged, conducting a self-conscious fight against the existing social order and its distributions of good things.

It is no accident, therefore, that most studies of stratification focus on basic inequalities and their consequences without paying much attention to the extent to which people become conscious of their situations and join in self-conscious groups aimed at altering their fates. The absence of well-formed, clear-cut classes does not make the study of inequality any less important. But we now know that we probably cannot expect those inequalities to result in the formation of self-conscious classes in the proximate future.

THE SHAPE OF THE SYSTEM: TODAY AND TOMORROW

The shape of the stratification systems in modern European societies, including the United States, then, is rather amorphous. It would be appropriate, we think, to visualize it as consisting of four distributions or ladders based on amounts of property, prestige, power, and education. There is some fair degree of correlation among the places people occupy on these ladders. But there is also considerable looseness; consequently, *status dissonance,* that is, differences in positions on the four ladders, characterizes many statuses.

The occupants of these statuses shift within and between generations, as various segments of the population experience upward and downward mobility. Small groups of people with common socioeconomic interests often coalesce into politically active units; but these are mostly temporary and mostly restricted in area and scope, and they tend to dissolve as quickly as they form. Both major political parties attempt to recruit supporters from all socioeconomic segments, though there is still some disproportionate support for the Democratic and Labor Parties by less-advantaged people and for the Republican and Conservative Parties by the more advantaged. Instead of traditional class consciousness, there is a great deal of income-level awareness. Instead of broadly based united action aimed at changing the system, there are temporary, narrowly based interest-group coalitions whose principal aim is to protect their existing interests; to increase their share of the wealth, power, and opportunity; or, at the least, to prevent their situations from deteriorating more than they otherwise might.

One can, if one wishes, divide each of these four ladders into various numbers of segments, or strata, and give to those segments such names as lower, middle, and upper class or higher and lower strata. If one does so, however, it must be understood that this is mostly a convenience for the purposes of dealing in simplified numbers of units and does not represent anything resembling the Marxist sense of class.

It is not possible on the basis of anything we now know to make confident predictions regarding the shape of the systems of stratification in the future. The amorphous structure that now exists is capable of becoming more firmly structured in any number of ways. The closest thing to a confident prediction one can make is that the amount of inequality in modern systems of stratification is not likely to deepen; and if any changes occur, they are likely to be in the direction of more equality. That probably means more equality in life chances, styles, institutional patterns, and ideologies as well.

That greater equality for most people could very well be accompanied by an even greater share of the wealth for a very small percentage of people we may call the super-rich and by an even smaller share for a very small percentage of people we may call the super-poor. In short, the extremes may grow even more extreme, while the majority, perhaps from the bottom 5 percent up to the top ninety-fifth percentile of wealth, power, education, and honor, become somewhat more equal or at least do not become more unequal than they are today.

NOTES

1. The most forthright statement of the Marxist view is in *The Communist Manifesto* by Karl Marx and Friedrich Engels. Weber wrote only briefly, but distinctly, about these matters in one fragmentary essay, "Class, Status and Party," which is to be found in *Max Weber: Essays in Sociology,* H.H. Gerth and C. Wright Mills, eds. (New York: Oxford University Press, 1946), pp. 180–95.

2. In Albert J. Reiss, Jr., *Occupations and Social Status* (Glencoe, Ill.: The Free Press, 1961), Chs. VI and VII.

3. Reprinted by permission of the University of California Press from Mary Jackman and Robert Jackman, *Class Awareness in the United States* (Berkeley: University of California Press, 1983), p. 73.

4. Ibid., p. 74.

5. W. Lloyd Warner et al., *Social Class in America* (Chicago: Science Research Associates, Inc., 1949).

6. Rolf Dahrendorf, *Class and Class Conflict in Industrial Society* (Stanford, Calif.: Stanford University Press, 1959), p. 245.

7. Ibid., p. 247.

8. Ibid., p. 247.

9. For a review of the comparative utility of nineteen different indicators of socioeconomic status, see Joseph Kahl and James A. Davis, "A Comparison of Indexes of Socioeconomic Status," *American Sociological Review,* 20 (June 1955), 317–75.

CHAPTER 14
SOCIOECONOMIC MOBILITY
Concepts, Measures, Trends

The study of socioeconomic mobility is an indispensable part of the study of social stratification. Data about inequalities in property, prestige, power, and education tell us how equal or unequal are the distributions of the good things of life at a given moment. The data about mobility, by contrast, tell us how much movement or change there has been or is currently going on between and among various positions on the ladders of stratification. How many people are moving upward? How many downward? How many are standing still? From where have the upward moving people risen? From where have the downward moving people descended? What kinds of people are standing still? How does the volume of upward movement compare with that of downward movement and/or no movement? How much of the upward movement is due to changes in the number of available places, and how much is due to new opportunities? New laws? New educational credentials?

The answers to those questions tell us about the amount of opportunity or openness there is in a society, and if we have such data on a number of societies, we can compare them with regard to their openness. An open society is one in which it is possible for young people to rise higher on the socioeconomic ladders than their parents did or to fall down to positions lower than their parents occupied. A society in which such rising and falling goes on over generational time is a fluid or open society: people acquire their statuses by achievement. By contrast, a society in which most children end up just where their parents were is considered a rigid, inflexible, or closed society; statuses are acquired by inheritance. Caste and estate systems are characterized by a great preponderance of such status inheritance. By contrast, the term *class* is usually applied to those systems in which there is a noticeable degree of status achievement even if there is also substantial inheritance.

The interest of sociologists in the openness of a society is due in large part to the high moral and political value placed on that openness in the western societies where most sociologists are located. The opportunity to succeed in accordance mainly with one's talents, and thereby to improve one's situation beyond that achieved by one's predecessors, is taken as the mark of a good society. A society is deemed to be fair when most achievement is based on merit, without advantage or impediment from one's origins, skin color, religion, sex, or any other such irrelevant characteristic. All western societies officially approve such equality of opportunity and deplore it when studies show it to be lacking or deficient.

Equality of opportunity, however, is not the same as equality of situation or outcome. The latter refers to the condition in which everyone receives equal amounts of the good things of life, whatever their talent, fitness, and performance. It is therefore eminently possible to have both equality of opportunity and inequality of situation in the same society at the same time. Even if everyone had perfectly equal opportunity, it would still be quite possible to reward the expectable different levels of natural talent and ability with unequal amounts of the good things and thus to create unequal situations and outcomes. Equal situations can be achieved only by altering the reward structure so that everyone is rewarded equally or, failing that, by redistributing the good things after they have been unequally allocated in order to achieve equal situations. The socialist ideal has always been "from each according to his ability, to each according to his needs," which means equal outcome in spite of unequal achievements or performances.

It is also possible to have inequality of opportunity side-by-side with equality of situation, or, at least, to have much more inequality in opportunity than in final outcome. Modern welfare states practice a version of this plan. Rewards are distributed unequally according to performance or other criteria; and then some of the resultant inequality is reduced by securing funds through taxation, which are then redistributed mostly to the less-well-off people.

But sociologists study socioeconomic mobility for reasons other than the moral and political value attached to openness and fairness. Primary among these is the supposition that the amount of mobility in a society may be importantly connected to a number of other societal features which would be most difficult to understand without taking account of mobility.

Among these are the degree of political freedom and democracy; the level of economic productivity; the amount of social and political solidarity felt throughout the society; the rates of various kinds of criminal acts; the amount of violence in social relations; the extent of participation in voting and other political processes; the changes in the role of the school system; and the quality of the networks of personal associations, including friendships, community groups, and even marriage patterns.

We do not now have the data that would decisively demonstrate that all those features of a society vary in accordance with the amount of mobility in the system. But one can trace the hypothetical ways in which degrees of openness might relate meaningfully to variations in such other features. For example, while poverty is not a major cause of most crimes, the extent to which poor young people feel they have a chance to make their ways by legitimate means must surely be reckoned as a possible connecting link between socioeconomic status and crime rates. In the same vein, if some groups in a society are experiencing rapid social mobility while others are not, the consequences may be very beneficial for the former while the latter, because of their relative deprivation, may show high rates of personality disorder and other pathologies. In that way a good deal of mobility, from which some are relatively excluded, may bring serious and costly disorders to the society.[1] Because of these possible influences of mobility on other important outcomes, mobility has become a matter of intense interest to sociologists.

WHAT KIND OF MOBILITY SHOULD BE STUDIED

If socioeconomic situations are made up of positions on the ladders of income, occupational prestige, power, and educational accomplishments, then, in principle, we should be interested in changes or mobility in all of these.

Various students have, in fact, focused on one or more of these four distributions to see what changes have occurred over generational time. As a result, we have studies of the distribution of incomes that go back numbers of decades, so that it is possible to say how many people in earlier times earned what amounts of income at an earlier date and what the shares of income were like at that time for various deciles or quintiles of the earning population. We have comparable studies of changes in the distribution of education and occupational achievements. But we do not have good studies of changes in power distributions because it is so extremely difficult to measure power. For now, therefore, we will ignore mobility in power and concentrate on income, occupation, and education.

It is always possible, indeed likely, that the three distributions will change in quite different ways and at quite different tempos; if we are to discover and represent socioeconomic mobility fully, then, we must examine and report changes in all three distributions. Practically, however, this is an enormous task. Perhaps the single greatest difficulty is in getting reliable information about income and educational levels of families over generational time. By contrast, it is today easier to get such information about occupations. If we ask young persons what kind of work their fathers did, we can get a more accurate report than if we ask how much education their father had or what the family income was at given points.

The greater accessibility of reliable information on occupations has been largely responsible for the fact that most studies of socioeconomic mobility today use occupation as the indicator of that mobility.

Several things commend that choice. First, we now have reasonably reliable ways of assigning prestige scores to categories of occupations. Moreover, the very high correlation (in the .90's) among the scores from one study to another, even across national boundaries, encourages us to consider those scores reliable measures of occupational prestige. Since prestige is one of the main socioeconomic ladders, it is obviously of great value to have such reliable scores, even if they represent only a portion of the totality of honor.

Second, because a great deal of research has been done on the relations between occupational levels and levels of income and education, it is now possible to use occupation to stand for all three things—prestige, income, and education. One has to be cautious, of course, since the correlations among these three are not impressively high. But they are high enough so that we can take occupation as a rough indicator, within specified limits, of the average income and average years of school achieved or required by members of an occupational category.

Table 14–1[2] (p. 136) shows the mean or average years of school and income for seventeen major categories of occupations in the United States for men aged twenty-one through sixty-four, for both 1962 and 1973. The occupational categories are arrayed in a descending order of prestige, as judged by their typical scores on the NORC scale of prestige. The general patterns of relationship are easy enough to see. As we go down the ladder of occupations and with that the levels of occupational prestige, we go down the ladder of educational and income levels as well. There are irregularities, to be sure; but the general patterns persist. at least enough to say that, within very broad limits and with a large margin of error, to know a man's occupational level is to know his educational and income levels as well.

PROBLEMS IN STUDYING MOBILITY

Movement within Categories

Various scholars have warned of a number of difficulties in the studies of change in occupations. First, the movements from one to another category of occupation fail to take account of many, possibly quite significant, shifts *within* any one category, where people can experience what they consider to be important changes. Within the category called managers, for instance, there are numerous and quite different levels, and movement among those levels is the essence of the mobility of managers. Yet in most mobility studies, those movements would be ignored, since they do not involve movement in or out of the large category. In general, much of the improvement (or deterioration) in title, salary, working conditions, autonomy, and power that people experience in their adult careers occurs within one occupational category rather than between several of them, and that movement is not caught in the studies of mobility.

Objective versus Subjective Mobility

A second critique is closely allied. It has to do with the distinction between the subjective meaning versus the objective facts about mobility. If a group of sons has moved up the ladder from the skilled labor positions of their fathers to their own white-collar clerk positions, but if the sons do not view this as real movement,

TABLE 14-1 Means and Standard Deviations* of Schooling and Income By Occupation: U.S. Men Aged 21-64 in the Experienced Civilian Labor Force, 1962 and 1973

	YEARS OF SCHOOLING		INCOME (1972 DOLLARS)	
Occupation category	1962	1973	1962	1973
1. Professionals, self-employed	15.55 (2.66)	15.89 (1.98)	15977 (12648)	24944 (21656)
2. Professionals, salaried	14.87 (2.33)	15.20 (2.16)	10443 (6897)	13412 (8362)
3. Managers	12.88 (2.69)	13.58 (2.38)	12748 (8671)	16450 (11931)
4. Salesmen, other	13.21 (2.33)	13.64 (2.13)	9717 (6317)	13777 (9016)
5. Proprietors	11.10 (2.96)	11.93 (2.71)	9785 (10564)	11495 (14085)
6. Clerks	11.84 (2.53)	12.42 (2.18)	7174 (3073)	9419 (4508)
7. Salesmen, retail	11.32 (2.55)	12.41 (2.30)	6550 (3640)	9025 (8119)
8. Craftsmen, manfuacturing	10.34 (2.51)	11.17 (2.30)	8856 (3227)	10964 (4976)
9. Craftsmen, other	10.23 (2.64)	11.19 (2.36)	7519 (3159)	9722 (4913)
10. Craftsmen, construction	9.70 (2.72)	10.57 (2.70)	6784 (3735)	9899 (6147)
11. Service	9.74 (3.19)	11.07 (3.02)	5444 (3236)	7569 (4515)
12. Operatives, other	9.50 (2.69)	10.47 (2.71)	6295 (3346)	8418 (4874)
13. Operatives, manufacturing	9.40 (2.70)	10.35 (2.70)	6661 (2606)	8415 (3851)
14. Laborers, manufacturing	8.32 (3.32)	9.90 (2.99)	5275 (2719)	7326 (4050)
15. Laborers, other	7.98 (3.50)	9.79 (3.36)	4245 (2800)	6953 (4941)
16. Farmers	9.00 (3.29)	10.56 82.98)	3972 (4921)	7647 (8610)
17. Farm laborers	6.97 (3.62)	8.26 (4.15)	2300 (2278)	4573 (3547)

* The standard deviation is a measure of the scatter or range of values around the mean. Take the mean years of schooling for professionals in 1962. It was 15.55 years with a standard deviation of 2.66 years (the figures in parentheses). That means that approximately two-thirds of all the professionals (self-employed) had completed between 15.55 plus and 15.55 minus 2.66 years, or between 18.21 years and 12.86 years.

because they do not feel any better off than their fathers, is this real mobility? In general, must the subjective experience of significant improvement (or deterioration) be present before we count a movement as a real one? We do not know now how to deal with these complications effectively. Yet we know that the influence of mobility on other social outcomes, such as rates and kinds of political participation, must surely depend to some degree on the extent to which the subjective experience of improvement accompanies the objective movement.

Absolute versus Relative Mobility

A closely related distinction is between absolute and relative mobility. A group of children may, for example, end up in occupations that are objectively more prestigious and better paid than those of their parents. But if they compare themselves with other groups who have moved even further from their parents' positions, the first group may judge the relative movement they have experienced as inadequate and unsatisfactory. So, though they have moved up absolutely, they have not moved enough, relative to others, to permit their improvement to yield a sense of satisfaction.

The Points between Which to Measure

Another problem in studying occupational mobility is the choice of the points between which mobility is to be measured. For instance, if we compare a son's occupation at the time he enters the labor force with his father's highest occupation, we will get a different score than if we compare a son's highest occupation with his father's highest, or a son's first with last occupation.

What Is a Son?

Another problem is involved in the identification of *son*. When we measure movement from father to son, shall we take the oldest son's occupational achievement? The youngest son's? The average of all sons? Suppose some of the sons have not yet achieved the highest point of their careers? How do we take account of that? Suppose, further, that the income and educational correlatives of the various sons' occupations are quite different? How do we allow for that contingency?

How Many Categories to Use

Another problem: How many occupational levels should be distinguished? There are over 20,000 different titles in the *Dictionary of Occupational Titles*. To how many categories shall we reduce these? How much by way of manageability gained is worth the loss of detail?

The Equivalence of Steps-up and Steps-down

Still another problem: Shall we count each step on the occupational ladder, however we construct it, as representing an equal amount of distance moved? Is the movement from the top of the blue-collar to the bottom of the white-collar level equal to a move from the lowest white-collar job to the second lowest?

Summing up All Movements

For a society as a whole, how do we add together the movements up and down the occupational ladder into a meaningful net score?

Structural versus Circulation Mobility

Another major concern in studying mobility is how to separate the mobility that is due to changes in the division of labor and labor supply from those that arise because of genuinely new opportunities for people who did not have such opportunities in the past.

This is a distinction between what is called structural as against circulation mobility.

Structural mobility, sometimes called forced mobility, means movement in and out of occupational categories or changes in the number of people in those categories that result from changes in the occupational structure itself, for example, the changed ratio of blue- to white-collar jobs. Such changes can come from a number of sources, including economic expansion and growth that make manual labor obsolete; differences in birth rates between levels of workers so that, for instance, the professional group may not produce enough children to replace itself; changes in death rates and rates of immigration that affect the number of people seeking and available for jobs.

By contrast, *circulation mobility*, sometimes called true mobility, refers to movements that occur as a result of the opening-up of opportunities in the system to kinds of people who did not have such opportunities before. Major factors here are laws that reduce discrimination against members of religious, racial, and sex groups; natural crises that require new and more kinds of labor; new educational opportunities that permit new kinds of people (as judged by their social origins) to acquire the skills needed for jobs their parents could not fill; and new attitudes on the part of those who serve as the "gatekeepers," such that they now welcome, or at least accept, as job applicants kinds of people they would not have accepted before. In short, anything that makes it possible for people to move into jobs from which they or their ancestors were barred or limited because of prejudice or lack of opportunities is called circulation mobility.

The movement into elite positions at the top of the occupational ladder of people from nonelite origins, so that the elites now come to be composed of quite different kinds of people from various origins, is called circulation of the elites. In popular parlance, "from rags to riches," or the Horatio Alger story, is the archetype of circulation mobility.[3]

While this distinction between structural and circulation mobility is certainly valuable to make, it must not be used to discredit the significance of structural mobility for the openness of the society. If new opportunities open up because of changes in the division of labor and the technological needs of the society and if this means that new kinds of people will be encouraged to train for these jobs and to enjoy the higher prestige and pay, it makes no sense not to consider these worthy of being included in the measure of openness of the society.

Intergenerational versus Intragenerational Mobility

A distinction also needs to be made between *intergenerational* and *intra-generational mobility*. The former refers to changes in the occupants of positions from father's generation to son's generation, for example, how many professional fathers have sons who become professionals as against sons who become managers, salesclerks, manual workers, and so forth and/or how many sons who are now professionals had fathers who were professionals, as against fathers who were managers, salesclerks, manual workers, and the like.

The first question, concerning the distribution of the sons of professional fathers, is called a matter of outflow. We are asking here what is the destination of those who flow out of each of the occupational categories in the father's generation. The second, which asks about the various kinds of sons who make up a given occupational category in the son's generation, is a matter of inflow. We are asking here what is the makeup of the population that flows into each of the occupational categories in the son's generation. Both outflow and inflow are important ingredients of intergenerational occupational mobility.

By contrast, intragenerational mobility refers to changes in the occupations held by people during the course of their lifetimes or working careers. Here we are interested in whether people enter the labor force at one level and remain at that level or move to other levels, and in what the factors are that lead to such changes.

One of the most important studies of occupational mobility[4] is very much concerned with occupational changes within one generation, that is, intragenerational mobility. It pays a good deal of attention to the extent to which father's education and occupation influence son's first and last jobs. In doing that, it is, in fact, considering the flow of forces both between and within generations. The main questions which the study addresses are: How can we best account for why various people end up in different places on the occupational ladder? What are the forces which influence their careers? How much influence is exerted by father's occupation and education? How much by their own? How much by their first job? The answers are put in terms of amount of variation in sons' jobs that can be attributed to each of these forces. The technology of the study is complicated but no more than is required by the questions and the desire for answers, in which one can be confident. Moreover, all of the problems confronting students of mobility that were just mentioned were faced and met as successfully as any other study has ever done.

CALCULATING MOBILITY

How then does one go about calculating rates of mobility? The most important figure is one which expresses the ratio of the amount of actual (observed) movement to the expected movement between occupational categories. To get this ratio, we use census or interview data, or both, to chart the distribution of a generation of sons in various categories of occupation, arrayed by their father's occupations. For example, we specify where all the sons of professional fathers ended up, where all the sons of managerial fathers landed, and so forth, down the ladder to the bottom category of sons of farm laborer fathers.

Table 14–2[5] (p. 141) shows these figures for 1962. Reading across the top row we see that 16.7 percent of all sons of professionals ended up as professionals, 31.9 percent ended up as salaried professionals, 9.9 percent landed in the category of managers, and so on.

Reading across the next-to-last row, for farm laborers we see that .2 percent of all sons of farm laborers ended up as self-employed professionals, 1.9 percent as salaried professionals, and so on.

> The last row, which represents the percentage distribution of the total labor force in the several occupations, serves as the standard against which all other percentages in the body of the matrix are compared [and becomes] the divisor in the ratio [we seek].
>
> By dividing each value in the matrix by the corresponding figure in the total row at the bottom of its column, we obtain an index of the influence of occupational origins on occupational destinations. This ratio, which has been termed the "index of association" or "social distance mobility ratio," measures the extent to which mobility from one occupation to another surpasses or falls short of "chance," that is, a value of 1.0 indicates that the observed mobility is equal to that expected on the assumption of statistical independence[6] (on the assumption that the father's occupation had no influence on the son's final destination).

Ratios larger than 1 indicate that the father's occupation had larger than a chance influence, and ratios smaller than 1 indicate that father's occupation had less than chance influence on son's occupation. Ratios larger than 1 indicate increasing degrees of inheritance; ratios smaller than 1 indicate decreasing degrees of inheritance.

Table 14–3[7] (p. 142) presents the ratios calculated from the figures presented in Table 14–2. Reading across the top row, for professionals we find that there were 11.7 times more sons of self-employed professionals who themselves became self-employed professionals than one would have expected if father's job had no influence on son's job; and, further, 3.1 times more of salaried professionals who became salaried professionals; 1.2 times as many managers; 3.0 times as many salesmen and other similar employees. All the other ratios are below 1, indicating, for example, that there were fewer sons of self-employed professionals who entered or landed in those lower-rated jobs than would have been expected on the assumption of independence.

Reading across the bottom row, we see that not until we get to the category *construction workers* do the sons of farm laborers reach the level of chance expectations. The ratio of observed to expected in the box for self-employed professionals is .1, meaning that the number of sons of farm laborers who achieved that high occupation were only one-tenth of what one would have expected by chance alone.

TABLE 14-2 Mobility From Father's Occupation to 1962 Occupation For Males 25 to 64 Years Old: Outflow Percentages

RESPONDENT'S OCCUPATION IN MARCH, 1962

Father's Occupation	1	2	3	4	5	6	7	8	9	10	11	12	13	14	15	16	17	Total[a]
Professionals																		
1 Self-Empl.	16.7	31.9	9.9	9.5	4.4	4.0	1.4	2.0	1.8	2.2	2.6	1.6	1.8	.4	2.2	2.0	.8	100.0
2 Salaried	3.3	31.9	12.9	5.9	4.8	7.6	1.7	3.8	4.4	1.0	6.9	5.2	3.4	1.0	.6	.8	.2	100.0
3 Managers	3.5	22.6	19.4	6.2	7.9	7.6	1.1	5.4	5.3	3.1	4.0	2.5	1.5	1.1	.8	.5	.1	100.0
4 Salesmen, Other	4.1	17.6	21.2	13.0	9.3	5.3	3.5	2.8	5.4	1.9	2.6	3.7	1.7	.0	.8	1.0	.3	100.0
5 Proprietors	3.7	13.7	18.4	5.8	16.0	6.2	3.3	3.5	5.2	3.9	5.1	3.6	2.8	.5	1.2	1.1	.4	100.0
6 Clerical	2.2	23.5	11.2	5.9	5.1	8.8	1.3	6.6	7.1	1.8	3.8	4.6	5.6	1.0	1.8	1.3	.0	100.0
7 Salesmen, Retail	.7	13.7	14.1	8.8	11.5	6.4	2.7	5.8	3.4	3.1	8.8	5.1	4.6	.1	3.1	2.2	.0	100.0
Craftsmen																		
8 Mfg.	1.0	14.9	8.5	2.4	6.2	6.1	1.7	15.3	6.4	4.4	10.9	6.2	4.6	1.7	2.4	.4	.1	100.0
9 Other	.9	11.1	9.2	3.9	6.5	7.6	1.5	7.8	12.2	4.4	8.2	9.2	4.6	1.2	2.8	.9	.3	100.0
10 Construction	.9	6.7	7.1	2.6	8.3	7.9	.8	10.4	8.2	13.9	7.5	6.2	5.2	1.1	4.3	.8	.6	100.0
Operatives																		
11 Mfg.	1.0	8.6	5.3	2.7	5.6	6.0	1.4	12.2	7.3	3.2	17.9	6.9	5.1	4.0	3.5	.8	.6	100.0
12 Other	.6	11.5	5.1	2.5	6.6	6.3	1.4	7.1	9.3	4.9	10.4	12.5	5.9	2.1	4.2	.9	1.1	100.0
13 Service	.8	8.8	7.4	3.5	6.0	9.0	1.9	8.0	6.4	5.4	11.7	8.1	10.5	2.7	3.3	1.0	.2	100.0
Laborers																		
14 Mfg.	.0	6.0	5.3	.7	3.3	4.4	.7	10.7	6.0	2.8	18.1	9.4	9.4	7.1	5.8	1.7	.9	100.0
15 Other	.4	4.9	3.5	2.5	3.5	8.7	1.7	7.7	8.2	5.7	12.7	10.6	8.1	3.4	9.9	.9	1.1	100.0
16 Farmers	.6	4.2	4.1	1.2	6.0	4.3	1.1	5.6	6.7	5.8	10.2	8.6	4.8	2.4	5.4	16.4	3.9	100.0
17 Farm Laborers	.2	1.9	2.9	.6	4.0	3.5	1.2	6.4	6.6	5.8	13.1	10.8	7.5	3.2	9.2	5.7	9.4	100.0
Total[b]	1.4	10.2	7.9	3.1	7.0	6.1	1.5	7.2	7.1	4.9	9.9	7.6	5.5	2.1	4.3	5.2	1.7	100.0

a Rows as shown do not total 100.0, since men not in experienced civilian labor force are not shown separately.
b Includes men not reporting father's occupation.

TABLE 14-3 Mobility From Father's Occupation to Occupation in 1962, For Males 25 to 64 Years Old: Ratios of Observed Frequencies to Frequencies Expected on the Assumption of Independence

RESPONDENT'S OCCUPATION IN MARCH, 1962

Father's Occupation	1	2	3	4	5	6	7	8	9	10	11	12	13	14	15	16	17
Professionals																	
1 Self-Empl.	11.7	3.1	1.2	3.0	.6	.7	.9	.3	.3	.5	.3	.2	.3	.2	.5	.4	.5
2 Salaried	2.3	3.1	1.6	1.9	.7	1.2	1.1	.5	.6	.2	.7	.7	.6	.5	.1	.2	.1
3 Managers	2.5	2.2	2.5	2.0	1.1	1.2	.7	.8	.7	.6	.4	.3	.3	.5	.2	.1	.1
4 Salesmen, Other	2.9	1.7	2.7	4.1	1.3	.9	2.2	.4	.8	.4	.3	.5	.3	.0	.2	.2	.2
5 Proprietors	2.6	1.3	2.3	1.9	2.3	1.0a	2.1	.5	.7	.8	.5	.5	.5	.2	.3	.2	.2
6 Clerical	1.6	2.3	1.4	1.9	.7	1.4	.8	.9	1.0a	.4	.4	.6	1.0a	.5	.4	.2	.0
7 Salesmen, Retail	.5	1.3	1.8	2.8	1.6	1.0a	1.7	.8	.5	.6	.9	.7	.8	.1	.7	.4	.0
Craftsmen																	
8 Mfg.	.7	1.5	1.1	.8	.9	1.0	1.1	2.1	.9	.9	1.1	.8	.8	.8	.6	.1	.1
9 Other	.6	1.1	1.2	1.2	.9	1.2	1.0	1.1	1.7	.9	.8	1.2	.8	.6	.6	.2	.2
10 Construction	.6	.7	.9	.8	1.2	1.3	.5	1.4	1.1	2.8	.8	.8	.9	.5	1.0	.2	.4
Operatives																	
11 Mfg.	.7	.8	.7	.9	.8	1.0	.9	1.7	1.0a	.6	1.8	.9	.9	1.9	.8	.2	.4
12 Other	.4	1.1	.6	.8	.9	1.0a	.9	1.0	1.3	1.0	1.0a	1.7	1.1	1.0	1.0	.2	.7
13 Service	.5	.9	.9	1.1	.9	1.5	1.2	1.1	.9	1.1	1.2	1.1	1.9	1.3	.8	.2	.1
Labor																	
14 Mfg.	.0	.6	.7	.2	.5	.7	.5	1.5	.8	.6	1.8	1.2	1.7	3.3	1.4	.3	.5
15 Other	.3	.5	.4	.8	.5	1.4	1.1	1.1	1.1	1.2	1.3	1.4	1.5	1.6	2.3	.2	.7
16 Farmers	.4	.4	.5	.4	.9	.7	.7	.8	.9	1.2	1.0a	1.1	.9	1.1	1.3	3.2	2.3
17 Farm Laborers	.1	.2	.4	.2	.6	.6	.8	.9	.9	1.2	1.3	1.4	1.4	1.5	2.1	1.1	5.5

a Rounds to unity from above (other indices shown as 1.0 round to unity from below).

By contrast, looking at the lowest right-hand box, we see that 5.5 times as many sons of farm laborers themselves became farm laborers as we might have expected if their father's occupations had nothing to do with where they landed. In effect, father's occupations had a very strong influence on their destined occupation.

OTHER USES OF MOBILITY TABLES

An interesting and useful figure results, too, when we compare the number of cells where the ratio is above 1 with those where the ratio is below 1. A preponderance of the former (both upward and downward movements) indicates much movement among occupational strata. So, too, if one draws a diagonal that goes from top left to bottom right, the cells with values above 1 that lie to the lower left of the diagonal line represent disproportionate upward mobility, while those with values above 1 that lie to the upper right of the diagonal represent disproportionate downward mobility.

One can then calculate the ratio of upward to downward mobility and use that as a measure of the prevailing direction in which mobility is taking place.

One can also compare short-distance moves with long-distance moves to see how far on the average sons of various fathers are moving when and if they move. Or one can analyze special patterns of individual occupations to see how those sons are faring compared to some other individual occupation. For example, are sons of clerical people more or less mobile, in what direction, and over what distance, as compared with sons of construction workers?

From these tables, too, one can analyze the flow of manpower that each occupation is supplying to the other occupations, for example, from what categories does the self-employed professional category receive its manpower. An analysis of this kind makes it possible to say such things as "...every occupational origin above the level of construction craftsmen sends more than one-fifth of its sons to only two of the seventeen occupations—salaried professionals and managers. A major reason is that these two occupational groups have been expanding rapidly while reproducing at a level somewhat lower than the rest of the population."[8]

Or from another matrix, which shows inflow percentages, that is, what proportion of men in each occupation were recruited from various occupational origins, one can discover such things as that in 1962, "every occupational group has recruited more than 10 percent of its members from sons of farmers. Three evident reasons for this are the large size of the farm category in the past...the rapid decline in the number of farmers in recent decades; and the exceptionally high fertility of farmers."[9]

With these same data, one can calculate what is called an index of occupational inheritance, or the percent of men in one category whose fathers were in the same one; and one can also calculate an index of self-recruitment, which is the percent of fathers whose sons continue in their occupational category. One can also analyze the data to discover how concentrated or dispersed are the inflows and outflows to and from various occupations.

All of these and still other observations and measures are the kinds of statements about the volume and patterning of mobility in a society that one can make on the basis of data about son and father's occupations. With those kinds of summary measures and statements about mobility, one can then compare various time periods to see what has happened to the volume and patterning mobility; and one can also compare the volumes and patterns of various nations.

SOME GENERALIZATIONS ABOUT MOBILITY

Blau and Duncan, on whose work we have relied very heavily here, venture a summary statement about American mobility patterns and volumes. They base these on three sources:

1. intergenerational movement from father's occupations to son's occupations in 1962
2. intergenerational movement from father's occupations to son's first occupations in 1962
3. intragenerational movement from son's first occupation to son's occupations in 1962

These three tables, they say, bring the main characteristics of the American occupational structure into "high relief." The conclusions include the following:

1. Occupational inheritance is in all cases greater than one would expect if one assumed perfect independence of father and son's occupations.
2. Social mobility is nevertheless pervasive.
3. Upward mobility is more prevalent than downward mobility.
4. Short-distance movements occur more often than long-distance movements.

Exceptional patterns include the following:

1. Industrial lines constitute stronger barriers to mobility than do skill levels within an industry.
2. Sons of craftsmen are more likely to move into higher than lower white collar occupations.
3. Sons of manual workers outside manufacturing are more apt to be upwardly mobile than those in manufacturing.
4. Downward mobility to first job is most marked for those in the highest white collar groups and for skilled craftsmen, while upward mobility to the first job is most common among both lower manual and nonmanual workers.

With regard to trends over time in the amount of mobility, some of the conclusions these authors reach include the following:

1. Mobility has slightly increased in the ten or fifteen years covered (as of 1962). At least there is no indication of increasing rigidity in the class structure.

2. The recent increases in overall chances of mobiltiy are due primarily to the expansion in the higher salaried positions to accommodate the upward flow of people, and it is the younger men in particular who have been able to take advantage of this expansion.

3. The amount of upward intergenerational and intragenerational mobility have both increased in the last decade.

4. Since World War II there has been no evident rigidification in the occupational opportunity system. The fear that the "land of opportunity" is giving way to a society with rigid classes is "premature" and perhaps "unfounded".[10]

Most of these generalizations were confirmed in a 1973 study by Featherman and Hauser[11] who replicated the 1962 study done by Blau and Duncan. They drew a sample from the 1970 Census that resembled the 1962 sample as closely as possible and to them they put almost all the same questions that had been asked in the earlier study.

Some of their most important conclusions were the following:

1. There is a great deal of movement both within occupational careers and between generations. More than 80 percent of the men in the 1973 sample had moved at least one level out of their fathers' occupations.

2. The trend was toward a greater volume of occupational mobility.

3. Upward mobility was far more prevalent than downward mobility.

4. There was, nevertheless, a moderate degree of correlation between occupational origins and destinations, both within and between generations.

5. The observed trends in mobility were due mostly to changes in the occupational structure, that is, in the numbers and kinds of jobs available, and only a small portion of the mobility was due to genuinely improved chances for mobility.

RACE AND MOBILITY

Featherman and Hauser[12] were also able to secure a sufficiently large sample of Black males so that they could study Black mobility and make some comparisons with White mobility. Among the most important findings were the following:

1. The mean difference between Black and White educational achievements was at an all-time low in 1973.

2. The payoff of education in occupations and incomes for Blacks, especially those with college education, rise sharply from 1962 to 1973. But the payoffs were still smaller than those for Whites.

3. The relative improvement in the socioeconomic status of better-educated Blacks was not matched by Blacks at lower socioeconomic levels. Instead, socioeconomic class lines within the Black community were drawn more sharply, and occupational inheritance among Blacks came to resemble that among Whites more closely than ever before. In sum, while the overall opportunities for Blacks had significantly improved, this was accompanied by greater inequality of opportunity *within* the Black population.

4.   Younger cohorts of Blacks experienced more extensive educational and occupational mobility between generations than their predecessors, and for those born after the mid-1930s the mobility rates compare favorably with those of the White population.
5.   Blacks born during and after World War II experienced occupational mobility (from fathers' to sons' current jobs) that far exceeded the mobility of older Blacks.

The authors believe that those trends in the Black population suggest a weakening in the influence of racial identity on socioeconomic standing and on chances for improvement across generations.

SEX AND MOBILITY

The 1962 and 1973 studies did not contain information about women's positions and patterns of mobility. Future censuses and special national studies are sure to provide this information. In the meantime, generalizations about women's patterns must rely on smaller studies, of which an impressively large number have been done since the early 1970s. Some of these have studied subsamples of representative national panels, but the total number of women studied in even the largest of these is far smaller than the more than 20,000 males studied in 1962 and 1973. Comparisons between the mobility patterns of men and women must therefore be made with considerable caution. We can report some of the findings from a few studies.

Treiman and Terrell[13] compared a small but representative national sample of women (1649 White and 875 Black) with a subsample of the larger group of men studied by Blau and Duncan. Their major findings include the following:

1.   Men and women are about equally well educated, and their educational attainments are similarly influenced by their parents (p. 197).
2.   Both the level and process of occupational attainment are very similar for women and men. The prestige of occupations held by women is roughly equal to the prestige of those occupations when held by men, and, for both women and men, attaining an occupation depends mostly on education and only slightly on social origins (p. 197).
3.   Wives earn about half as much as their husbands. Less than half of this difference is attributable to the fact that wives worked less and have worked only part of their adult lives. The remainder of the difference is due to a combination of three factors: direct discrimination against women, lack of equal opportunity for married women, and norms that lead or force women to take account of nonincome aspects of their jobs. These inferences are supported by the fact that single women earn substantially more than married women, while still earning less than men (p. 198).
4.   In regard to income, Black women are more like Black men than are White women like White men. But Black women are paid much less than Black men, even when they are as well educated, perform comparable work, have as much experience, and work as many hours (p. 198).

The foregoing findings on White women and men were largely supported by a later study by McClendon,[14] who also found that the number of children at home had no influence on the occupational status of women.

Still another study by Featherman and Hauser[15] also supports the major themes of these studies and adds the finding that sexual discrimination accounts for about 85 percent of the difference in the earnings of women and men, both in 1962 and 1973.

Taylor and Glenn[16] examined the evidence about the popular assumption that there is a direct correlation between the physical attractiveness of women and the occupational prestige of their husbands. The implication in this notion is that more attractive women are able to secure high-standing men, on some principle of exchange of attractiveness for status. The authors studied a nation-wide sample drawn in 1972 and found that the attractiveness of women is not nearly as influential as it is believed to be. The influence was insignificant in the marriages of women who came from families with higher social standing, and its influence was significant but only at a low level in the marriages of women from lower social origins. Among all women, educational level was more influential than attractiveness or social origin.

Another widespread assumption holds that because women spend more time at domestic affairs even when they are employed, there is a degrading effect on their earnings. Shelly Coverman[17] examined this matter in a study of a national sample of persons, aged 16 and over, who were working for pay for 20 hours a week or more, in 1977. She found that spending time at domestic labor significantly decreased the wages of both men and women. The wages of working-class men were most influenced, and nonworking-class women's wages were depressed by domestic labors more than the wages of working-class women. The author suggests that if wage differentials between men and women are to be reduced, domestic labor must be more evenly divided.

Only one major study[18] suggest that there are significant differences in the status acquisition patterns of men and women. This involved a 1975 follow-up on a sample of people who had been seniors in Wisconsin high schools in 1958 and had been studied at that time. The researchers report that the effect of post-high school education on first jobs was twice as great among men as among women, and the effect of first jobs on current jobs is one-third greater among men than among women. But they also found that by midlife the total effect of schooling on job status had become the same for both sexes, and that childless women closely resemble men in the patterns of occupational attainment.

With the exception of this one study, there is a consensus among researchers on two major findings: (1) the general patterns of status attainment that hold true for men also apply to women, with education and first job being most important in determining final job, while social origin is less influential;(2) while women have achieved educational parity with men, they still show significantly lower occupational and income levels. This difference is due to the persistence of their normative roles which involve marriage, child bearing, and domestic work, along with jobs, and to the continuation of prejudice and discrimination against women in the job market. The implication here is that if and when discrimination reduces or ceases, and if and when the traditional views about the proper roles for women and men move toward greater equality, the achievement levels of the two sexes will show comparable equalization.[19]

INTERNATIONAL COMPARISONS

How then does the picture of opportunity and mobility in the United States compare with that of other nations? Is America more or less the land of opportunity than others? Can immigrants from abroad still count on the United States as a place where one can start from very humble origins and by diligence, education, and training climb high on the ladder of occupational prestige and income?

More important, from a sociological point of view, are such questions as the following: What kinds of economic and industrial organization are correlated with what amounts and patterns of mobility? Do countries with similar levels of economic development have different volumes and patterns of mobility so that we must turn to noneconomic factors to try to understand the differences? Do countries with higher rates of upward mobility show less or more internal disorders, social pathologies, and participation in political processes? In short, the same kinds of questions that one asks about the significance of mobility within any one nation can be raised about the differences between nations.

To answer these questions one needs equally good data from all the countries one wishes to compare. While competent sociologists are at work in all western European countries on many of the same problems and while the techniques and methods for measuring mobility are available to all, we do not have sufficiently good comparable data to be able to answer many of the questions about comparative amounts and kinds of mobility in various countries. Many problems plague the person who tries to make international comparisons.

In general the difficulties involved are precisely the same as those one encounters in trying to measure mobility within one country, magnified and multiplied now by the necessity to get genuinely comparable data from several countries.

Yet studies of comparative mobility rates have been made by various scholars since the early 1960s.

The soundest comparisons are those that restrict themselves to selected portions of the total picture of mobility, for example, by whom are the elite or top educational ranks and jobs being filled? Alternatively, various comparisons have been made of the movement of the sons of blue-collar fathers into white-collar occupations. To do this requires that one condense the ladder of occupations into two large groupings, and, naturally, much detail is lost in the process.

From these and other studies, it is possible to venture a number of generalizations, albeit tentative ones, about mobility patterns in the United States and other western European industrialized democracies.

1. Rates of mobility in all industrial societies are high and there is little difference between them.

2. While rates of upward mobility, as well as of upward and downward combined, seem somewhat larger in various European countries when measured by movement across the blue-collar–white-collar line, the overall rate of mobility, taking more detailed distinctions into account, is probably not very significantly different and may indeed favor the United States, but not by much.

3. The greater degree of egalitarianism in America, as expressed particularly in its system of education, has served in the past, and continues to serve to a lesser degree, as one of the main sources of American mobility. It has been reflected in the past in the greater movement in the United States of sons of manual and other lower-category workers into elite positions at the top of the occupational ladder. At the same time, the greater degree of indifference to social origins in the United States probably has made the transition for mobile sons easier, at least so far as acceptance in the ranks of elites is concerned. These latter differences in ease of transition probably still persist.

4. The former superiority of the United States to other European countries as measured by wealth, or GNP per capita, has by now virtually vanished; and indeed a number of other European countries now outrank the United States in wealth per capita and have more egalitarian distributions of wealth. To that extent, the former greater ability of people in the United States to enjoy higher standards of living, without correlative changes in occupations, has probably by now been eliminated or equalized.

5. Shifting economic fortunes and shifting structures of occupational opportunities in the United States and Europe (and Japan) make it perilous to predict the future shapes of occupational opportunities and the related mobility rates. The very sharp decrease in the well-being of certain basic industries in the United States probably has produced depression in the educational and occupational fortunes of the children of workers employed in those industries. Many of the same observations apply to European countries as well.

6. The single, safest prediction one can make about the future of comparative mobility rates is that as all the countries involved become more alike in their political and economic structures, as they are in the process of becoming, the more similar do they become in their rates and patterns of mobility.

NOTES

1. See Melvin Tumin, "Some Unapplauded Consequences of Social Mobility in a Mass Society," *Social Forces*, 36, 1 (October 1957), 32–37.

2. Reprinted by permission of Academic Press from D.L. Featherman and R.M. Hauser, *Opportunity and Change* (New York: Academic Press, 1978).

3. See, for example, Suzanne Keller, *Beyond the Ruling Class: Strategic Elites in Modern Society* (New York: Random House, Inc., 1963).

4. Peter M. Blau and Otis Dudley Duncan, *The American Occupational Structure* (New York: John Wiley and Sons, Inc., 1967).

5. Ibid., p. 28. We also use Blau & Duncan's formulations in explaining various of the measures and in specifying the uses of mobility tables. All page numbers in parentheses refer to that volume. Reprinted with permission of The Free Press, a division of Macmillan, Inc. Copyright © 1967 by Peter M. Blau and Otis Dudley Duncan.

6. Ibid., p. 35.

7. Ibid., Table 2.5, p. 32. Reprinted with permission of The Free Press, a division of Macmillan, Inc. Copyright © 1967 by Peter M. Blau and Otis Dudley Duncan.

8. Ibid., p. 38.

9. Ibid., p. 38.

10. Ibid., p. 113.

11. David L. Featherman and Robert M. Hauser, *Opportunity and Change,* (New York: Academic Press, Inc., 1978). All the findings reported here are taken from pp. 135–38 of this book.

12. All the observations on Black mobility patterns are drawn from pp. 325–29 and 381–84 in Featherman and Hauser, *ibid.*

13. Donald J. Treiman and Kermit Terrell, "Sex and the Process of Status Attainment: A Comparison of Working Women and Men," *American Sociological Review,* 40 (April 1975), 174–200. (Page numbers in parentheses refer to this article.)

14. McKee H. McClendon, "The Occupational Status Attainment Processes of Males and Females," *American Sociological Review,* 41 (February 1976), 52–64.

15. David L. Featherman and Robert M. Hauser, "Sexual Inequalities and Socioeconomic Achievement in the U.S., 1962–1973," *American Sociological Review,* 41 (June 1976), 462–83.

16. Patricia Ann Taylor and Norval D. Glenn, "The Utility of Education and Attractiveness for Females' Status Attainment Through Marriage," *American Sociological Review,* 41 (June 1976), 484–98.

17. Shelley Coverman, "Gender, Domestic Labor Time, and Wage Inequality," *American Sociological Review,* 48 (October 1983), 623–37.

18. William H. Sewell, Robert M. Hauser, and Wendy C. Wolf, "Sex, Schooling, and Occupational Status," *American Journal of Sociology,* 86 (November 1980), 551–83.

19. Each of the works cited in footnotes 12 to 19 contains extensive bibliographical citations to other works in the field of sex differences in status attainment.

CHAPTER 15
SOME THEORETICAL PROBLEMS

Intense and widespread debate is a persisting feature of the literature on social stratification. Three of the main issues on which there is serious disagreement are the following:

1. Is stratification inevitable?
2. Is stratification efficient for societal well-being and survival?
3. Why is stratification so widespread now, as it has been in most previous societies?

To answer these questions we must first specify a core of agreements about social inequality as follows:

1. Some form and amount of socioeconomic inequality is found in all societies of the world today and probably has always existed.
2. Some of that inequality arises when, in accordance with the norms, unequal rewards are assigned to various statuses.
3. Another portion of inequality gets into societies as a result of the disparities between the inequality that the norms call for and the actual amount of inequality that develops. These disparities are due to factors such as power to secure more than one's share; illegal conduct; inadequate calibration of reward to assessed social importance of the statuses; imperfect monitoring of the reward system; the play of market factors outside the status-reward system; and the influence of particular personal characteristics, such as strength, intelligence, skill, beauty, guile, charm, and charisma.
4. Since nothing in innate human nature or the nature of societies commands any particular form or amount of stratification, it must be assumed that the distribution of good things in any society results from human decisions, consensual or other, to shape the distribution.
5. Those decisions can and do vary between dictatorial decrees, on one extreme, and wholly consensual, democratically decided patterns on the other. The shape of a

system at any given time therefore represents the outcome of the competition between opposing forces in the society. At times there is no competition because it is ruled out by powerful elites or because those with the power to do so establish the prevailing norms and reinforce them by powerful punishments, both secular and sacred, for deviation. At other times, as in modern democratic societies, there is open and often bitter and widespread disagreement and conflict over how to distribute the good things.

6.   The systems of inequality throughout the world vary greatly along a number of dimensions including:

   (a)   The depth of inequality on any one of the distributions

   (b)   The span or scope of stratification, that is, how many of the good things are distributed unequally and into what other areas of life do these inequalities extend their influence: life chances, institutional patterns, life styles, and attitudes and beliefs

   (c)   Their shape and internal arrangements of strata; the range is from virtually classless, unstratified societies, on the one extreme, to rigid, closed, hierarchical systems, such as those called castes, on the other

   (d)   The amount of openness or mobility in the system

   (e)   The extent to which the distribution of any one of the good things tends to match or be correlated with the distributions of the other. Such correlations normally tend to be high, so that positions on the ladder of property are accompanied by comparable positions on the ladders of honor and power. This matching is due not to any inherent strain in the system so much as to the conscious efforts by those with unequal amounts of good things to preserve their privileged positions, the inability of the less fortunate to change the situation, or the acceptance of the situation by most of the people.

   (f)   The degree of endurance and persistence over time. Some systems last for decades and centuries virtually unchanged. Others, such as modern, industrial societies, undergo frequent and often substantial change, mostly toward greater equality. The speed and amount of change depends on the balance of forces among opposing segments of the population with their differing interests in, and ideas about, the right way to distribute the good things.

7.   When mobility begins to take place in a society, it occurs most often along only one of the distributions, for example, only wealth or only honor. In earlier periods, mobility onto higher levels of property was the most usual pattern. Today mobility onto higher-education and job-prestige levels is the most common pattern. Such mobility in one dimension, without accompanying mobility in the others, introduces status dissonance. This is seen as a source of tension and strain that may produce efforts to reduce the dissonance by attempting to increase shares in the good things not yet attained, for example, more honor or power to accompany the increased property or education.

8.   Fundamental changes in systems, such as the change from feudal, estate, or caste systems to open, classlike, democratic systems have almost always required political revolutions to displace ruling oligarchs and change the norms and laws that govern the distributions of good things.

9.   The growth in the wealth of a society does not automatically or naturally produce greater equality in the distribution of wealth. Nations can become much wealthier without any significant reduction in the inequality of the distribution of wealth. Specific measures aimed at altering the distribution seem required if greater equality is to be achieved.

10.   Growth in the equality of opportunity in a society—as indicated by mobility—is not necessarily, automatically, or naturally accompanied by growth in equality of situation. Equality of opportunity can coexist, side-by-side, with inequality in actual condi-

tions of life. Only deliberate policies aimed at redistributing wealth more equally can produce that equality.

11.. There is an evident coincidence in contemporary democratic societies among (a) the amount of political freedom; (b) the degree of equality of distributions of good things; (c) the amount and type of mobility; and (d) the wealth or productivity of the nation. Each of these seems to increase with the others, but not regularly or evenly. The causal connections among these four variables are not clear.

12.. None of the variant forms and amounts of inequality in social systems can be shown to be more natural, more logical, or more responsive to imperatives of human nature or of social organization. Societies obviously endure, often for very long periods of time, under very different circumstances.

The foregoing twelve sets of statements sum up some of the more important agreements about systems of stratification. With those as base lines, we can now address the theoretical questions raised at the outset.

IS STRATIFICATION INEVITABLE?

Three of the factual findings make it extremely dubious that more than minimal stratification is inevitable. The first is the great variability in the depth, scope, and shape of systems, a variability that includes at least some systems that approach equality and classlessness, or the absence of formed strata. The second is the absence of persuasive evidence that something in the imperatives of human nature or of organized social life commands socioeconomic inequality. The third is the finding that the shape and scope of any system of stratification at any given time represents the outcome of the interplay among political, economic, and social forces in the society. In short, human decisions determine how much stratification, if any, there will be.

The people of a society can *decide*, and some have decided, to organize themselves so that there is something approaching total equality in the good and scarce things of life. That being the case, stratification cannot be said to be inevitable or inescapable.

Yet certain inequalities are sure to be found everywhere, even when the society has decided to practice total equality. Primary among these is the unequal power that various role-players, for example, parents, teachers, governors, and so forth, must have if they are to discharge their normative responsibilities. These role-specific inequalities can be great or modest, once again depending on how the people of the society decide they want to conduct their affairs. Such unequal, role-specific power need not, however, spill over into relationships outside the role context.

The answer then to the question of whether stratification or inequality in the good things of life is inevitable is a qualified "yes." Some inequality is probably inescapable, if only as a result of the slippages and discrepancies between ideal standards and actual practices. Otherwise, the only inequalities that seem inevitable are those in role-specific powers, and those have no necessary spillovers into other areas. Nothing in the imperatives of human nature or of social structure seems to require more inequality than that. There will be as much inequality in a society as the members of that society permit, or want to have, or believe it is right or necessary to have. All depends on prevailing values and on the distribution of power to decide those matters.

IS STRATIFICATION EFFICIENT? FOR WHOM? FOR WHAT?

Inequality may not be inevitable in any absolute sense, yet there may be other good reasons why inequality occurs everywhere. One major school of thought, called the *functionalists,*[1] argue that if societies are to be efficient about getting their most important tasks done well by the most talented people, they must induce those talented people to undergo the needed training and then to perform their importnat tasks efficiently; and the only way, or the most efficient way, to do this is by promising and giving them unequal amounts of property and prestige. They claim that most of the inequality found in societies is due to the fact that societies have discovered the necessity and the efficiency of unequal rewards for securing efficient task performance. They call stratification *an unconsciously evolved device* by which efficient task performance is insured.

The underlying assumption here is that there is a fundamental strain in human nature that makes it difficult if not impossible to get people with unequal talents to take on and perform their tasks without the promise of unequal rewards. But this is manifestly untrue, at least so far as general human motivation is concerned. The contrary evidence is seen in family life in this and every other society. All over the world people are socialized, trained, and motivated to take on the burdens of parenthood and to discharge them to their maximum efficiency, without any regard for rewards of any kind except those that come out of the intimate relations and gratifications of family life. These are highly desired but also infinitely abundant in the sense that the amount of such gratifications secured by one does not in any sense affect the amount available for others. Moreover, if people have unequal talents for engineering, medicine, and carpentry, they surely also have unequal talents for parenthood. Yet at all levels of talent people perform their parental roles with extraordinary conscientiousness.

We know, too, why this is so. In addition to the great normative pressures to be good parents, there is the additional pressure that comes from the fact that parents immediately and fully experience the pleasures of their successes and the pains of their failures in family life. The combination of external normative pressures and the immediacy and fullness of the consequences of one's behavior appears to work very effectively indeed.

One may argue that one cannot duplicate family conditions in large-scale bureaucracies and that therefore different motivational schemes have to be used to secure effective task performance in those impersonal contexts. That is probably true. But we remain quite unsure about the array of possible ways in which people can be motivated to give their conscientious best without consideration of unequal rewards. Could they not be threatened with dire consequences if they did not? Or could they not be taught that giving one's conscientious best is an absolute moral imperative? And that acceptance as a decent citizen and access to a decent share of good things will depend on such conscientiousness? Could not duty, morality, obligation, and acceptance achieve the desired ends? We do not know. But no one has demonstrated satisfactorily that these are not workable possibilities. Until that demonstration is forthcoming, one cannot claim the necessity of using unequal rewards as motivators.

That still leaves open the question of the efficiency of unequal rewards. For even if people can be motivated to be conscientious by other means, perhaps unequal rewards yield the highest motivation and the highest degree of conscientious excellence in task performance.

Three separate but connected things are at stake here. One is the question of the efficiency of the promise of unequal rewards in recruiting the most talented people and inducing them to take on the training necessary to become excellent. A second issue is the efficiency of the scheme of rewarding talented people unequally to secure from them their most conscientious excellence. A third is whether there are costs that societies pay for promising and giving unequal rewards that may diminish or negate whatever efficiency such unequal rewards may produce.

On the matter of recruitment of talent: How does one know if the system of unequal rewards has been efficient in discovering and recruiting the highest talents for the most valued tasks? One piece of evidence is found in the comparison of the aptitude scores of candidates for admission to schools of medicine, law, and engineering. That comparison shows that while some of the most talented people are admitted to these schools, many equally talented people are rejected. Their rejection is due simply to the scarcity of available places.

That scarcity is due in turn to the decision by those who control admission policies to limit the number of people who will be trained. Keeping the numbers of trained people low ensures higher levels of income for the successful candidates and for all members of the professions. By the same token, the contrived scarcity of professionals makes their services less available to the public and forces the public to pay more for these services than they would have to pay if there were more practitioners available.

Moreover, we really do not know how many people have the talents required to perform the most skilled tasks efficiently. Those who apply for advanced training may be only a portion of all those who might have qualified, but who never had a chance to think about, much less pursue, such career possibilities because of the disadvantaged positions of their parents. The stratification system, in short, may diminish the efficiency with which a society can identify, recruit, and train its most talented people for the most skilled positions.

Is it, then, mostly the promise of high rewards that attracts the most talented people to these opportunities? Or are other factors also influential? Here there is an instructive contrast between corporation lawyers and equally talented lawyers who specialize in public interest law or who serve in the public sector. On the average, the former earn far more annually than the latter. Why should the latter choose to earn less if they could earn more? Apparently, factors such as the desire to serve public interests, to have a substantial degree of independence, and to pursue intellectually interesting and varied themes are influential in shaping the career choices of these lawyers. Similar considerations seem to influence those doctors who chose careers in research or in public health rather than in the more lucrative private practices they might have pursued.

These observations cast doubt on the functionalist claim that the promise of high monetary rewards is indispensable to attract talented people and motivate them to excellent performance in tasks of high social importance.

The next issue is that of the quality of performance of those who are trained for the most valued statuses and who are rewarded with relatively large amounts of property and prestige.

Do doctors, engineers, lawyers, and others, such as corporation executives, perform excellently? We have no way of knowing. Indeed, the matter is so uncertain that any one of three hypotheses is as good as any of the others: namely, the most highly paid, most highly skilled people are doing better than, or about as well as, or significantly less well than one could reasonably expect.

The uncertainty is due to the absence of any effective ways to measure excellence in performance. Careers marked by high incomes and prestigious practices do not tell us anything necessarily valid about the excellence of the people involved. The gap between the knowledge possessed by skilled professionals and the knowledge of the public who must consume their services is so very great, or is assumed to be, that the consumers normally have no way of knowing whether the goods and services produced by the skilled practitioners are excellent, good, fair, or poor. To that difficulty one must add the absence of anything but the loosest of professional scrutiny, reinforced by the right of the professions to police and monitor themselves, and by the well-known reluctance by professionals to testify about the competence of any of their colleagues. It has required the development of dedicated public sector attorneys and of lucrative legal practices concerned with product liability and malpractice to bring to light some of the most egregious cases of incompetence and often of criminal damage.

The corporate world, in spite of its claim to rationality in its conduct, is perhaps the most uncertain about the excellence of its most highly paid executives. Only in rare cases is it possible to tell decisively whether a corporation is doing as well (or as poorly) as it is doing because of its executives, or in spite of them, or in indifference to them. So many other variables enter into the determination of the success of a corporation that the claim that the best people have been chosen for the most skilled jobs is most difficult to prove.

If, then, there is so much uncertainty about the excellence of those who are in the most highly rewarded positions and if the evidence necessary to test out that excellence is so difficult to secure, one must seriously doubt the claim that unequal rewards ensure excellence in performance.

These questions can now be moved on to the level of the total society and its efficiency. Can it be shown that societies are efficient in proportion to the depth and scope of the inequality in their distributions of their rewards? Are the most unequal societies the most efficient, or are the most equal societies more efficient? Or is there a middle point of inequality at which efficiency is maximized? Or are inequality and efficiency simply not correlated at all?

To answer these questions, we are forced to use a very limited indicator of societal efficiency, namely, economic productivity as measured by the Gross National Product, or GNP. The GNP tells us about the total amount of goods and services produced in a given year by a society, and variations up and down in the GNP are taken as marks of increases or decreases in the productive efficiency of a society.

We also need a measure of the amount of inequality present in a society's distribution, and here too we use a very limited indicator that tells us only about the distribution of incomes mainly the incomes from wages and salaries. As we recited at length in the chapter on property, the measurement of societal inequality is most imprecise and incomplete, even when confined to incomes alone.

Let it stand for the moment, however, that we have indicators of both economic productivity and inequality. When we examine the correlations between the positions of various nations on those two ladders—productivity and inequality—we find so much uncertainty about the outcomes that we are unable to say anything concrete about the relationship between those two features of a society. Some of the wealthiest nations are among the most unequal—Saudi Arabia and Quatar, for example. Some are among the most equal—Denmark, Sweden, and Japan, for example. Some of the most equal nations are relatively low on economic productivity. Some of the most unequal nations are at the bottom of the ladder of GNP per capita, for example, the majority of nations in Africa, Asia, and Latin America.

To be sure, the differences between the average GNP for all such developed nations and the GNPs of less developed nations are quite striking, but so too are the differences in their amounts of inequalities. The pattern seems vaguely to be one of a modest correspondence between relatively low amounts of inequality and relatively high amounts of economic productivity. Yet the historical and contemporary factors that might be producing these results are so numerous and complex that one cannot claim either that equality produces high GNPs or vice versa, or that the two factors are causally connected at all.

Even if we confine our comparison to countries at comparable levels of economic development, that is, the western, capitalist democracies, we find a random scattering of higher and lower GNPs on the distribution of inequality and vice versa.

It may be that the western nations are as well developed and rich as they are because of the relative equality they exhibit, because of the inequality in their reward systems, or because of other factors having nothing to do with inequality. There is no way to decide this question at the present time. Hence there is no way to support the claim that unequal rewards result in national efficiency.

The third issue to be considered is that of the costs that societies pay for practicing inequality in scarce and desired rewards. Do those costs vitiate or negate the gains made by unequal rewarding? Do societies that concentrate their attentions greatly on the efficient production of material wealth suffer significant deficiencies in other valued outcomes, such as internal order, the level of popular and elite culture, the sense of loyalty to the system, spiritual richness in daily life, the quality of personal relations?

Here we are involved in value trade-offs where something other than scientific measurement is required to make the necessary judgments. People with different degrees of wealth and value systems are likely to judge the worth of the trade-offs in quite different ways.

As one distinguished sociologist, Robert Merton, has put it, "The criteria of the 'essential' are of course heavily dependent on the social system as it exists at a given time. In actual practice, functional sociologists devote little attention to alternative roles 'essential' to the modification of a social system in determinate directions."[2]

Merton is saying, in effect, that it is as relevant to ask what kinds of changes ought to be made in the existing scheme and how might they be made, as to ask what is it that needs to be done to serve the society as it is. Those in privileged positions tend to ask the latter question, while those in lesser positions tend to ask the former question. Between the advocates of these two sets of orientations there are sure to be substantial disagreements on what is important, what the reward structure ought to be like, and what other values ought to be considered.

CONSEQUENCES OF INEQUALITY IN PROPERTY FOR A SOCIETY

In spite of such problems, it is possible to assess some of the consequences of inequality for the society at large.[3]

We may hypothesize that when a society distributes its wealth and honor unequally so that some are very rich, others are very poor, and all others are unequal in varying degrees, the following consequences may ensue:

1.   Differences in wealth will produce fairly distinct strata of people who will be separated from each other by those differences and who may come over time to form quite distinct social units.

2.   Such segmentation of the society lessens the possiblity of social solidarity and, in turn, of societywide consensus on the most important issues, such as the uses of public funds.

3.   The unequal earnings of people in different positions may produce unequal commitment to the society's norms and laws and result in higher rates of deviant behavior, such as crime, than might otherwise occur.

4.   Strata that are separated by unequal wealth and the unequal ability to purchase basic life chances, such as education and health, are likely to engage in hostile or conflictual encounters as they struggle for shares of wealth.

5.   Very low income and honor may produce high rates of pathologies, such as mental disorder, physical illness, shortened life, crime, and high rates of accidents.

6.   The chance to achieve full equality of opportunity for all and, with that, a high degree of fairness in the system will be lessened as wealthier people use their wealth to give their children special advantages over the children of poorer families.

7.   Through such transmission of unequal advantage over generations, the social divisions among people may become hardened.

8.   The discovery of the full range of talent in the society is likely to be less effective when mobility is restricted by the transmission of advantages from parent to child.

9.   Low income may make it difficult to induce the less well rewarded people to give their conscientious best to the tasks for which they are suited.

In light of these possible negative consequences of inequality, it is clear that any system must be willing to pay some very severe prices for whatever gains it believes it achieves through the unequal distribution of wealth.

Frequently we put the most emphasis on the modes of *producing* wealth. These observations about the importance of the *distribution* of wealth reveal the inadequacy of an assessment of a society that does not take its mode of distribution importantly into account.

All the welfare states of the modern world are aware of this. In these systems the state deliberately intervenes to supplement the smaller shares of income when they are considered inadequate to meet the basic needs of decent life. Such interventions illustrate how deliberate, conscious acts by a society are both required and effective in the achievement of conditions that are considered desirable when the unregulated interplay of social forces results in conditions considered less than desirable. That is a considerably larger view of matters than that which is implied in the functionalist explanation of stratification as an *unconsciously evolved device* by which societies ensure their well-being by seeing to it that the most talented people are recruited and motivated to perform the most important tasks conscientiously.

WHY IS STRATIFICATION SO WIDESPREAD?

If the system of unequal rewards is not inevitable, nor necessary for social survival, nor demonstrably more efficient than other schemes for producing wealth and well-being, and if it can generate many negative consequences, why then is it so widespread and so persistent?

One part of the answer is that most people do not know the facts we have presented. They believe inequality is both inevitable and efficient, and they have no visible contrary evidence in the form of attractive, enduring societies that practice full-scale equality. Yet even if people did know the facts and the arguments it is dubious that they would then rush to institute equality in their societies. To the contrary: The belief in the inevitability, efficiency, and justness of inequality in rewards is so widespread, even in modern western societies, that facts that raise these matters into question are neither likely to be heard well nor attended to.

Inequality has been the dominant practice for so long, how could most people *not* believe that inequality is inevitable, efficient, and fair?

We noted earlier that in the beginning of organized society sheer physical power must have determined who got large or small shares of good things. Self-designated elites, starting with dominant males in small family bands and going on to self-proclaimed rulers, including nobles, kings, slave owners, bishops, and assorted oligarchs, used all their powers to seize lands and other material resources, forced others to work for them and fight for them, required others to pay taxes, imposts, and duties to replenish their coffers, and saw to it that all instruments of education and indoctrination preached the rightness of elite rule and elite monopoly of good things. Sometime early in human history, such elites also brought to bear the power of divinities they invented, and they used the threats of supernatural sanctions to reinforce their favored positions. Thereby they created a pervasive culture of massive inequality and all the structures needed to keep it operating according to their will.

In the western hemisphere, it took about four hundred years of uprisings, civil wars, and revolutions, starting around 1500, to alter these systems of absolute rule and elite monopoly of good things and to introduce new ideas about how decisions ought to be made and how the good things ought to be divided.

But the bourgeois classes that emerged out of these changes did not abolish the right of the propertied and powerful groups to rule society as they saw fit and to arrogate to themselves such very large shares of the good things as they desired. Instead, the bourgeois, with their new economic and political power, included themselves among the privileged elites of their societies.

The idea of inequality was challenged effectively only once, by the Bolshevik Revolution in Russia. The outcome, as is well known, was not the abolition of inequality, but the replacement of the former elite of nobles and propertied land-holders by a new oligarchy of elites who became absolute rulers of the Society, the State, and the Party. Thus, though there may be somewhat less economic inequality today than under the Czar, there is more economic inequality in the Soviet Union than in any of the capitalist societies of the West, and the political inequality is probably even greater today than in Czarist times.

Yet the western, capitalist democracies that developed after the bourgeois revolutions did effect some major transformations which seriously affected the distribution of good things. They overthrew and evicted tyrannical, monopolistic rulers; they instituted rules of quasidemocratic government, including free speech; they vested supreme power in civil authorities, displacing military and church hierarchies; they democratized military service; they opened up new opportunities for school and jobs so that the children of the new middle classes were able over time to move into elite posts of command and privilege; they devoted themselves assiduously to the creation of wealth so that it was possible for a relatively small number to remain very wealthy while some additional well-being was also spread lower down on the class ladders. All of those, we see, involved a lessening of the former inequality in property, prestige, and power.

Some students of these matters, especially those who call themselves Marxists, deplore the methods by which the capitalist democracies became wealthy, citing their histories of imperialism, colonialism, harsh factory capitalism, and the destruction of indigenous populations. While acknowledging with Marx that the bourgeois revolutions were needed to "break open the bonds" of feudalism, they argue that today's capitalist systems have outlived their usefulness; they cannot and will not willingly reduce inequality any further; they will spread benefits only as much as is necessary to appease the underprivileged classes and thereby to maintain themselves in positions of privilege.

Yet it cannot be denied that the idea and practice of more equal sharing of good things has diffused widely through western societies. Major changes, especially recent ones, have been put in place through reforms that sum up to the name of *welfare state*. None of those reforms challenges the basic justice of inequality, but only of excessive versions thereof. Yet significant redistributions of wealth and opportunity for education and jobs have taken place in western societies, especially since World War II. These have helped to mitigate the harshness of former inequalities and have made it possible for western societies to develop their human and material resources beyond anything previously assumed possible. The coincidence of wealth, freedom, mobility, and modest inequality in these western states gives them an impressive stability and reinforces the notion that existing norms of modest inequality in wealth, prestige, and power work better than the more extreme versions in older societies.

Most citizens of western democracies accept the notion that some version of the current systems of producing and distributing wealth is probably the best available. With that they accept the idea that there shall be unequal pay for unequal jobs, though they may disagree sharply on how much more some positions should receive than others.

The unequal wealth that results from unequal pay is seen as justified only if everyone has had an equal opportunity to secure a relevant education, have their marketable talents trained, and have a fair chance to secure the positions for which they are best suited. In the absence of such equal opportunity, the unequal wealth that results from unequal pay is seen as reflecting advantages that have been unfairly inherited by privileged youth. By the same tokens, the poverty and low standards of living that many experience are seen as unfair results of an unfair system and hence the redistribution of wealth in the form of welfare programs is required.

Of particular relevance to the stability of democratic societies is the widespread acceptance of the rightness of unequal pay for unequal performance. For that means that little or no coercion is required to keep the general features of the system in place. The only opposing doctrine with any strength at all is that of socialist equality, under whose terms all would receive relatively equal pay however unequal their talents, so long as everyone contributed their conscientious best to the production and distribution of goods and services. The Marxist doctrine ''from each according to his ability, to each according to his needs'' has great humanistic appeal. But it is unavoidably associated in the minds of most of us with totalitarian and brutal systems such as those of the Soviet bloc in which there is no freedom, little fairness, and very much less wealth than in the West. Though that Marxist doctrine has never been implemented in the Soviet states, it is seen as part and parcel of the Soviet system and hence utterly without appeal.

Some argue that the capitalists, who control the western societies, including their mass media and school systems, have brainwashed the populace into acceptance of capitalist inequality and into unthinking rejection of the socialist notion of equality. There can be little doubt that the most powerful people and groups in the western societies favor the continuation of the western-style system and do their best to make it endure. But that is not the same as saying that the publics of the West have been mindlessly brainwashed into unthinking acceptance of the major premises and values of that system.

One cannot say whether social evolution will produce a different consciousness about inequality than now seems dominant. It is possible that there will be increasing pressure to reduce economic inequality much further. It is possible, too, that the continuing strong assertion of the right to political equality will result in a perception that economic inequality prevents the full realization of political equality and that the former must therefore be sharply reduced to make the latter more possible. All these trends are now visible, but they are not very potent. Perhaps as people press for a greater share of political power, a new vision of different ways to realize freedom, wealth, and fairness may emerge.

If we focus alone on western societies for the moment, the answer to why there is still so much inequality is that first, there is much less inequality than before; second, there may be even less in the proximate future; but, third, the idea of inequality, inherited from previous societies, still permeates the basic attitudes, beliefs, and ideologies of people from all socioeconomic levels. It will endure as long as the well-being that accompanies it causes the majority of the people to see it as better than any alternative arrangement in sight.

NOTES

1.   Kingsley Davis and Wilber Moore, "Some Principles of Stratification," *American Sociological Review,* 10 (April 1945), 242–49.

2.   Robert Merton, "Discussion," *American Sociological Review,* 13 (April 1948), 168.

3.   See Melvin Tumin, "Some Principles of Stratification: A Critical Analysis," *American Sociological Review,* 18 (August 1953), 387–93 for an earlier and longer analysis of these matters. See also Jack L. Roach et al., *Social Stratification in the United States* (Englewood Cliffs, N.J.: Prentice-Hall, Inc., 1969), especially Chapters 1 and 2, pp. 3–73, for an excellent survey of differing assessments of the sources and functions of inequality.

INDEX

Abramson, J.H., fn. 69
Achievement vs. ascription, 37-39
Ackerman, Frank, fn. 57
Adult education, participation by class, 111
Aristotle, social theory, 9-10, fn. 17
Assessment:
  compared to ranking, 23-24
  defined, 20
  elites, 27-28
  societal, 25-28
Astin, Alexander, W., fn. 108
Attitudes, as consequence of stratification, 7

Bernstein, Basil, 113, fn. 118
Blacks:
  adult education participation, 111
  distribution of attainment, 93; table, 94
  educational level and earnings, table, 95
  English, 113
  income, white vs. nonwhite, table, 85
  life-expectancy 102-3
  mobility among, 145-46
  mortality rate, 101-2
  occupational distribution, 90; table, 85
  suicide rate, 104
Blalock, Hubert, M., fn. 69
Blau, Peter, 17, 144-45, fn. 95, fn. 149
Bronfenbrenner, Urie, 106, fn. 109
Broom, Leonard, fn. 69
Burstein, Paul, fn. 109
Bushmen, stratification among, 2

Campbell, Angus, fn. 118
Caste society:
  comparison with class society, 44, 45; table, 45-47
  described, 5-6
  in South Africa, 42, 45
Child rearing:
  class differences, 106
  means of transmitting norms, 3-4
Class consciousness:
  defined, 12
  in defining classes, 126
  factors affecting, 43
  false consciousness and mobility, 126
  in the U.S., 127-29
Classes, social:
  adult education differences, 111
  association membership differences, 110-11
  comparison with caste system, 45-47
  consumption patterns, 112
  crime rates, 104-5
  Dahrendorf's view of, 127
  defining, 120, 123, 124, 126-29
  economic basis, 11-12
  emergence, 11
  fertility differences, 101
  language patterns, 112-13
  life-expectancy differences, 102-3
  Marxist view of, 120, 126-28
  measurement of number of, 121
  and mental illness, 104
  mortality rates, 101-2
  physical disorder rates, 103

political attitudes, 116-18
religious patterns, 107-8
solidarity of, 126
television viewing, 112
value systems, 115-16
Warnerian view of, 124-25
Weberian definition of, 120
work ethic, 114-15
Closed society:
  characteristics of, table, 45-47
  and mobility, 132-33
Commensalism, 67
Community:
  conditions necessary for forming, 13, 120, 124-28
  Weberian definition of, 13
Conflict theory, 16-17
Conformity, characteristic of stratification, 3-4
Connubialism, 67
Consumption patterns, class differences, 112
Convivialism, 67
Coverman, Shelly, 147, fn. 150
Crime:
  class differences in commission, 104
  class differences in victimization, 105
Cultural patterns, See Lifestyles, 110-18
Cutright, Phillip, fn. 109

Dahl, Robert, fn. 81
Dahrendorf, Rolf, 127-28, fn. 130
Davis, James, A., fn. 131
Davis, Kingsley, 16, fn. 162
Depth (of stratification):
  defined, 36
  of educational differences, 91-95
  of income differences, 84-87
  of prestige differences, 87-91
Deviant behavior (See Crime)
Differentiation, role:
  characteristics of, 19-22
Disease, class differences, 103
Divorce, class differences, 105
Duncan, Otis, D., 17, 88, 122, 144-45, fn. 69, fn. 95, fn. 149

Economics (See also Income, Power, Property):
  as dominant institution, 39
  Marxist view of, 120
  and rewards, 32-34
  social theory of, 11-14, 16
Education:
  college and success, beliefs about, 113-14; table, 114
  correlation with income and occupation, 77, 92
  distribution by race and sex, 93; table, 94
  and income, 93, 95; table 95
  and income by occupation, table, 136
  and occupational achievement, 91-92
  path diagram of, 92
  and status specification, 23
  study of quality of colleges attended, 100; table, 101
Elites:
  and power, 77-78
  and rewarding, 34-35
  and task assessment, 27-28
Engels, Friedrich, fn. 130

Equilibrium theory, 16-17
Erlanger, Howard, S., fn. 109
Evaluated Participation, (EP), 124-25
Evaluation:
  social patterning of, 63
  of statuses, 64

Family (*See also* Kinship):
  class differences, 105-6
Fauman, Joseph S., fn. 69
Featherman, David L., 145-47, fn. 118, fn. 149
Fertility, class differences, 101; table, 102
Freeman, Linton, fn. 81
Functionalism, 16-17, 154-58
Functional prerequisites, 19-20, 23, 25

Gerth, H., fn. 18, fn. 130
Gini coefficient, 56
Glenn, Norval D., 147, fn. 150
Glick, Paul C., fn. 109
Glockel, Galen L., fn. 109
Goode, William J., fn. 109
Guest, Avery M., 116, fn. 118
Gusfield, Joseph, fn. 69

Hacker, Andrew, fn. 17
Hatt, Paul, 58-59
Hauser, Robert M., 145-47, fn. 149
Hobbes, Thomas, "social contract" theory, 10
Hodge, Robert W., fn. 69
Hoggart, Richard, 113, fn. 118
Hollingshead, August B., fn. 108
Honor (*See* Prestige and honor)
Hunter, Floyd, fn. 81
Hyman, Herbert, fn. 118

Ideologies (Beliefs and Values):
  defined, 99
  described, 113-18
Illness, mental, class differences, 104
Income (*See also* Property, Rewards):
  comparison of white and non-white, table, 85
  defined, 51
  distribution of: family income, table, 85; aggregate
    income, tables, 85, 86
  earned, 51
  and education, 93-95; table, 95
  and education by occupation, table, 136
  mean, 84, 85
  measurement problems, 51-53
  measuring inequality in, 53-57; table, 55
  median, 84, 85
  ratio of reported to actual, 52
  unearned, 34, 51
Index of Status Characteristics, 15, 124-25
India:
  patterning of evaluation in, 63
  stratification in, 5, 45
Inequality (*See also* Stratification):
  among Bushmen, 2
  causes of, 31-32, 151
  consequences of, 158-59
  efficiency of, 154-58
  inevitability of, 153-54
  in Israeli Kibbutz, 5
  measurement of income, 53-57
  and mobility, 17
  and power, 34, 74-75
  and property, 48-49
  in rewards (*See also* Rewards), 30-31
  in social importance and rewards, 34
Inheritance of status:
  ascription vs. achievement, 37-39
  Platonic theory, 8-9
  and political power, 4, 16
Inkeles, Alex, 116, fn. 69, fn. 118
Instability, social, 4-5

Institutional patterns of conduct:
  as consequence of stratification, 6
  defined, 6, 99
  described, 105-8
Institutional tasks, 26-27
  emphasized area, 39-40
Israel:
  patterning of evaluation in, 63
  property in, 48
  stratification in, 5, 45

Jackman, Mary, 117, 124, fn. 118, fn. 130
Jackman, Robert, 117, 124, fn. 118, fn. 130
Job evaluations (*See also* Occupation):
  in differential rewarding, 29-30
  Hatt-North study, 59
  honor and income, 61
  preferability and popularity, 60-61
Jones, F. Lancaster, fn. 69

Kahl, Joseph, fn. 131
Karabel, Jerome, fn. 108
Keller, Suzanne, fn. 149
Kinship:
  and mobility, 139, 143-47
  Platonic theory, 8-9
  reward system, 29-30
  transmission of norms, 3-4
Knoke, David, 107, fn. 109
Kohn, Melvin, 115, fn. 118
Krauss, Irving, fn. 108
Kron, Joan, fn. 70

Language patterns, by class, 112-13
Lenski, Gerhard, 114, 115, fn. 69, fn. 118
Lewis, Oscar, 115, fn. 118
Life chances:
  compared to life-styles, 113
  as consequence of stratification, 6
  defined, 99
  described, 100-105
Life expectancy, class differences, 102-3
Life-styles:
  compared to life chances, 113
  as consequence of stratification, 6
  defined, 99
  described, 110-13
Lipset, S. Martin, 106, fn. 109, fn. 82
Lunt, Paul S., fn. 70
Lynd, Helen, fn. 81
Lynd, Robert, 14, fn. 81

Machiavelli, Niccolo, 9, fn. 17
Malewski, Andrew, J., fn. 69
Marriage (*See also* Divorce):
  rates and stability, 105
Marx, Karl, 11-12, 43-44, 120, 126, 127, 161, fn. 130
Marxism, 32, 42-44, 120, 126, 161
McClendon, McKee H., 146, fn. 150
Measurement:
  of classes, 121, 124-25
  of prestige, 87-91
  of property, 50-53
  of power, 75-77
Memberships, voluntary, class differences, 110-11
Merton, Robert K., 158, fn. 162
Middletown (Lynd), 14
Mills, C. Wright, 15, 78; fn. 18, fn. 82, fn. 130
  power structure, table, 79
Mobility:
  Blau-Duncan study, 7, 144-45
  compared to Western Europe, 148-49
  conclusions, 144-49, 152
  as element of system of stratification, 41
  and false consciousness, 126-27
  Featherman and Hauser studies, 145-46, 147
  and inequality, 17
  intergenerational vs. intragenerational, 139
  measurement of, 139-40, 143

Mobility (*cont.*)
  measurement problems, 135-39
  occupation as indicator of, 134
  and race, 145-46
  relationship to other societal features, 132-33
  and sex, 146-47
  structural vs. circulation, 138
  tables, 140, 143; table, 141-42
  Treiman-Terrell study, 146
Moore, Wilbert, 16, fn. 162
Mortality, class differences, 101-2; table 102
Mulvihill, D., fn. 109

Neugebauer, Richard, fn. 108
NORC ratings, of occupation prestige, 88
Norms, transmission of, 3-4
North, Cecil, 58-59
Norton, A.J., fn. 109

Occupation: as a status factor, 58-61
  determining factors, 145-48
  distribution of employed workers, table, 89
  distribution by sex and race, table, 89
  and education and income, table, 136
  Hatt-North job evaluation, 59-60; table, 59
  and mobility, 135-43
  preferability and popularity of, 60-61
  prestige and income, table, 90
Okner, B.A., fn. 57
Okun, Arthur, fn. 57
Open society:
  characteristics of, table, 45-47
  and mobility, 132-33
Parsons, Talcott, 15-16
Parties, Weberian definition of, 120
Performing arts, audiences by class, 111
Plato, 8-9
Politics:
  class differences, 106-7
  inheritance of status, 4
  and power structure, 12-15
  values, 116-17
  voting patterns, table, 107
Poverty (*See also* Inequality):
  minimum subsistence level, 87
  official index, 87
Power:
  contexts of, 72-74
  defined, 1, 71
  elites, 77-78; table, 79
  inequality in, 74-75
  legitimate vs. illegitimate, 72
  Marxist view, 11
  measurement of, 75-77
  in politics, 4
  and prestige, 61-62
  and property, 49
  as reward, 78-80
  and rewards, 34
  social patterning of, 74
  sources of, 71-72
  variations in distributions, 80-81
  Weberian view, 13-14, 77
Prestige and honor (*See also* Status):
  criteria of, 66-67
  defined, 58
  depth of inequality in, 87-91
  Hatt-North job evaluation study, 58-59
  and income, 61; table, 90
  and incongruence with income and power, 62-63
  occupational, 87-91; table, 89; by sex and race, 90; table, 89
  and power, 61
  reference groups, 66, 97
  social patterning of, 63
  study of occupational, 58-60; table, 59
  tests of equality of, 66-67
  universal quest for, 65
Production, means of:
  Marxist view of, 11-12, 120

Property (*See also* Income):
  consequences of importance of, 49-50
  defined, 1, 48
  Marxist view of, 11
  measurement of, 50-53
  Parsons view, 15-16
  Platonic view, 9
  and reference groups, 51-52
  and subjective perceptions, 50
  uses of, 48-49
  Weberian veiw of, 13
Psychic gratification (*See also* Motivation), 1, 49
Puerto Rico:
  association membership in, 111

Ranking:
  characteristics of, 22-24
  compared to assessment, 23-24
  criteria for, 22
  defined, 20
Redlich, F. C., fn. 108
Reisman, David, power structure, table, 79, fn. 82
Religion:
  class differences, 107-8
  as dominant institution, 39
  work ethic and success, 114-15
Reputational approach, 124-25
Rewards:
  criteria determining level of, 40-41
  disparity between importance and, 32-33
  efficiency of unequal, 154-58
  inequality of, 31
  justification for differential, 31-33
  psychic gratification, 1
  relation to assessment, 26
  in status differentiation, 21, 29-35
  in Western societies, 30-31
Rivlin, A. M., fn. 57
Roles (*See also* Status):
  assessment of, 25-28
  ranking of, 19-24
  specification of, 23
  in status differentiation, 21-22
Rose, Arnold, 111, fn. 118
Rossi, Peter, H., fn. 69
Rushing, William, 104, fn. 108

St. Augustine, fn. 17
Sanctions (*See* Rewards)
Sawyer, Malcom, fn. 57
Schwartz, Michael, fn. 69
Segal, David, fn. 69
Sewell, William H., fn. 150
Shape of stratification systems:
  defined, 119-20
  measurement of, 120-25
  in modern societies, 129-30
Smith, Adam, 31
Social institution:
  defined, 22
Socialization (*See also* Childrearing):
  in inequality of rewards, 30-31
  as societal prerequisite, 19
Social theory:
  early theorists, 8-11
  equilibrium vs. conflict schools, 16-17
  Marxist theory, 11-12
  stratification theorists, 14-16
  Weberian theory, 12-14
Society:
  defined, 19
  prerequisites for survival, 19
Socioeconomic Scale (SES):
  construction of, 122
  as measure of power, 77
Span:
  of consequences, 100-118; causal analysis of, 96-100
  of stratification, 37
Speech, as status indicator, 112
Status (*See also* Rewards):
  by achievement, 37

Status (*cont.*)
  acquisition and maintenance of, 37-39
  by ascription, 37
  assessment of, 25-28
  conspicuous consumption and, 68
  criteria for, 67
  differentiation of, 26-28
  evaluation of, 54-55
  incongruence (dissonance) 62-63, 129
  by influence, 38
  by inheritance, 38
  job evaluations, 59-60
  prestige, 58-69
  and property, 49
  ranking of, 22-24
  rewarding, 29-35
Status anxiety, 68
Status groups, 13, 120
Strata:
  characteristics of systems of, table, 45-47
  and class consciousness, 43
  determining criteria, 120, 123-24
  determining number, 121-22, 124-25
  distinctiveness of, 42
  objective factors, 42
  objective vs. subjective criteria, 123-24
  subjective factors, 43
Stratification:
  causes, 159-162
  characteristics, 1-7, 44
  consequences of, 6-7, 97-118, 158-59
  contrasting types, 5, 36-47
  defined, 1
  depth of, 36, 87-95
  efficiency of, 154-58
  emphasized institutional area, 39-40
  history of, 1-2
  inevitability of, 153-54
  instability of, 4
  Marxist views, 32, 42-44, 120
  mobility in, 41
  modes of acquisition of statuses, 37-39
  processes (criteria), 20-24, 25-28, 29-36
  shape of, 119-30
  span of, 37, 96-118
  stability of, 3, 4

variation in systems of, 36-47, 152
Suicide, class differences, 104

Taylor, Patricia Ann, 147, fn. 150
Terrell, Kermit, 146, fn. 150
Treiman, Donald, J., 146, fn. 69, fn. 150
Tumin, Melvin, M., fn. 70, fn. 109, fn. 118, fn. 149, fn. 162

Unemployment, 103; table, 103
U.S.S.R.:
  income inequalities in, 34-35
  institutional areas emphasized in, 39
  power distribution in, 80
  property ownership in, 48

Validation of status, 38-39
Values:
  in assessment of tasks, 26, 27, 28
  as consequence of stratification, 7
Variables:
  continuous vs. discrete, 120-21
  dependent, 96-98
  independent, 96-98
  intervening, 96-98
Veblen, Thorstein, 68, fn. 70
Voting (*See also* Politics):
  by class, 106-107
  patterns, tables, 107

Wages and salaries, 30, 34-35
Warner, W. Lloyd, 14, 15, 66, 124-25, fn. 70, fn. 130
Weber, Max, 12-14, 77, 120, 125, fn. 70
Wolfgang, Marvin, fn. 108
Wolf, Wendy C., fn. 150
Women:
  and income, table, 90
  and mobility, 146-47
  occupational distribution, table, 89
Work (*See* Occupation)
Work ethic and work values:
  class differences in, 115
  religious differences, 114-15
Wright, Charles, fn. 109

"Yankee City" studies, 14, 66, 124-25

BETH CIOTTA
out of eden

HQN™

If you purchased this book without a cover you should be aware
that this book is stolen property. It was reported as "unsold and
destroyed" to the publisher, and neither the author nor the
publisher has received any payment for this "stripped book."

Recycling programs
for this product may
not exist in your area.

ISBN-13: 978-0-373-77443-2

OUT OF EDEN

Copyright © 2010 by Beth Ciotta

All rights reserved. Except for use in any review, the reproduction or
utilization of this work in whole or in part in any form by any electronic,
mechanical or other means, now known or hereafter invented, including
xerography, photocopying and recording, or in any information storage
or retrieval system, is forbidden without the written permission of the
publisher, Harlequin Enterprises Limited, 225 Duncan Mill Road,
Don Mills, Ontario M3B 3K9, Canada.

This is a work of fiction. Names, characters, places and incidents are
either the product of the author's imagination or are used fictitiously,
and any resemblance to actual persons, living or dead, business
establishments, events or locales is entirely coincidental.

This edition published by arrangement with Harlequin Books S.A.

For questions and comments about the quality of this book
please contact us at Customer_eCare@Harlequin.ca.

® and TM are trademarks of the publisher. Trademarks indicated with
® are registered in the United States Patent and Trademark Office, the
Canadian Trade Marks Office and in other countries.

www.HQNBooks.com

Printed in U.S.A.

This book is dedicated to my brother, Bob Miller—
a courageous and inspiring spirit. Ride that bull!

ACKNOWLEDGMENTS

This is where I get to thank the awesome people who helped
give this story life.

Two very special ladies brainstormed and critiqued this tale
from beginning to end. Barb Hisle and Cynthia Valero—if I
baked, I'd whip you up a lifetime of mouthwatering brownies!

Two other very special ladies provided me with never-ending
cyber hugs and support. Mary Stella and Julia Templeton—
clinking my cyber champagne glass to yours!

One very special husband put up with my cranky moods
and crappy housekeeping when in the throes of deadline hell.
Steve Ciotta—are you feeling the love?

One special agent who "gets me" and "champions me."
Amy Moore-Benson—I'm saving a dance, any dance,
for you.

One special editor who handled this story
and the creator with tender loving care. Keyren Gerlach—
you're one of a kind.

One special soul who bid on a mention in this tale via a
donation to an extremely worthy cause. Kerri Waldo—
your generous spirit gave a character life. Enjoy!

Countless special individuals at HQN who worked together
to create a fantastic package (love my cover!) and to market
this story far and wide—my heartfelt gratitude.

Last, but most importantly, a mega-huge, very enthusiastic nod
to booksellers, librarians and YOU, the reader. Without you,
I wouldn't be able to share the stories of my heart.

Thank you all!

Also available from

Beth Ciotta

and HQN Books

Evie Ever After
Everybody Loves Evie
All About Evie

**And be on the lookout for Beth's fabulous
new contemporary romance**

Into the Wild

Coming in September 2010!

out of eden

"Yes, but this was Jack. It's supposed to be different with him."

CHAPTER ONE

"YOU ARE A HEEL. A chunky heel. A chunky, *boring* heel. Please don't take this personally, but I'm over you."

"I knew it was a mistake to let you drink cosmopolitans."

"I'm not drunk."

"You're talking to your shoe."

"I *was* talking to my shoe. Now I'm talking to you." Sensible slip-on in one hand, toxic cocktail in the other, Kylie McGraw leaned back against the red vinyl seat of one of the four booths in Boone's Bar and Grill and frowned across the table at Faye Tyler, two of her—strike that—one of her splendiferous best friends. They'd grown up together in Eden, Indiana—*Paradise in the Heartland* according to the slogan emblazoned on the green water tower planted on the outskirts of town. Someone had even painted red apples on the elevated tank so that the tower resembled a, you got it, apple tree. This was, after all, Eden, a place where most residents lived out their years because who would want to leave paradise? Except for the occasional thrill-seeker and random oddball. Although sometimes fate intervened and even *they* stuck around. Kylie and Faye were prime examples.

Kylie sipped her drink and studied her friend, reflecting on how they'd come to this moment.

Faye, who'd wanted to be a rock star, was married with two kids and owned the local bed-and-breakfast.

Kylie, who'd wanted a husband and kids, was single and running a business she should have inherited. Nothing was going according to plan. Even her dream of touring Asia, a dream she'd nurtured since the age of thirteen, seemed doomed. It's not that her life was horrible—just horribly boring.

This morning she'd woken up another year older, thinking about another year of the same. Three-hundred-and-sixty-five days of ordinary. She'd barely made it through the long, uneventful, dull-as-the-mayor's-speeches day. Then Faye had picked her up for her birthday celebration and it was official. Kylie had reached the end of her extraordinarily vast and famous patience.

Faye and her slightly blurry twin snapped their fingers two inches from Kylie's face. "Earth to McGraw. Are you zoning or comatose?"

Kylie adjusted her black oval glasses and blinked away the double image, conceding cosmopolitans packed a mighty punch. Either that or Boone had screwed up the ingredients. Possible, since he'd referred to a mix recipe and his reading glasses were forever perched *on top* of his balding head. "Okay. Maybe I am a teensy bit tipsy, but I am not, absolutely *not* drunk. And even if I was—" she grappled for a righteous excuse "—it *is* my birthday."

"I'm not saying you aren't entitled to cut loose," Faye said, nursing a frosty mug of Budweiser. "It's just that you always drink beer."

"Exactly!" Kylie jabbed her shoe in the air to emphasize her point. "I always drink beer."

Faye sighed. "I have no idea what that means."

"It means I can't take it anymore."

"Define *it?*"

"The predictability. The routine. The mundane. The run-of-the-mill, unremarkable, habitual sameness—"

"I get the picture."

"Today is my birthday."

"September 15. Same day every year."

"And every year we spend my birthday together."

"Since you turned twelve, yes. We've yet to miss a celebration, which goes to show how much I love you. I could be home watching MTV."

"You see my point."

"Not really."

"Same ol', same ol'."

Faye shrugged, smiled. "Not following."

"Every year we celebrate my birthday the same way. Pizza King. Movie. And since we turned twenty-one, Boone's Bar and Grill."

"Except we skipped the movie this time and came straight to Boone's," she said with a frown. "It's 7:00 p.m. We're the only ones here aside from a few guys throwing back happy hour brewskies and you're already half tanked."

Kylie scrunched her nose. "I heard that mobster flick's more violent than *The Godfather* and *The Departed* combined. Did you really want to see it?"

"Not really. But since the Bixley only runs one feature, it's not like we had a choice. We could have closed our eyes during the gory parts."

"We would've missed three-quarters of the movie!"

"That's not the point! We always celebrate your birthday the same way. Pizza. Movie. Boone's. It's *tradition*."

"It's boring." Maybe it was the alcohol, but Kylie could swear the curls of Faye's bleached hair drooped along with her smile. "Not you," she clarified, "tradition."

She glanced at her friend's manicured fingernails. Tonight they were metallic blue. Tomorrow they could be vivid orange or neon pink. Sometimes she even adorned them with decals and rhinestones. She was nearly as creative with her hairstyles, although she changed the shade every other month rather than every other day. Her thrift shop wardrobe ranged from 1960s Annette Funicello to 1990s Madonna. "You," Kylie said with sincere admiration, "are the Gwen Stefani of Eden."

Faye tucked her shoulder-length platinum curls behind her ears and quirked a thinly tweezed, meticulously penciled brow. "I take back the scathing remark I mentally slung your way."

"Thank you."

"You're welcome."

Kylie was not so adventurous with her appearance. Her wardrobe was casual. Loose-fitting clothes in muted, earthy tones. Minimal makeup and accessories. She came from the less-is-more camp. She wasn't sexy or funky or feminine. She was...sensible.

She was also miserable.

She set aside her right shoe—the left was still on her foot—and wrangled her natural blah-boring brown, overly thick, overly long hair into a loosely knotted ponytail. "It's hot in here."

"Blame it on the cosmos or your heated rant," Faye said. "It's the same as always—comfortable. Boone keeps the thermostat set at sixty-eight year round. You know that."

Kylie wanted to scream at yet another example of predictability. Instead, she propped her elbow on the table, footwear in hand. "My life is like this shoe. Sensible. This town is like this shoe. Practical."

"Hello? Your family's motto? Practical shoes for practical people. It's written on the plaque hanging behind the cashier counter."

Kylie narrowed her eyes. "That plaque is so gone. In fact, I'm going to redecorate the entire store," she said on a whim. "Bright colors. Maybe even pink. Pepto-Bismol pink with banana-yellow trim. Acrylic racks. Leopard seat cushions. Art posters splashed with funky period high heels. I saw this Andy Warhol print on the Internet. *Diamond Dust Shoes.* Weird, but fun."

"You know me," Faye said. "I'm all for kitschy. But that's radical. If your mom and grandma were here—"

"One would applaud my vision. The other would nix it." She didn't know which woman would take what stance. She just knew they'd take opposing views. They bickered constantly and Kylie was forever playing mediator. She'd been given a short reprieve since they were currently enjoying (or not) the Alaskan cruise Grandma McGraw had won at the church's silent auction, but they'd be back. "I'm bypassing the debate and making an executive decision as the store's manager."

"Without consulting Spenser?"

Kylie bristled. When her treasure hunting brother had been presented with an opportunity to host a cable series on the Explorer Channel, she hadn't thought twice about taking full responsibility and running McGraw's Shoe Store.

A: Because she loved Spenser to pieces.

B: Unlike her brother, she had an actual interest in shoes and the business as a whole.

It's just that she hadn't expected to be in charge for so long without an extended break.

Closing the store for a month was not an option, and she was too territorial to trust the business to a nonfamily member. Leaving the store in the hands of her mom and grandma was unthinkable. They'd kill each other. Or the business. Or both.

Last month when she'd talked to Spenser, he'd said he'd be coming home after he finished a shoot in Egypt, which meant any day now. She'd intended to discuss her dream trip then. In person. Except this morning, when he'd called to wish her happy birthday, he'd explained that he and his cameraman had finally obtained permission to visit Pitcairn—the secluded island inhabited by the ancestors of Fletcher Christian and the other mutineers of the *Bounty*.

"This is a once-in-a-lifetime opportunity, Kitten," he'd said.

They were all once-in-a-lifetime opportunities.

"Just a few more weeks," he'd said.

Which in Spenser-speak meant a few more months, maybe years.

Okay. That was overdramatic. But as sure as Kylie opened the store every day, Tuesday through Saturday at 9:00 a.m., he'd be broadening his horizons while hers flat-lined. "I know the store's in Spenser's name," she grumbled, "but he saddled me with the responsibility."

"Temporarily," Faye said. "Although I admit his idea of 'temporary' differs from most folks. Still, if I recall, you're supposed to run things status quo. Knowing your brother, I don't think he'd be keen on pink walls and weird posters."

"Spenser can kiss my—"

"Ashe sent this over." Wanda, Boone's wife, who usually manned the kitchen whipping up her locally famous kick-butt chicken wings, seasoned mozzarella sticks and other assorted yummies, was currently working the floor due to a server shortage. She set another cosmo on the table. "Be warned, the silver-tongued dog paid Boone for a double shot of vodka."

"Happy birthday, Kylie," Ashe called from his bar stool.

He probably thought that winking thing was sexy. Smarmy was more like it. "Thanks." She saluted the cocky car dealer with a dismissive smile. Ashe Davis had been trying to score with her since her almost-fiancé, make that *ex*-almost-fiancé, fled paradise last year. At no point in time had she suggested he had a snowball's chance in hell, but the man was persistent. Handsome and successful, thirty-six and never married, he was considered by some the perfect catch. Only thus far he'd proved too slippery for any of the eligible women in Eden and even a few of the not-so-eligible. With Ashe it was all about the hunt. Once he bagged his prey, he lost interest. If Kylie wanted a brief, hot fling, he'd be the perfect choice. That is, if she could stomach sleeping with a self-absorbed womanizer.

"He's thinking tonight's his lucky night," Faye said with a roll of her blue-shadowed eyes.

"I'd have to be blitzed out of my gourd to sleep with Ashe."

"Drink that third cosmo and consider yourself boinked," said Faye.

Kylie pushed her glasses up her nose and focused, sort of, on Wanda. "Do I appear inebriated to you?"

"I did see you talking to your shoe, dear."

"That's because this shoe represents the crux of my discontent."

"Don't ask," Faye said, then sipped her beer.

"Giving you blisters?"

Faye slapped a palm to her forehead, metallic-blue nails glittering.

Ironically, or maybe not, someone punched A12 on the jukebox—Kylie knew that jukebox by heart—flooding the bar with the retro hit: "These Boots Are Made for Walking." Probably someone was making fun of her current shoe fixation, but she was more inspired than insulted. The music provided the perfect background for her on-the-spot promo.

"These," she said, displaying the slip-on for Wanda's keener inspection, "are Aerosoles. Padded insoles. Lightweight and flexible. They do not cause blisters. A smart buy for someone who spends a lot of time on their feet. Someone like you."

"You introduced me to that brand the last time I was in your shop," Wanda said while snapping her gum. "Felt like I was walking on clouds, but Boone would have a cow if I paid that kind of money for one pair of shoes."

"Yes, but they'd last longer than the bargain canvas sneakers you're wearing, plus they'd offer proper arch support. Given your occupation, don't your feet deserve better?"

"Stop trying to sell my wife fancy shoes!" Boone shouted over the music while sliding a beer down to Ashe.

"They're not fancy!" Kylie shouted back. "They're practical!"

"I'm thinking it's a birthday crisis," Faye said to Wanda. "Did you wig out when you turned thirty-two?"

"No." Gaze fixed on the far wall, she shifted and tapped the empty tray against her thigh in time with the music. She blew a pink bubble and when the bubble burst, spoke her mind. "Although I did go through a funk when I turned thirty-nine. All I could think was, I'm one year from forty. Then of course, I panicked when I turned the big five-oh. Who doesn't?"

"You're a size seven, right?" Kylie asked, bulldozing over their talk of a birthday crisis. This wasn't about age, although it was about another passing year.

"Yes, but—"

"Take them." Desperate to take action, any action to shake up her life, she shoved her right shoe in Wanda's free hand, toed off the left and handed that over, as well. "They're yours."

"They look brand-new." The redheaded, gum-cracking woman flipped them over, inspected the soles and heels. "No scuffs, no wear."

"I've worn them three times max."

"Are you sure you want to give them up?"

"Trust me. I've got loads of sensible shoes."

"Shoes, schmooze!" someone complained. "What's a guy gotta do to get some chicken wings around here?"

They turned their attention to the grumpy complainant, Max Grogan, the town's retired fire chief, seventy-two and prickly as a porcupine. Armed with two bottles of beer each, he and his cronies—Jay Jarvis (of J.J.'s Pharmacy and Sundry), Ray Keystone (Keystone Barbershop) and Dick Wilson (the town mayor)—were engrossed in their biweekly game of cards.

"Keep your pants on, Max!" Wanda shouted.

"An image I can do without." Faye shuddered. "Max's dingy."

"You can tell you've got a five-year-old at home," Wanda said with a grin. "Dingy. That's cute, hon. Thanks for the shoes, Kylie, and Happy Birthday," she added before leaving.

"I wish." Kylie downed Ashe's alcoholic gift in two swallows, then slid aside the empty glass with a snort. "Didn't taste stronger than the first two."

"Probably because your taste buds are numb." Faye pursed her cherry-red lips. "Good thing I'm driving."

"Wash those hands before you handle my wings!" Max yelled when Wanda disappeared into the kitchen.

"I wouldn't mind seeing dingy's Max," Kylie said, tripping over her words. She pinched the end of her tongue. Also numb. Dang. "I mean Max's dingy."

Her friend groaned, then leaned forward. "You have *got* to be kidding. I know you've been sexually deprived since the asshole split town, but you cannot be *that* desperate for a thrill."

"Actually, I am." Although, it was spurred by lack of zest, not sex. She'd felt melancholy and hollow since Spenser's phone call this morning. She wasn't a stranger to disappointment, and usually she sucked it up and moved on, doing what she had to do, doing what was best for all involved even if it didn't feel best for her. But today she hadn't been able to wrangle the disappointment, and as the day crawled by, depression had given way to desperation and uncharacteristic behavior. She mentally kissed her nurturing, passive self goodbye. Time to take action. Time to shake up the life she was stuck with.

"At least it would cause a sensation," Kylie said, shocked at the vehemence in her tone. "Can you imagine the headlines?" She mimicked a newspaper barker, shouting her concocted news just as the song ended and the noise level dipped. "Max Grogan drops his pants in protest of tardy service!"

"I ain't flashing my willy just because you're bored, Kylie McGraw." Max grunted as he dealt a new hand. "Kids."

"Kids who don't know when they've had enough," said the mayor. "Even worse."

"Maybe you should switch to soda," called Mr. Keystone.

"Maybe you should mind your own beeswax," said Kylie.

J.J. tsked. "She's usually so nice."

"Yeah, but tonight she's fun." Ashe approached Kylie

with another cosmo and a smarmy grin. "I'll show you mine, if you show me yours."

Kylie dropped her head in her hands with a groan.

"Go away," Faye said. "And take that evil drink with you."

"Hey, I'm just trying to please the birthday girl. She said she wants a sensation."

Kylie banged her fists to the table and frowned up at the man. "I'm talking about something *extraordinary,* you thick-skulled bozo. People expect you to seduce me and they expect me to fall under your spell. Boone knows Max and gang will show up twice a week to play pinochle and *they* know they'll get two-fer beers, kick-butt chicken wings and a comfortable room temperature of sixty-eight. Faye expects me to drink beer because I always drink beer. I expect Faye to whine about her summer guests because she always whines about her summer guests. The majority of Eden will watch *Into the Wild* Saturday night and gossip about Spenser's adventures most of Sunday. The Bixley will never expand to a multiplex theater and storefronts on Main Street will always look as they did in 1955, because progress moves at a snail's pace in Eden! Nothing out of the ordinary *ever* happens!" Kylie vented, voice slurred and shrill. "You can set your watch by this town. *We* are boring people!"

"Ooo-kay." Ashe backed away with the drink, his free hand raised in surrender.

But Kylie wasn't done. "I bet I know what you've been talking about," she said to Max and friends. "*Omertà.* That's all you ever talk about because you're obsessed. Never mind the mob series is off the air and you're just now catching up compliments of DVD. That's typical. Out of step with fashion and the arts. Yup. That's us! Behind the times. Boring and passé."

"I came in here for cards and beer," shouted Max. "Not to be insulted!"

"That does it," Boone called from behind the bar. "You're cut off, Kylie."

She jabbed a finger in his direction. "I *knew* you'd say that."

"Predictable," Faye grumbled.

"Exactly."

"But wise." Looking harried, the normally unflappable woman rooted in her oversize purse and pulled out her Orchard House souvenir key chain, *available at the front desk for the bargain price of $3.99.* "I'm taking you home," Faye snapped. "You're making a spectacle of yourself."

Fueled by years of frustration and three cosmopolitans, Kylie pushed out of the booth, her compact body trembling with Godzilla-like rage. "Well, get used to it. All of you! Because starting tomorrow there's a new Kylie McGraw in town. I'm going to shake up paradise. Just you wait and see!" She made it halfway across the hardwood floor before her nylon footies slid out from under her and Kylie tumbled butt over heels.

J.J. whistled low. "Wasn't much of a wait."

Dazed, she squinted at the sea of faces spinning above her. "Stand still, you guys."

"We aren't moving." Faye stooped and inspected Kylie's noggin. "How hard did you hit your head? Are you seeing double?"

"Of course she's seeing double," Boone said. "She's shit-faced."

Swearing, Faye tried to pull her friend to her feet, but Kylie's arms and legs went all noodly. "I could use some help getting her in my van," she said to the men.

Ashe, the smug, blurry dog, rubbed his paws together and smiled. "I'll do it."

"Touch her, Davis, and I'll kick your ass."

It was a voice she hadn't heard in a long time, but one she'd know anywhere and in any state of mind.

Ashe knew it, too. "Just trying to help."

Knowing the dog's true intention, the circle of faces that had been staring at Kylie snorted, then turned their attention to the don't-challenge-me stranger. Only he wasn't a stranger. He was one of Eden's own. Or at least he used to be.

Jack Reynolds. Kylie's first major crush. Although *crush* was putting it mildly. Best high school bud of her infuriating brother, this man had made tofu of her teen hormones and ruined her for other men well into her twenties. He'd also broken her heart. Three times, to be exact. Not that he knew it, but that wasn't the point.

She adjusted her crooked glasses and blinked up at the obsession of her youth. Dark cropped hair. River-blue eyes. A buff body and a warrior's heart. Hands on denim-clad hips, the most handsome man in the universe *ever* towered above her. Then again, she was flat out on the floor. She hadn't seen him in years, and usually her stomach fluttered when she did. Either she was completely over him or the mass quantities of vodka had paralyzed her vital organs along with her limbs. "Heard you were back in town."

"No secrets in Eden."

No kidding. That's why Kylie generally guarded her words. Jack's sister, on the other hand, vented to anyone who would listen. Jessica Lynn shared Jack's good looks, but none of his good sense. A self-centered former beauty queen, it was always: *Enough about you, let's talk about me.* Hence, most everyone knew about the feud between the estranged siblings, plus some of the particulars. Kylie noted the *particular* of most interest to her. "So, did you accept the job as Eden's chief of police?"

"I did."

She quirked a hopeful grin. "You been in here long, Chief Reynolds?"

"Long enough."

"Going to arrest me for drunk and disorderly behavior?"

"No."

"Shoot," she complained as he hauled her off the floor. That would have brought Spenser running.

Dizzy, she rested her head against Jack's shoulder, her face nuzzled against his neck.

God, he smelled good.

He tightened his hold and suddenly she was hyperaware of where she was.

In Jack Reynolds's arms!

That's when she felt it. Her traitorous stomach fluttered. Or maybe she'd overindulged in pepperoni pizza and cosmopolitans. Yeah, that was it. Crushing on Jack was hazardous to her heart. Better to battle an upset stomach than a doomed attraction. At least she could cure the former with Alka-Seltzer.

CHAPTER TWO

JACK REYNOLDS HAD BEEN in town for four days. Settling into his new home. Meeting with the mayor. Being courted by the town council and snubbed by his sister. Mostly he'd been reacclimating. Even though he'd grown up in Eden, he'd spent a lifetime in New York City, working for the NYPD. Big difference between the Big Apple and Eden. His friend's little sister didn't know how good she had it. Unless that was the alcohol talking. Either way, she'd just provided Eden with a week's worth of gossip.

Jack had never seen the squeaky-clean McGraw sauced. Then again, he'd been avoiding Eden for years. Ever since he'd clocked his sister's husband on their wedding day. He'd refused to tell Jessie why—effectively severing their dysfunctional relationship. Instead of going to hell, as she'd demanded, he'd returned to NYC. Over the next ten years, he made homicide detective, got married, got divorced, and tempted the devil as he took accelerated risks on the streets.

His wake-up call had come last month in the form of a young woman. A victim of a mob hit. He'd seen a lot of death. He knew how to manage his emotions. How to temper the revulsion and outrage. But how the fuck did you manage numb? Maybe he'd gone to hell after all. Jack Reynolds. Zombie cop. He'd sworn long ago that if he ever stopped feeling, he'd get out.

Easier said than done.

He'd resorted to drowning his misery and indecision in whiskey.

His sister's crisis had kicked his drunken ass into action. When he'd learned through the grapevine that Jessie's bastard husband had deserted her and her daughter, he'd sworn off the hard stuff and given his notice. Time to look after his own. The job opening for chief of police had been coincidental. Or maybe it was fate. In the end it had been too convenient to pass up.

Jack made eye contact with every man and woman in Boone's as he carried Kylie out of the bar. These people, this town, would be his salvation. At least that was the plan. Reconnect with your roots, reconnect with your soul.

As for Kylie…he couldn't get over how much she'd changed. He'd seen her briefly at her dad's funeral eleven years ago, but they'd both been preoccupied. Mostly, he remembered her as the gawky, skinny kid who'd shadowed her big brother. Spenser used to run her off with a smile and teasing words. Spense loved his sister, but he was a daredevil and she was an angel. Spunky, but sweet. Kitten, he called her.

Jack tempered a smile, flashing on the episode that made it impossible for him to think of her as *Kitten*. An episode he'd sworn to a then fourteen-year-old Kylie he would never reveal to her brother. A promise he'd kept.

He glanced down at the woman in his arms, recognizing the big chocolate eyes and thick wild hair and little else. He was keenly aware of her compact curves and her quirky, pretty features. No wonder Ashe was sniffing. Kylie was an interesting package.

She pushed at his shoulder. "I can walk."

"Whatever you say, Tiger." He set her on her stocking feet but kept his arm around her waist in case she faltered. She did.

"I don't get it," she lamented as he escorted her outside and onto the sidewalk. "I can usually hold my liquor."

"You usually drink beer," Faye said.

"I wouldn't reference *the usual* just now," Jack told Kylie's eccentric friend, though the harm was already done. He shook his head as the youngest McGraw launched into another gripe about routine.

"I don't know what's wrong with her," Faye told Jack. "Except the obvious, of course." The bleached-blonde unlocked the passenger side of a cherry-red minivan.

He'd never imagined the girl who dressed like a retro pop star would drive a minivan. He'd never imagined her as a mother, either, but the toys and books scattered in the backseat along with the Spider-Man sun shield confirmed what he'd heard. Faye Tyler, formally Powell, was married with children. Children she'd named after nineties musical icons.

Jack helped Kylie, who continued to vent, into the van while Faye answered her ringing cell. "What do you mean Sting threw up? Does he have a fever? He *what?* Where were you when... Yes, I know you can't stomach vomit, Stan. For crying out loud. Okay. Yes. *Yes.* Be right there." She tossed her phone in her purse, looked at her friend, then Jack. "There's a bit of a crisis at home."

"Is Sting okay?" Kylie asked, struggling to fasten her seat belt.

"He got into the freezer—don't ask how—and ate an entire tub of double-fudge ice cream. He'll be fine, which is more than I can say for my husband when I get hold of him."

Jack remembered Stan Tyler. A short but solid man, former captain of the high school wrestling team. He didn't figure Faye could take him, but it would be fun to watch her try, especially since he knew Stan would cut off his hand before raising it to a lady. "You live in the converted carriage house next to the B and B, right?"

"Right," she said. "And Kylie lives in the opposite direction in the boonies. Do you think—"

"Sure." He unbuckled the seat belt Kylie had just managed to fasten. "Come on, Tiger."

"Stop calling me that." She batted away his hands and glared at him through her oval, plastic-rimmed glasses. No-nonsense glasses, black, like her no-nonsense clothes—

cropped, wide-legged pants and a loose-fitting blouse. He thought about the no-nonsense shoes she'd given away and decided she must've gone out on the town straight from work. "And I don't need a ride home. From you, I mean. Max lives out my way."

"Max plays cards from six until eight," Faye said as she scurried to the driver's side. "He's got another forty-five minutes to go. He's not going to break away early for anything other than a four-alarm fire."

"I'll wait." Shoeless, Kylie strode unsteadily toward Boone's Bar and Grill.

"Stop where you are. Hello? Splinters! Broken glass!" Faye snapped, clearly in mother mode. "Jack?"

"Yes, ma'am." He stepped in and hauled Kylie over his shoulder. "Drive safe, Faye. Best to Stan."

She saluted and pulled away from the curb.

Kylie kicked like a swimmer on speed. "Put me down, darn you!"

He pressed the lock release on his key fob as he reached his Chrysler Aspen. The new SUV would serve as his personal and professional wheels. Though he didn't have a weak stomach like Stan, he hoped Kylie didn't hurl on his new leather seats.

"I'm serious, Jack. Don't make me hurt you."

He quirked an amused brow. "You wouldn't assault an officer of the law, would you, Miss McGraw?"

"Would you throw me in jail?"

"No."

"Dang. What's a girl gotta do to get tossed in the clink?" she asked as he poured her into the passenger seat.

"Why are you determined to spend the night in jail?"

"Because it would set this birthday apart from all the others."

"I can think of more pleasurable distinctions," he said while buckling her in.

She nabbed his shirt collar and got in his face. Her hair tumbled free of the ponytail, overwhelming her delicate face and ramping her sexuality ten points. "You offering up a distinctive pleasure, Jack?"

Kylie, flirting? The kid who got tongue-tied when Spense teased her about boys?

Only she isn't a kid anymore.

Jack held her sultry gaze, breathed in her flowery scent and cursed an unexpected boner.

"Touch her," he could hear Spenser saying, *"and I'll kick your ass."*

He wouldn't blame his friend for trying. He'd threatened to do the same to Ashe Davis, a serial womanizer. This was Kylie, for Christ's sake. Sweet. Naive. *Drunk.*

She licked her lush lower lip. "Well?"

"Let's not go there, Tiger."

"Too bad for you. I'm a yoga geek." She raised one brow. "You know what *that* means."

"Flexible?"

"Like Gumby."

The retro green guy that could bend every which way and back.

Christ.

He shut her door, rounded the Aspen and claimed the driver's seat. "Where am I headed?"

"Route 50, a half a mile past Max's place. Do you remember where Max lives?"

Flicking on his headlights, he eased onto Adams Street and headed north. "The boonies." A twenty-minute drive from town, midway between Eden and Kokomo. Corn and soybean fields. Patches of woods. Pig farms. Pastures of grazing cows and horses. Sporadic century-old farmhouses and the occasional contemporary modular home. A wide-open area where the nearest neighbor lived a mile or a half mile away. He shot her a look. "You live alone out there?"

She smirked. "I'm single, if that's what you're asking."

"I'm asking if you live alone. No roommate?"

"I like my privacy."

"You could live alone here in town."

"I like the solitude."

He couldn't argue with that. He'd rented a home on the outskirts of town, an old two-story brick house on two acres of land. He, too, liked the idea of solitude. Peace and quiet. The exact opposite of what he'd had when he'd lived in the high-rise in Brooklyn. Difference was he was a trained cop, capable of handling a crisis in any form. She was...Kylie. Kylie all grown up, he thought, raking his gaze over her body.

"I didn't used to live alone. I used to be almost engaged. Are you shocked?"

"That you were almost engaged? Or that you were living in sin?" he teased.

"Either, or."

"Neither."

"His name was Bobby Jones. You wouldn't know him. He was a free spirit."

You mean a freeloader. "Spenser mentioned him." Jack kept in touch with his friend via e-mail. Mostly they talked sports and global affairs, but they always touched on family.

"Spenser never liked Bobby."

That was putting it mildly, but Jack held his tongue.

"I'm not fond of my brother right now."

"Because he didn't approve of Bobby?"

"Because he's an insensitive boob."

Jack swallowed a laugh. "Did he forget your birthday?"

"No. He forgot I'm human."

"Meaning?"

"Meaning I have dreams, too."

He started to ask specifics, but she'd slumped against the window, eyes closed. She'd either passed out or clammed up. One thing he'd learned on the force, sometimes the easiest way to learn something was not to ask. He'd let it go for now and she'd talk when she was ready.

He tapped the radio media key, scanned his presets and chose a local classic rock station. The same music he'd listened to in his teens while cruising these back country roads. He grinned at the irony when the speakers rattled with the Cars' "Shake It Up." What did Kylie plan on doing, anyway? TP-ing every tree in town? Spraying Eden's sacred water tower with graffiti? Streaking down the center of Main Street?

A vivid image of the woman sitting next to him exploded in his mind. Ivory flesh and toned curves. It was the second time in less than twenty minutes he'd imagined Kylie McGraw naked. Damn. He shifted in his seat, frowning when "Shake It Up" segued into "Keep Your Hands to Yourself." Seemed the DJ had coordinated a playlist specifically fitted to Jack's evening. He lowered the volume and concentrated on the road, not Kylie. The scenery, not Kylie.

She'd changed. He'd changed. But aside from a random new home, this rural area had remained the same. Between the music and landscape, he easily slipped back in time. He soaked in the serenity as if it were a restorative drug.

Ten minutes later he zipped by Max Grogan's place. The antique fire engine parked in the drive had been in the old man's possession for more than twenty years. He wondered if Red Rover still ran. He relived a few choice memories regarding that red hook-and-ladder truck while keeping an eye out for Kylie's house. A half mile past Max's place, she'd said.

He was about to wake her when he spied a lone mailbox and rolled to a stop. Brightly colored shoes were painted up and down the white post and McGraw was scripted on the box alongside #312. He turned his SUV into the crushed-stone drive that led him into the woods and soon after his headlights flashed on a mobile home. Not only did she live alone in the boonies, she lived in a disaster waiting to happen. Eden was smack in the middle of Tornado Alley. If a twister touched down, she'd be gone with the wind. What was she thinking? Why hadn't Spenser intervened?

She stirred along with his annoyance. "You found it," she said in a slurred, husky voice. "Great. Thanks for the lift." Then her lids drifted back shut and Jack smiled in spite of his unease. Damn, she was cute.

Three seconds later he sidestepped potted flowers and carried the dozing woman toward her green mobile home. Moonlight bathed the tended lawn. The warm evening breeze rustled the leaves of the surrounding oak and maple trees and the bamboo wind chimes hanging from a wrought-iron pole rooted next to a bird feeder. He smelled earth and flowers and perfume. "Kylie?"

"Hmm?"

"Keys."

"Purse."

"Where?"

She furrowed her brow.

"Let me guess. You left it at Boone's."

"No problem. Mat."

"Who's Matt?"

"Doormat. Hey, it's like a *knock-knock* joke. Funny," she said with a loopy smile, then slipped back into la-la Land.

If he hadn't been pissed about her obvious hiding place for the spare key, he would've laughed. The joke wasn't funny, but she was. "When you're sober, you and I are going to have a talk about home protection, Tiger."

He fished the key from under the mat and unlocked the door, no easy feat while juggling a living rag doll. Once inside he flicked on a wall switch, bathing the compact living and dining area in muted light. "Spotless" was his first thought, quickly followed by "sparse." Minimal furnishings with an oriental flair. He noted the framed prints on the wall. Japanese temples and landscapes. A movie poster of *Crouching Tiger, Hidden Dragon*. Huh.

He located her bedroom, wishing she hadn't mentioned her agility, compliments of yoga. Oriental images of an erotic nature flashed in his mind as he laid her on her black-and-red comforter.

Time to leave.

He took off her glasses and placed them on the nightstand, noted a book on Zen and travel brochures on China and Japan. Spenser had never mentioned her obsession with the Orient. He wondered if he knew. He thought about what she'd said earlier. *"I have dreams, too."* After one peek at her living quarters, any idiot could deduce her dreams involved Asia. He filed away the knowledge, slipped into the bathroom and nabbed a glass of water and two aspirin. He returned and nudged her awake. "Take these and drink this. You'll thank me in the morning."

Bleary-eyed, she complied, then fell back on the pillow with a groan.

"Sleep tight, kid." *I'm outta here.*

Warm toes skimmed up his T-shirt and across his lower back. "Jack?"

Wary, he turned back and nabbed Kylie's adventurous foot. The wide pant leg slid toward her body, revealing a toned thigh and a glimpse of red panties. *Damn.*

"I'm not getting any younger," she said.

Hit the road, Jack. "Meaning?"

"Meaning if I wait for what I want, I'll never get it. At least that's the way it's worked so far." She shoved her hair out of her eyes, then wagged a finger in his direction to emphasize another thought. "Although, I did grab the bull by the horns once, if you catch my drift, and I know you do, and I didn't get what I wanted that time, either. I gotta tell ya, life has been one big-butt disappointment."

She sounded pitiful and angry at the same time, and he cursed himself a pig for imagining the pleasure zone beneath those satin panties. He released her sexy foot and tugged her pant leg back past her knee. Against his better judgment, he sat on the edge of the bed. "Sorry to hear that."

"Today in particular stunk."

"Want to tell me what Spenser said or did to ruin your birthday?"

"It's what he didn't say or do."

"You're losing me."

"It's not about my birthday, but my life."

"Definitely lost."

"But it is what it is so I need to make the most of what I have, which isn't much. I've got my work cut out for me."

He pressed a finger to his temple, rubbed.

"Creative visualization is a beautiful thing. I *will* have my adventure, just you wait and see."

"Back to shaking up things in Eden, huh?"

"I was planning to start tomorrow, but you know what they say…" She quirked a brow, waited.

"No time like the present?"

Her full lips curved into another of those loopy grins. "For the past year, I've spent every night in this bed alone. It would certainly break my blah, boring routine if you—"

"No."

"—kissed me."

Shit.

"It's the least you could do."

"For?"

"Refusing to be my first."

He scratched his forehead, reflecting on the episode he'd sworn to take to his grave. "You were fourteen."

She scrunched her brow. "So? How old were you when you first—"

"That's different."

"Why? Because you're a guy? That's a stupid argument," she slurred, "but I'll let it slide and point out that I am now thirty-two."

"You're also blitzed."

She narrowed her eyes. "What if I was sober?"

"You'd still be Spenser's little sister."

She heaved a dramatic sigh. Then she stretched like a languid cat, teasing him with thoughts of Gumby flexibility.

"I know," he said, only half kidding. "My loss."

"My stinky birthday." She stuck out her lower lip in a contrived but alluring pout.

He knew when he was being played. His ex had been a master manipulator. Not that Kylie was in Amanda's league. Kylie was drunk. He scrambled for a graceful exit without hurting her feelings.

She mistook his hesitation as an invitation. "A pleasurable distinction," she whispered, then pressed those pouty lips to his.

Soft. Sweet. *Hot.*

Holy shit.

He froze.

She sighed. "Thanks for the birthday kiss, Jack."

He grappled for a casual response.

"Too bad I didn't feel anything."

CHAPTER THREE

ANOTHER DAY IN PARADISE.

Hell would have been preferable.

As was his routine for the past seven years, Travis Martin rose at 6:00 a.m. He showered—using bargain-brand soap, shampoo and shaving cream. He dressed in Lee Dungarees Carpenter Jeans, a plaid shirt and beige work boots. Breakfast consisted of oatmeal, white toast and a cup of Folgers. He scanned the local newspaper while he ate. The only upset in this routine was the absence of his wife. She'd died three months earlier. Life had been difficult before. Now it was painful.

Still, Travis stayed the course.

At 7:00 a.m. he pinned on his name tag and tugged on a cap embroidered with his employer's logo: Hank's Hardware.

At 7:05 he was out the door of his run-down farmhouse and behind the wheel of his 1995 Chevy pickup. The truck, like his clothes, was nondescript. He blended with the male population of Eden. He was just another hardworking, blue collar stiff who occasionally attended church on Sunday mornings—not that he got anything out of the preacher's sermons. Now and then he dropped by Kerri's Confections where he indulged in doughnuts and coffee. What he really wanted was a cannoli and espresso, not that he ever asked. Once in a while, like most of the men in these parts, he made an appearance at Boone's Bar and Grill, where he tossed back a couple of beers. Last night he'd been sitting at the end of the bar, nursing a bottle of Pabst and craving a glass of Chianti, when Kylie McGraw, who was typically as unassuming as himself, went a little *oobatz*. Unlike anyone else in Boone's, Travis had empathized.

Like Kylie, he despised the tedium of this Midwestern mom-and-pop town.

Unlike Kylie, he had no intention of shaking things up. He'd flirted with danger a month earlier, a moment of weakness. A mistake he'd quickly rectified. Drawing attention to himself was not an option.

Or was it?

At 7:40, Travis parked his pickup in the alley behind the hardware store. He entered through the back door, traded greetings with his boss and two coworkers. He tidied his work station and skimmed new orders. He did everything exactly as he always did, only this morning, like that one unfortunate night, he couldn't calm his inner self. His true self.

At 8:00 a.m., his boss opened for business and Travis struggled to maintain his composure, his wife's last request ringing in his ears. *"Don't do anything stupid."*

Unfortunately, as his loneliness and frustration escalated, the warning packed less punch.

CHAPTER FOUR

KYLIE WOKE UP WITH a blinding headache and a gross taste in her mouth. Her memory was splotchy, too, but it could have been worse. She could have woken up next to Ashe. Or she could have puked up her guts. Although, if she had slept with Ashe, she would have felt wretched and not because of a hangover. She didn't care how good-looking he was, the man was a bed-hopping sleaze with a checkered past, and she had scruples.

She also had a stabbing pain behind her dust-dry eyeballs.

Who would have thought a trendy drink could be so lethal? Except she'd had three, four if you counted the third as a double, over a short period of time. She regretted taking a spill at Boone's—not exactly a shining moment—and she sort of felt bad for lashing out at Max and gang. But she didn't regret her vow to shake things up. She'd meant every word, well, the ones she remembered. At the very least, she could attack her own dull-as-dirt existence. *She* could be bold. *She* could take risks.

A moment blipped in her mind.

Her. Jack.

She smacked her forehead, winced.

"Stupid cosmos."

She had a big-butt hangover and one mortifying memory. Her lame attempt at seducing Jack Reynolds. He'd resisted her flirting. He'd tolerated her kiss. She didn't know what else to call it. He didn't jerk back, but he didn't reciprocate. But that wasn't the shocker.

There'd been no spark!

Considering the Mount Fuji-size crush she'd had on the man for most of her freaking life, she'd expected to go up in flames the moment she'd sampled that sexy mouth. Instead, she'd felt nothing, nada, *numb*. Either the alcohol had obliterated her senses or she really was over him. *Completely*. She chose to believe the latter. Otherwise, living in the same town with him, again, would be torture.

She still couldn't believe he'd moved back to Eden in the first place. He'd devoted his life to fighting the bad guy. Even as a kid, Jack had been the first to stand up to school-yard bullies, usually in defense of others, because you'd have to be nuttier than a squirrel's hoard to tangle with Jack Reynolds. He and Spenser were both motivated by macho protector instincts. Only Jack gravitated toward fighting crime in the big city, and Spenser had joined the fight against evil on foreign soil. Kylie had never been to New York City, but she knew it brimmed with art, music and literature, diverse cultures and interesting people. So much to do and see…unlike in Eden. Plenty of criminal butts to kick…unlike in Eden.

"The man will be bored to tears within a month," she mumbled into the murky predawn. Good thing she was no longer crushing on him, because he wouldn't be here for long. Unlike Kylie. The way things were going she'd be here until she was six feet under. Not that she wanted to leave Eden forever. Just for a while. Just long enough to experience the beauty and wonder of Asia. Although at this point, an adventure on any level would do.

"You can hide under the blankets feeling sorry for yourself or you can attack the day with gusto, McGraw." Despite the nauseating pulse behind her dry, bleary eyeballs, she swung her bare feet over the edge of the bed. "Gusto it is." She grimaced at the aftertaste of the nacho chips she'd wolfed down, compliments of the midnight munchies. "But first I'm brushing my teeth."

"How THE HELL DID YOU get my toothbrush? Oh, shit. Wait. *Shit*."

Note to self, Jack thought as the stray mutt peed on his bathroom floor, *don't yell at the dog.* Any time he exhibited frustration, Shy—he had to call her something—peed. Not a lot, just a nervous sprinkle. Still. "Damn."

He grabbed a wad of tissue and soaked up the mess.

Shy cowered on the bath mat.

Two nights earlier, he'd found the midsize stray cowering under the old rocker on his back porch. She was scared of thunderstorms. She was scared, from what he'd witnessed so far, of everything. Starved, wet and frightened, the pitiful thing had allowed him to coax her inside. Next, he'd called animal control, but no one had reported a missing dog that looked like a miniature German shepherd. He'd told himself, and Shy, that he'd only keep her until he found her owner or a suitable home. The way things were going, that day couldn't come too soon.

He adopted the casual manner he used to soothe victimized humans. "Easy, girl." He flushed the soiled tissue, then washed his hands. Noting the dog's stricken look, he ruffled her bowed head. Five seconds later, she trotted after him and into the kitchen, tail wagging.

He opened the fridge and nabbed the makings of a mushroom omelet.

Shy circled twice, then curled on the braided rug in front of the sink.

"Don't get too comfortable. You're coming with me today." Yesterday, she'd destroyed one of his shoes, two books and a magazine. Either she'd been pissed because he'd left her alone, or bored. He wasn't a doggy shrink, but this pup had issues. She was a complication he didn't want or need. His goal was to simplify.

Jack beat three eggs, then poured them into a heated skillet, his mind veering to another complicated doe-eyed female. Kylie McGraw. Her goofy smile and fiery spirit. Her red panties and lush lips.

That freaking birthday kiss.

Too bad I didn't feel anything.

It's not like he'd put any effort into it. Still. He'd felt something and she hadn't. Then again, she'd passed out seconds later. Maybe she'd been too trashed to feel anything. His ego demanded a second shot. Logic said, let it go. The only thing worse than a mutual attraction would be acting on it. This was Kylie. Sweet and responsible. *Except when she's trashed.* She was the marrying kind and he was the kind who wrecked marriages.

Shy barked.

"A recipe for disaster, huh?"

Another bark.

"Right."

Jack fed the mutt a half a can of beef kibble, then loaded up his own plate with an omelet and toast. He ate standing up at the counter. Sipped coffee. Flipped through *Law and Order* magazine and contemplated his first official day as chief of police.

He wondered if Kylie would go through with her threat to shake things up or if she'd lose her nerve when she gained her sobriety. He had better things to do than reading her the riot act for disturbing the peace. Like organizing his new office and finding a home for Shy. There were also security issues pertaining to the upcoming Apple Festival.

One thing he wouldn't be doing was investigating a gang shooting or a mafia hit. Those two factions didn't exist in Eden. Hell, there hadn't been a murder of any kind in this town for several decades. No atrocities. No risk that he'd experience that damned numbness that made him wonder what he'd become. No self-disgust binge drinking.

Who needed a shrink, he thought as he topped off his coffee. He had Eden.

A SLICE OF DRY TOAST, one banana, two cups of strong black tea and a hot shower later, Kylie felt rejuvenated enough to attempt gusto. Wanting to shake up her routine straight away, she raided her closet in search of anything bold. She passed over conservative ensembles and settled on a flared black skirt and a fitted black T-shirt featuring a sequined green-and-red dragon breathing sparkly gold fire. Bypassing a dozen pairs of sensible shoes, she snagged the flower-power combat boots she'd ordered and never worn. Whimsical and daring. "The new me."

Feeding off nervous energy, she skipped morning meditation, although she did chant affirmations as she applied mascara and lip balm and tamed her thick hair into her signature ponytail. "I will act out of the ordinary in order to attract and promote change. Change is exciting. Change is good."

She repeated that three times while staring at her reflection in the mirror, although her mind trailed off to the *un*-extraordinary. She considered her pale freckled cheeks, her juvenile ponytail, her poor vision. Maybe she should experiment with cosmetics and a stylish haircut. Investing in laser surgery seemed extreme, but she could definitely afford new glasses. Her body benefited from years of yoga, but typically she hid her toned form beneath loose clothing, choosing timeless classics over here-today-gone-tomorrow trends. She'd never fussed over style, choosing instead to focus on inner beauty. Thing was, men were visual creatures, stimulated by what they could see and touch.

She knew Jack's type and she wasn't it. That explained his lack of enthusiasm when she'd leaned in for a kiss. Plus, she'd been drunk and vulnerable, and wouldn't that be so Jack—a gentlemen even when you ached to be ravished.

Been there. Lived through the embarrassment. *Twice now.*

She sighed and turned away from the mirror. There were other ways to shake up her life aside from burning up the sheets with Jack Reynolds. Not that she was tempted to do so. She was, thank goodness, over him. No, she was going to concentrate on her daring decision to renovate McGraw's Shoe Store.

Sporting a devilish grin, she called Faye while tugging on a pair of thick green socks.

Her friend picked up after the second ring. Despising telemarketers, Faye always screened her calls. "You're alive."

"Rough around the edges, but a lesson learned. What about Sting?"

"Rough around the edges, but a lesson learned."

Kylie frowned at Faye's gruff tone. "What about Spice? Did she survive her first slumber party without getting her undies frozen?" Spice was Faye's thirteen-year-old daughter. As quirky as her mom, but not as outgoing. Her first slumber party—the kid wasn't exactly Miss Popular—had been a very big deal. Maybe it had been a disaster.

"She had a blast."

Kylie waited for details. None came. She squirmed as the silence stretched. What the heck? "Are you mad at me?"

"Why would I be mad at you?"

Kylie pursed her lips and racked her fuzzy brain. "Because I made a spectacle of myself?"

Faye grunted. "Do you even remember last night?"

"Most of it. Okay. Parts of it."

Another long stretch of silence.

Kylie bristled. So, she'd had too much to drink. So, she'd gotten a little loud, given away her shoes and taken a spill in Boone's. It wasn't like Faye to be so easily embarrassed. "Aren't you going to ask me about Jack?" Kylie blurted, because normally that's exactly what her friend would do. Faye knew all about Kylie's longtime infatuation, although she didn't know about the never-to-be-mentioned-*ever* episode. "He gave me a birthday kiss. Actually, I *stole* a kiss. He just sort of sat there. Disappointing."

"You expected Jack to take advantage of you?"

"I expected fireworks."

"You always expect fireworks," Faye said. "And you're always disappointed."

"Yes, but this was *Jack*. It's supposed to be different with him."

"It's supposed to be different with someone who sets your soul on fire. I thought you were over Jack."

"I am."

"Are you sure about that? For someone who's having a hard time remembering parts of last night, you have a damn clear recollection of that kiss."

"You *are* mad at me." Kylie padded to her medicine cabinet and nabbed a bottle of aspirin. Between the hangover and Faye's snippy mood, she felt queasy. To make matters worse, Stan shouted something in the background and Faye shouted back. Okay. So maybe she'd just caught her friend at a bad time. "Are you guys fighting about Sting and the ice cream fiasco?"

"Not exactly." Faye blew out a breath and lowered her voice. "Just do me a favor, Kylie. Don't drink any more cosmopolitans."

"Trust me, it's not on the agenda." Stomach rolling, Kylie popped an antacid along with the aspirin.

"So what instigated that birthday meltdown, anyway?"

A change of subject and a softer tone. Sort of. She'd take it. "Spenser."

"Let me guess," Faye said. "He extended his shooting tour. Which means you have to postpone your trip. Again."

So far Kylie had missed out on two opportunities to travel the Orient. Both times due to a family crisis. The latter had wiped out her bank account. Now, after years of living frugally and saving *(again)*, she finally *(almost)* had enough money to fund her dream trip. Problem was, Spenser's change of plans put a glitch in her plans. "Maybe it wasn't meant to be."

Faye snorted. "Maybe you should *tell* Spenser why you need him to come home and to take responsibility for the business *he* inherited."

"I don't want to step on his dream. *Into the Wild* is a huge hit. He's in his fifth season and the ratings are consistently high."

"What about *your* dream?"

Kylie faltered. Her gut said she needed to attack the here and now. The real world. *Her* world. "If I went to Asia now," she said sensibly, "I'd still have to deal with my dull existence when I got back."

"Meaning?"

Kylie shoved on her glasses, glanced at the shoe-order confirmation and the paint samples she'd printed off the Internet. She smiled. "Meet me at the hardware store in two hours."

CHAPTER FIVE

JACK STEERED HIS SUV into the chief of police's designated parking space. He glanced at the black-and-white parked to his left—one of two department cruisers. Chief Curtis had used his own wheels. Jack opted to do the same. Small towns have small budgets. Police vehicles were costly. Better to allocate funds to staffing, programming and equipment. Besides, driving an unmarked vehicle suited his purpose as did his semicasual uniform.

He cut the engine, looked at Shy over the metal rims of his polarized Oakleys. Instead of the backseat where he'd put her, she now sat on the passenger seat. Slobber streaked the partially open window. Short blond hairs coated his black dashboard. His new car didn't look so new anymore. Didn't smell new, either. Was there such a thing as dog Beano?

"So is this because of the canned kibble?" Jack asked, waving off the noxious odor. "Or because you're nervous?"

Shy barked.

"Uh-huh."

Maybe a trip to the vet was in order. Not that he planned on keeping her. But as long as Shy was in his care, he didn't want her stinking up his air.

"Okay. Listen up. The squad's still mourning Curtis. They're not sold on me. I have no idea how they feel about dogs."

Shy angled her head, whimpered.

"Relax. I'm not locking you in the car for eight hours. Just...behave. No chewing. No peeing. No farting."

Her tail wagged.

"You don't understand a word I'm saying, do you?"

She barked again.

"Right." He climbed out and jerked a thumb. "Let's roll."

Shy leaped to the sidewalk. He half expected, half hoped she'd run. Run home. Run off. Anything to relieve him of this newfound responsibility.

She sat by his side.

Great.

New job. New life. New, and unwanted, complication.

In an effort to root himself, he scanned Main Street and assessed the area. No skyscrapers. No public transportation. No street vendors or homeless beggers. Just a scenic grid of two-story buildings, antique street lamps, and meter-free curbside parking.

Eden, Indiana.

Smalltown, U.S.A.

Four eateries: Pizza King, The Box Car, Boone's Bar and Grill and Kerri's Confections.

One grocery store. One hardware store. One barbershop, beauty salon, car dealership, car wash, Realtor, dollar store, library, shoe store and pharmacy/sundry. One convenience store—Circle K. One department store—Kmart. Two churches—both Protestant. Two gas stations and one bank. Two dentists. Two doctors. Two lawyers—one of those being his brother-in-law, Frank Cortez, or as Jack called him: the Cheating Bastard.

Jack shook off the thought of the man who made him see red. His numbness did not extend to TCB. He breathed in the crisp autumn air and a heady dose of Americana.

Considering where he'd spent the past several years, he felt as if he'd traveled back in time. Kylie was right. Eden hadn't changed in decades. The storefronts looked exactly as they had when he'd been a kid. J.J.'s place still had a soda fountain. A red-and-white-striped barber pole spun outside Keystone's and the Bixley still showed feature films at bargain prices.

Unlike Kylie, he found comfort in the familiar. Especially when the familiar included old-fashioned values. His *CSI* cynicism could use a dose of *Leave It to Beaver* innocence. Dog at his side, he strode toward the station house, soaking in the sunshine and breathing smog-free air.

To think he'd blown out of paradise the day after he'd graduated high school. He'd been hungry for purpose and action. Jessie had accused him of having superhero syndrome. She'd said it like it was a bad thing.

Turned out, she was right.

As soon as she stopped giving him the cold shoulder, he'd concede and give her a chance to say I told you so. At least it would mean they were talking.

He shoved aside thoughts of his sister. She wasn't the only one's favor he needed to gain. He needed to earn the respect of his new unit. A skeletal crew divided among three shifts for twenty-four-hour coverage. His second in command, Deputy Ed Ziffel, worked 7:00 a.m. to 3:00 p.m. Officer Andy Anderson covered the 3:00 p.m. to 11:00 p.m. The night shift belonged to Officer Bo Hooper. Dorothy Vine, their administrative assistant, pulled nine to five. Jack would float, working longer hours and where needed. He'd get to know the unit, but it would take time.

Prepared for the morning shift, Jack entered the station house along with the perky-eared, stink-ass dog.

Ed Ziffel sat at a dinged metal desk immersed in a book while devouring a powdery pastry. Ziffel had graduated high school two years behind Jack. They'd never been friends, but they weren't enemies, either. After an hour in the man's company yesterday, Jack knew why the town council hadn't promoted from within. Some men are born to lead. Some…aren't.

Jack cleared his throat.

Ziffel jerked his nose out of the book and brushed crumbs from his dark blue tie. He noted Jack's attire. "Chief Curtis dressed in the official EPD uniform," he said by way of a greeting.

"I know." Part of the reason Jack had deviated. Dark blue Dutymax cargo pants and black LITE*Speed* running boots. He wore a white T-shirt under his tan polo shirt and a lightweight nylon blue jacket with Police embroidered on the right. His gold badge was clipped to his belt. His .40 caliber semiautomatic Glock was holstered at his hip. His headgear of choice—a blue ball cap—was embroidered with stark white letters: EPD.

His goal was to appear official yet approachable. According to the mayor, the former police chief had fallen out of touch with the populace. Burned out? Maybe. Probably. Christ. The man had been on the job thirty-five years. Shit happens.

Jack knew shit. He also knew people. He was an expert at reading personalities. An expert at blending. He could converse and connect with butchers, bakers and cold-blooded killers. His goal to bond with the citizens of Eden was both professional and personal.

"Guess you're more comfortable in plainclothes seeing as you were a detective."

Jack didn't argue. He didn't want to speak ill of Ben Curtis. He didn't feel obliged to explain his clothes, though not official EPD attire, were in fact regulation. He took off his Oakleys, slid them into his inner jacket pocket. "Any activity I should know about?"

"Hooper got a call from dispatch at 2:31 a.m. Mrs. Carmichael reporting a possible break-in. Or vandalism. She swore someone was skulking around her house."

The E911 Dispatch Center also dispatched calls to the Eden fire department, ambulance service, and to the animal control officer. Jack wondered how they kept up. Then again, this was Eden. They probably got four calls a day, total. "And?"

"Hooper drove out even though he knew he wouldn't find any threat."

Jack raised a brow.

"We get calls from the old woman at least once a week."

"Regardless, Hooper investigated."

"Bo Hooper's a good man."

"Didn't mean to imply otherwise."

Ziffel pursed his lips, nodded.

Jack bypassed his office—a disorganized nightmare—and drifted toward a pot of freshly brewed coffee. Shy slinked along. "So what did Hooper find?"

Focused on a manila file, Ziffel grunted. "A tree branch scraping against her upstairs pane."

"I remember Sally Carmichael," Jack said as he filled a blue ceramic mug to the brim. "Sunday school teacher."

"Retired now."

"Married forever."

"Until Harry died."

"Now she's widowed, alone. Skittish."

"Starved for attention," Ziffel added.

"Lonely."

The man nodded. "That's our take. Especially at night."

"Anything else?"

"This town doesn't see much action." Ziffel cast a subtle line. "At least not the kind you're used to."

Jack didn't take the bait. He sipped coffee.

Ziffel didn't take the hint. He fished deeper. "Folks are speculating on why a gung-ho cop like you would ditch New York City—maybe the most exciting city in the whole U.S. of A.—for hum-drum Eden."

In other words, he was the subject of town gossip. He wasn't surprised. He did, however, want to douse speculation. "I burned out on big crime."

"Oh." Ziffel looked disappointed by the straightforward answer. No drama. No scandal. No dancing around the subject. "Burnout is common in high-stress, high-risk professions," he said. "So instead of melting down, you transferred out of a toxic environment into a wholesome community. Smart."

Jack saluted the man with his mug. "No place like home."

Shy whimpered.

The deputy peered over his desk. He noted the mutt leaning against Jack's leg, frowned. "You brought your dog to work?"

"She's a stray. I'm her caretaker. Temporary." Jack gestured from canine to deputy. "Shy, Ziffel. Ziffel, Shy."

"You named her?"

"Had to call her something."

Ziffel, a rail-thin man with a face only his mother—and wife—could love, drained his mug, then joined Jack for a refill. "Should've stuck with 'Dog.' Once you give an animal a name, you've made it personal."

Jack didn't comment. Ziffel was a pain-in-the-ass know-it-all, but he didn't care that he hadn't been promoted, and according to the town council, he was a conscientious lawman. Jack needed a reliable deputy, a man who knew Eden and its citizens like the back of his hand. A man the squad already respected. Ziffel fit the bill.

Jack refilled their mugs.

Shy sat and leaned into Jack's leg.

"*She* thinks she's your dog," Ziffel said, stirring two packets of sugar into his coffee.

"She's anxious."

"You mean attached."

Jack sipped. "Hazelnut?"

Ziffel nodded, then shifted. "Chief Curtis liked Maxwell House Dark Roast. Day in, day out. Don't seem right, drinking his brew without him. Thought I'd try something different."

"It's good."

"Dorothy won't like it."

Jack's gaze flicked to the assistant's vacant desk. "Speaking of Ms. Vine…"

"This ain't typical," Ziffel said in her defense. "Dorothy's one of the most punctual people I know."

"Should I be worried?"

"She's seeing to Chief Curtis's…worldly possessions. He was a widower," Ziffel explained. "No children."

"I get it, Deputy." No wife. No kids. No one to see to his affairs after he'd keeled over unexpectedly from a heart attack. Jack was in a similar position. No wife. No kids. Just a sister who resented him and a niece who didn't know him. "Ms. Vine gets here when she gets here."

"Right-o, Chief Reynolds."

"Jack'll do.

Ziffel smiled and Jack got the feeling he'd just risen a notch in the man's eyes. "Know what you need with that coffee, Jack? Kerri's apple strudel. I bought a half dozen. Help yourself."

According to Ziffel, Kerri's Confections was famous countywide. The proprietor, Kerri Waldo, a fairly recent addition to Eden, had a gift for creating heavenly desserts. Her recipes were spiked with secret ingredients and the daily special was usually a one-time affair. The freshly baked scents wafting from the box on Ziffel's desk promised a decadent delight.

Jack wasn't hungry, but this was a chance to bond with his new right-hand man. If it meant sampling strudel, so be it. He moved to Ziffel's desk and dipped into the box. Two seconds later, nirvana. "Wow."

"I've asked her to marry me three times," said Ziffel.

"Aren't you already married?"

"In this case my wife would consider bigamy a blessing. She's addicted to Kerri's sweets."

Jack cracked a smile, sampled more strudel. Shy licked his fingers. He couldn't blame the dog. Hard to resist heaven.

"Just so you know," Ziffel said, narrowing his eyes on Shy. "Dorothy is a neat freak."

"Really." Jack's gaze flicked to his office.

"Chief Curtis's office was off limits. Said he had his own system. Knew where everything was. If Dorothy shifted so much as a pencil, he had a conniption fit."

"Yeah, well, I don't know Curtis's system. Ms. Vine can shift all the pencils she wants, and while she's at it, I could use help organizing files."

"That she'll like. *That*," he said, pointing to Shy, "she won't."

Jack had only met Dorothy Vine briefly, but long enough to know she'd view Shy as a hairy, four-legged disruption. He looked down and met the mutt's baleful brown eyes. Could she be any more needy? "Ms. Vine will have to deal. Shy's destructive when I leave her home alone." He refreshed his coffee and moved into the disaster zone.

Ziffel followed. "Separation anxiety. Saw a special about it on Animal Planet. Stems from fear of abandonment. Especially prevalent in rescued strays."

Jack sat at his desk and opened that day's edition of the *Eden Tribune*—the rural voice of Miami County. Although the paper included state news, it typically focused on feel-good articles, local sports and community events. Far and away from the bleak and stark reports of the *New York Times, Daily News* and the *New York Post*. There was something to be said for Americana newspapers, especially by someone suffering big-city burnout. This week the paper brimmed with stories and advertisements for Eden's upcoming Apple Festival.

Jack skimmed the classifieds while Ziffel spouted the advantages of hiring a dog trainer. "I don't need a trainer. I'm not keeping her." No mention of a missing dog in the lost-and-found section. "Figured I'd walk her around town. See if anyone recognizes her."

"Without a collar and leash?"

Jack glanced up. "We have a leash law I don't know about?"

Ziffel sniffed. "No law. But what if she attacks someone?"

"Shy's afraid of her own shadow."

"Doesn't mean she won't attack if provoked. Just because she's meek... Where is she, anyway?" Ziffel turned, stiffened.

Jack saw what he saw—Shy with her nose in the red-and-white signature box marked Kerri's Confections. *Shit.* "Don't—"

"Hey, you thieving mutt!"

"—yell." Jack was on his deputy's heels. The sight of Shy crouched and trembling with apple goo and flaky crumbs on her snout made him smile.

Ziffel was not amused. "You…scrounge. You… *menace!*"

He gripped the man's bony shoulder. "You can't blame the dog for wanting to sample something that smells so good."

"She not only ate all the strudel," he complained, "she peed on the floor."

"That's because you yelled. Relax. I'll clean it up." Jack patted Shy's bowed head, then swiped several tissues from Dorothy's desk.

"The strudel—"

"I'll buy more."

"Probably sold out already." He swiped up the damaged box. "Dang nabbit!"

Dang nabbit? What the hell? Cops cursed. Most of them crudely and often. At least in Jack's experience. Then again, this was Eden—paradise in the heartland. An old-fashioned town with old-fashioned values.

While Ziffel cleaned up the pastry disaster, Jack made a mental note to clean up his language—when in Rome— although he refused to substitute *dang* for *damn* or *fudge* for *fuck*. Although, *damn,* fuck should probably go. This should be interesting. Amused, he flushed the soiled tissue, then washed his hands.

The roar of an engine drew them both to the station's front window.

Jack noted the rider with a raised brow. Was that… Holy shit. It *was*. On the heels of surprise came a jolt of lust. Typically he wasn't attracted to biker chicks, but this one was sexy as hell in her short skirt, denim jacket and… Christ…were those combat boots?

"Spenser would have a fit if he saw Kylie on that motorcycle," Ziffel said.

Jack wrestled with his own misgivings. "Because it's not a Harley? Or because it's dangerous?"

"Both."

He was right. Spenser wouldn't approve. Mostly because of the safety issue. Motorcyclists were twenty times as likely to die in a crash than someone riding in a car.

Great.

Now Jack felt compelled to lecture Kylie on the perils of the road as well as home security.

At least she was wearing a helmet.

He watched as she parked the sleek silver motorcycle in front of Hank's Hardware. Given her obsession with Asia, he wasn't surprised she'd chosen Kawasaki. "That her regular mode of transportation?"

"Her car's in the shop. Usually she drives a Honda Civic."

"She has a sudden aversion to the usual."

"A sudden aversion to modesty, too," Ziffel noted. "Who rides a bike in a skirt? What was she thinking?"

About shaking things up.

Jack noted her tousled ponytail when she whipped off her helmet, the way the flared skirt kissed the back of her toned, creamy thighs. He wondered about the color of her panties—bright green like her socks?

Touch her and I'll kick your ass.

"Are those army boots?" Ziffel asked.

"Something like." He couldn't make out details, but he made out splashes of color. Yellow, pink and blue on black. Definitely different. Hardly sexy, yet he had the mother of boners.

What the hell, Reynolds? Jerk off. Nail a loose woman. Do not approach the temptress.

Ziffel looked at his watch. "Nine-fifteen. McGraw's Shoe Store always opens at nine prompt."

"So?"

"Kylie always opens the store. Always. What do you think she's up to?"

"Trouble."

"Kylie McGraw?" Ziffel snorted. "That girl's a pussycat."

Jack believed otherwise. *What's your game, Tiger?* "Keep an eye on Shy."

"Where are you going?" Ziffel asked as he pushed through the door.

"Making a strudel run."

"Good Lord," he heard behind him. "What's that *smell?*"

CHAPTER SIX

KYLIE WAS THREE STEPS from Hank's Hardware when she caught a fragrant whiff of baked goods and java. She wasn't a coffee drinker, but she'd read that caffeine tames headaches. Just her luck, her hangover had magnified on the bumpy ride into town. In lieu of more aspirin, she'd settle for a big honking cup of dark roast. She swiveled toward Kerri's Confections…and saw Jack.

Just. Her. Luck.

She almost did a one-eighty—hang the coffee—but she couldn't avoid the man forever. Best to get this over with. *About last night…*

Standing her ground, she smiled at the approaching lawman and cursed her skipping heart. She told herself she was reacting to his official appearance, not his hunky bad self. Just because she was over him, that didn't mean she was blind to the pulse-tripping package. He looked more like a SWAT guy than Eden's chief of police. The ball cap, the cargo pants and tactical running boots. The badge clipped to his taut waist.

S-e-x-y.

She thought about the previous night. Her botched seduction. Her *second* botched seduction. Her cheeks flamed. Not that he'd bring it up.

A gentleman even when you ached to be ravished.

Dang.

He stepped from the street onto the sidewalk. "Kylie."

"Jack."

His eyes were hidden behind a pair of cool cop sunglasses, but she sensed his amusement when he noted her funky but incredibly *un-sexy* boots. No doubt he preferred his women in strappy four-inch heels. Jack went for glamour girls. Stunning beauties with hourglass figures. Kylie wasn't voluptuous or blond, but—thanks to yoga— she did have nice legs. Not that she wanted Jack to go for *her*. She was, after all, over him, and he'd be over Eden in a month, if not sooner. Pursuing an intimate relationship would only end in heartache. She mentally recited that affirmation three times as her traitorous heart raced.

He focused back on her face. "About that kiss…"

Oh, *God*. If he was compelled to address her drunken advance, then he felt he had to set her straight. *You're a sweet girl, but…*

Kylie scrambled to preserve her dignity. "I'm so not attracted to you."

He regarded her over the rims of his tinted glasses.

Her knees weakened at the sight of those river-blue eyes. Her stomach constricted as she thought she'd maybe, possibly insulted him. Normally she went out of her way *not* to hurt someone's feelings. "Not that you're not attractive. I mean you're gorgeous. In a, you know, beefcake sort of way."

He raised a brow.

"But I'm not the beefcake type," she rambled on. "I mean, you're not the type for me. That kiss was just…well, I was drunk and you were there."

"So if Ashe…"

"Exactly," she lied. "What can I say? I was pretty blitzed."

"No argument there."

Embarrassed and oddly provoked, she hitched the purse she'd just picked up at Boone's higher on her shoulder and hiked her chin a notch. "I'm just saying you don't have to worry about me stalking you or coming on to you, because I'm over you. Completely. That schoolgirl crush? History. So…there. We're okay. Right?" She stuck out her hand, offering a truce, retaining her dignity. "Friends?"

He clasped her palm, stroked his thumb over her skin.

Heat shot up her arm and burned a path from her heart to her... *Uh-oh.*

He smiled. Just a little. Just enough to make her insides gooey. "Join me for a cup of coffee?"

She blinked. "What?"

"You were heading toward Kerri's."

"Yes, but..."

"Friends confide in each other."

"Sure, but..."

"The beef you have with Spenser. Maybe I can help."

Kylie stared, his words not registering as much as his touch. He was still holding her hand, still stroking her skin. She tingled everywhere. *Eh-ver-ree-where.* Even her *hair* tingled. How was that possible? How could she get zip from a kiss and zing from holding hands?

Then again, this morning she was sober.

This was bad. Not the sober part. The zing part.

Really, really bad.

Kylie jerked free. "Thanks, but...I'm late." She spun back toward the hardware store.

"Thought you were heading for the café," Jack said with a smile in his voice.

Was he *teasing* her? The thought occurred that he'd done that thumb-stroking thing on purpose, just to see if she really was cured of her schoolgirl crush. Curiosity? Arrogance? Although, it wasn't like Jack to lead a girl on.

"I was," she said over her shoulder, feigning an easy smile. "But now, thanks to our chat, I'm late. Meeting someone. Gotta run." She intentionally left the identity of that someone to his imagination. Hopefully, he'd imagine a guy. Maybe even—*eew*—Ashe. She sure as heck didn't want him thinking she was hopelessly single, which she was, but that wasn't the point.

Flustered, Kylie rushed over the threshold of Hank's Hardware and slammed into Faye.

"You're twenty minutes late."

"Sorry." Kylie wanted to spew about the unnerving encounter with Jack, but she felt stupid. Just this morning, she'd sworn she was over him. Actually, she'd declared her undying love dead the day she'd learned he was getting married—much to Faye's relief. Faye, who'd endured years of Kylie's unrequited pining. Faye, who apparently had problems of her own. As soon as they had a private moment, she'd have to ask why she and Stan were on the outs.

"I left this at the bar last night," Kylie said, flashing her purse and hoping it excused her delay. "Had to stop and pick it up."

"You drove without a license? Are you nuts?" Faye snapped her fingers. "Ah, yes. The new you. The rebel rouser. What next? Picketing the Bixley? Expand or else?"

Again with the sarcasm. Kylie refused to take offense. If she stayed upbeat, maybe she could lighten her friend's dark mood. "I could zoom my bike down Main Street topless," she teased while glancing at the signs hanging above the aisles. "That would cause a stir."

"Speeding. Indecent exposure." Faye sighed and shook her head. "You're determined to land in jail, aren't you?"

Kylie snorted and moved toward aisle seven. "Jack wouldn't arrest me. It would piss off Spenser."

"Spenser's half a world away."

"Don't remind me." Kylie gestured to her flower-covered Doc Martens. "What do you think?"

"So that's how you're going to shake up Eden. Impractical footwear."

"For a start."

"Nice ensemble," Faye said, gesturing to the rest of Kylie's attire. "Sort of retro Madonna. Except...you rode your bike in a skirt?"

"Yep."

"No tights or leggings?"

"I'm a little backed up on laundry."

"Tell me you're wearing shorts."

"I'm wearing shorts." Kylie stopped in the aisle stocked with paint supplies. "So about renovating McGraw's..."

"I can't believe you're going through with this."

"Believe it." Kylie surveyed the shelves. Brushes, pads and rollers. Drop cloths. Sandpaper. Solvents and thinners. "I have no idea what to buy."

"Don't look at me," Faye said. "The only thing I know how to paint is fingernails."

"Ha."

"I'm serious. I haven't the slightest clue as to what you'll need to paint the store. That's what you have in mind, right? You're going to make good on your threat? Pink walls, yellow trim? Spenser's going to kill you."

Kylie waggled her brows. "Spenser's half a world away."

"Can I help?"

"Hi, Travis."

"Kylie."

Travis Martin was a long-time employee of Hank's Hardware. Tall. Fit. His huge puppy-dog eyes and fleshy lips softened his hard-angled face. His red hair clashed with his olive skin. His nose had a weird bump and dent. She'd asked him about that once. An old baseball injury, he'd told her. He also had a scar dissecting his left eyebrow. He wasn't handsome, but he *was* attractive, even with the unflattering hair color. She didn't know his ancestry. Irish-Italian? Spanish-German? She didn't even know where he'd lived specifically before moving to Eden, although she'd heard through the grapevine Montana. Or was it Wyoming? She never could place the accent.

She did, however, know his shoe size.

Mostly he purchased his footwear at a nearby department store—*shudder*—but he occasionally shopped at McGraw's. She wasn't sure she'd call him a satisfied customer. Although she always sold him what he asked for, he always seemed apathetic. Then again, he was a man, and men didn't generally fuss over shoes. Especially the practical, silent type.

She indicated his latest purchase. Insulated work boots—waterproof and rugged. Suitable for manual labor. "How are those holding up?"

"Good."

"Because if you don't like them—"

"Like 'em fine."

"I have a new shipment of boots coming in."

He noted her Doc Martens. "With flowers?" He quirked an excuse for a smile. "No, thanks."

"We want to buy some paint," Faye interrupted. "Maybe. If it's not too expensive. Or too pink."

Kylie rolled her eyes. "I'm going to redecorate McGraw's Shoe Store. Inside and out."

"Out?" Faye echoed.

"A total makeover. In addition to changing the color scheme, I want new shelves and lighting. I have pictures." She dug in the pocket of her denim jacket and produced photos she'd printed from the Internet, plus pages she'd ripped from a shoe supply catalog. "I ordered some of this stuff online last night."

Faye groaned. "In a drunken stupor? That's not good."

Kylie ignored her. "These shoe displays, these mirrors. And check out these prints I found on Art.com."

"Interesting mix of abstract and art deco," he said. "Nice."

"Sure. If McGraw's was in a cosmopolitan hotspot," said Faye. "But it's in *Eden*."

"Please don't mention cosmopolitans," Kylie said, massaging the dull pulse at her temples. "Anyway," she pressed on, "I was thinking about painting the walls this color with these accents. Maybe something similar for the exterior? And wall-to-wall carpet. I like this color. Or maybe this."

Travis nodded. "Bold."

Faye looked around his shoulder. "Disastrous."

"I get what you're going for," he said.

"Yeah," Faye said. "Spenser's boot up her butt."

Kylie smirked. "Ha."

"Do I look like I'm kidding?" Faye asked. "Spenser will

have a cow. And what about your mom and grandma? What about tradition?"

"The only tradition I care about is Kabuki Theater and *zongzi*."

"I'll bite," said Faye. "What's *zongzi?*"

"A glutinous rice dumpling wrapped in bamboo leaves."

"I take it back. I won't bite. Sounds disgusting."

"It's the food of honor at the Dragon Boat Festival."

"Still disgusting."

"You don't know that. Maybe it's orgasmic. Not that I'll ever know," Kylie muttered. The way things were going, she'd never make it to Japan or China, let alone both. She'd be lucky if she ever made it across state lines. She glanced at Travis, who was still studying her photos. "Since you get what I'm going for, would you please box up everything I need?"

Travis raised a brow. "Everything?"

Kylie nodded.

Faye nudged her. "Don't you think you should get an estimate?"

"If you're talking an extensive renovation," Travis said as he moved to his work station, "it could get expensive. Especially when you factor in labor."

Kylie scrunched her nose. "Hadn't thought about hiring help."

"Don't tell me you planned on handling everything yourself," Faye asked.

"Not *all* by myself."

Faye's eyebrows rose to her bleached hairline. "*Me?* You expect *me* to help? I'm not good with simple home repairs, let alone an entire renovation."

"You renovated the Orchard House."

"I picked out colors and furniture. *Stan* renovated the building." Faye blinked, smirked. "Oh. You expect me to rope Stan into helping."

Kylie smiled. "Free shoes for the family for a year?"

"As tempting as that sounds…"

"In addition to some sort of cash fee, of course," Kylie added. Maybe that's why Stan and Faye were fighting. Money troubles. "I wouldn't dream of taking advantage of anyone, especially your husband. You guys are like family."

"Stan won't take money from you. Same reasoning. Family."

"What about the shoes?"

"What about the B and B? We have a business to run and I can't do it alone. Not with two kids in the mix. Besides, we're knee-deep in our own spiffing-up. The Apple Festival is next week. Starting midweek we're booked solid and…" Faye broke off and looked away.

"What?"

"Never mind."

"But—"

"Just when did you plan to start your renovations?" Faye asked, swinging the subject back around.

Kylie's head spun. "Today."

"Naturally."

"I know it'll be hard work," Kylie babbled, flustered by Faye's ongoing sarcasm, "but, I want to reopen McGraw's on opening day of the festival. I ordered a special line of stock. Shoes that'll appeal to the tourists and…" She flushed when she noted her friend gaping at her like a widemouthed bass. "You're right. What was I thinking? I can't expect you and Stan to…never mind."

"We would if we could, Kylie."

"I know. It's okay. I didn't think things through. Drunken stupor and all that. Obviously, I'm going to have to hire a crew or at least one very productive man."

"I have an estimate," Travis said.

Kylie and Faye moved to the counter. They looked at the figure Travis had scratched on a yellow pad. Kylie swallowed. "That much, huh?"

He slid her Internet printouts under her nose and picked up a pencil. "If you cut this and this—"

"Nope. Gotta have those."

"What about these?" Faye said.

"I've had my eye on those for months. Spied them in *InStep Magazine*."

"You could cut cost by renovating the interior only," Travis said.

"Yeah," Faye said. "It would save time, too. Also, Spenser would only be half as mad."

It was the exact wrong thing to say. Kylie shook her head. "I want the whole sushi roll." She nabbed the pencil from Travis and scribbled her own figure. "This is how much I have to spend on supplies and labor. Obviously, I need someone who'll work cheap. And fast. Oh, and I'll throw in free shoes."

Travis looked at the figure.

Faye looked at the figure. She whistled. "You're taking that out of the business account? Without Spenser's approval?"

"No. I'm dipping into my personal account."

"Dipping? It'll wipe you out! What about your dream trip?"

"It's just that, Faye. A dream. Sometimes you have to make lemonade out of lemons." She shrugged. "Or in this case, cider out of apples."

"I can't believe you're giving up," Faye said. "You've worked so hard. Skimped and saved. *Again.* I can't—" Her cell phone blared—ringtone of the month, Evanescence's "Bring Me to Life." "I have to take this," she said after checking the screen. "Hi, Miss Miller." Sting's kindergarten teacher. "He did what? He...I can't hear you. You're breaking up. Hold on." Faye gestured to Travis and Kylie she needed to move outside.

Kylie wondered what planet she'd been on when she'd thought about enlisting Faye and Stan's help. They had full lives. A business. A family. A marriage. They didn't have time to indulge her life crisis. Especially when they were, possibly, immersed in their own crisis. Except, if that were the case, why hadn't Faye confided in her? Which brought

Kylie back to her initial worry that Faye's anger was actually directed at her, not Stan. But why?

Dang.

"What about me?"

Kylie blinked out of her musings and focused on Travis. Her temples throbbed as she processed. "You're offering to help me renovate?"

"I am."

"But you work full-time and I'm on a tight schedule."

"I have vacation time coming."

"Wouldn't you rather spend that time somewhere else? Somewhere out of Eden?"

"I would, but I can't."

Hmm. Maybe he was strapped for funds. "You could relax—"

"I prefer to keep as busy as possible these days."

Or maybe he didn't want to travel alone. She suspected keeping busy kept his thoughts off of his deceased wife. Three months back, Mona Martin had succumbed to cancer. Travis had been devastated. He was still damned somber. How long did it take to get over a spouse's death? She hoped to never know.

Kylie crossed her arms over her middle, trying to decide what to make of the man's offer. She asked straight out. "Why would you want to do this?"

"To shake up my life?"

Had he been in the bar last night? Had he heard her rant?

"Maybe you miscalculated that figure I jotted. To be clear, I can't pay you close to what you'd deserve for your time and effort."

He almost, sort of, smiled. "Happy belated birthday."

CHAPTER SEVEN

AT 10:00 A.M., TRAVIS entered his boss's office and put in for vacation time. If Hank had refused, he'd been ready to quit. But it didn't come to that. The man felt sorry for him. Assumed he was still mourning Mona—which he was. Only this wasn't about Mona. This was about two people stuck in a rut.

By 10:45 a.m., Travis had loaded several cans of paint and various other supplies into the bed of his truck. Hank didn't carry the kind of lighting fixtures Kylie wanted. Not wanting to wait weeks for an order to come in, she'd been ready to settle for something more conservative. Travis didn't want her to settle. He told her not to worry. He'd track down those contemporary fixtures or something damn close.

At 11:15 a.m., Travis pulled into his driveway. A burst of adrenaline made his hands shake. He'd broken his routine. He'd tempted fate. Again. He wasn't one-hundred-percent sure how he felt about that. But this time he wouldn't turn back.

He raided his work shed for a ladder and toolbox. He pulled a roll of canvas and a bin of paint brushes out of his attic. The whole time he'd been at work boxing up everything Kylie needed, he'd been mentally ticking off items he could bring from home. He'd try to save her what money he could. It bothered him that she'd given up on a dream. He knew all about giving up something important. It ate at your soul. It was too late to save his, but maybe he could save Kylie's.

Mona wouldn't approve. She wouldn't understand why he'd stick his neck out for a person he barely knew. He couldn't explain it. All he knew was that Kylie McGraw had unleashed the part of him that he'd kept locked away for seven long years. Time to shake up the life forced upon him.

Eleven-forty-five. He stashed his name badge and work hat in a drawer. Changed into a fresh T-shirt and a clean but paint-splattered long-sleeved button-down. He tugged on an Indiana Colts ball cap. In his heart, he rooted for the Eagles.

Lunch consisted of a ham sandwich—white bread, yellow mustard and American cheese, Lays potato chips and a Coke. Of the times they'd shopped together, three times Travis had reached for a package of provolone. Mona had nudged him away.

"They don't eat provolone," she'd reminded him after they'd reached the sanctity of home.

Not typically. Typically *they* ate American, Swiss or Cheddar. Travis had grinned. "I feel daring."

"No, you don't," she said as she put away the groceries. "You feel like everyone else in this county. You dress like them, talk like them, eat like them…." She bobbled a can of Campbell's soup. It should have been Progresso. "Anything out of the norm—"

"—is dangerous. I know." He'd hated the fear in her voice. He'd pulled her into his arms and hugged her. He'd assured her that American cheese was just fine.

Only it wasn't. And Mona was no longer here to reassure.

By 12:40 p.m., Travis was on the road and on his way to McGraw's Shoe Store. Renovating Kylie's business called to his artistic side. He'd liked the pictures she'd shown him, although he'd suggested slight variations in the color scheme so as not to deter the male clientele. He'd also recommended scattered throw rugs—a mix of abstract and art deco—as opposed to the wall-to-wall carpet. Less expensive. More impact. Splashes of vibrant color against the dark hardwood floors. Kylie had applauded his vision, naming him a kindred spirit. He didn't know about that. But he sure liked the way she made him feel.

Alive.

He popped open another can of Coke and floored the Chevy. He knew he'd work hard and work late tonight. Maybe he'd reward himself later...with a bottle of Chianti and a wedge of provolone.

CHAPTER EIGHT

JACK SAT BEHIND HIS DESK sorting through old newspapers, budget reports, trade magazines and assorted mail. A daunting task, complicated by the fact that he couldn't concentrate. He'd played with fire this morning. First to soothe his ego. Then to satisfy his desire. He'd *wanted* to hold Kylie's hand, to stroke that ivory skin. Watching her blush and ramble had been a turn-on. The more she denied an attraction, the keener his arousal. Growing up, given their four-year age difference, he'd never paid much attention to Kylie-the-kid. But Kylie-the-woman…she was a fascinating enigma.

Mesmerized, he'd imagined her in his arms, in his bed. He'd imagined her flexibility and fiery spirit. He wanted to lose himself in all that spunk and sweetness. He wanted to protect her from men like Ashe Davis and Bobby Jones. In that split second, he'd felt possessive of Kylie Ann McGraw. A sign that he was in deep shit. He wasn't sure if he could shovel himself out. Worse. He wasn't sure he wanted to. Spenser was always bragging about his sister's grounded, caring spirit. Connecting intimately with all that goodness could do wonders for Jack's cynical soul.

Tempting.

The desk phone rang, jerking him out of his destructive musings. "Chief Reynolds," he answered.

"Personal assistant to Chief Reynolds," Dorothy Vine replied.

Jack frowned at the woman's caustic tone. "What is it, Ms. Vine?"

"As requested, I phoned your sister on your behalf and invited her and her daughter to your house—or anyplace of their choice—for dinner."

It had been a desperate act on his part, asking the squad's administrative assistant to act as a liaison of sorts. But dammit, he'd been in town for almost a week and Jessie had avoided him at every turn. He knew she had to be heartbroken. She'd finally learned the truth about the Cheating Bastard. Frank Cortez was ruled by his dick, not his heart. That's *if* he had a heart. Jack wanted to help Jessie through this. He wanted to help his young niece.

"Jessica Lynn asked me to give you a message," said Ms. Vine.

"Okay."

"She said…"

"Go on."

"Fuck off."

Disappointing, but not unexpected. Almost amusing coming from straight-laced Ms. Vine. "Thank you."

"You're welcome."

Jack hung up and focused back on his paper-ridden desktop. Better than obsessing on his fractured relationship with his sister and nonexistent relationship with his niece. Better than obsessing on Kylie. According to Ziffel, Chief Curtis had had a filing system. Damned if Jack could figure it out, and he wasn't about to ask Ms. Vine. Not today. The squad's administrative assistant, a fifty-something woman with choppy silver hair, green cat-eye glasses and a fondness for polyester suits, had rolled in an hour late— eyes swollen from crying over the former chief, manner brusque. Ziffel was right. She didn't like the coffee and she didn't like Shy. She'd spent the next hour sweeping, dusting and dousing the air with pine-scented Glade.

Shy cowered under his desk. He didn't blame the dog. She probably felt like Toto hiding out from the Wicked Witch of the West. He had to admit, Dorothy Vine was a little scary. Then again, grief caused people to act in strange ways.

Take the parents of the victim who'd instigated Jack's breakdown. Instead of wanting revenge or, at the very least, demanding justice, they'd swallowed their misery and moved on. Their emotional lockdown had made Jack hyperaware of his own numb state.

"Chief."

Jack looked up. His expression must've been fierce because Ziffel stepped back. "What is it, Deputy?"

"Got a call from dispatch. Disturbance at 1450 Main."

McGraw's Shoe Store. Given his previous dark thoughts, Jack tensed. "Define disturbance," he said as he rose.

"Kylie's making a scene."

Shaking things up. He almost smiled. He definitely welcomed the distraction. Jack braced himself for another encounter with the woman—*Just don't touch her for Christ's sake*—and nabbed his jacket. "Let's roll."

Shy scrambled out from under the desk and followed them into the administrative office.

Jack tugged on his EPD cap, glanced at Dorothy who was tapping away at the computer. "Do you think—"

"Not a dog-sitter."

Right.

Head down, Shy zipped ahead of the two men.

Dorothy spritzed the air.

"You," Ziffel said to Shy as they left the building, "stay downwind."

"You're not the boss of me, J.J."

"Maybe not, but you don't call the shots either, missy."

"Stop talking to me like I'm ten years old!"

"Then start acting like a responsible adult," said Ray Keystone.

Arguing with her elders wasn't Kylie's style. Nor was airing her dirty laundry, especially in broad daylight directly in front of McGraw's. But she'd already been knocked dizzy by Faye's prickly mood and Jack's unsettling touch. She'd be danged if she'd be bullied into

ditching her home-spun adventure just because these
fuddy-duddies were opposed to change! Insulted, Kylie
smacked a hand to her racing heart. "I *am* responsible. My
family owns this store and we're renovating."

"Anyone in your family know about that aside from
you?" asked Max.

Kylie felt a small pang of guilt for not running the idea
by her mom and grandma. Although they'd never taken an
active interest in the business end of things, they did
consider McGraw's a family venture. As for Spenser, well,
someone had to take a progressive role. Moving McGraw's
into the twenty-first century would shake things up in a
good way. She hoped. Besides, it wasn't as if she could
easily contact her brother or her mom and grandma due to
their current exotic locales. *That* thought only fueled her
determination.

"Just as I thought," Max said. "She's acting solo."

J.J. and Keystone chimed in, citing last night's inebriated rant and a pre-midlife crisis.

Kylie fumed at being ganged up on. First the owner of
the pharmacy, then the owner of the barbershop. The two
businesses flanking hers. She'd never known these two men
could be such curmudgeons. To make matters worse, Max,
who still had shaving cream on his chin, had followed Mr.
Keystone out of the barbershop to add fuel to the inferno.

"Since when do you fan flames instead of putting them
out?" she blasted.

"Just doing my civic duty," said Max. "Wouldn't be
right if I let you deface property."

"Damn right," said J.J.

"I'm not…I'm just…" Spitting mad. She was so dang
mad she couldn't think straight. She lost her train of
thought as a crowd gathered.

"Is that pink?" someone asked.

"Prissy pink," said Max.

J.J. tsked. "If Spenser was here—"

"Well, he's not," Kylie snapped.

Keystone shook his finger at Travis, who was perched on the top rung of the ladder, painting the trim of McGraw's storefront. "I'm warning you, Travis. One more swipe and—"

"You're not the boss of me, Keystone." He didn't look down. He didn't stop painting.

Kylie refrained from sticking her tongue out at the barber, but couldn't hold back the "Ha."

"That's mature," said J.J.

"Listen, you…" She trailed off as the crowd parted and Jack showed up on the scene. Darn. She met his bluer-than-blue gaze and ignored the flutter in her heart. *Just friends,* she told herself, then focused back on her dilemma.

All business, Jack looked to the crotchety trio. "What's the problem, gentlemen?"

"No problem," Kylie said.

"Big problem," said J.J.

"Huge problem," said Max. "She's ruining the integrity of the landscape."

"Sissifying our block," Keystone groused.

"Since when is jazzing up and adding color sissifying?" Kylie shouted. "If you'd get your heads out of your—"

"Play nice," Jack warned.

J.J. tsked. "She used to be polite."

"You mean passive." Not that she didn't appreciate the benefits of meditation, but she was sick of squashing her restlessness.

"She's bored," said Max.

"Aren't you?" Kylie asked, blood burning. Of course he was. A career fireman forcibly retired due to his age. She knew he'd rather be at the firehouse, but he'd made a pest of himself and they'd restricted his visits. Now he hung out at Boone's, Kerri's and Keystone's.

"If you're bored," said J.J., "get a hobby. Don't mess with history."

"She tried to get me to drop my trousers," Max told the ten or so bystanders.

They snickered and whistled.

Kylie flushed head to toe. "No, I didn't! I just...I..."

"Deputy," said Jack.

"Sir?"

"Move the spectators along."

"Will do," he said, and he did.

That's when she noticed the dog. A midsize pooch with big sad eyes—sort of like Travis's. Instead of leaving with the gawkers, the dog leaned into Jack. "Who's that?" she asked.

"Shy," he said.

"Yours?"

"No." He gestured to Travis. "Who's that?"

"Travis Martin." She knew he didn't know Travis. The Martins had moved to Eden long after Jack had moved to New York. But she didn't offer further information. Actually, aside from the fact that Travis worked at Hank's Hardware, was a widower and wore a ten-and-a-half shoe, she didn't have much information to offer.

"Mr. Martin," he called. "Stop what you're doing and join us."

Travis abandoned his post, set aside his brush and wiped his hands on a rag.

"I'm Jack Reynolds."

"The new chief of police." Travis nodded. "Welcome to Eden."

"Jack's a native," Ray said.

"I used to make him chocolate Cokes when he was a kid," J.J. said.

Travis just nodded.

Kylie shifted as the two men studied each other. She sensed some tension, which was weird. They'd never met before today. "I'm doing some renovations," Kylie said, wanting Jack to vamoose. "I'm allowed."

"No, she isn't," J.J. said.

"My family owns this business."

"Doesn't matter," said Keystone. "It's part of a historical block."

"You're allowed to maintain the look of your store-front," J.J said. "But you can't alter it. Not drastically. You have to get a permit for that."

"You're kidding." She'd never heard of that. Then again, her family had never tried painting the storefront anything other than what it had been before. *Tradition.*

Jack folded his arms over his chest, studied the store-fronts. "Deputy?"

"Anything to do with the building's exterior is governed by the Historic Preservation Society," Ziffel said. "She needs approval from them *and* the town zoning board."

"Told you," said J.J.

Kylie narrowed her eyes. "*That's* mature."

"Kylie," Jack said.

"Yes?"

"Get a permit."

J.J. and Keystone chuckled.

Max, the contrary cuss, said, "Ha."

Kylie wanted to smack them all. She envisioned knocking Jack off his black utility boots with a side kick. But if she'd learned anything from her two years of jujitsu, it was self-discipline. She clenched her fists at her side and took a cleansing breath. It didn't help.

Deputy Ziffel cautioned the men about disturbing the peace and herded them back to their respective stores. The mutt stayed put.

Jack glanced at the paint cans lined alongside the building, then focused on Travis. "Got any white paint?"

"I could get some."

"Cover up your handy work until Kylie gets a permit."

Travis didn't say anything. He just left. To get some white paint, she presumed.

Dang.

"How do you know that guy?" Jack asked.

How do you know that dog? "He works at the hard-ware store."

"What's he doing here?"

"Working for me."

Jack squinted at the trim. "Pink?"

"Moroccan spice."

"Looks pink."

Kylie just smiled. Actually, it was a muted tone compared to what she'd first had in mind.

Jack met her gaze. He didn't smile back. "You want to piss off your brother? Get a permit."

"You said that already." Kylie couldn't say what set her off, specifically. She was miffed about a lot of things. Not knowing about the permit, for one. Travis, for two. She'd felt some sort of bond with the man. He'd taken vacation time for her, committed to her cause. Then, at the first sign of trouble, he'd thrown in the brush. Okay, so Jack was the law and Travis was a law-abiding citizen. Still, she felt deserted and disappointed. Much as she had with Faye.

"I will act out of the ordinary in order to attract and promote change. Change is exciting. Change is good."

She turned on her rubber heels and commandeered Travis's brush. She eyeballed the stern-faced chief and, ignoring the skip in her pulse, dipped her weapon in Moroccan Spice.

"Don't do it," Jack warned.

"Don't worry," Ziffel said as he returned to the scene of the almost crime. "Kylie's a sensible girl."

It was the exact wrong thing to say. She climbed the ladder, gripping the rungs with one hand, holding the paint-slathered brush with the other.

"Used to be modest, too," she heard Ziffel say. "Although her undies ain't what I'd call sexy."

Kylie froze two rungs from the top. "Are you looking up my skirt, Ed Ziffel?" She glared down. "You are!" And so was Jack.

He grinned. "Boxers?"

"They were the only clean shorts I had!" Any further explanation was silenced when she misstepped. She grabbed the ladder with both hands, bobbled the brush. Her heart pounded in her ears, muffling Ziffel's curse.

She glanced down and saw the slash and dribbles of pink—er, Moroccan Spice—on the deputy's dark blue uniform. The brush had bounced off his shoulder and landed on the sidewalk. "Sorry," she squeaked as the paint-splattered cement zoomed up to her face in some weird 3-D movie illusion, then slammed back down to earth.

"You shook things up," said Jack, sounding half amused, half pissed. "Happy now?"

"Not really."

"Climb down."

She would if she could, but her legs wouldn't move.

"Now."

She broke out in a sweat, her vision blurred. She cursed the cosmos—the liquor kind—and her hangover. Hugging the ladder tight, she focused straight ahead. Which put her at eye-level to the sign with her family's motto: *Practical shoes for practical people.*

"Not for long," she whispered through clenched teeth.

"I won't ask twice," Jack said.

"New crowd gathering," Ziffel muttered, then switched to an authoritative tone. "Move along, people. Nothing to see."

She tensed when the ladder creaked under more weight. She felt a couple of soft bounces, then a hard body climbing up behind her. Every nerve in her body pulsed. She told herself it was because she'd had a fright. Not because Jack's front was plastered to her back.

Pursuing an intimate relationship would only end in heartache.

"When did you get so damned stubborn?" Jack said close to her ear.

No way was she going to admit to a hangover-induced dizzy spell. Aside from all the nerve pulsing, she felt slightly better. Probably because she was focused on the feel and smell of Jack and not the long drop down. She relaxed against him, and next thing she knew she'd been plucked from the ladder. Her knees buckled when her boots hit the sidewalk, but she didn't crumple due to Jack's hold on her waist.

"You can go, Ziffel," he said. "Drop your shirt at the cleaners and be sure to send Miss McGraw the bill."

"Hey," she complained. But Ziffel was already stalking off and Jack was hauling her inside McGraw's. She pried at his hands. "Stop manhandling me."

He let her go, but backed her up against the wall in between the gumball machine and the cashier counter.

She didn't like being bullied. She especially didn't like the erotic thrill she got when he braced his hands on the wall and fenced her in. Or the heat between her thighs when he leaned close. Or the fluttery feeling in her stomach when his gaze slid over her mouth.

"Find a new hiding place for your spare key, Tiger."

What?

Then she flashed on the night before. Jack driving her home. Lost purse. Locked door.

Oops.

He made eye contact and her stomach flipped. Ice-blue eyes on fire.

Yikes.

"Under the doormat? Why don't you leave the door open and a plate of cookies on the table for the burglars and rapists?"

His sarcasm grated. "Don't you think you're being a little dramatic, *Chief* Reynolds?"

"Another thing. Hire someone to install motion-detector lighting and think about an alarm system. You live in the fu—" he glanced away and back "—frickin' middle of nowhere."

Kylie scrunched her brow. "Is this a lecture on home security? Is my trailer even in your jurisdiction? I'm pretty sure I'm suppose to call the county police if I need help, which I won't, since nothing ever happens in the *frickin' middle of nowhere.*"

BETH CIOTTA   77

"You left your purse at Boone's last night."

Did he just skate over her rant? "So?"

"I assume you keep your drivers license in your wallet."

Uh-oh.

"It's unlawful to operate a motor vehicle without proof of license."

Well, duh. "So lock me up."

He quirked a humorless smile. "No."

"Then let me go."

He didn't budge. "What's with the motorcycle?"

"This conversation is giving me whiplash."

"What's the projected repair time on your car?"

"A week or so, depending on when the part comes in. Not that it's any of your business."

"Are you aware of the statistics on motorcycle accidents?"

"What are you? Standing in for my brother?"

"Someone has to look out for you. You've gone a little loopy, hon."

"Loopy?"

Breathe, Kylie, breathe.

No. Don't breathe. Blow!

"Just because I want to redecorate the store? Just because I own a motorcycle? Or is it my flower-power boots? You lived in New York City. Surely you've seen more outrageous shoes than these. Stop trying to squash my spirit, Jack Reynolds!"

Her skin burned with fury...or something...when his gaze dropped to her boots and slowly skimmed up her bare legs, over her funky attire, settling at long last on her mouth. Oh, *God*. Was he going to *kiss* her?

Her brain and body sizzled with dread and hope. What if she felt something this time? What if he reignited her crush, full flame? Then she'd be doomed to be alone *forever*, because no other man would ever measure up!

"I wouldn't dream of squashing your spirit, Tiger. Long as you don't break the law." He pushed off the wall, severing the anticipation, the tension.

Relief and disappointment warred, making Kylie snap. "You're not the boss of me!"

Doh! Was it any wonder he still thought of her as Spenser's kid sister?

This time his smile was downright cocky. He tugged at the brim of his EPD cap. "Where the law is concerned, yeah, I sort of am."

Out of the corner of her eye, she saw the pointy-ear dog that wasn't Jack's peek out from under a chair and follow him outside. Had she been in here the entire time?

Travis walked in, carrying gallons of paint and a roll of tarp. Had he been out there the entire time? Listening?

Kylie flushed and smoothed her disheveled hair.

He flashed a sympathetic look. "I'll start on the interior. You get the permit."

And just like that, she didn't feel so alone in her quest for adventure.

CHAPTER NINE

TRAVIS PULLED INTO HIS driveway and cut the engine. He glanced at his luminous watch—12:05 a.m. He rubbed his hands over his weary face. He was exhausted.

Mentally.

Emotionally and physically.

He sat in the dark, not wanting to go inside. Not wanting to go to sleep. When he slept, he dreamed of another life. His old life. It made him melancholy. It made him angry.

At least when Mona had been alive he'd had someone to confide in. She had similar dreams. Sometimes they'd lie in the dark and talk about the past. Friends. Family.

Enemies.

Enemies were the reason they couldn't be with friends and family.

It was why they ate jarred sauce and American cheese. Why he drank beer instead of Chianti. Why he spoke with a nasally twang instead of his native Philly accent. Why he dressed in jeans and flannel shirts instead of Armani suits. He hated that he'd attended Mona's funeral wearing cheap oxfords. She deserved better. But if he'd worn the Ferragamo slip-ons he kept hidden away, she would've rolled over in her cheap-ass coffin. God rest her soul.

Travis gripped the steering wheel and endured a fresh wave of grief. Mona's suffering had started long before the cancer. He'd never forgiven himself. He'd tried to make it right, though. He'd sacrificed everything to make it right.

Today, he'd taken another step in that direction. While

painting the walls of Kylie's store and listening to her lovingly brag and gripe about her family, he couldn't help thinking about the way Mona would reminisce about her family. Did the Vespas reminisce about her? Had they mourned her death? Had her brother gotten the letter he'd sent? Circumstances prohibited him from contacting them directly. But he'd followed procedure. He'd done the right thing. He realized in the midst of Kylie's ramblings that he'd been hoping to hear back from someone, anyone from their past. The silence made him wonder. Had his letter gone missing?

Don't do anything stupid.

He should've called WITSEC, but he was still pissed by his new contact's lack of response to Mona's death. The U.S. marshal/inspector originally assigned to them had been transferred, which made Travis feel even more isolated. At least he and Burton had a history. He'd never even met his replacement face-to-face. Obviously, Travis Martin was no longer a priority.

Feeding off Kylie McGraw's determination to buck the system, he'd taken a break and made a quick trip to the library. He'd borrowed a computer terminal, created a bogus account and sent an e-mail. He'd taken more risks in this one day than every day of the last several years combined. He felt anxious. He felt empowered.

He squinted through the windshield, expecting the new chief of police to appear out of the shadows. He'd been anticipating a visit from the man all night. No dice. Either Reynolds was letting him stew or he hadn't yet read the file. One thing was certain, he'd riled the cop's interest. He'd seen it in his eyes.

"This is bad," he could hear Mona say. But Travis barely cared.

Don't do anything stupid.

Too late.

If not for today, he probably could've avoided contact with the new chief of police for a good long while. Maybe forever. He didn't know Jack Reynolds, but he knew he wasn't a rube like Ben Curtis. A former NYPD detective, Reynolds had experience with men like Travis. Or at least the man he used to be. The question was, would he allow Travis to exist as he had for the past seven years? Or would he make waves?

If only he hadn't offered his services to Kylie. But when she'd shown him those pictures and when he'd expanded on her vision, he'd gotten that old rush. He was born to create, not to corrupt. Certainly not to kill. He was the defective son, the troublesome brother. A disappointment to the family. He'd tried to conform. He *had* conformed. As had been expected of him, he'd married a nice Italian girl. Instead of going into interior design, he'd become a lawyer, the mouthpiece for the family business. Able to finesse his way around the stickiest legal issues, those in his circle had dubbed him the Artful Dodger. He'd been respected, revered even. But then he'd broken with convention. That one indiscretion had instigated a bloodbath.

The memory of those final days still sickened him. Their reaction. His retaliation. Vengeance went both ways. He had a lot of regrets, but there was no way to mend that bridge. He couldn't go back. But, dammit, he was sick of Travis Martin.

He reached across the seat and snatched the brown paper bag filled with his late-night booty. Red wine, provolone cheese and pepperoni. Three of the Artful Dodger's culinary favorites.

CHAPTER TEN

JACK AWOKE AT 3:15 A.M. with a hard-on. He'd been dreaming about Kylie. Kissing Kylie. Stroking Kylie. Rolling in the sheets with Kylie. He'd never had a woman get under his skin so fast. She wasn't even his type. Not that he hadn't sampled a variety of women, but he had a definite weakness for fair-haired women in distress. Something he'd discovered when he'd gone to a marriage counselor with Amanda. A fascination rooted in childhood. When he was twelve, he saw Alfred Hitchcock's *Vertigo* and fell in love with Kim Novak, or rather the character she portrayed in the film. He not only lusted after her, he wanted to rescue her. Since then, he'd always gravitated toward curvy, classic beauties. Most of them blond. All of them needy.

Kylie had a petite, athletic build. She had dark, quirky features and a modest sense of style—usually. She ran a business and looked after her mom and grandma. She didn't *need* a man, although he was surprised no man had snatched her up. Unless the men of Eden were scared off by her competence and stubborn streak. She'd proved herself a handful today. He couldn't say what fired him up most—her contrary spirit, her shapely legs, the striped boxer shorts or that sassy mouth. Horny and pissed, he'd backed her against the wall.

He'd wanted to shake her.

He'd wanted to kiss her.

Neither action seemed prudent.

So he'd lectured. Home security. Motorcycle safety. He'd

pissed her off. He didn't feel bad about that. She'd pissed him off when she'd climbed that ladder. Something told him they'd knock heads again. Fine. If they kept pissing each other off, maybe the attraction would fizzle. The "kid" barrier was history. The face that intrigued him, the body that tempted him, belonged to a thirty-two-year-old woman.

Except she's still Spenser's sister. She's a nice girl and you're a cynical bastard.

Getting physical with Kylie would be disastrous. He could list a dozen reasons.

Maybe he *should* list the reasons. Right now. Mentally. Like counting sheep.

It was that or a cold shower.

Christ.

He rolled over and got a face full of fur. Thanks to the vet, at least Shy didn't smell bad. "What are you doing up here?"

The dog groaned and curled into a tighter ball. At least someone was getting a good night's sleep.

Jack thought about nudging Shy off his bed, but he didn't have the heart. She'd probably spent the last month sleeping in the woods or in a random barn or shed. He'd walked her around town today. No one recognized her. He dropped her at the vet for an examination. Aside from being malnourished and flea-bitten, she was healthy. For her gas, Dr. Price had suggested a high-quality pet food. No dairy products or table scraps. Jack had purchased a small bag of the recommended dry food. Enough to last until he found her a home. To Shy's dismay, she'd been shampooed, deloused and groomed. A flyer featuring her picture now hung on the animal hospital's bulletin board: *Free to a good home.*

Jack thought about his niece. He wondered if she liked dogs. Yeah, *that* would go over well with his prissy, snobby sister.

Shy barked a split second before he heard the sharp knock on the front door. He glanced at his clock as he swung out of bed—3:25 a.m.

He pulled on jeans and a T-shirt. He braced for something bad. People don't drop by in the middle of the night with good news. He should know. He'd paid many a nocturnal visit while working Homicide.

After motioning Shy to stay, he tucked his Glock in the back of his waistband and navigated the stairs in the dark. He peeked through the living room curtains. What the hell? His sister—the woman who'd been avoiding him for days—stood on the front stoop, balancing a little girl, his niece, on one hip and a bulging backpack on her shoulder.

Alarmed, he switched on a light and opened the door.

"Sorry to wake you," Jessie snapped before he could ask *what's wrong?*

"No problem." He quickly surmised she hadn't been in a car accident or house fire. No blood, no bruises, no burns. Maddie looked okay, too. Oddly wide awake for the middle of the night, but fine. He focused back on his sister. She looked frazzled. Pale and fidgety. No makeup. Lopsided ponytail and ill-fitting clothes. This woman didn't look anything like his confident, pageant queen, fashion-conscious sister. This woman had fled home in the middle of the night in a panic. Had the Cheating Bastard shown up? Called? Harassed her? Scared her? He didn't want to ask in front of the kid.

"We couldn't sleep," Jessie said.

"Our house is sad," Maddie said in a small voice.

Chest tight, Jack relieved his sister of the weighty backpack. "Come in."

"Are you my uncle Jack?" Maddie asked as they moved into the sparsely furnished living room.

"Sure am, sweet pea." He hated that she had to ask. Hated that he'd allowed work and pride to interfere with family.

"Where's your badge?"

"Upstairs."

Her eyes twinkled. "Can I see it?"

"Not now, Madeline." Jessie set her daughter on the couch. Jack set the backpack on his recliner. He noted the little girl's pink pajamas, her bunny slippers and the colorful bear clutched to her chest. He recognized that bear. He'd sent her that stuffed animal as a Christmas gift two years earlier. Jessie and Frank had made it clear he was unwelcome in their home, their lives. Naturally, he thought they'd deprived Maddie of the gifts he'd sent over the years. Jessie had intimated as such. It warmed him to learn otherwise.

Throat thick, he smiled even though he knew something was wrong. "Can I get you ladies, anything? Milk and cookies?"

Maddie glanced at her mom, at Jack. "We don't eat cookies."

"Why not?"

"Too fattening."

That was his sister talking. A woman—thanks to years on the pageant circuit—obsessed with body image. No five-year-old should be worrying about her weight unless she was obese, which Maddie wasn't. She was a skinny little thing with long black hair and big brown eyes.

"Well, I eat cookies," Jack said, cursing himself for not being a better uncle, or for that matter, a better brother. "And I could use a late-night snack."

He wondered if Jessie ever snacked. Hell, he wondered if she ate, period. He'd have to refrain from force-feeding her an entire bag of Fig Newtons. She looked rail thin in her baggy jeans and shapeless shirt. She'd always been thin, but this was troubling.

He smoothed a hand over Maddie's silky hair. "I need your mom's help in the kitchen. We won't be long. Do you want to lie down?"

"Can't sleep." Maddie hugged the bear tighter—a chubby teddy he'd stuffed himself at one of those Build-A-Bear stores. Patches looked worn and loved, and suddenly he didn't feel like the worst uncle in the world, just a lame one.

"Do you have a DVD player?" Jessie asked.

He nodded.

She unzipped the front pocket of the cartoon backpack they'd brought. "Here." She passed him a DVD. A Disney flick.

Jack put the disk in his player and fired up the movie without comment. He wanted Jessie in the kitchen. He wanted answers.

"Who's that?" asked Maddie.

Jack turned and saw the pointy-eared mutt sitting at the bottom of the stairs. So much for following orders. "That's Shy."

Mother and daughter spoke at the same time.

"Does she bite?"

"Is she yours?"

"No and no. We'll be right back," he said to Maddie, while motioning Jessie to follow.

Once inside the kitchen, he spoke frankly. "What's wrong?"

"Nothing I can't fix. But I can't do it tonight." She tucked her hands under her armpits and paced. "I feel like I'm coming out of my skin. I hate this."

So did Jack. Until he knew what was wrong, he couldn't fix it. If he pressed too hard, too fast, she might bolt. Considering they'd been estranged for years, Jessie being here like this was a breakthrough. He didn't want to screw it up. "How about some hot tea?"

"How about something stronger?"

Given his recent battle with booze, he hadn't stocked the house with hard liquor. "All I've got is beer."

"I'll take it."

As far as he knew, she never drank anything other than wine spritzers. Damn, he itched to press. *What's wrong?* Instead he got her a beer and poured a glass of milk for his niece.

Jessie paced and chugged. "I wouldn't be here if I had any other choice."

"That's flattering," he said while loading a plate with cookies.

"Look. I know we've never been on great terms. As kids or adults," she said in a tight, brittle voice. "But I...we... Madeline and me...need a place to spend the night."

He should have said *okay*. Plain and simple. But there was nothing simple about their relationship. And he'd be damned if he'd let her freeze him out in his own house. "Why? Did Frank show up? Does he want to move back in?"

"No."

"Did he call? Threaten you?"

"I haven't talked to Frank in two weeks."

"He calls to speak with his daughter, right?"

She didn't answer.

Jack looked over his shoulder. "You're kidding."

She wouldn't meet his gaze. "Frank never wanted... Madeline was..."

An accident? Unexpected? So what? Just when he thought his opinion of his brother-in-law couldn't sink any lower. "You can stay here as long as you like, Jessie."

"I don't like it at all," she said, still pacing, still drinking. "But I can't impose on friends and I can't afford the Orchard House."

Jack blew over the personal jab and focused on the financial. "Are you telling me that fu—" He glanced toward the sound of cartoon voices and cheery music. "That Frank's not supporting you?"

"I don't want his money. I don't want anything to do with him or anything that belonged to him—including the house. We'll be fine. Madeline and me. I just want...I need to make my own way. And I will. Starting tomorrow. I mean, later today."

Jack worked his jaw. She'd shut him out of her life for years. Avoided him like the plague since he'd returned home. He couldn't help himself. He had to push. "What happened between fuck-off and showing up on my doorstep, Jessie? It had to be damned bad for you to come to me, in the middle of the night, no less."

"I don't want to talk about it. I...I can't."

He noted the crack in her voice, the trembling of her hands. "Okay."

"Please don't grill me."

"Fine."

"Or think you have to save me."

"You want to make it on your own."

She stopped in her tracks. "You don't think I can?"

"Didn't say that."

"Just because I didn't finish college or devote my life to some noble cause..." She trailed off and looked for a place to ditch the beer. She looked embarrassed, upset and exhausted.

"Why don't we revisit this discussion after some shut-eye?" Jack relieved her of the empty bottle, then grabbed the milk and cookies. "You keep Maddie company while I change my sheets."

"I wish you wouldn't call her that. Nicknames are...I don't know."

"Humanizing?"

"Undignified."

"Jessie is undignified?"

"My name is Jessica. Jessica Lynn."

"Sounds stuffy," said Jack.

"To you, maybe. But it's my given name and I'm proud of it."

"Okay."

"So you'll call me Jessica? And Madeline, Madeline?"

"Probably not."

She blew out a frustrated breath. "Why do you have to be so headstrong?"

He looked at her and smiled. "Runs in the family."

She opened her mouth, closed it. After a thoughtful pause, she changed the subject. "Why do you have to change your sheets?"

"No furniture in the other two bedrooms yet," he explained. "You and Maddie take my bed. I'll take the couch." Before she could argue, he slipped into the living room. His niece was fast asleep. So was Shy. They were curled up side by side—one hand, one paw on the stuffed bear.

Jessie groaned. "I hope she doesn't get attached to that dog."

Jack hoped the exact opposite.

CHAPTER ELEVEN

KYLIE WOKE UP EXHAUSTED. Three hours of sleep will do that to you. It wasn't even three restful hours. Bleary-eyed, she schlepped to the shower. Her mind still churned on the things that had plagued her the night before.

She fretted over her upcoming appointment with Eden's Historic Preservation Society, otherwise known as the HPS. She hated that she hadn't been able to get that over with yesterday. Nope. They'd insisted she wait until their scheduled weekly meeting. Thank goodness that was today. The suspense, the delay, was killing her. Although, it wasn't like her renovation was on hold. Travis had made tremendous, no, *amazing* progress on the interior. He'd worked tirelessly. And, although he hadn't been keen on her helping to paint the walls, he did coach her in redecorating the chairs she already owned instead of purchasing new ones. She appreciated the cost-saving suggestion and his creative tips. Who knew a hardware guy could be so artsy? She also admired his energy. She'd pooped out around 6:00 p.m., plus she wanted to get home before dark. Travis had stayed on. He'd said he was in a groove. She suspected he was avoiding his lonely house.

Kylie scratched shampoo through her hair, feeling a little lonely herself. She blamed the chief of police. Celibacy was a lot easier when you weren't battling desire. Once she'd finally drifted off last night, she'd dreamed about Jack pinning her against a wall. Jack undressing her with his eyes, his hands. Jack touching her, kissing her.

In McGraw's Shoe Store.

Her family's place of business.

She'd been squirming with thigh-quaking lust, begging the hunky lawman to boink her senseless when suddenly she'd spotted her dad. Not for real. But in the dream. Unfortunately it had been a lucid dream. So in addition to experiencing erotic thrills compliments of Jack, she also sensed Dewy McGraw's shock and dismay. Kylie had spent her entire life trying to win her dad's approval. Now he was gone and she was still proving a disappointment.

She rinsed the herbal-scented suds from her hair, pondering the relevance of that weird dream. It had to run deeper than her dad frowning on public displays of sex.

At least he hadn't materialized in her second dream. Her mortification would've been off the charts. She'd gotten down and dirty with Jack in a jail cell. Handcuffs were involved. Just thinking about the things he'd done to her made Kylie ache.

"Crushing on Jack is stupid," she told herself as she cranked the cold water. "He's not attracted to you. If he was, he would have kissed you in the store. He didn't even flirt."

She continued to talk herself out of the attraction as she soaped her body. Only, her mind kept flashing on the handcuffs, iron bars and lots of naked flesh. Suddenly she was touching herself everywhere Jack had touched her. Or at least everywhere her subconscious wanted him to touch her. The cold water pelting her body did little to cool the heat between her legs. Frustrated, she nabbed the handheld shower massage, turned the dial and directed the fast and hard pulsating stream to where she ached most. She exploded with a quaking orgasm in two seconds flat.

Breathless, she wilted against the wall of the cramped stall. Seconds later, her heart settled in her chest, and instead of satisfied, she felt a twinge of guilt and regret.

"Why can't I make you come like that?" Bobby had once asked after he'd urged her to pleasure herself.

She didn't know, and it frustrated her that it bothered

him so much. It's not like she didn't enjoy sex with him. In fact, she went out of her way to please him. It made her feel good when she drove him over the edge. Why couldn't that be enough?

She'd assured him that it wasn't his fault. *"I've only been with two other men and I didn't have orgasms then, either."* That didn't make him feel better. In fact, two weeks later he left on a travel assignment and never came back. She didn't want to believe it was because she was wired wrong, so she convinced herself, and everyone else, he'd simply gotten cold feet.

In a way, she wished she was promiscuous. Maybe she'd benefit from more experience.

Unfortunately, Kylie had never been able to wrap her mind around sex without an emotional attachment. If she could, she would've indulged in casual affairs in search of a skilled lover with the magic touch. A lover who'd show her the orgasmic stars.

In her dreams, Jack was that man. She hated that she couldn't wipe those erotic sensations and images from her mind. She hated that she was contemplating risking her heart in order to fulfill a primitive yearning. Maybe she wasn't wired wrong. Maybe she just hadn't been with the right man. Maybe she could handle a fling with Jack because she *was* emotionally attached to him. Maybe if she knew going in that it wouldn't be forever.

"Wow," she said as she toweled off. "Given the proper motivation, a girl can talk herself into anything."

Thoughtful, Kylie swiped her hand over the steamy mirror and frowned at her reflection. "When Jack looks at you, he sees Spenser's kid sister." She hated that, too. "Maybe it's because you haven't updated your look in, well, *ever.* Maybe it's because he's used to slick city chicks and you look like a frumpy bumpkin."

Inspiration struck. Or rather, an intense urge to shake things up.

She stared into the mirror, tried to envision a new haircut and color. She couldn't.

"But Faye could."

They'd never gotten that private moment yesterday. Faye had blown back into the hardware store, saying she had things to do at Orchard House, then she'd blown back out. The tension had been worse than before. At a loss, Kylie had decided to give her friend space and time.

That meant trusting her makeover to Petunia, the owner and primary stylist at the local beauty shop. Most of the woman's clients walked out with a perm or last year's hot celebrity cut. Seeing as Kylie wasn't big on poodles or Posh, visiting a big-city stylist might be a safer bet. Except, she couldn't afford the long drive. Couldn't afford missing her meeting with the HPS. Plus, she probably couldn't get an appointment for today, anyway, and she wanted a makeover *now*. She'd just have to be firm about what she didn't want and hope for the best.

Change is exciting. Change is good.

"Right."

Minutes later, dressed in jeans, a long-sleeved cream tee and orange high-top sneakers with hot pink laces, Kylie made an appointment with destiny, aka Petunia of Petunia's Hairdoodles.

OPERATING ON LITTLE SLEEP and no coffee, Jack worked a crick from his neck as he drove into town. He'd dressed quickly and split without breakfast, hesitant to wake his guests. He figured they needed the rest, even though it meant Maddie missing another day of kindergarten. Apparently, she'd skipped the day before, claiming a tummy ache. But when tucking her into Jack's bed, Jessie had confessed that it wasn't Maddie's stomach that hurt, but her feelings. Kids were making fun of her, calling her names. This bothered Jack, but, damn, maybe the kid would fare better if Jessie focused on inner strength as opposed to outer beauty.

Then again, what the hell did he know about kids.

Except that they liked dogs.

He'd contemplated leaving Shy at home, more time to bond with his niece, less irritation at the stationhouse. But Jessie had indicated she had plans today. Wherever she went, she'd take Maddie. Which would leave Shy alone. Shy who'd gotten into the trash that morning and eaten a paper towel laced with cookie crumbs.

So, once again, the dog rode shotgun.

This time Jack rolled down the window so Shy wouldn't slobber on it while looking at the passing scenery. The grooming had resulted in less shedding, and the dry food had cured her stink. Things were looking up.

Jack cranked the classic rock station, anticipated Kerri's featured pastry and ticked off a mental to-do list. Ten minutes later, he turned on to Main Street. Traffic was moderate and flowing. No gridlock. No blaring horns. The sidewalks in NYC would have been teeming, even at this early hour. He noted three pedestrians—total. All was calm. Quiet. *Routine.* Kylie would hate it.

As he neared McGraw's Shoe Store, he looked for her motorcycle. Even though she'd closed the store for renovations, he imagined she'd show early in order to put in a full day. According to Ziffel, who'd heard it from Boone, who'd heard it from Stan, who'd heard it from Faye— Kylie and her lone hired hand were handling the bulk of the work, and Kylie wanted to reopen in time for the Apple Festival. They'd need to pull long hours to make her goal. But instead of a sleek silver motorcycle, he spied a beat-up blue pickup.

Jack pulled to the opposite curb and watched as Travis Martin hefted a box of supplies from the bed of his Chevy, then let himself inside McGraw's. Kylie must've entrusted the man with a key. *Bad move, Tiger.* Something about Martin bothered him. Just because he had a clean record— and Jack had checked—didn't mean he was harmless.

Jack sat tight, observed. Not that there was anything to

see. Kylie or Travis, or both, had draped a black tarp over the front windows, concealing whatever changes they were making inside. Given Kylie's gripe with the ordinary, Jack envisioned pink walls, zebra-cushioned seats and displays featuring impractical shoes. Or maybe practical shoes with a playful twist. Like her flowered work boots.

He wondered if he should alert Spenser. Not because the store was in his name—Spenser had never cared about shoes—but because Kylie's actions affected her mom and grandma, too. If she ran the business into the ground, they'd all suffer. On the other hand, who knew? Maybe she'd breathe new life into the old business.

"Maybe I should wait and see how she fares with the HPS."

Shy barked.

"Right."

Just then Kylie roared by and parked her bike behind the Chevy. The first thing he noticed, aside from her cute ass, was her modest clothing. Denim jacket, jeans. Nothing scandalous. Nothing whimsical. Although, wait, were those sneakers orange? Uncommon, but not as unique as the flowered combat boots. Had she already ditched the idea of stirring things up by dressing out of the ordinary?

Too bad. The boots had been cute, but it was the short skirt he missed. And the boxers. They shouldn't have been sexy, but they were. Mostly because he'd speculated on the panties beneath the boxers. Bikini? Thong? Or maybe there were no panties. Maybe she'd gone commando. He wondered if those thoughts had crossed Ziffel's mind. Not that he was jealous—hell, no—just protective of his friend's sister.

As he watched her dismount the bike, his thoughts turned to another man. What if she'd decided to shake things up by fooling around with the hardware guy? Or maybe Martin sensed she was vulnerable and intended to seduce her. Not that it was Jack's business.

Damn.

If he sat here any longer, he'd end up inside McGraw's. "Under what pretense, jackass?"

"Arrff!"

"Right." Better to move on. Put his Aspen in gear and drive directly to the station house. Instead, he opened his door and jerked a thumb at Shy. "Let's roll."

CHAPTER TWELVE

KYLIE WAS LOST IN THOUGHT as she pulled off her bike helmet and looped the chin strap over the handlebars. Even though the store would be closed for business, she'd planned a full day. First, she'd put in time with the renovations. Then she'd hit Petunia's for her hair makeover. This afternoon she'd plead her case with the Historic Preservation Society. At some point today, she'd at least *try* to get in touch with Spenser. On the ride into town the thought occurred that *not* informing him about the renovations wasn't so much daring as cowardly. If he balked, she'd just have to convince him that change was good. If she could convince the stuffy HPS, she could convince her adventurous brother.

She recited her argument in her head for the umpteenth time. She gripped the doorknob of McGraw's just as someone said her name. That *someone* was Jack. *Drat,* she thought as she turned to face the man of her dreams. She'd hoped to avoid running into him until *after* her meeting with the HPS. The man mucked up her concentration. Although, she hadn't run into him. He'd sought her out— along with the dog that wasn't his.

Flashing back on their last confrontation, she hiked a brow. "Want to see my driver's license?"

"I'd like to buy you a cup of coffee."

Kylie's heart fluttered, which was nuts. It's not like he was asking her out for drinks and dinner. This was…she didn't know what it was. She furrowed her brow. "You made that same offer yesterday."

"Is that a 'no'?"

"It's a 'why'."

"I need to talk to you."

Her frown deepened. "What did I do now?"

His lip twitched. "Nothing. As far as I know." He sobered then. "It's about my sister."

"Jessica Lynn?"

"Her life's in turmoil, and since we've been on the outs, I don't know specifics."

"It's not like she confides in me." Kylie tried to wrap her mind around this unexpected conversation. "We don't even run in the same circles."

"But you both live in Eden and this town feeds on gossip. I'm sure you've heard talk."

She'd heard talk, all right. Mostly about Jessica Lynn's husband, Frank Cortez. It wasn't pretty. "You won't like it."

"Better than being in the dark."

He sounded so earnest, looked so sincere, and just the teensiest bit desperate. Never in a million years would she have expected Jack Reynolds—super-man, super-cop—to come to her for help. "Why me? You could ask Deputy Ziffel, or Boone or—"

"Because I know you'll keep whatever's said between us private. Because if you needed help with Spenser, I'd have your back."

Well, dang. How was she supposed to say no to that? Especially since just yesterday she'd declared them friends. It's just that this talk struck her as awfully intimate and she was trying very hard not to fall for Jack. *Again*. Lust was one thing. Love…she didn't want to think about it.

She covered her heart, a silly protective gesture. She glanced at the store, wishing Travis would stick his head out and call her inside, any excuse for a getaway.

"Heard Travis Martin is a competent, hard worker," Jack said, as if reading her thoughts. "I'm sure he can do without you for a half hour."

Dang.

"Kerri's Confections is a short walk away."

"Not Kerri's," Kylie blurted. "First, no dogs allowed." She glanced down at the mutt sitting quietly at Jack's side. "Are you sure she's not yours? She seems awfully attached."

"She attaches herself to whoever offers food and affection."

Meaning Jack must dote on her. Kylie smiled at that. "Second," she said, keeping the conversation on track, "do you know how busy Kerri's place is in the morning? How many ears would strain in our direction? If you don't want Jessica Lynn to know we were talking about her, we should go somewhere private." *Just not too private.* "Although I could use a cup of tea." *And a moment to gather my wits.*

She'd known Jack all her life, but she'd never had a private, serious discussion with him regarding family or anything else for that matter. Her birthday exchange didn't count—she'd been drunk. Yesterday's heated exchange in McGraw's didn't count—he'd been lecturing. Even the many-moons-ago, never-to-be-mentioned exchange didn't count because they'd both been walking on eggshells.

Nope. This was a first. It felt weird and important. He wanted her help and she didn't want to let him down.

"What about one of the park benches near City Hall?" Jack asked.

The Appleseed Memorial. A beautified area maintained by the Garden Club. Not too private, but private enough on a weekday morning. Kylie nodded.

"I'll get the tea and coffee," Jack said. "You take Shy. I'll meet you both there in five."

Five minutes to gather her wits. Great.

Not willing to waste a second, she reached into her backpack and snagged a peanut butter cookie from her snack pack. She broke off a piece and offered it to Shy.

"The vet said not to feed her people food," said Jack.

"Do you want her to follow me or not?" But it wasn't the cookie Shy seemed as fond of, as the attention Kylie paid her with a hug and a kind stroke. "She's awfully sweet."

"Like you."

Kylie frowned into Shy's fur. Jack thought she was *sweet?* If only he was privy to her erotic dreams. Cheeks burning, she straightened and headed for the park. "Come on, Shy!"

Thank God, the dog followed.

Thank God, Jack headed for Kerri's.

Four minutes to gather her wits.

USING HIS SISTER AS AN excuse to steal time with Kylie had been spontaneous and inspired. Jack sincerely wanted insight into Jessie's situation. And he honestly did believe he could count on Kylie to share what she'd heard without embellishing and keep their discussion on the QT. His sister wouldn't appreciate his digging, but since she wasn't forthcoming, he didn't have a choice. He'd be damned if he'd sit by while she was in an emotional tailspin.

Jack stepped up to the counter of Kerri's Confections, and just like the day before, Kerri Waldo herself insisted on taking his order. She was young, pretty, flirtatious and the Goddess of Baked Goods. Normally, he would've considered asking her out, but he was preoccupied with three other women just now—one of them waiting a mere block away.

"Are these for you and Deputy Ziffel?" Kerri asked sweetly as she bagged the beverages and pastries. Even though she was an East Coast transplant, she played the small-town-where-everybody-knows-everyone's-business game as if she were, what they called in Eden, a lifer.

"No," he said honestly. "I'm treating a friend to breakfast." He swore the noise level dipped, sensed the café's patrons leaning his way.

"Anyone I know?" Kerri asked with a bright smile.

Jack smiled back. "I'm sure you do. How much do I owe?" Kylie had been right. This place was a gossip mill. Amused, he paid up and said a congenial "good day" to Ms. Waldo and folks who toasted him with red-and-white-checkered coffee cups. As he left the café and crossed the street, he imagined everyone clamoring to the window to see where he was going. He rounded the corner, out of sight. He could almost hear their disappointed sighs. Although, now they could spin scenarios to their hearts' content. He hadn't escaped being the subject of gossip, but at least they wouldn't overhear Kylie sharing news about his sister.

Jack neared the Appleseed Memorial Park. It was small—a few oaks, an apple tree, a fountain, a statue of Johnny Appleseed and a half-dozen beds of flowers—but it was scenic and quiet.

Instead of sitting on a bench, Kylie was playing fetch with Shy. He watched as the needy mutt retrieved the stick and smiled when Kylie lavished attention on her. His ex-wife would never have risked getting dirty to play with a dog. In fact, most of the women he'd dated over the years had been obscenely focused on the shallow things in life. According to the marriage counselor, Jack gravitated toward these women because they were needy. Then he'd suggested they were safe because Jack didn't want to connect with a woman on a deeper, more intelligent level. He'd listed the possible reasons and Jack had shot them down. But those reasons sporadically ran through Jack's mind.

"Breakfast is served," he called.

Kylie tossed the stick aside and settled on a bench. Shy circled, then curled on the grass next to her backpack. Probably smelled more cookies.

Jack sat, unsure whether to be amused or insulted when Kylie scooted away. She crossed her legs, and he noted those orange chucks had vibrant pink laces. Cute, and more whimsical than he'd first thought. Smiling to himself, he opened the bag and offered her a cup of hot tea, a napkin and a cannoli.

"Thanks." Brow scrunched, she inspected the crispy, cream-filled shell. "What is it?"

"Kerri's pastry of the day."

"Yes, but what *is* it?"

"You've never had a cannoli?"

She shook her head.

"It's an Italian pastry filled with sweet ricotta cheese and, typically, vanilla cream. This one's filled with chocolate cream and topped with almonds and a cherry."

"Sounds interesting, but I already had breakfast."

Jack lifted a brow. "You can resist Kerri's pastries?"

She snorted. "Yeah, right. It's just that I'm not hungry. Mind if I save it for later?"

"Mind if I indulge? I got hooked on cannolis when I policed Little Italy. Never thought I'd get one here." He sampled and groaned. "Unbelievable."

"That good, huh?" She pursed her lips. "All right. Maybe just a taste. Who says you have to be hungry to eat?"

Jack watched as she bit into the cannoli, smiled when her eyes lit up. "Rivals anything from Little Italy," he said. "Impressive, since Ms. Waldo isn't even Italian."

"It's amazing. The flavor. The texture. Light but rich. How does she *do* that?" Kylie asked as she took another bite.

He couldn't remember ever enjoying watching a woman eat, as if it were a sight to behold. Concerned with maintaining a svelte figure, Amanda had always nibbled at her meals. Jessie, too. Kylie didn't nibble, she ate with gusto. Messy and sexy. "You have a little something…"

"What?"

"The corner of your mouth."

"Crumbs?"

"Cream."

Her tongue darted to the left side of her mouth, a sexy maneuver made even sexier because it was innocent.

Christ. "The other side." He wanted to get it for her. With *his* tongue.

She swiped at her mouth with her finger, then sucked off the cream. "This chocolate stuff is to die for. What is it? Mousse? Pudding? *Yum.*"

Yum came to his mind, too, only he wasn't thinking about the chocolate. Jack schooled his expression, shifted to hide his arousal and scrambled for a distraction. "About my sister…"

"What do you want to know?"

"Everything you know about the decline of her marriage."

"You at least know that Frank left her for another woman, right?"

"That I know."

"No warning. No apologies. No chance to work things out. Just up and left—his wife and kid. His home and job. Creep."

"That's putting it mildly."

Kylie wrapped up the remainder of her treat and wiped her hands and mouth with a napkin.

Shy popped up and licked crumbs from her pant leg.

"You never liked Frank," Kylie noted, while petting the dog's head. "I always thought that was strange since everyone else in this town respected the guy. Charming, friendly and successful. A lawyer who fought hard for his clients. But knowing what I know now… You must have a heck of an intuition."

Jack sipped coffee and braced himself. "What do you know?"

"I don't know anything. Not for a fact. I've just heard things." Kylie fidgeted. "I hate spreading gossip."

"I appreciate that. What did you hear?"

She leaned in and lowered her voice. "Frank was unfaithful. Rumor has it he had multiple affairs and that they had been going on for years. He must have been slicker than a hog on ice, because nobody knew. Well, the women he cheated with knew, but they never said anything. Although, why would they? He was married. Some of *them* were married. The only reason it came out was because one of those women confided in Jessica Lynn after Frank took off. She said, *"You're better off,"* then confessed she'd had an affair with Frank and that he'd burned her, too. That woman was one of Jessica Lynn's snooty friends, by the way. Part of her Garden Club circle."

"That sucks."

"It gets worse," Kylie said. "Are you sure you want to know?"

"Spill."

She sipped her tea, wet her lips. "Well, it was like this weird trickle-down effect. Jessica Lynn blew up at her friend."

"Understandable."

"At a country club event."

"Shit."

"I think the only reason Jessica Lynn was there to begin with was to distract herself from Frank's desertion. But she wigged out and blasted the woman and a lot of people overheard. Next thing you know, a few other bitter, jilted women slipped up and basically said, *"Frank screwed you, too?"* Kylie blushed. "I'm guessing they meant both ways."

Jack tugged at the brim of his EPD ball cap, shielded his eyes from the bright morning sun. Mild temperature. Clear skies. A perfect fall day except for the crap he was learning about his brother-in-law—not that he was surprised. He focused on Kylie, a ray of sunshine in a shitstorm. "I notice you're not naming names."

"You mean of the women Frank seduced?" She shrugged. "If you really need to know, ask Deputy Ziffel or Boone. Like I said, I don't like to spread gossip."

Jack smiled in spite of his dark mood. "You're a good soul, Tiger."

She frowned at that, then narrowed her eyes. "Why aren't you more upset?"

"I'm upset."

"You don't look it."

"Trust me." Jack set aside his coffee. "Anything else?"

Kylie cleared her throat and pushed her glasses up her nose. "It's twisted if you ask me, but everyone in Jessica Lynn's social circle? They don't want anything to do with her. I don't know if they're scandalized or just uncomfortable, but…it's like she's paying for Frank's sins. And everyone else in town? Can't say they have much sympathy."

Kylie blushed. "Forgive me for saying so, but Jessica Lynn has always been uppity. She's snubbed a lot of folks—"

"Including you."

"Including me. I always thought your sister was self-involved and I never much cared for her, but I wouldn't wish this scandal and heartache on anyone."

Jack felt a pull in his chest. He ached for his sister, but he ached for Kylie, too. He wanted to pull her into his arms, to soak in her goodness. A selfish desire that shamed him. He felt like a fucking vampire, starving to feed off of someone else to fill a need. "Anything else?"

"Isn't that enough?"

More than enough. But it didn't explain Jessie showing up at his house in the middle of the night. There had to be something more. Something that had pushed her over the edge. Something he'd have to investigate. He reached over and squeezed Kylie's hand. "Thanks for being open with me."

She squeezed back, smiled.

Heat burned a path up his arm and wrapped around his heart. He didn't want to let go and was surprised when Kylie didn't pull away. He registered a connection, more powerful than a physical attraction, although that was damned strong, too. He wanted to lean in and kiss her, a deep, scorching kiss. He wanted to make her feel, burn. He looked into her big brown eyes and noted empathy, desire and, oh, hell, alarm. Talk about mixed signals.

"I should go," she said, looking flustered. "I have obligations and appointments and...stuff." She broke contact, ruffled Shy's head and swiped up her backpack.

Jack stood. "I'll walk you back."

"That's not necessary."

"It is if I want to get my wheels," he teased. "I'm parked across the street from McGraw's."

"Oh. Right. I forgot." She didn't say anything more, just hurried ahead.

Jack kept pace with Shy tagging behind. "How are the

renovations going?" he asked, hoping to break the sudden tension.

"The interior, great. The exterior...I have a meeting with the HPS later today."

"Good luck."

She grunted. "Like you mean that."

He held her elbow as they crossed the street. "I do mean it. If you get the permit, you'll be within your legal rights to alter the storefront however you want."

She glanced over at him with a smart-ass grin. "Afraid I'll alter the storefront no matter what?"

"A little, yeah."

"Would a sweet girl break the law?"

"A sweet girl with spunk might."

"You think I've got spunk?"

"I think you've got something."

Kylie slowed as they neared his SUV. She didn't meet his gaze. "Thanks for walking me back. And thanks for breakfast. If I can help with Jessica Lynn, well...just give a shout." She tweaked Shy's ear, then saluted Jack. "See ya."

He nabbed her wrist, felt her racing pulse. *Why so skittish, Tiger?* He glanced at the store, wary of the man inside. "Kylie."

"What?"

"My intuition?"

"What about it?"

"Nine out of ten times it's dead-on. There's something suspicious about Travis Martin."

She screwed up her pretty face and lowered her voice. "That's insane, Jack. He's—"

"Just...be careful."

CHAPTER THIRTEEN

KYLIE'S HEART POUNDED as she blew into McGraw's Shoe Store. So much for not crushing on Jack. And, although he hadn't blatantly flirted, she'd sensed a blip of romantic interest on his part. It was actually a little scary. Theirs had always been a one-sided love affair. *What now?*

Kylie fell back against the door, caught her breath, then duly lost it again. "Oh, my God."

"You hate it."

"No. I'm just…amazed." Kylie pushed off the door and stepped deeper into McGraw's. Thoughts of Jack took a temporary backseat to the radical changes of the store. She was bowled over by how much Travis had accomplished since yesterday evening. The walls and ceiling were painted. He'd revarnished the old cashier counter purchased by her great-grandfather in the late 1800s. Presently, Travis-the-miracle-worker was perched on a ladder, attaching funky new lighting tracks to the chic new ceiling. "Did you work straight through the night?"

"Knocked off before midnight."

Holy cow. "And you've been back at it since…"

"Early this morning. I'm motivated."

"I'll say." Kylie dropped her backpack at her feet, spun around and soaked in the changes. Instead of four stark white walls, McGraw's now boasted walls of contrasting but coordinated colors. Two were painted a cross between cranberry and mahogany—Caliente, Travis called it. The third wall was a rich, creamy yellow—Starburst. The fourth—antique white. The ceiling—black. It all blended beautifully with the walnut hardwood floors. But when she envisioned the Andy Warhol prints hanging on the vibrant walls, her hand-painted chairs, the abstract shoe displays, the eclectic throw rugs and her not-so-practical incoming stock, she imagined various patrons rolling their eyes and taking their business elsewhere.

"Are you disappointed we went with bold instead of bright?" Travis asked.

"Absolutely not. You were right. If I'd gone with hot-pink and banana-yellow, I could've kissed all of our male customers goodbye. Now I'll only drive away maybe eighty percent of our clientele."

She was only half joking.

Imagining the drastic renovations and seeing them for real were two different beasts. Faye was right. Spenser was going to freak. Her mom and grandma were going to faint. Or maybe one would faint and the other would applaud. It's not like they ever agreed. One thing was sure. This wasn't her great-grandpa's store. Or her grandpa's. Or her dad's.

What have I done?

She didn't know whether to celebrate or puke.

"Most of the guys around here shop for shoes at Sears or Kmart," Travis said not unkindly. "Including, usually, me."

He was right. Even though McGraw's offered a fair selection of casual shoes and work boots, they couldn't compete with department store prices. Not without forfeiting quality. One thing her dad and grandpa had always insisted on, aside from practicality, was quality. Kylie agreed wholeheartedly on that score.

"If I recall, aside from the customized sneakers you bought to cater to the Apple Festival tourists, the majority of the new stock you ordered is targeted at trend-conscious women."

"It's not like they don't exist in Eden," Kylie said as she wandered the store, envisioning fashionable displays. "Take Jessica Lynn Cortez and the snooty women of the Garden Club. They travel all the way to Indianapolis or

Chicago to buy their shoes. I figure if they want to blow good money on pretentious designer shoes, they might as well blow it here. At the same time, I want to offer a trendy selection for those on a stricter budget as well as the younger set. Faye's daughter, Spice, always complains about how they can't get any cool shoes around here. This town may be stuck in the past, but kids are still influenced by what they see on TV. They want to dress like Hannah Montana and Paris Hilton. The Gossip Girls. I'm pretty sure those celebrities don't wear Hush Puppies."

"Sounds like you're attuned to a new wave of potential consumers."

She moved to the base of the ladder. "Meaning I should stop second-guessing my decision to renovate?"

"Meaning you should trust your instincts."

It had been easier when she'd been fueled by cosmopolitans. "What if I run the business into the ground?"

"Is that you talking? Or your dad?"

What was he, psychic? "Why would you say something like that? You didn't know my dad. You barely know me."

He shrugged. "I've lived here awhile. People talk."

Her cheeks burned. A) Because she'd just *talked* to Jack about his sister and her cheating husband. B) Because at some point people had *talked* about her dysfunctional relationship with her dad.

Intensely private, Kylie strived to keep her personal life, well, personal. She'd never complained about the way her dad patronized her. Never whined about the fact that he'd left the business to Spenser, even though she was the sibling who'd inherited the sales savvy and the passion for shoes. She never vented. Never bared her soul. (Except that night at Boone's.) Yet people *talked* about her pitiful attempts to impress her dad?

Kylie curled her fingers into her palms. *Breathe.*

At some point," Travis said, concentrating on the lighting fixture, "a person has to stop living for others and start living for themselves. Usually that involves risk."

"Nothing ventured, nothing gained." One of Spenser's favorite clichés. He always said it with a twinkle in his eye. Just before he did something risky. He rarely failed, and when he did he shrugged it off. If *he'd* had the inclination, he would've painted McGraw's hot-pink and banana-yellow without flinching.

I can be bold. I can take risks.

Travis slipped his tools in his utility belt and climbed down. He opened a minicooler, nabbed two Cokes and handed one to Kylie. "I know about trying to live up to family expectations. I know about not being appreciated for who you are."

Even though he was concentrating on his pop-top, she felt as though he was looking into her soul. It was both weird and wonderful.

"I spent my whole life trying to impress my dad," she said, popping open her own can. "Don't get me wrong. He loved me. But he worshiped Spenser."

It was hard to blame him. After all, she worshiped Spenser, too. He was carefree and kind. Honorable and courageous. Smart and motivated. *Fun.*

"Sometimes it's hard to shine in a big brother's shadow."

Kylie sipped her soda. "You speaking from experience, Travis?"

Another shrug.

She angled her head and studied him hard. Something was different about him today. Not in his appearance, but in his manner. He'd always been so reserved. Today he was downright talkative. She'd never known he was so smart. So well spoken. His word choice and views suggested he was highly educated. Yet, he mixed paint in a hardware store.

There's something suspicious about Travis Martin.

Kylie shook off Jack's warning. Truth was, before yesterday, she'd never had a meaty conversation with Travis. Just short exchanges about shoes—shoes he'd never been thrilled with. Maybe he'd always been this worldly. Suddenly she was curious as heck about the man.

"So who did *you* disappoint?" she asked.

"Who didn't I disappoint?"

She noted his skilled work, thought about his creative advice. "You should be an interior designer."

"In a perfect world, yes."

"In a not-so-perfect world?"

"I'm grateful for the chance to renovate McGraw's." Travis drank his Coke, stared up at the exposed wiring. "Trust your instincts, Kylie."

She glanced around the store, considered all the time she'd spent here as a kid and a young adult. All she'd learned from her grandpa and dad. There had to be more to her life than McGraw's Shoe Store, but at the same time, she took great pride in the family business. If Spenser trusted her to run things, then he should trust her judgment. It's not like he had his finger on the pulse of footwear *or* Eden. She was sick of playing it safe. Sick of just getting by. Department stores and the Internet were killing small businesses like McGraw's. Shaking things up wasn't a purely selfish act, she told herself. Shaking things up was a matter of survival. *Nothing ventured, nothing gained.* "What can I do to help?"

"Don't take this as an insult, but just now, nothing."

"Don't take this as a cop-out, but good. I have an appointment." She hadn't expected to lose the morning to Jack. Hairdoodles was at the other end of town, and Petunia, who'd squeezed her in, had impressed the importance of being on time.

"No problem," said Travis

"I'll be gone for two hours. Three, tops."

"I'll tackle lighting and trim."

"The new shelves and mirrors, the stock—they'll be arriving between today and tomorrow. I paid extra for express shipping," Kylie said. "If I'm not here, would you sign for them?"

"Sure."

Travis's pep talk rivaled a double cosmo, stoking

Kylie's anxious spirit. She felt giddy and light-headed. Drunk on the potential power of change. "I'm getting a makeover today," she blurted.

"Why?"

"Because this store isn't the only thing that needs beautifying."

His puppy dog eyes flicked over her denim-clad body. "You don't need beautifying."

Embarrassed, she glanced away and shoved her fingers in her back pockets. "I wasn't fishing for compliments."

"I know."

"It's not like I think I'm ugly. I'm okay-looking. But I'm a product of my family's mind-set. Sensible. Practical."

"Subtle."

"I don't want to be subtle. I want to pop. I want to *wow*."

"Ah."

She frowned. "What do you mean, 'ah'?"

"You want to catch a man's eye."

"Maybe."

"Chief Reynolds?"

"*No.*"

Travis's fleshy lips twitched as he snagged another lighting fixture from a cardboard box.

Kylie flushed. "Am I that obvious?"

"No."

"You're lying."

"I'm lying."

"Dang."

He smiled and climbed the ladder.

She snagged her backpack and headed out.

"Kylie?"

"Hmm?"

"Don't let Petunia give you a perm and don't let her cut your hair above your shoulders. You need length to offset your round face. And if you're going to change your color, go with subtle highlights. Auburn would make those whiskey-brown eyes of yours *really* pop."

Dazed, she hovered on the threshold. In addition to a fancy vocabulary, Travis-the-hardware guy had an impressive flair for interior *and* hair design. Who knew? Certainly not anyone in Eden or she would have caught wind. That was gossip fodder for sure. "You used to be in another profession, didn't you?"

He concentrated on the wiring. She noticed he didn't look quite as confident with the electrical aspects of the renovation. She also noticed his clenched-jawed silence.

It only fanned her curiosity. Surely he'd been an artist of some kind. Or at least a wanna-be artist. Had he lost his business? His passion? Had there been some sort of scandal? Was he worried he'd be laughed out of town if people knew he'd been a craft artisan or a window trimmer? "*Were* you an interior designer?"

"No.

"A fashion consultant?"

"Hell, no."

"What did you do?"

"You don't want to know."

CHAPTER FOURTEEN

Philadelphia, Pennsylvania

CARMINE "CHICKIE" Mancini sank into the leather armchair across from Dr. Bennett. It was his second visit. The second time he'd ignored her offer to recline on the tapestry-covered couch. He wasn't crazy, he was dying. He was sure of it. The dizzy spells. The heart palpitations. The dreams.

His family doctor, Salvatore Aversi, M.D., had assured him he wasn't suffering from a fatal disease. However, he was flirting with a heart attack. Tests had verified high blood pressure and high cholesterol. In addition, he was overweight and over fifty. Aversi had prescribed medicine, a healthier diet and exercise. He'd also targeted stress as a contributing risk factor. Obsessing on his eminent death was only hurrying it along.

Obsessing, my fucking ass.

Carmine didn't believe he could cheat fate by altering his lifestyle. Besides, who wanted to live without living to the fullest? No red meat? No salt? Cut down on tiramisu and sign up at a gym? Fuck that. But that stress thing… That he could not ignore. He'd had an episode during a business meeting last week, although he'd stepped outside before the boys had witnessed the worst of it. His consigliere, Jimmy "Buddah" Cerone, had driven him to the emergency room. From the way Carmine was sweating, gasping for air and gripping his chest, Buddah had assumed a heart attack. Carmine, too. He'd almost pulverized the attending physician who'd diagnosed his condition as an anxiety attack. Mafia bosses did not suffer *anxiety* attacks. Even after Aversi returned his call and concurred, Carmine didn't believe it.

He'd sworn Buddah to secrecy. He didn't want to worry his wife or his girlfriend. He didn't want his nephew, Mario "Turk" Gallo, the acting underboss of the Mancini Family, to sense weakness. He didn't want word to leak to the commission that he was knocking on death's door or, worse, falling apart. He didn't want anyone moving in on him before he'd made things right. In the recent string of prophetic dreams, his mama kept saying, *"You gotta make things right."* He knew what she meant or at least he thought he did, but he didn't know how he was supposed to mend that bridge. And what if he was wrong? What if she was referring to some other wrong? *"Do it, Carmine,"* she warned. *"Before it's too late."*

Just thinking about that dream gave him fucking palpitations. He needed to buy more time. He needed to analyze that dream. To curb this damned anxiety.

Buddah had suggested Dr. Susan Bennett, a psychiatrist with a few shady patients. *She's discreet,* he'd promised. She also has a stick up her ass, Carmine thought after ten seconds in her company. At least she had nice legs

"So what's on your mind this morning, Mr. Mancini?"

The same thing that had been on his mind last night and the day before. *He-who-shall-not be-named.*

Carmine ignored the flutter in his chest, toyed with his pinkie ring and met Dr. Bennett's cool blue gaze. "Family."

CHAPTER FIFTEEN

JACK WAS CONTEMPLATING his sister's dilemma and his attraction to Kylie when he walked into the station house an hour behind schedule. Not that he was punching a time clock and Ziffel would've called if he was needed, but he was beginning to feel like a slacker. He was used to working a case. Currently, there were no open cases in Eden. The streets were safe. Hard crime was nonexistent. Even though he'd wanted a break from the never-ending bleakness of working Homicide, he needed to keep busy. Otherwise, he'd feel useless. Which probably added to this obsessive need to solve Jessie's problems and to dig deeper into Travis Martin's background. He'd bet his badge they were both hiding something.

"You look like you could use something to brighten your morning," Ziffel said. "Try a cannoli."

Jack looked to where the deputy pointed. The red-and-white bakery box sat on top of the gray metal filing cabinet, well out of Shy's reach. Grinning, he reached for the coffeepot. "Thanks, but I already had one this morning."

"Have another."

"Maybe later." If he overindulged in Kerri's baked goods, in a matter of weeks he'd have a gut. He envisioned the former chief of police—overweight and unmotivated. He noted the desk of the woman who mourned him. "Where's Ms. Vine?"

"In your office. Organizing."

Thank you, Jesus.

Ziffel gestured to Shy. "Still haven't found her a home, huh?"

"Working on it. What are you reading?" Jack gestured to the book in the deputy's hands. Ziffel wasn't a pretentious know-it-all, he actually did know a lot. Jack attributed that to the man's voracious reading habit.

Ziffel flashed the cover in Jack's direction. *"Omertà— Behind the Scenes."*

Jack barely refrained from rolling his eyes. "You, too?"

"What do you mean?"

"Last night I stopped at Pizza King for a slice. The cook and cashier were comparing notes on season two. Also heard two assistants at the vet's arguing about an episode from season five."

"I'm midway through season four," said Ziffel. "I'd be further along if there wasn't such a wait. We've got two video outlets. Mac's Video Circus and the library."

"There's always Netflix," said Jack.

"What's Netflix?"

"Never mind."

Ziffel stowed the book in his desk. "I'm sensing you're not a fan."

"Of the mob?"

"Of the show."

"I'm not a fan."

Ziffel brushed crumbs from his tie. "I'm thinking that's because you've tangled with the real deal. Experienced the true crimes. You think the series glamorizes the mafia."

"Something like that." Gut tight, Jack refilled his coffee.

Ziffel leaned forward, eyes bright. "Ever meet anyone from the Five Families?"

The infamous New York factions of the Cosa Nostra. "I have." One of them had been responsible for the grisly death of a woman who'd broken *omertà* (the code of silence). Jack's last case. Connie Valachi hadn't been a made man, of course, but she'd been screwing one.

"Are they anything like the mobsters in *Omertà?*"

"Yes and no."

"I'm sensing you don't want to talk about it."

Jack sipped coffee.

"Right-o." Ziffel sighed and wiped his sticky fingers. He glanced at a file. "Ready for the morning briefing?"

"Hit me."

"Night shift reported nocturnal activity in McGraw's Shoe Store. Hooper investigated. Just Travis working late on renovations."

Jack raised a brow. "How late?"

"At 11:05 p.m."

"Long shift."

"He told Hooper they were on a tight schedule. Said he'd be working a lot of overtime for the next few days."

"What do you think Martin charges for twelve-hour days?"

Ziffel shrugged. "Kylie's frugal. I'm sure they agreed on a price ahead of time."

"If she's frugal, then we're not talking a lot of money. Why would Martin take vacation time only to work hard for little pay?"

"Maybe it's not about the money."

"A favor for a friend?" Jack flashed on his previous thoughts. "Are Travis and Kylie close?"

"Not that I know of."

"Maybe he's lending his services in hopes of getting close."

"You mean in a romantic way?" Ziffel shook his head. "Travis recently lost his wife. Took it hard. According to Hank, his boss, the man's still grieving."

Jack didn't ask why Hank had shared that information with Ziffel. In Eden everyone blabbed about whatever was on their mind.

"On the other hand," the deputy went on, "Ashe Davis has been trying to *get close* to Kylie for months. Arrogant cuss. He's certain he can..." Ziffel trailed off, fingered his collar.

Christ, was the man blushing? Jack waited. And waited. "What?"

"You know."

"Not a clue."

Ziffel glanced at the chief's office then nabbed his mug and approached Jack. "Man to man," he said in a lower voice, "word has it... That is... It's not like Kylie's never dated, but she doesn't—" he cleared his throat "—reciprocate. The only long-term relationship she ever had was with that travel writer. I'm surprised he stuck around as long as he did given...well...a man has needs."

Jack applied what he knew to what Ziffel didn't say. The travel writer was Bobby Jones. The guy who'd lived with Kylie for a year. Was he saying the bastard split because Kylie didn't put out? "Hold up." Even though Jack wasn't comfortable gossiping about Kylie's love life, he was definitely intrigued. From what he'd experienced, she was a healthy, hot-blooded woman, and by her admission, flexible as a bendable toy icon. "Are you saying Kylie's a virgin?"

"He's saying she's frigid." Ms. Vine popped out of the office with a bulging garbage bag. "So it's rumored."

Jack processed that statement while reaching for the trash. "Let me do that."

"I've got it." She shook her head in disgust as she hauled the garbage outside. "Men are the worst gossips."

Jack winced when the door slammed. "Don't think I scored any points just now."

"She'll come around," Ziffel said.

Before Jack could counter that the door slammed back open and his sister stalked inside. She looked more herself today, dressed in a flared skirt and a matching blouse, her long hair twisted into a sophisticated bun, her makeup subtle but perfect. Her manner was familiar, too. Self-absorbed. She didn't even acknowledge Ed Ziffel's presence. "I need to speak with you, Jack."

Ziffel backed away before Jack could comment on her

rudeness. Shy must've sensed the brewing storm, because she disappeared under Dorothy's desk.

"Coffee?" Jack asked.

"I won't be staying that long."

"Figured. Just thought I'd be *polite* and offer."

She blinked, then followed Jack's line of vision. "Oh. Hello, Deputy Ziffel."

"Mrs. Cortez."

"Not for long." She zipped past Jack and into his office.

He closed the door behind them. Was this about the divorce? He knew the court date was scheduled for next week. "Where's Maddie?"

"In school. Though I got her there forty-minutes late. Why didn't you wake us?"

"Thought you could use the rest."

"Life goes on." Jessie slammed an envelope onto his clutter-free desk. "What's this?"

"The money I left you for groceries?"

"We don't need your charity, Jack."

His back went up. "It's not charity. You're a guest in my house. I'm not going to ask you to pay for food. You and Maddie are fussy eaters. Even if I shopped I wouldn't know what to buy."

"We're not fussy. We're health conscious."

Jack noted his sister's frail frame. "Is that anything like anorexic?" Oh, hell. "Sorry." He caught her bony wrist before she made it out the door. "I can't help it if I'm worried about you, Jess."

Her cheeks flushed. "You don't even like me."

"That's not true."

"Think about it," she said, then slipped his grip.

Troubled by the accusation, he followed her into the administrative office. "I made a call this morning. There'll be furniture in the spare bedroom by tonight. Just in case you decide to stay. Nothing, by the way, would make me happier."

She blew him off and, posture pageant-perfect stiff, blew out the door.

Dorothy passed Jessie on her way back in. "Some are saying she had it coming. Not me, of course," the woman said with a disapproving glance to Jack and Ziffel. "I'm not a gossip."

CHAPTER SIXTEEN

KYLIE SAT RIGID IN PETUNIA'S white leatherette styling chair. "Wait."

Aluminum foil and bleach goop ready, Petunia sighed. "Do you or do you not want me to highlight your hair?"

"I do. I think. I'm not sure."

"You leafed though four hair magazines. You chose a color and style—"

"I know." But what if she'd chosen wrong? Faye would know what suited her face and lifestyle best. Unfortunately, Kylie didn't feel comfortable calling her yet. All she had to go on was Travis's suggestions, and though he was talented with interior design, he wasn't exactly a fashion plate. Yes, she wanted to shake things up, but not at the cost of looking like a beauty-school-project-gone-wrong. "Maybe I should postpone."

"Up to you," said Petunia. "But just so you know, I'm booked solid for the next two weeks. The only reason you got in was because Mrs. Carmichael canceled. A flare-up with her arthritis."

"Is she okay?"

"I'm sure it's nothing. You know Mrs. Carmichael."

Everyone knew Mrs. Carmichael. A kindly lady who'd been the Sunday School teacher for a bazillion years. She'd also run a day-care service for a spell. Now she was retired, widowed and miserable. Always suffering some hardship, only nothing was ever really wrong. People said she made things up to get attention. Mostly everyone sympathized because they knew she was lonely. Kylie felt sorry for the widow. Her own grandma had gone through a tough time after she'd lost her husband after fifty-five years of marriage, then not long after, her only son. Sally McGraw had filled the void by filling her home with stuff. Stuff she'd purchased on the Home Shopping Network. Cookware and vacuums. Jewelry and handbags. With her obsession turned addiction, she'd shopped herself into deep debt. By the time Kylie learned the truth, her grandma's financial situation was dire. She cringed just thinking about that bleak time. On the flip side, the crisis had generated a special bond between Kylie and her grandma.

Petunia rearranged a collection of combs and scissors, the impatient clinking analogous to drumming fingertips. "Take me or leave me, Kylie. Time's ticking."

"Two weeks, huh?" By then the Apple Festival and the opportunity to impress tourists would be over. She couldn't unveil the new and chic McGraw's looking like the old, blah Kylie! Plus, she wanted to impress, okay, *wow,* Jack.

Kylie bolstered her spine and channeled Spenser. "Nothing ventured, nothing gained."

Petunia smiled. "Let the fun begin."

Kylie focused on a copy of *Glamour* while Petunia had *fun.* She tried not to think about the end result. She tried not to listen to the gossip flying around the salon. Impossible. *But* she could at least refrain from participating. Instead, she studied celebrity shoe trends and contemplated future orders for the store. She lost track of time, tuned out the gossip. But then something caught her attention.

Silence.

Kylie looked up and saw Jessica Lynn Cortez standing at the receptionist's desk. As always she was impeccably dressed, her ink-black hair twisted into princesslike updo. She looked sophisticated, uptight and completely out of place at Hairdoodles.

Petunia kept working, as did Becky the manicurist, but all eyes were on the woman whose husband had slept all over town. The woman who'd snubbed places like Hair-doodles and the people who frequented it. The woman bending Loretta, the receptionist's, ear.

Two seconds later, eyes wide, Loretta scooted over to Petunia. "You're not going to believe this," she whispered.

"What does she want?" Petunia grumbled.

"A job."

"I don't believe it."

"Told you."

"Doing what?" Petunia snapped, slapping more bleach on Kylie's hair.

"She said she's a skilled makeup artist."

"That's true," Kylie found herself saying. "Must be all those years on the pageant circuit. Her makeup always looks incredible." She wasn't sure why she spoke up for a woman who always spoke down to her. Except that she was Jack's sister and Jack was worried about her. Plus, the woman, though beautiful, looked kind of pathetic just now.

Petunia grunted. "We don't need a makeup artist."

"She said she's willing—"

"We're not hiring," Petunia said.

"I told her that," Loretta said, "but—"

"I'll tell her." Petunia plunked her brush in the cup of bleach, then split.

Loretta followed.

Kylie tried not to worry about the time factor and her half-foiled head.

Seconds later, Jessica Lynn retreated from the shop.

Petunia returned and snatched up another square of aluminum foil. "I can't believe she had the gall to ask me for a job! She's never set foot in my salon. In fact, she bad-mouthed me. Called me a *hack*. She didn't think that wouldn't get back to me? People talk, you know."

I know, Kylie thought. Tonight the town could well be talking about her striped hair. Not that *she* considered Petunia a hack, but she was seriously second-guessing the highlighting process. Mostly because Petunia had blabbed the whole time she'd brushed the goopy dye over chunks of Kylie's hair, wrapping uneven amounts in aluminum foil. What if she'd used too much or too little?

"Travels two hours to get her hair done by some big-city stylist," Petunia rattled on as she checked the egg timer. "Heard she pays a hundred bucks for a cut and blow-dry. I provide the same service for twenty-five!"

"She's a stuck-up nitwit," said Becky, while filing Mrs. Roper's nails. "Always has been."

Kylie couldn't disagree about the stuck-up, nitwit part. If the shoe fits and all that. Still, she felt sorry for Jessica. She'd led a charmed life. She'd won a scholarship to a pre-stigious college. She'd had a shot at being Miss America. She'd given up a higher education and a lifelong dream for love. Even though she was self-centered and shallow, she'd devoted her life to her husband.

Only to be betrayed.

Kylie had been devastated when Bobby had deserted her. But they'd only been together for one year, not eleven. And they didn't have a child. Kylie had never liked Jessica Lynn much, but imagining her pain certainly softened her heart.

"Why do you think she needs a job?" asked Mrs. Roper, admiring her newly polished nails. "Frank's loaded. Surely she'll rake in the alimony."

"Maybe there's something we don't know," said Petunia. "Maybe Frank has something on Jessica Lynn."

"Even if he does," said Becky, "it's not like his butt don't stink. I recently heard something that would set your hair on fire."

All of the women leaned forward, except Kylie, who touched her fingertip to her foiled head. She was curious about Frank, but she wasn't keen on that flaming-hair image.

"Sorry," said Becky. "My lips are sealed. A young woman's reputation is at stake. A very nice, very *young* woman."

"You mean the Cortez's babysitter," Petunia said.

Becky gaped. "I can't believe you broke my confidence!"

Petunia rolled her eyes. "It's not like I revealed her name."

Except everyone knew the Cortez's regular babysitter was Mya Unger. Mya was only seventeen. Frank was in his thirties. Kylie cringed.

"Ick," said Loretta.

"Pervert," said Mrs. Roper.

"Here's my take," said Petunia. "Frank's a crackerjack lawyer. Probably knows a ton of loopholes. He's going to cheat Jessica Lynn out of her due and she knows it. Hence the job-hunting. She's desperate."

Becky grunted. "I'd feel sorry for her if she weren't such a witch."

The women continued to gossip. Kylie thanked God she wasn't Jessica, then directly wondered what was so great about her own personal life. Although, she *was* trying to spice things up by attracting Jack. She glanced at her reflection in the mirror, frowned. She looked like one of those nuts who donned tinfoil hats to ward off mind-controlling aliens. "Don't you think this goop has been on long enough?"

Petunia peeked between two layers of foil. "Nope."

Loretta rushed over. "For you," she said, handing a cordless phone to Kylie, who hoped for Faye but got Travis.

"Your grandma's on the other line," he said.

"What other line?" She only had one incoming line.

"I'm calling you on my cell phone. She's on your business land line. What should I—"

"Tell her to call this number."

"I did, but she said she can't."

Kylie's stomach fluttered with dread. She wasn't supposed to touch base with her mom and grandma until they hit Anchorage, two days from now.

"She says it's an emergency."

Kylie flung the cordless at Becky, flew off the chair and out the door. She hopped on her bike and zoomed six blocks, cape flying. Her brain pounded with horrific thoughts. Lungs burning, she exploded over McGraw's threshold and snatched the receiver. "What happened? What's wrong? Did you break a leg? A hip? Did mom fall overboard? Did you two get thrown off the ship for excessive bickering?"

"Don't be silly," said Grandma McGraw.

"Then, what's the emergency?"

"The world's gone topsy-turvy."

Kylie slumped into the chair Travis shoved under her butt. "What are you talking about, Grandma?"

"Your mom was right. For once."

"About?"

"She had a bad dream. Woke up feeling like something was wrong at home. Couldn't shake it all day. I got tired of her pacing a hole in our cabin's carpet and spoiling my fun. Decided to call ship-to-shore, hang the cost. Thought you could ease her mind by telling us everything's fine. Same as always. Only it's not the same as always. I call the store and you're not there. Mr. Martin, who normally works at the hardware store, is there. Said he's handling some renovations. Said you're getting your hair done."

"I *was* getting my hair done." Kylie fingered the foil, some of which she'd lost in the wind. Should she pull the rest off? Leave them on? Which was worse?

"You closed the store on a weekday to get a haircut? That's so unlike you, dear. And what's this about renovations?"

"Nothing severe," she lied. She didn't want to break the news over the phone. What if they freaked? What if she ruined their trip? No way was she going to rain on anyone's dream trip. "Just some maintenance, Grandma. A little sprucing up."

"In preparation of the Apple Festival?"

"Yes." It was the simplest truth.

"Did you have a nice birthday celebration with Faye?" she asked, switching subjects.

"It was one for the memory books. Are you having a nice time with Mom? Strike that. Are you having a nice time?"

"One for the memory books. Except today. Your mom was a real drip."

"So you said. Where is she, anyway?"

"I sent her on a fool's errand. Just in case."

"In case what?"

"In case something was terribly wrong."

"Nothing's wrong, Grandma. Tell Mom...same ol', same ol'."

"I'll tell her exactly that." The old woman sighed. "Wish you were here, dear."

Just now, Kylie couldn't imagine being anywhere but Eden. She always finished what she started, and her homespun adventure was barely off the ground. "I'd only cramp your style," she teased, then turned serious. "I should go. This call is probably costing big time."

"Such a sensible girl," said Grandma McGraw. "Such a good girl."

They signed off and Kylie battled melancholy. What was that line? Good girls finish last?

Travis gestured to her alien-protected head. "Think you can kiss the same ol', same ol' goodbye."

CHAPTER SEVENTEEN

IT IS GOOD TO HAVE AN END to journey toward; but it is the journey that matters, in the end.

Kylie mentally chanted that Zen quote after Petunia informed her she'd have to wait forty-eight hours before repairing the botched dye job. She repeated the chant two hours later when the wrong display shelves were delivered to McGraw's. Believing there was a grand purpose in all these bumps and glitches kept her focused and in the game.

Travis hadn't flinched when they'd unboxed the vintage pewter racks (she'd ordered modern acrylic). *"We can work around this."*

He'd said the same thing about her hideous highlights. Following his suggestion, she'd pulled her flaming hair completely off her face, knotting it in a tight bun at the nape of her neck. The sophisticated style tempered the wild color. Since she had an important meeting to attend, he'd also suggested a stylish hat and bold lipstick. She'd purchased both at Kmart, and by gosh he was right. Not a look she'd want to live with forever, but one she could live with for now.

So, although she couldn't see how the vintage racks would complement the new look of the store, she trusted Travis's judgment. "Go for it," she told him, then slipped through the storage room and into her office. Anxious, she changed into an outfit more suitable for her meeting with the board of the historical society. She zipped herself into the black sheath dress she'd brought from home and stepped into a pair of four-inch wedged espadrille sandals.

Pushing her glasses firmly up her nose, she studied her reflection in the full-length mirror hanging on the back of her door. *Not bad.* Topped with her new black beret and a swish of earth-red lipstick (that smartly matched the red poppies on her shoes), she almost looked business chic. Manga hair notwithstanding.

Looking around the tiny private office, Kylie realized she hadn't asked Travis to make any changes in there. She wouldn't, either. A) She didn't want to impose further on his already generous help. B) Although she loved the work he'd done thus far, she wanted to get her hands dirty, as well. True, she didn't have the eye for design that he did, but no one ever saw this office aside from family. She could tinker and experiment. She could make it her own…even though it was really Spenser's.

She glanced at the phone. *Call him.* Even though he was on a remote island, since Spenser carried a satellite phone she stood a chance of connecting.

"I will," she said to herself. *After the meeting.*

Breathing deep, Kylie leaned over the desk and brought the computer to life. She checked her e-mail. *Yes!* Confirmation that the customized sneakers she'd ordered to appeal to the Apple Festival tourists and Eden's high school students would be here in two days. Just in time for her grand reopening. Things were looking up!

Smiling, she left for her appointment at city hall.

Minutes later, she entered a small meeting room…and faltered just over the threshold. "Am I too early?"

"You're right on time," said Mayor Wilson, a key member of Eden's HPS.

"I thought I had a private meeting with the board."

"Board meetings are open to the membership," he said, waving her forward.

"Oh." *Crap.*

She thought she'd be pleading her case in front of five people. Instead, she counted approximately twenty. Most were retired seniors. Most had been frequenting McGraw's

Shoe Store since her grandpa had been at the helm. Some, like Ray Keystone and J.J. Jarvis, had been close friends of her dad's. They all purchased McGraw's most practical, sensible shoes. They wouldn't appreciate the new look and inventory of the store.

Or maybe some of them would.

Why assume the worst? she asked herself in a spontaneous pep talk. Maybe there were a few restless souls in this room. Maybe they were as bored with the same ol', same ol' as she was.

Her positive mind-set dwindled as she moved through the bug-eyed crowd to get to the frowning board members.

"What the heck did you do to your hair, Kylie McGraw?" Mr. Keystone asked.

"Red lipstick?" said J.J. "What next? Breast enhancement?"

"Are those cherries on her shoes?" someone asked under their breath.

"No, flowers."

"How can she walk in those heels?"

"How can she go out with that hair?"

Cheeks burning, Kylie ignored every whisper, every comment. She would not lose it. She would not make a scene. If she really wanted to shake things up, to make major changes to the store's exterior, she needed the permission of this society. She drew on Zen. She summoned serenity. She had her argument memorized and she would deliver it with calm conviction.

I can do this, she thought as reached the board members. They were seated side by side at a long table. They didn't look happy. Undaunted, she smiled and made eye contact with each one. Mayor Wilson, Max Grogan, Bernard Peterson (the elementary school principal), Vicky Crowne (the president of the Garden Club) and Ida Rathbone (a rival of Grandma McGraw's). She took a deep breath, then launched into her opening line. "Change is exciting. Change is good."

"You call orange hair good?" cracked Ida. "I call it radical."

"Shocking," said the mayor, eyes wide.

"Surprised it's not pink," said Max. "She has a thing for pink," he said to his fellow board members.

Be calm. Stay focused. "Could we please stick to the subject?"

"We are," said Vicky. "The subject is change."

"Change is bad when your objective is to preserve history," said Principal Peterson. He then proceeded to read her the mission statement of the Historical Preservation Society. It was detailed and lengthy and obliterated Kylie's vision for the facade of McGraw's. When he finished several members cheered.

She clenched her fists at her sides and glared at the board. "You've already made up your minds."

"We have," said Ida.

"Afraid so," said the mayor.

Max nodded. "Don't take it personally."

Fury burned its way from her toes to the tips of her ears. "If you had no intention of granting me a permit, why the heck did you agree to let me plead my case?"

Principal Peterson shrugged. "Because it's your right."

"But no matter what I say, you're going to order me to conform."

The mayor nodded. "It's in Eden's best interest."

"In history's best interest."

The room erupted in applause.

The mayor rapped a gavel on the table, then said to Kylie, "Go on."

She blinked. "You're kicking me out?"

"No, dear," Ida said with a condescending smile. "He's inviting you to plead your case."

"Why?"

"It's your right."

Unbelievable! Seconds ago they'd assured her that no matter what she said they wouldn't grant her permission to make changes. Even now the board's body language said, "You're wasting your breath." If pleading her case was fruitless, why plead? She'd save her argument and energy for another day, thank you very much.

Frustrated to no end, Kylie turned on her wedged heels. "This isn't over!" she railed as she stalked from the room. She wasn't sure of her next move, but that wasn't the point. She just wanted the last word.

She pumped her arms as she race-walked down the hall, muttered under her breath. "I should just ask Travis to make the changes in the middle of the night."

But she wouldn't. First, she'd never ask someone to break the law. Second, after hearing that mission statement, she truly did understand the whole historical angle. That didn't mean she had to like it. Nor did she like the notion that *different* was weird or wrong. Maybe she *should* dye her hair pink. Flamingo-pink. That would show them. Although it probably wouldn't bode well for her efforts to attract Jack.

Speaking of… Had he insisted she get a permit, suspecting she wouldn't be granted one? Was it a way of controlling her? He hadn't seemed any happier about the storefront changes than Max and gang. Was it because he didn't think Spenser would approve? Yet, this morning, he'd wished her good luck. She didn't know what to think, and she was so dang mad, she couldn't see straight.

Tears burned her eyes as she neared the outer door. She needed some air. She needed some space. She'd never wanted to punch something so bad in her life. She mentally chanted her Zen quote. When that didn't work, she fell back on one of Spenser's clichés: *Everything happens for a reason.*

She couldn't imagine the *reason* for her sudden run of bad luck. Every time she tried to change something, it backfired. She wanted to shake up Eden, but so far, the only citizen she'd managed to knock off kilter was herself.

"…but it is the journey that matters, in the end."

"I must have one big-butt lesson to learn." Frustrated,

she pushed through the double glass doors...and smacked into Jack.

Just. Her. Luck.

"Easy, Tiger."

His steady hold on her shoulders only threw her more off balance. "Here to gloat?" she snapped, silently cursing the erotic thrill his casual touch invoked.

"Here to speak with Mayor Wilson," he said, doing a head-to-toe visual and releasing her like a hot potato.

"Yes, I know." She gritted out the words while readjusting her glasses. "I have orange hair. I also have small breasts. We can't all be Charlotte Avery, you know." With that, she stomped past him and down the concrete stairs. Throwing his senior-high sweetheart in his face had been childish, but just now she wasn't at her best. Just now, Jack, as chief of police, represented rules and conformity. The urge to rebel was fierce.

"Hold up, Kylie."

Despite what he'd said yesterday, he was not her boss. She didn't stop. She didn't look back. Instead she did something she'd never done before. Flipped him the bird.

She half expected him to follow, to give her the riot act, but—oh, yeah—he had a meeting with the mayor. The more she thought about them conspiring to button up and tie her down, the madder she got. She was halfway down the block when she felt a hand clamp around her wrist. White-hot desire sizzled up her arm.

Jack.

"I want to talk to you," he said, keeping pace.

"Not a good time."

"Too bad." He tugged her off the sidewalk, into the alley, and backed her up against the side of the library.

The air crackled with energy and tension. Her body hummed with sexual awareness. She wanted to shove him away, but she couldn't move. Rooted by anger and desire. *Dang.* The combination was volatile and infuriating.

"What was that crack about Charlotte?" he asked in a low voice.

"The HPS shot me down," she snapped.

"Given your mood, I gathered. What about Charlotte?"

"You knew they wouldn't give me a permit," she persisted.

"No. But I knew the chances were slim."

"Why didn't you warn me? Why did you let me get my hopes up?"

"You told me not to squash your spirit. Besides, you had every right to try for that permit. You tried and failed. Let it go."

"Don't tell me what to do."

"Don't take your frustration with the HPS out on me." He leaned closer. "Why did you bring up Charlotte Avery?"

Kylie blew out a breath and averted her gaze. "Because she's blond and big-chested, just like every other woman you've ever been attracted to, including your ex-wife." There. She'd said it. And damn, she felt petty.

"Not every woman."

Something in his voice...something...intimate. A sensual thrill chased up her spine. She met Jack's gaze and shivered.

"I find you very attractive, Kylie."

"But...I have orange hair."

"I noticed."

"And small breasts."

"Perky breasts." His blue gaze smoldered. "I noticed."

Anger gave way to confusion. "But back there, when we collided...after you took a good look at me..."

"I pushed you away. I know." He worked his jaw. "I manage the attraction better when I'm not touching you."

So it *hadn't* been her imagination. He *did* feel something. She could scarcely breathe. "Why do you want to manage it?"

"Because I want you for the wrong reasons."

Meaning just for sex? *Breathe, Kylie, breathe.* "Maybe I don't care."

"You don't want this, Tiger."

"Don't tell me want I want."

He arched a brow. "All right, then. *I* don't want this."

Now, in addition to being confused, she was embarrassed. "But—"

His cell phone rang.

Jack pushed off the wall and took the call. "Chief Reynolds." *Pause.* "Understood, sir. On my way." He snapped shut his phone.

"I know. You have to go." Anger was preferable to mortification, so she focused on the humiliating encounter with the HPS.

"We'll finish this later."

"Can't wait," she said with a roll of her eyes. *I'm attracted to you, but I don't want to act on it.* Gee. Fun conversation.

Jack turned to leave, then paused. "I know you're pissed about the HPS decision, just…"

"What?"

"Don't do anything stupid."

It was the exact wrong thing to say.

Burning, she peeled off in the opposite direction. The brisk four-block walk to McGraw's did nothing to cool her temper. It felt as if everyone was controlling her life, even Jack. She unlocked the store's door and stomped inside.

Travis, who was attaching shelves to the walls, looked at her and frowned. "I guess you didn't get the permit."

That was only half of it, but the part she'd focus on since she didn't want to ask Travis for relationship advice. "You should have heard the run-around they gave me!"

"I can imagine. Did they say anything about your sign?"

"What? No. I don't think so." She tried to remember the details of the mission statement. "It was all about the storefront and trim. Paint. Colors. Oh, and the awning. Sorry. I'm just so dang mad, I can't think straight." She hugged herself to keep from pacing. She didn't want to scuff the polished hardwood floors. They looked so great. Everything looked great, including the vintage pewter display racks. "You're amazing, Travis. The store…well, it's what I imagined only different."

"Good different?"

Touched by the concern in his voice, she smiled. "Perfect different."

He smiled back, and it occurred to her, once again, that Travis was an attractive man…even with his crooked nose and that scar. He took off his ball cap and sleeved sweat from his brow. Hunched over like he was, she got a prime view of his scalp and—*gasp*—dark roots. No wonder his red hair didn't look quite right with his olive skin. Why would he dye his dark hair red? She itched to ask, but it seemed rude.

Instead, when he pulled his cap back on, she took off her beret and smoothed a palm over her own dye job. "Thanks again for all the hair tips."

"Except the highlights didn't go well."

"That wasn't your fault. So…how is it you know so much about hair color and styles, anyway?" Oh, *that* was subtle.

He turned away to screw a bracket into the wall. "Mona used to be a hairdresser."

"Really?" She'd had no idea. Not that she had known Mona all that well. Like Travis, the woman had kept to herself.

"That was a long time ago. Another life." He glanced at his watch. It seemed to her that he did that a lot. As if he had to be somewhere at a certain time—all the time. "It's close to five and you've had a rough day," he noted. "If you want to take off, I can handle things here."

She must've hit a sore spot, making him think of his wife. Empathy rose, but she didn't know how to help. She thought about him going home to his lonely house, or rather, avoiding it and staying here until all hours. "What about you? Ready to knock off? Maybe I could…I mean…I'd like to treat you to dinner. You've worked so hard and I'm paying so little—" she gestured to the extensive renovations "—considering."

"It's not about the money." After an awkward moment, he glanced over his shoulder. "I appreciate the dinner invitation, Kylie, but I'm on a roll, so I'll probably work well into the night, if you don't mind."

"I don't mind." But she did feel guilty. "Can I help?" She meant that in more ways than one.

He smiled again before turning back to his work. "You already have."

CHAPTER EIGHTEEN

BY 5:10 P.M. TRAVIS HAD assembled the last display rack. He threw empty boxes into the trash bin behind the store. Kylie had changed back into jeans and sneakers, and was on her way home. She'd plastered on a smile when she'd said goodbye, but he knew she was upset. About the HPS, her hair, plus she mumbled something about Faye not taking her calls. Travis had wanted to hug her on her way out, but he didn't dare. She might mistake his affection for a sexual overture. It wasn't like that. Could never be like that. But he didn't plan on explaining—about his affections or anything else. If all went well, in two days he'd be on a plane to France. A long-lost dream resurrected by Kylie.

At 5:15 p.m. Travis examined the weather-beaten sign that had previously hung above the awning of the store.

McGraw's Shoe Store
"Practical Shoes for Practical People"

The style and message no longer reflected the interior or stock—or its proprietor. Travis envisioned an overhaul that would complement the renovations without violating any codes.

If anyone knew how to get around red tape, it was the Artful Dodger.

Screw the Historical Preservation Society. If they thought they were going to silence Kylie's cry for change, they were wrong. He knew what it was like to crave something different. He knew the anguish of being denied.

"Don't make this about you," he could hear Mona saying.
Too late.

At 6:10 p.m. Travis admired his work. In less than an hour he'd tackled both the exterior sign and the interior plaque that used to hang above the cashier counter. He popped open his sixth can of Coke and contemplated what still needed to be done, undaunted by the hard work, inspired by the challenge.

Interior decorating had been his first passion. Even as a kid, he'd spent days rearranging his ma's furniture. While his older brother had his nose stuck in a graphic novel, Travis flipped through the pages of their aunt Maria's home decor magazines. When it came to furnishings and window treatments, he always had opinions on colors and styles. Even as a teen, the passion never died, but it *was* snuffed—by his pop, his uncle and his brother.

Tradition dictated Travis go into the family business. Interior design was for fairies and pussies. Except Travis wasn't a chip off the old man. And he wasn't anything like his brother. He couldn't stomach physical intimidation. But he was smart. Smart and personable. He could talk anyone in circles and dodge any problem—hence his nickname.

So they sent him to law school. Having a lawyer in the family was beneficial, and even though he didn't love the work, he was good at it. Because he loved his family, he ignored his true self. Just as he'd ignored the realization early on regarding his sexual preference. He'd conformed and been miserable.

He didn't want Kylie to buckle under town pressure and conform. He'd do everything in his power to transform McGraw's into the shoe store of her unique vision. As for her dream trip, he planned on making that happen, too. But he had to work fast. The last thing Travis wanted was to bring danger into Kylie's life. He couldn't shake the bad feeling

that he'd stirred up trouble by breaking routine. By sending that e-mail. He couldn't get Mona's voice out of his head.
   "Run!"

CHAPTER NINETEEN

THE SUN SAT LOW ON THE horizon by the time Jack drove out of town. Shy sat in the passenger seat, head out the window, ears ruffling in the wind. Not a care in the world.

Jack focused on the road, his mind clogged with the day's events. Problems out the ass.

After his tense encounter with Kylie, Mayor Wilson had dragged him into an uncomfortable meeting with the town council. They'd hired Jack to keep the peace. Kylie was proving a nuisance.

"I was hoping this crisis of hers would play out when she sobered up," said the mayor. "Unfortunately, she's still acting out and promised there's more to come."

"If Kylie sabotages the success of the Apple Festival," said Fred McCourt, president of the First National Bank, "she's going to rile the town merchants and tarnish her reputation."

"We'd hate to see folks turn on that girl just because she's having a rough time," said the mayor.

"We're counting on you to curtail her sudden rebellious streak," said Max Grogan, who, although retired from the fire department, seemed to hold several other civic positions.

"How do you propose I do that?" Jack asked, not liking the gist of the conversation.

"Use your imagination," said McCourt.

"Or your influence as a friend of the family," said Max.

"Or your badge," said the mayor.

Even though they'd had the best interests of Eden and,

seemingly, Kylie, at heart, he'd left that meeting unsettled. Being ordered to manipulate Kylie, by any means, chafed on several levels. The situation was complicated by their mutual attraction.

The afternoon had digressed when Ms. Vine hit him with a ton of paperwork and Ziffel reported gossip about Jessie applying for jobs all over town. Jessie had never worked a real job. She'd never wanted to. She'd married well and lived the good life. And now she was willing to work as a hostess, cashier or salesperson? Clearly, the woman was desperate, yet no one had been willing to hire her. At least that was the scoop according to Ziffel. Maybe Jessie would inform him differently.

Jack pulled into his driveway and cut the engine of his SUV. He swiped off his sunglasses and rolled back tense shoulders. Loud thumping distracted him from his thoughts. He glanced over at Shy, who was sitting in the passenger seat. Her wagging tail thwacked against the leather seat. He looked to where she looked and spotted Maddie sitting on the front porch swing, alone and focused on a book. He smiled. First, because it meant Jessie had decided to stay on another night. Second, because it was good to see his niece.

He thought back on their brief interaction last night. He hadn't expected Maddie to be so timid. So...polite. Jessie had been an outgoing kid, always vying for attention. Maddie was the extreme opposite. She'd stolen his heart in a blink of her baby browns. It blew Jack's mind that Frank had walked away from that sweet little girl. Although, he'd heard through the grapevine that he'd never been a doting father. Probably because he was too busy screwing everything in a skirt.

Jack tucked away furious thoughts as he approached his somber niece.

Shy bolted forward and surprised the kid by jumping on the swing. Maddie tossed aside her book and hugged the dog, burying her face in Shy's sleek fur.

"Hi, sweet pea," Jack said as he scaled the front stoop.

Her pale skin flushed as though she'd been caught doing something wrong. She nudged away Shy and swiped dog hair from her pink dress—a lacy, poofy thing, embroidered with flowers. Jack noted her white leggings and shiny black shoes. Her long black hair was brushed to a high gloss and...were those rhinestones on her headband? *At least it's not a tiara,* he thought, wondering if Jessie dressed her daughter like a princess every day.

He stooped in front of Maddie, noted the sadness in her eyes. "How was school?" he asked casually.

She glanced away, shrugged.

Not wanting to force their relationship, he respected her silence and glanced at the house. "Your mom inside?"

"Making supper."

"I'll lend her a hand."

"Okay."

He noted the way Maddie kept stealing looks at the dog. He ached to see her smile, to hear her laugh. "Shy's been cooped up all day," he said as he stood. "Would you do me a favor, hon? Run her around? Maybe throw her a stick? She likes playing fetch."

Maddie's eyes sparkled, but she didn't move. "I'll get dirty," she said in a small voice.

That was Jessie talking.

"I'll square it with your mom."

She glanced at the badge clipped to his belt. A smile tugged at the corner of her mouth. "Okay."

Maddie pushed off the swing and ran into the yard, poking around an old oak, looking for a fallen branch. Shy followed, and soon after the two were engaged in a playful game.

The minute Jack saw a genuine smile on the girl's face, he moved inside. He wondered at Jessie's mood. Wondered if she'd fill him in on her day or if she'd shut him out. Wondered how he could make *her* smile.

He tugged off his EPD cap and shrugged out of his nylon jacket. He caught a whiff of tangy sauce and garlic toast. He couldn't remember the last time he'd had a home-cooked meal, cooked by someone other than himself. Although he could say for certain, he'd never had a meal cooked by Jessie. Mouth watering, he followed his nose.

His sister was shaking oregano into a saucepan when he walked into his kitchen. He moved closer and looked over her shoulder. "Spaghetti and meatballs?"

"With garlic bread. I know," she said before he could comment. "You were expecting rabbit food."

Jack heard the hurt in her voice. "I'm sorry about that anorexic crack, Jess."

"A loss of appetite and an unwillingness to eat are two different things."

"I know." Jack noted his sister's frail frame. She'd always been conscious of her weight, but this was beyond maintenance. He blamed stress. Trying to lighten her mood, he indicated the boiling pasta and simmering sauce. "So, tonight you're hungry?" Maybe things were looking up.

"It's for Madeline. She had a bad day. I'm trying to cheer her up."

"Thought she looked a little glum when she greeted me on the porch."

"No offense, but I think she was more interested in greeting the dog."

"I don't blame her," he said with a smile. "Shy's more fun than me. They're in the front yard playing fetch."

"Oh, for..." Jessica frowned over her shoulder. "She'll get dirty."

"Dirt washes off. So why does Maddie need cheering up?"

She focused on the sauce. "Another incident at school. Kids making fun of her. Calling her names."

"Like what?"

"Fancy-Girl. Priss-Butt. Only this time a little boy stuck up for her and there was a fight. He got in trouble and... she's upset for multiple reasons."

"Jessie."

"What?"

"Maddie does look like a Priss-Butt."

"What?" She abandoned the wooden spoon and turned to glare.

"You dress her up like a little princess. Like a mini pageant queen. She's a five-year-old. Let her be a kid."

"And you're qualified to give advice on children because?" She threw up her hands and turned back to the stove. "Never mind."

Jack backed off. He nabbed two beers from the fridge, set an open bottle next to Jessie, then took a pull of his own. "I'm glad you decided to stay."

"It won't be forever." She took a sip of Bud, then poured the boiled pasta into a strainer. "Just until I can afford to rent a place."

Again he wondered why she couldn't or wouldn't stay in her own home. Four thousand square feet of luxury. As far as he knew, the house was paid off.

"I got a job," she blurted. "As a server at Boone's Bar and Grill."

Jack paused midsip.

"I start tomorrow," she plowed on. "Wanda said I lucked out. Said her day server, Missy, wants to switch to nights so she can attend classes at ITT Tech in Fort Wayne. Still, the day shift is 10:00 a.m. to 6:00 p.m. Which means I need to find someone to watch Madeline for a few hours after school. I can't ask our old sitter. I...I just can't."

"Why Boone's?" He had an idea, but he wanted to hear it from Jessie. Couldn't be good keeping her feelings bottled. Maybe if she opened up about the job hunt, she'd open up about Frank.

Embarrassed, she busied herself transferring the toasted bread from the oven to a napkin-covered plate. "Boone and Wanda were the only ones who'd hire me. They're desperate for help. I'm desperate for a job."

"Why?"

"I told you. I don't want Frank's money."

"Why?"

"Because…just because!"

Jack eyed his sister's stiff spine. Jessica Lynn Cortez, former pageant queen, wife of a prominent lawyer, a woman who'd earned a reputation as a snob, serving up suds and chicken wings to the locals? Jack was impressed with her determination to earn her own money—no matter the cost to her pride.

Jessie shoveled spaghetti into a large bowl, then poured on the sauce and meatballs. "Would you please tell Madeline to wash up? Dinner's ready."

"I'll pick up Maddie from school," Jack said, backtracking to avoid a total freeze out. "If I can't, I'll have Ziffel do it. I usually get off at five, so we just need coverage for a couple of hours." He angled his head. "What about Mrs. Carmichael? She has a lot of experience with children and I think she'd appreciate the company. I'll look into it."

Jessie bristled.

"What?"

"You're doing that superhero thing. I don't want to be saved. I want to take control of my own future, but…"

"What?"

"I can't refuse your offer or your suggestions. I know I can trust Madeline with you and Deputy Ziffel and…Mrs. Carmichael. She's perfect." She blew out a tense breath. "Thank you."

"You're welcome."

"Now, would you please call in Madeline?"

"Sure." He swigged more beer, then set the bottle on the counter. She could've complained about her humiliating day of job hunting. Or about Frank's philandering. She could've asked her big brother to beat the shit out of her piece-of-shit husband. The old Jessie would have done all those things. Instead, she seemed determined to endure this life-altering debacle in stoic, if not stubborn, silence.

"I thought about what you said this afternoon. You were right, Jessie. I didn't like you, or rather what I saw of you when we were younger. I love you. You're my sister, for chrissake. But you always ticked me off. I thought you were self-centered and insensitive, as a kid and an adult."

She swallowed hard. "And now?"

"I think Dad was right," he said while turning to fetch his niece. "There's more to you than meets the eye."

CHAPTER TWENTY

LIVING IN THE FRICKING middle of nowhere had its advantages.

For instance, no one saw Kylie wipe out on her bike when she cut too sharply and peeled into her gravel driveway. She'd been going too fast, obsessing on her crappy day. The bike was okay, which was more than she could say for her pride and bruised thigh. But at least no one, especially Jack, had witnessed the embarrassing display.

Mad at herself, she'd parked the Kawasaki in the shed, then hobbled toward her humble abode. She'd invested in the 1989 single-wide mobile home for three reasons.

1. It was a goodly distance from the home she'd grown up in. The home still occupied by her mom and grandma. Two women who bickered even when they agreed. (How was *that* possible?)

2. It was cheap. Her dream trip wasn't. And so far she'd saved for it twice.

3. Privacy.

No one was in her business thanks to the seclusion of Hawkins Woods. So when she'd paused two feet from her doorstep and screamed her frustration to the darkening sky—no one heard. When she kicked the bird feeder in her Zen garden—no one saw. Unfortunately, the outburst hadn't quieted her chaotic emotions.

Once inside, she'd changed out of her ripped jeans into comfy black yoga pants and an oversize Godzilla T-shirt. She'd checked her answering machine—no messages, flipped though her mail—all junk, then schlepped into the kitchen, realizing, on top of everything else, she was lonely.

Distracted, she'd burned her dinner, so she'd settled on a bowl of frozen raspberry yogurt and a cup of mint green tea.

She was heartsick about her hair, frustrated with Jack, confused by her feelings for Jack, lonesome for Spenser, concerned about Travis and anxious about Faye—who'd yet to return two of her calls. Yes, she'd broken down and reached out first. She was mad about that, too.

Kylie was sitting on a cushioned mat in her living room, in the lotus position, seeking inner calm, when her friend blew into the trailer, her big purse in one hand, a tie-dyed tote in the other. "Got here as quick as I could." She dropped on her knees in front of Kylie. "I'm so sorry."

They'd parted on heated terms yesterday—at least, Faye had. They hadn't talked all day, a first. Yet suddenly here Faye was, in person and apologizing. For what? Kylie decided to skip over yesterday's mystery tiff, for now, and focused on today's trials. "Sorry about my hair? Or about the historical society's ruling?"

"Both. I got your messages. I meant to call back. It was one thing after another today."

"Tell me about it."

"I stopped by the store, but you'd already left. Travis told me you were pretty upset."

"Yeah, well—"

"He wouldn't let me inside."

Kylie flinched at her friend's wounded tone. "I told him I didn't want anyone to see the interior until we were through."

"Since when am I just anyone?"

"You're not. You're you. You're…special." Kylie's cheeks burned. "I should have specified—"

"Never mind." Faye waved off the apology and squinted at Kylie. "Let's shed some light on the supposed catastrophe." She reached over and flicked on the dragon table lamp Kylie had purchased on eBay.

Maintaining her cross-legged position, Kylie loosened her tightly wound bun and shook her head.

"Yikes."

"Told you I look like a character out of a Manga graphic novel."

"I thought you were exaggerating."

"I wasn't."

"I can see that."

How could Faye be so calm? Oh, right. She'd had purple hair once. By choice. Kylie wasn't Faye. Yes, she'd wanted a change. But this… "My hair is striped. *Striped.*"

"I can see that."

"The highlights are orange. Not auburn. Not blond. *Orange.* Like the fruit. Like a carrot. Like a flipping pumpkin!"

Faye hugged her tote. "I can fix that."

Kylie teared up. Partly because it seemed as if she and Faye were back to normal. Partly because she'd offered to do what Petunia had declared impossible. "Petunia tried some sort of toner, but it didn't help. She said I need to wait a couple of days before she tries something else. Her schedule's packed and my hair's too fragile."

"Petunia can kiss my patootie."

Kylie laughed and sniffed back tears.

"You know me. I know hair. Mostly I've always colored my own and mostly it comes out okay."

"Mostly." Kylie opted not to dwell on the time chunks had broken off of her friend's hair due to overbleaching. That bungle had resulted in Faye chopping her long hair into a funky boyish cut.

"If you'd rather wait—"

Kylie grabbed her friend's hand and tugged her toward the bathroom. "In spite of everything I said on my birthday— strike that—mostly everything I said, in this instance I'd give anything for ordinary." Kylie quirked a hopeful smile. "Please tell me you have a box of blah-boring brown dye in that tote."

"I've got espresso. A shade darker than your mocha-brown, but it's the closest match I could find. Be warned, the color won't grab the same to your orange streaks as it will to your natural chunks."

"So I'll still be two-toned?"

"Yes, but two-toned brown. Hopefully."

Kylie groaned.

Faye shrugged. "It's an art, not a science."

"Have at it, maestro." Kylie removed her glasses and set them on the vanity. She sank onto the toilet seat of her cramped bathroom while Faye snapped on latex gloves. She wondered about yesterday's mystery tiff. Wondered if things were okay between Faye and Stan. She chided herself for being self-absorbed and sought to reconnect with her friend. "So, how was your day?"

"Busy. Stressful." Faye draped a towel over Kylie's shoulders. "Got another call from the school. Spent an hour in Principal Peterson's office. Sting punched a kid."

"What? Why?" Sting was mischievous, like most five-year-old boys, but he wasn't mean.

"Apparently some kids have been picking on Madeline Cortez, calling her names, making her cry. You've met Madeline. Unlike her mom, she's shy and sweet. Sting attacked the meanest of the bullies in her defense."

Kylie smiled.

"I know. I'm proud and worried at the same time. I don't want him to think violence is the solution to all problems. I told Stan we need to be more strict about what he can and can't watch on TV. Even cartoons glamorize violence."

"Everyone's desensitized these days," Kylie said as Faye squeezed dark goo on her neon hair. "Fifteen years ago folks would have been shocked and disgusted by the graphic killings on *Omertà*. Now they seem to revel in it. The bloodier the better."

"If even one-quarter of what's depicted on that show is true to life, can you imagine some of the horrors Jack has seen? I mean, the mob is rampant in New York, right? No wonder he burned out."

"Who said he burned out?"

"I heard it from Kerri who got it from Deputy Ziffel who got it straight from Jack. Said he burned out on big crime."

Kylie stiffened. She couldn't help feeling jealous of the pretty, successful and normal-colored-haired Kerri Waldo. "Why is Kerri prying into Jack's personal business? For that matter, why is Ed Ziffel running off at the mouth about his boss?"

"You're kidding, right? Jack's a homegrown hero returned home. The only thing that would instigate more gossip is if your brother moved back."

"Ha! Like that'll happen."

"Like you want it to."

Kylie's stomach knotted. "What's that supposed to mean?"

"Never mind." Faye stripped off the gloves then glanced at her watch. "Tell me about the meeting with the board."

The knot tugged tighter. "Not much to tell. They shot me down before I even stated my case. It burns my buns that I can't alter the storefront and all because McGraw's is part of a historical block."

"Hey, at least they didn't stop you from renovating the inside."

"If I didn't know better, I'd think you were siding with the HPS."

Faye didn't respond.

Kylie frowned. "You are taking their side."

"I'm being realistic," she said, digging through her big purse. "Eden benefits financially from the tourists who frequent the Apple Festival. Those folks enjoy the town's old-fashioned ambience as do most of the people who live here." Faye leaned into the vanity and swiped red lipstick over her puckered mouth. "Why do you think Stan and I retained the Americana look of the Orchard House? It's good business."

Kylie crossed her arms over her chest. "Being unique is good business, too."

"The historical block *is* unique, Kylie. It's provincial. It's nostalgic. Locals and tourists appreciate the 1950s facades, a reminder of simpler, better times. If you modernize McGraw's exterior by painting it funky colors and swapping the green awning for leopard print or pink-and-yellow stripes, you'll ruin the unified quaintness of the historical block. What if it has a negative impact on business? I'm not just talking about McGraw's. I'm thinking about the other store proprietors. Jay Jarvis and Ray Keystone, for example. Normally you'd consider them, too."

Kylie blanched. No one had ever accused her of being selfish.

Faye sighed. "I miss you, Kylie."

"What do you mean? I'm right here."

"Not the Kylie McGraw I know and love." Her friend spun away. "I shouldn't have come here tonight. I'm going to make hot tea. Want some?"

Kylie stared after her. "No, I don't want *tea*." Perplexed, she held tight to the towel around her shoulders and followed Faye into the kitchen. "I want an explanation. You were snippy with me all day yesterday and now... What's going on with you?"

Faye filled the brass kettle with water and clanged it to the gas stove.

Kylie's stomach turned. "If you're mad at me, just say so."

"I'm mad at you. I thought I was over it, but I'm not."

"What did I do?"

"For starters, you betrayed my confidence."

Kylie flinched. "When?"

"During your drunken tirade at Boone's. You told the whole bar that I whine about our summer guests at the Orchard House. First, I didn't realize you considered my venting, whining. Second, it got back to Stan, who took my *whining* personally."

So *that's* why they'd been fighting. "Oh, Faye. I...I..."

Kylie stumbled for an excuse, only there wasn't one. Worse, she didn't even remember her slip. "I was tipsy, and stoked, and rambling—"

"I know. I was there."

"I'm sorry."

"Apology accepted."

"But you're still mad at me."

"Yes."

"For?"

"For flipping out. For acting recklessly. For blowing your dream-trip fund on a whim!"

Rattled by Faye's vehemence, Kylie plopped onto a kitchen chair. "It wasn't a whim, exactly. I've been itching to reinvent McGraw's for a while now, but I felt bound by…"

"Tradition?"

"Exactly. I imagined the smallest changes causing Dad and Grandpa to roll over in their graves. I spent a lifetime trying to win their approval. It's a hard habit to break. But then I snapped and suddenly there was no turning back. I *had* to renovate McGraw's. I confess I had second thoughts this afternoon, but Travis told me to trust my instincts. He said there comes a point when a person has to stop living for others and start living for themselves."

Faye folded her arms, cocked one brow. "Sounds like you and Travis had a real heart-to-heart."

"Weird. I know. I mean, he's always been so private."

"You mean aloof."

"I feel sorry for him. I think he's stuck with a life he doesn't want. Kind of like you and me."

Faye's face burned red. "I'm not *stuck* with anything. I love my life. I love Stan. I love my kids!"

"I know you do!" Mortified, Kylie shot to her feet. "I didn't mean it like that. I just meant…you wanted to be a rock star."

"*You* wanted to backpack across Asia!"

"Why do you keep harping on that? I've saved before, I'll save again. When the time is right, I'll go."

"No, you won't. If you really wanted to go, you wouldn't have blown your savings on this spontaneous renovation."

"I just explained—"

"You would have told Spenser about your dream trip when he called you on your birthday," Faye plowed on. "You didn't tell him because you knew he'd come home. He wouldn't deny you your adventure. Only, you don't want him running McGraw's, even temporarily. What if he liked it? What if he took over permanently? It would kill you because—brace yourself—you love being in charge. You love that shoe store and you love watching over your mom and grandma even though they drive you nuts. You're a caretaker, not a risk-taker. I don't think you had that birthday meltdown because you're bored. I think you're unhappy. Not with Eden, but with your…circumstances."

"Thank you, Dr. Freud." Kylie was so dang stunned, so furious, her brains were leaking out her ears. She swiped at the goo with the corner of her towel. Not brains. Dye. "Is it time to wash this stuff off yet?"

Faye glanced at her watch. "No. And you don't have to be sarcastic, by the way."

"You just psychoanalyzed me and it wasn't pretty!"

"I didn't mean to be so blunt, but I've given this a lot of thought. Childhood dreams and adult needs are two different things, Kylie. Maybe you should give up Zen, because it sure as hell hasn't gotten you in touch with your feelings. You're clinging to the past and afraid of the future. Stop chanting other people's epiphanies and listen to your heart. Figure out what you really want and go for it. Take Jack, for instance. I know you're still crushing on him. Travis mentioned he's the reason you wanted a makeover."

"I can't believe you two dished about me."

"I can't believe you confided in Travis!"

Kylie blinked. "Is that what this is about? Because I bonded with someone other than you?"

"You *bonded* with hardware guy? You don't even know

him! Oh, wait. Oh, no." She smacked her hand to her forehead. "So *that's* why he jumped at the chance to work for you. Long hours, little pay."

"What are you driving at, Faye?"

"He's trying to get in your pants."

Kylie gaped. "He just lost his wife!"

"Three months ago. He's miserable and lonely. You're pretty and lonely."

"You know what?" Kylie snapped. "You need to leave."

"You know what? You're right." Faye stalked out of the room and returned two seconds later with her purse and tote slung over her shoulder. She handed Kylie her glasses and a folded paper. "Just follow the directions."

Kylie perched her glasses on the end of her nose, trying not to smear the ear temples with dye goo. She stared down at the printed paper as Faye slammed out the door. *Apply color and check after twenty-five minutes.*

Oooh-kay. And Faye had applied the color *when?*

Great. Just great. Although Kylie didn't much care what shade of brown her hair ended up, so long as it wasn't orange.

She stormed back to the bathroom, Faye's words ringing in her ears. *"You're a caretaker, not a risk-taker."* Faye had said a lot of hurtful things, but that particular observation cut to the core. Along with her grandma's comment that she was a sensible girl, and J.J.'s remark that she was usually *so nice.* And what had Jack called her? *Sweet!* He'd also told her not to do anything stupid, which griped her fanny as much as the HPS ordering her to conform.

Every fiber in her body burned to rebel. To make a statement. To shake up Eden.

She stared into the vanity mirror. "What would Spenser do?"

A memory popped into her head and she smiled. "I'll show them."

CHAPTER TWENTY-ONE

Philadelphia, Pennsylvania

"FUCK!"

That had to hurt. Carmine watched his nephew spring off the sofa, after sitting on a four-inch stiletto. He tried not to smile. "Hey. *Babbo.* Keep your voice down. It's almost midnight."

But it wasn't just the late hour. Wiped out from a forty-eight-hour creative binge, a session of wild sex and two celebratory bottles of merlot, his mistress was dead to the world. Carmine welcomed the quiet. Dixie Darling was a fucking ball of energy. She never stopped, never shut up—except when she was smoking Carmine's sausage.

Mario glanced up the stairway of the rented brown-stone, waited. Satisfied he hadn't woken Sleeping Beauty, he glared at the glittering offender. "One of Dixie's creations?" he asked at a muted volume.

Carmine nodded. "She's obsessed."

"It's whacked."

"It's one of her classier results. You should've seen the sneakers she's been decorating for the past two days."

"Who would buy this shit?"

"Someone with whacked taste."

Mario set the high-heeled shoe on the gleaming cocktail table and rubbed the seat of his tailored trousers. He eyed the sofa again before sitting down. "Why was a shoe wedged in between the cushions?"

Dressed only in boxers and a tee, Carmine shook off the remnants of satiation and opened a bottle of sambuca. "Dixie was modeling them for me earlier tonight and…" *we got naked and kinky* "—one thing led to another." *How's that for exercise, Dr. Aversi?*

Mario took the proffered glass of liquor and winked. "You're a lucky man, Chickie."

Luck had nothing to do with it. He was used to getting what he wanted. He wanted Dixie. She was a breath of fresh air in his stale life. She took his mind off his worries. Made him forget about his impending death. That's why he'd been risking his wife's fury by spending more time with his mistress. He loved Marisa, but she was part of his fucking reality. A reality plagued with health issues and prophetic nightmares.

Dixie was a blessed distraction, a remedy of sorts. Like Dr. Bennett. Bennett tended his demons, while Dixie showed him the stars. Carmine's pole twitched just thinking about the way she'd sashayed into the living room wearing a sheer pink nightie and those four-inch fuck-me pumps. He'd had to tear his gaze away from her luscious ta-tas when she'd asked for his opinion on her latest custom-decorated shoes. Since he'd wanted her to ride him sore, he'd noted the blinding combination of sequins, rhinestones and metallic paint with a proud smile. "*Beautiful, baby,*" he'd lied. "*Like you,*" he'd added honestly. Then he ridded her of that flimsy nightie, telling her to strut her stuff—wearing nothing but those *beautiful* FMPs.

"No offense," Mario said, "but Dixie's a little *oobatz.* Though I guess you don't mind what with her being—"

"Yeah?"

"Uh, so easy on the eye."

He meant a walking sex toy. But Mario knew better than to disrespect Carmine's mistress. As for being a little crazy, sure, Dixie was all foam, no beer, but she'd been blessed with a stunning face, killer body and a voracious sexual appetite. She used to hawk drinks at the Candy Stripper.

Now she was his *goomah*. So what if she had a loose screw? She had a heart of gold and a mouth that worked magic. "She's got a Web site now."

"For what?"

"Bada-Bling!"

Mario blinked.

"That's the name of her business."

"She's got a business? Since when?"

Since she softened me up with a hummer that melted my brain cells. "Since two weeks ago." Carmine raised his glass in a toast. *"Salute."* He sipped the strong licorice liquor, weighed his words. He didn't want to give the wrong impression. He wasn't pussy-whipped like his brother-in-law. What he was, was head-over-sparkly-heels in lust.

"Dixie's...motivated. She's got a lot of energy," he said. "A lot of ideas. She approached me about selling her custom-decorated shoes over the Internet and I thought, why the fuck not? Something to keep her occupied, *capiche?*"

He'd also enrolled her in a culinary class. Yeah, yeah. So she wasn't Italian. She hadn't been weaned on home-made pasta and gravy. But freaking ragú?

Mario frowned. "What if *Bada-Bling!* takes off? What if she can't keep up and has to hire help? You want strangers traipsing in and out of here? You want to attract attention? The don who rebuilt this organization on a low-profile mentality?"

Carmine sipped his drink and watched his nephew's ears turn red. Mario had earned the nickname "Turk" because of his aggressive tendencies. In time, and with maturity, he'd make a strong leader, if not a great one. It's not that the kid was short-tempered, just that the oddest things set him off. Once the fuse was lit, watch the fuck out. "Mario."

"Yeah?"

"Dixie can barely balance her checkbook. Chances are good she'll run *Bada-Bling!* into the ground before it ever takes off. Or she'll get discouraged. Do you know how many handmade, special-made, custom-designed, uniquely yours Web sites there are on the Net? *Bada-Bling!* has been up and running for two weeks and she's had one sale. Granted, it was a mass order. I think she decorated somewhere around forty pairs of shoes. But she gave the woman a deep discount. Between minimal sales and little profit…" He snorted. "I'm not worried. Now, give me the nut before Dixie wakes up and spoils this little party. What couldn't wait until morning?"

Focused once more, Mario hitched back his leather jacket and leaned forward. "It's about *He-who-shall-not-be-named.*"

CHAPTER TWENTY-TWO

JACK WAS WRESTLING with insomnia when he heard a loud knock. He glanced at the bedside clock—12:31 a.m. Shy groaned when he rolled out of bed. He pulled on jeans and a shirt, tucked his Glock in his waistband and moved quietly into the hall.

Jessie peeked out of the spare bedroom. "Who is it?"

"I don't know." Jack noted his sister's worried expression. Did she think it was Frank? Although she wouldn't discuss the man, he sensed there was more to the breakup than the Cheating Bastard's infidelities. Whatever it was, it had driven Jessie out of her own home and shaken her to her core. He hoped it was Frank knocking. He had a few choice words for that fucker.

"Whoever it is," Jack said to his sister, "I'll handle it. Go back to bed."

He descended the stairs before she could comment. Shy trotted along. He swung open the front door ready to coldcock Frank Cortez. But it wasn't the shifty lawyer. It was an anxious uniformed cop. "What's wrong, Hooper?"

"We have a jumper, Chief."

The words registered, but the emergency didn't. "There isn't a building in Eden that exceeds three stories."

"She's on the water tower, sir."

"She?"

"Kylie McGraw."

KYLIE RACKED HER BRAIN for a positive affirmation, but one thought raged. *I'm going to die.*

Toes precariously close to the edge of the narrow circular walkway, she gritted her teeth and squeezed the steel railing. She was locked in a half squat. She couldn't straighten. She couldn't sit. She couldn't *move*.

She heard a siren. The second siren in the last few minutes. Fire truck? Squad car? Ambulance? She didn't know who or what was down there. Only that someone had blinded her with a powerful searchlight and that someone—not Jack— kept barking at her through a bullhorn. *"Climb down!"*

She sincerely wished she could.

Her arms, though toned from yoga, felt noodly after the strenuous climb. Her leg, bruised from her cycle mishap, throbbed. Her backpack, weighted down with two cans of yellow spray paint and a super-bright lantern, cut into her shoulders. She'd take it off, but that would mean letting go of the railing. If she let go, she'd fall. It was a two-hundred-foot drop.

Splat.

"Don't puke. Don't puke."

"Kylie, it's Jack. I need you to climb down, honey."

Unlike the previous person on the bullhorn, Jack didn't snap nervous orders. He delivered a calm plea. The endearment made her insides squishy, even though she knew it was probably a professional tactic. It also made her nervous. It intimated concern. Were he merely irritated, he would've said, *"Climb down. Now."*

"You've got a lot of people worried, Tiger. At least wave so we know you're okay."

She couldn't wave and she wasn't okay. But she did glance toward his voice, a kneejerk reaction that backfired. The earth slammed up and back. Her vision blurred. She screamed. "Jack!"

"I'm coming up. Don't move."

If only she could!

Kylie registered a wash of white headlights and red sirens before she jerked her gaze back to the horizon. How many *people* were down there?

The searchlight shifted to light the police chief's way.

Were she capable of romanticizing the moment, she'd think of herself as a damsel in distress and Jack as her knight in shining armor. *"I'll rescue you, m'lady."*

Unfortunately, her thoughts were grim. "I'm going to die." If not from the fall, from fear.

How did Spenser scale mountains and shimmy into cramped dark caves? How did he face spear-wielding tribes and jungle beasts without freezing up? She'd have to ask him. That's if she didn't croak before night's end.

Heart pounding, Kylie gripped the railing tighter. Her headlamp, an adventure gadget Spenser had sent her for nighttime mushroom hunting, cut a brilliant streak into the black night. But since she was in the flipping stratosphere and since there were no birds flying in her direct line of vision, she saw nothing. She pretended she was in her Zen Garden staring into Hawkins Woods in the dead of night— grounded in more ways than one. Still her pulse raced and her body trembled. Though the air was chilly, she was soaked with sweat. Looking down made her nauseous and dizzy. Similar to how she'd felt on Travis's ladder, only a billion times worse. Logic told her she'd developed a fear of heights. Sometimes that just happened, right? Like people who loved carnival rides as a kid, then lost their lunches as adults?

She was definitely scared out of her newly dyed gourd. Why she'd been able to scale the water tower without hesitation, she couldn't say. Then again, she hadn't been looking down. She'd been focused on each rung of the metal ladder. Then on the green tank as she sprayed one of the red apples yellow. She'd been so pumped, so determined to make a statement, it wasn't until she'd packed up and turned to descend that she froze.

"Mind if I join you?"

Jack's voice, so near, so gentle, warmed Kylie to her chilled bones. "Please do," she gritted out.

"I know you had a bad day, hon—"

"Try awful. But I'm not suicidal, if that's what you're getting at."

"Never crossed my mind, Tiger."

"No, you're probably thinking this is another one of my ploys to shake things up."

"Isn't it?"

"No. Well, yes. But it sort of went wrong."

"We'll talk about that later."

"You mean you'll lecture me later." She was too nervous to turn her head, but she could feel him creeping closer. "I can hear it now," she babbled, then affected a deep voice. "I told you not to do anything stupid, Tiger."

"Actually," Jack said, "I think climbing the water tower is more crazy than stupid."

"Great. So you don't think I'm suicidal but you do think I'm certifiable. I bet you didn't call Spenser crazy when he climbed up here and spray painted *Spense loves Nancy* for the world to see."

"Nope. Called him…well, let's just say it wasn't complimentary. He only did that because Nancy promised him a certain sexual favor."

"Ick." She didn't want to know that kind of stuff about her brother. Thank you very much.

"What am I dealing with here, Kylie?"

"An unexpected and paralyzing fear of heights."

"Okay."

"No. It's not okay. It's mortifying. It's terrifying."

"It's acrophobia."

"Every time I look down, I get dizzy and my vision goes wonky."

"Vertigo. Ever see that movie?"

What the…? She had one foot on a banana peel, the other over a grave, and he was talking movies?

"Alfred Hitchcock flick. James Stewart. Kim Novak."

"Yes, yes. Of course I've seen it. Who hasn't? It's a classic. Oh, I get it. You're trying to distract me. I've seen this on TV. The cop negotiator talking down the jumper.

Only, trust me, I have no intention of taking a dive. Hence my death grip."

"I had it bad for Kim Novak."

He was close now. Maybe a foot away. She didn't dare look. "Of course you did. She was blond and stacked. Hollywood gorgeous."

"It was more about her persona. That fragile air. The need to be saved."

Kylie snorted. "In that case, I must be looking pretty good right now."

Jack chuckled. "You're not fragile or needy, Tiger."

"Not usually." She nearly wilted when she felt his body flush against hers. The backpack proved a wedge, but he maneuvered his arms around her, wrapped his warm hands over her clammy ones. He offered his protection, just like on the ladder, only this time she didn't relax. She couldn't.

"Some really awful thoughts are going through my head, Jack."

"Like what?"

"Like what if this platform isn't built to withstand our combined weight? What if we fall through? Or what if this railing gives and we fall over?"

"We're not going to fall. We're going to back away from the ledge."

"That would entail *letting go* of the railing."

"Hold on to me instead."

He's only doing his job, she told herself, yet his tone was so intimate. Seduced, she relaxed her fingers and the next moment she was in his arms. She didn't remember turning. She didn't remember him pulling her against the tank's wall. But the feel of his ripped body, of his strong embrace, of his hand swiping off her headlamp to grab a fistful of her ponytail, was imprinted on her brain for life.

"I just wanted to make a statement," she whispered against his chest. "I wanted to prove something to the HPS. To Faye. To myself. I didn't know about the acrophobia. It's awful."

"I know, hon."

"I'll never make it down. I keep thinking about slipping like I did on Travis's ladder. What if I fall? What if I take you with me? What if…?" She faltered, her brain misfiring as he cradled her face and angled her head. "What are you doing?"

"Giving you something else to think about." He smothered her with a kiss that fried common sense. Think? Who could think?

But she could feel. Tonight, her senses weren't numbed by alcohol. Tonight, Jack was the aggressor and she was…overwhelmed. By his heat. His urgency. His passion. She felt his mouth on hers, his tongue sweeping in and over. Tasting. Devouring. She felt his right hand anchoring her head. His left, palming the small of her back. She felt herself give over to the lust she'd been harboring for eons. Her heat. Her urgency. Her passion.

Bobby had been a good kisser. But Jack…Jack was better than good. The not-so-great kiss on her birthday had been a fluke. She'd been drunk. He'd been a gentleman. This moment the man seduced. This kiss ignited a fire in the pit of her stomach. It scorched her brain and sizzled through her blood. Moments ago she'd been chilled. Now she burned. Grim thoughts went up in smoke as she imagined them in bed. Making love.

Magic.

"Not that we don't enjoy a good show," someone groused over the bullhorn. "But some of us would like to go home."

Max.

But of course the busybody was on the scene. Even though he was retired he still knew every move the fire department made. This was probably the most excitement he'd had in a month. It was certainly the highlight of her year.

Jack eased back and, begrudgingly, Kylie opened her eyes.

They were in the spotlight.

Literally.

Once in Jack's arms, she'd forgotten about that annoying

searchlight. She should have been embarrassed, but she was too spellbound. Mesmerized by Jack's earnest, dark gaze and tender touch, she blew out a shaky breath. "Wow," she whispered. "If that was a negotiating tactic—"

"That was a don't-scare-me-like-that-again response."

"Wow."

He adjusted her crooked frames, kissed her forehead. "We'll talk about this later."

"You keep saying that. Why don't we skip the talk and move straight to the other thing."

He relieved her of her backpack, slipping it over his own shoulders. "And that would be?"

Heart pounding, she flicked a nervous tongue over her kiss-swollen lips. "You're going to make love to me."

"You think so?"

"I know so. Even though you think it's a bad idea." *It's meant to be.*

"What if I have something else in mind?"

"Like?"

"Fucking you senseless."

Holy crow. His crude language only stoked her desire. He made it sound so…primal. "Are you trying to scare me off?"

"Yes."

"It's not working."

His mouth grazed her ear. "I'm not husband material."

"Thanks for the heads-up."

"Consider yourself warned."

She felt the earth move. No, *she* moved. While she'd been trying to think of a sexy retort, Jack had maneuvered her closer to the ladder. *Closer to the edge.* "Oh, God."

He squeezed her hand. "I'll go first. Slip in under me, then we'll descend together. Slowly. Don't look down. Focus on the rungs."

Kylie didn't argue. She wanted to climb down. She wanted him to boink her senseless. She was determined for something to go right in this disastrous week. Making love with her first love was better than right. It was mind-blowingly perfect.

Kylie attacked the ladder one rung at a time. She did as Jack suggested, she didn't look down. She stared straight ahead, at the trunk of the tower.

One rung at a time.

Soon she heard voices. No bullhorn. *We're close!*

She slipped and bobbled. Jack was there, but she panicked. Suddenly, she was dangling. His grip on her wrist hurt, but she endured. No way was she going to die when she was this close to getting down and dirty with Jack Reynolds. With her free hand, she groped for him, for the ladder.

"Stop struggling, Kylie. I'm going to let go."

What? She gawked up at his calm, handsome face. Wasn't he supposed to say, I'll *never* let go?

"There are firefighters directly under you. They'll catch you."

Oh, God.

Spenser's voice whispered in her mind. *"You can do this, Kitten."*

"Don't look down. Close your eyes. Trust me, Kylie."

She flashed on his daredevil days with her brother. Reflected on stories she'd heard regarding his stint with the NYPD.

She closed her eyes.

She let go.

CHAPTER TWENTY-THREE

"HAPPY NOW?" Jack shut the jail cell door with a resounding clang.

Kylie looked at him from the inside, eyes wide behind those sexy librarian glasses. "Am I under arrest?"

"You broke the law." Jaw tight, he pocketed the key. For the umpteenth time, he imagined her scaling that tower, alone, in the dark. She could've fallen and broken her damned neck. That thought had steered him back to the station instead of her trailer. Shaking things up was one thing. Putting her life at risk was another.

On the scene, he'd harnessed his emotions, falling back on his training and experience. He'd handled Kylie with professional detachment. Except for the kiss and the promise to fuck her senseless. Right now, he was mad as hell.

"But—"

"Trespassing. Vandalism." Jack crossed his arms, glowered. "Surely you knew there'd be consequences to your actions."

"I didn't plan on getting caught."

"Aside from the obvious—that doesn't make it right—you shouldn't have broadcast your presence."

She gripped the bars and raised her voice. "I dressed to blend with the night!"

True. Black jeans, black sneakers and a black hooded sweatshirt. Even her hair was black, a drastic change from this afternoon's tropical orange. Still… "You lit up the tower like a Christmas tree, Tiger."

Two people had phoned E911 reporting lights and movement on the town's water tower. Mrs. Carmichael, who had insomnia and a vivid imagination, had called in a jumper.

"But I needed the headlamp to see when I climbed," Kylie explained, "and the additional lantern so I could see what I was painting!"

Her reasoning was almost humorous. "You shouldn't have been on the tower in the first place. Jesus, Kylie. You risked your neck to paint one frickin' red apple yellow?"

"It's symbolic!"

"Of what?" Jack asked.

"Of me! Just because I live in paradise, that doesn't mean I have to look or behave like all the other apples on the tree!"

Jack rubbed a hand over his face. He was attracted to a lunatic. "Is that why you keep changing your hair color?"

She shrugged, then tightened her sleek ponytail. "Not that this is much better, but those orange streaks were a hideous mistake."

"I thought they were interesting. Or maybe it was the whole package. Dress. Heels. Beret. You had a sexy Parisian thing going on."

"You think I'm sexy?"

"I think you're trouble."

Her tantalizing lips curved into a flirty grin. "You want me."

"That's a separate issue."

"One we'll explore when I'm out of the clink?"

He refused to smile. "This is serious, Kylie."

She furrowed her brow. "What's the charge?"

"Criminal mischief." There'd been no formal arrest, but he did want to deter further dumb-ass behavior. She'd been angling to get herself thrown in jail for days. Maybe a few hours behind bars would scratch that itch. That and making the headlines tomorrow.

"Jack," she said when he turned to leave. "I'm sorry I scared you."

Wanting to make her squirm, he said, "You'll be sorrier when Spenser finds out."

IT WAS WRONG. Carrying on in public. But thrilling. Some sort of kinky fantasy come to life. The prisoner being felt up by the warden.

No. Not warden. Police chief.

Jack had her handcuffed to the jail cot. He'd stripped her naked. He was taking advantage. Taking his time.

"Kylie."

"Stop teasing, Jack. Touch me. Make me—"

"Wake up."

Wake up? Her body tingled with pleasures she'd never known. His hands. His mouth. She moaned, flexed.

"You're killing me, hon."

A gentle shake broke the spell. Kylie fought her way through an erotic haze and reluctantly opened her eyes. *Jack.*

His blue gaze smoldered with something that only intensified the ache between her legs. "You were dreaming."

Dreaming? Bleary-eyed, she pushed herself to her elbows and squinted at her surroundings. She was exactly where she'd been for the past several heart-pounding minutes. In a jail cell, on a bed, with Jack. Only now they were fully clothed. And he wasn't sprawled on top of her. He was sitting beside her.

Her cheeks burned. "I…I must've fallen asleep."

"Between the late hour and the water tower escapade, I'm not surprised. You must be exhausted." He stroked her cheek…then abruptly stood.

"I manage the attraction better when I'm not touching you."

Smiling to herself, Kylie groped for her glasses.

"Someone showed to speak in your defense."

"Faye?"

"Max."

"Grogan?"

"Is there another Max in Eden?"

Kylie swung her legs over the cot, feeling disoriented. "What time is it?"

"Two in the morning."

Faye was no doubt asleep and oblivious to the tower episode. If she knew Kylie was in jail, she would've come.

Or maybe not.

Kylie was still reeling from her friend's angry outburst.

"The old guy got home and had a guilt attack," Jack said of Max. "He's worried the HPS pushed you over the edge. He called the mayor. The mayor called me."

Kylie blinked. "So they're going to reverse their decision about McGraw's?"

"No. But where the tower's concerned, there'll be no formal charges."

She frowned. "Oh."

"That's a good thing, Tiger." He guided her into the administrative office.

The smell of strong coffee permeated the air. Shaking off the last remnants of sleep, Kylie saw Bo Hooper answering the phone and Max standing nearby looking sheepish.

"Max insists on giving you a ride home."

Kylie glanced up at Jack, his sexy promise and that erotic dream fresh in her mind. "Oh, but…"

"It's for you, Chief," said Hooper. "Your sister. Wants to make sure you're okay."

"Be right there."

"Guess that means you two are on good terms," said Kylie.

"Better terms. Jessie and Maddie are staying with me for a while."

Which meant she wouldn't be getting down and dirty with Jack at his place. "Heard that through the grapevine. But I don't believe everything I hear."

Jack regarded her with a strange smile. "Neither do I."

Kylie fidgeted. Had he heard something about her? But of course he had. The question was, what? Hyperaware of Hooper and Max looking on, she wasn't about to ask. "I guess I should go."

Boy, this was awkward. They'd shared a passionate kiss on the tower, yet she felt timid about instigating a chaste kiss good-night. Well, she certainly wasn't going to shake his hand. Instead, she nodded. "Thanks again for, you know, rescuing me."

"My pleasure."

She moved to leave, but Jack grasped her fingers.

"Would you have dinner with me tonight?"

She blinked.

"We're well into Saturday morning," he clarified.

"I know. I just…" Her heart fluttered. "You mean like a date?"

"Unless you have other plans."

Sheer willpower kept her from hopping with joy. "Are you kidding? I mean…" A date was more special than just a lusty boink. And would probably *lead* to the lusty boink. Had she croaked after all and gone to heaven?

Hooper cleared his throat, waggled the receiver.

Max grunted. "She'd love to have dinner with you. Damn, Kylie. No wonder your social life stinks." He gestured to the door. "Can we go now?"

Flustered, she smiled at Jack, said good-night to Bo, then hurried out into the still night with her crotchety, but good-hearted neighbor.

Max chuckled under his breath as he helped her into his Ford pickup. "Bet you're not sorry you're stuck in Eden now."

CHAPTER TWENTY-FOUR

Philadelphia, Pennsylvania

"WHAT'S ON YOUR MIND, Mr. Mancini?"

Carmine resented Dr. Bennett's calm tone. She knew he'd had another attack this morning. He'd been this close to shaking hands with St. Peter. He didn't care what the resident at the emergency room had said. He'd had a fuckin' heart attack, brought on by his nephew's shocking news and another one of those prophetic nightmares. But, because he was a stubborn motherfucker, he did not succumb. Yet.

"I'm dying, Doc."

"You're not dying, Mr. Mancini."

"Not at this particular moment. But it is in my future."

She remained expressionless. "Death is in everyone's future."

"You're a cold bitch."

"Not cold, Mr. Mancini. Realistic."

He grunted at that.

"Are you comfortable?"

He'd surrendered to the couch. The piece of psycho-babble furniture he'd sworn he'd never touch. Only this morning, he'd been so desperate, he'd reclined and clung to the tapestry-covered sofa like it was his anchor to earth. "Everything said here is confidential, right?"

"That's right."

"Not that this is about me. I have this friend. Joe."

"Is Joe troubled by something?"

"He is. You see, there was this man, this family member, a brother, actually."

"Go on."

"This brother, uh, Art, he was weak, but kind and smart. So Joe took him under his wing, gave him a place in the...world. Things were good for a while. Great, even. Until he learned something about Art. Something unholy. Something that could not be tolerated. So Joe, in his disgust and anger, disowned his little brother."

"That must have been difficult," said Dr. Bennett.

"Yeah." He shrugged. "So Joe told me."

"Go on."

"I don't want to get into specifics, but word got out to some...business partners. Men who'd worked closely with Art."

"About Art's unholy behavior," she guessed.

"That's right. Things got ugly. Real ugly. In retaliation, Art broke a promise. A sacred promise, Doc."

"He betrayed someone."

"He betrayed family." Carmine ignored the pain in his chest. He had to get through this. Time was of the essence. "Breaking this particular oath is unforgivable."

"Perhaps circumstances—"

"Right is right and wrong is wrong."

She lifted a brow. "No gray areas?"

He twisted his pinkie ring. "Typically no. Thing is, these *partners* acted without permission."

"I'm not sure I follow."

"You don't need to. Let's just say that their wrong was as bad as Art's wrong. They were...reprimanded."

"What happened to Art?"

"He went on the lam, uh, into hiding."

"How did Joe feel about that?"

"Relieved. It meant he didn't have to...deal with his brother's betrayal." *Joe* wasn't pissed about the shitload of money Art had stolen from him—well, at least not anymore. Considering the fallout, Art sort of deserved the dough. But the other thing… The stupid bastard had ratted to the feds about the Gambelli family. Past rivals Joe had worked hard to make peace with in order to conduct joint business. Art had broken *omertà,* a transgression punishable by death.

"Sounds like Joe loved his brother, even though he disowned him."

"He realized the bond was still there when he heard those fucks had beaten Art within a fraction of his life. If it weren't for Art's wife…" Carmine sighed and rubbed a hand over his face. "In hindsight, Joe wishes he would've handled things differently. Wishes he would have been more…"

"Tolerant?"

"Yeah. Tolerant. He's thinking maybe he should make peace with his brother before, well, before one of them bites the big one. If you know what I'm saying."

"Hmm."

"Joe's ma blames him for putting the younger brother in harm's way. She keeps telling him to make it right. Otherwise, he'll burn in hell."

"Does Joe believe that?"

He cut her a look. "How would I know?"

She didn't answer.

Carmine sniffed. "Anyway, last night Joe received information that could ultimately pinpoint his brother's location. This presents a dilemma."

"Why is that?"

Was she really so dense? She knew *the world* he circulated in. "Use your imagination, Doc."

"That's not helpful, Mr. Mancini."

Damn. Just thinking about this gave him *agita.* "Joe is honor-bound to…address his brother's betrayal. Failing to do so would mean disgrace."

"Couldn't he address the betrayal by forgiving him?"

"Not an acceptable solution."

"What if Joe ignored this information and didn't seek out his brother?"

"Others would."

"Thereby taking the pressure, the responsibility, the moral repercussions off of Joe."

This time Carmine held silent.

She tapped her pencil on her pad. "What is Joe going to do?"

"He doesn't know."

"What is he waiting for? Looking for?"

He didn't know. Carmine rubbed his tight chest, considered. "A sign."

CHAPTER TWENTY-FIVE

KYLIE WOKE WITH A START, squinted at her bedside clock. "Crap!" She never slept this late! Not even on her days off. Although the store was closed for renovations and she hadn't told Travis she'd be in at any particular time, she felt guilty because she just *knew* he was hard at work. The man was abnormally driven. At the rate he was going, she'd be able to reopen ahead of schedule. All she was waiting for were the new shoes she'd ordered.

Somewhat recovered from yesterday, she sprang out of bed...and winced. "Ow."

Every muscle in her body screamed. Partly from her tower escapade. Partly from her motorcycle mishap. She glanced down at her throbbing, discolored thigh. If she got naked with Jack tonight, he'd ask about that bruise, because, man, it was huge and ugly, impossible to miss. "Dang." She wanted a mind-blowing seduction, not a lecture on safety.

Kylie swiped her tangled hair out of her face and shoved on her glasses. She limped into the living room and checked her phone messages. There were none. No call from Grandma, saying Mom had a feeling something bad had happened. That was good. No call from Spenser, asking what the frig was wrong with her? Which meant Jack hadn't contacted him about the tower. Also good. No call from Faye, saying, I'm sorry I freaked out or can we talk about this?

Not so good.

Kylie felt bad about slipping and causing friction between Faye and Stan, but she was also stinging from a few of her friend's harsh observations. This time Kylie was the one who needed a little time and space. When she next spoke with Faye, she wanted to have a better grip on what she wanted out of life.

Meanwhile, she refused to pout. She had a business to renovate. She had a date. With Jack. *Tonight!*

She kicked up her heels...and winced.

Forty minutes later, Kylie was half way to town on her bike. Okay. She was speeding, but if she got pulled over, at least she had her license. Her mood was high...until she spotted the water tower.

She slowed to get a better look. Then jumped the road and took off across an open field to get a *closer* look. "It can't be."

But it was.

All of the apples were *red.*

She didn't know whether to scream or cry. Of course, she'd known someone would cover up her statement, eventually. That water tower was the pride and joy of Eden. But even Spenser's graffiti love note to Nancy had lasted twenty-four hours before Public Works had painted over it. Had her yellow apple even made it to dawn? Had anyone, aside from the person who painted it red, seen it? Had she risked her neck in vain?

Frustrated and angry, Kylie turned her bike back around and sped toward town. *Someone* was going to get an earful.

AT 12:20 P.M. TRAVIS was operating on sheer will, a pot of coffee, Kerri's cheese Danish and two cans of Coke. He'd been at it since 5:00 a.m. He'd knocked off late last night, thinking he'd sleep like the dead. Only he'd dreamed about sleeping with the fishes. Mona kept shouting, *"Run!"* He'd woken up in a cold sweat twice. It wasn't that he was a coward, but he didn't want to die. Not before he sampled what Paris had to offer.

At 3:00 a.m., he'd given up on sleep. He'd showered and

dressed, sorted through his closet and drawers. He wouldn't be taking much with him, just a carry-on suitcase and a briefcase full of essentials, including a phony passport he had in the works. He'd lingered over some of Mona's belongings, remembering how she'd hated her new persona. Drab hair. Drab wardrobe. Although, she'd once quipped, she'd take drab over dead. On her good days, she'd still been able to joke.

Before his indiscretion, before he'd torn their world apart, she'd been a vibrant personality with a dry sense of humor. After...he wasn't sure what haunted her more. Seeing her husband savagely beaten and hearing what those gorillas planned to do with his balls or seeing Dutch Gambelli's head explode when she popped him with the Beretta they kept for emergencies.

Travis swore to himself that, once overseas, he'd celebrate who she'd been born as and not who she'd become because of him. He'd always loved her, in spite of his urges, and in spite of his urges, she'd loved him.

Enough to kill.

The bloody episode remained somewhat fuzzy in Travis's mind. Through his beaten haze, he faintly remembered Joey the Enforcer bobbling his knife after Mona shot Dutch. Joey went for his gun and Travis grabbed the knife, stabbed. Travis had been close to unconscious at that point, his face as raw as hamburger meat. Mona had been in shock. Soon after, the cops had arrived. Then the feds—the beginning of their end.

Bleary-eyed, Travis focused back on his work. Hands on hips, he turned in all directions, marveling at all he'd accomplished in so little time. For the most part, his work here was finished. All he needed was Kylie's opinion on the sign. That sign would be her calling card. He didn't feel right about hanging it until he knew she approved.

He glanced at his watch.

Twelve-forty-five.

Where was she?

KYLIE BLEW INTO Boone's Bar and Grill, knowing Max and gang typically met there for lunch on Saturday afternoons. It had been their routine for the past ten years and sure enough there they were. Max, J.J., Keystone and Mayor Wilson, chowing down on burgers and fries.

"Why?" That's all she got out. Her throat was clogged with frustration and road dust.

Four of Eden's most esteemed silver-haired citizens calmly abandoned their Wanda Wonder-Burgers.

"Told ya she'd be peeved," said J.J.

"I was hoping she'd be thankful," said Keystone.

Max wagged an arthritic finger. "We did you a favor, kiddo."

She clenched her fists at her side. "I risked serious injury or—hello—*death* climbing that tower to make a statement. There are all kinds of apples, gentleman. Delicious. Granny. McIntosh. They don't all look, smell or taste the same. And yet every apple on that tower is red."

"That's because the tower represents one tree," said J.J. "When have you ever seen a yellow and red apple on the same tree?"

Kylie gawked. "That's not the point."

"*Your* point isn't Eden's point," said Mayor Wilson.

"What's that supposed to mean?"

"It means don't sabotage this town just because you've got a bug up your butt. That tower is part of Eden's history. A conversation piece. Starting Monday," the mayor went on, "people from all over will be driving in and out of Eden for a week's worth of clean-cut hoopla. We want them talking about the church-sponsored Chicken Noodle Dinner and craft bizarre. The flea market, the Little Miss Eden Pageant, the tractor races and the parade."

"Don't forget about the firehouse hog roast," said Max, "and the car and truck show."

"The apple pie and cake baking contest, monster arm wrestling and live music in the Pavilion," said J.J.

"The moonlight sock-hop, square-dancing and carnival rides," said Keystone.

"Every business in Eden benefits from the Apple Festival," said the mayor. "People return again and again and spend oodles of money. They return expecting to see the same quaint town and to experience the same old-fashioned fun."

"Tradition," said Max.

Mayor Wilson punctuated the air with a French fry. "The *last* thing we want is for folks to leave here lamenting the modernized look of one of the stores on the historical block and a vandalized water tower. We do *not* want folks worrying that Eden's going to hell in an apple bushel and maybe choosing to go elsewhere next year."

"The citizens and business folk would not be happy," said Keystone.

"They'd blame you," said J.J.

"That's why we covered up your statement," said Max.

"We've known you since you were knee high to a grasshopper," said Keystone. "We care about you, Kylie."

J.J. frowned. "Was a time, you cared about us, too."

Kylie's shoulders slumped. How was she supposed to argue with their calm logic? On top of it, like Faye, they made her feel like she'd been insensitive and selfish. "I do care about you," she said in a soft voice. She'd known these men all her life. All good friends of her grandpa and dad. Good men, period. Until her birthday meltdown, they'd never shared cross words. "I'm still me," she went on, aware that everyone in the bar was listening. "I'm still…nice. I just want…I want something more. Something different."

Mayor Wilson raised a bushy brow. "Heard you have a date with Chief Reynolds."

The four men smiled.

The mayor added, "That's something more."

J.J. winked. "That's different."

There were murmurs throughout the bar, and Kylie

knew everyone was gossiping about the lusty kiss Max and the emergency team had witnessed last night at the tower. Eden's Busybody Squad may have covered up her artwork, but they couldn't erase the memory of that kiss. That was something.

"Can we buy you lunch?" J.J. asked.

"Maybe we can help you sort through this life crisis," said Mayor Wilson.

"Lord knows I've had my share of upsets," said Keystone.

"I'm thinking we should give her some dating tips," said Max.

Kylie's cheeks burned. First of all, they thought she needed dating advice? Second: It would be like discussing sex with her grandpa. Self-conscious, she fussed with her ponytail. "Um. Thanks, but—"

"Right off, I'd tell you to let your hair down," J.J. said.

"In more ways than one," said Keystone.

"At least it's no longer orange," said the mayor.

"The black is sort of nice," Max said, squinting at her new hair color. "Exotic. Men like exotic."

"Show some cleavage. Men love that."

"Maybe you should buy one of the marvel bras."

"Wonderbras. Good idea."

"And don't talk about your past boyfriends. Men hate that."

"Don't play hard to get."

"But don't be too clingy."

"Don't, uh, do the deed on the first date."

"But don't wait too long."

"And make sure Jack wears a rubber," said Max.

J.J. elbowed him. "The polite term is condom."

"Or prophylactic," said Mayor Wilson.

"I always called it a love glove," said Keystone.

Kylie had wanted to excuse herself the moment the mayor had suggested a marvel bra. Now she wanted to die.

Luckily for her, since she seemed incapable of making her own escape due to paralyzing mortification, a waitress swooped in to save the day. Pushing Kylie out of the spotlight with a gentle hip nudge, she set four bottles of Bud on the table. "Another round of beers, gentlemen."

"But we didn't—"

"You're welcome." When she turned to leave, she took Kylie with her. "That was rough," she said in low voice.

Kylie couldn't believe her eyes. Jessica Lynn? She was dressed down in jeans and a baggy maroon T-shirt that advertised Boone's Bar and Grill in big white letters. She'd pulled her hair into a simple ponytail and hadn't bothered with any makeup other than pink lip balm. Surely Jessica Lynn, former pageant queen, snooty wife of a slick lawyer, wasn't waiting on people?

But sure enough, she was holding a serving tray.

So, she'd finally landed a job. At Boone's. Wow. Not wanting to embarrass the woman, Kylie focused on Max and gang. "I'm not sure which was worse," Kylie grumbled. "The part where they cautioned me against ruining Eden or the part where they lectured me on dating?"

"On the other hand," said Jessica Lynn, "it was also touching."

"Touching?"

Jessica nodded toward Max and gang. "They spoke and acted out of concern. For you. They respect you. They like you. And rightly so. For as long as I can remember, you always put other people's needs ahead of your own. I used to think you were a pushover. Then again I was self-centered—so I'm told." Jessica blew out a breath. "I'm sorry I dissed your family's shoe store."

Kylie racked her brain. "Are you talking about the time you called our selection—"

"Yes."

"That was, I don't know, ten years ago?"

The woman shrugged. "I'm making up for…I'm making up. I hope. I'm sorry for anything and everything I ever said or did to offend you. As for my brother…and dating…just be yourself."

She whisked off before Kylie could say *what* or *huh* or *run that by me again*. Jessica Lynn Cortez apologizing for rude behavior? For anything?

In the words of her grandma, the world had gone topsy-turvy.

CHAPTER TWENTY-SIX

J.J.'S PHARMACY AND Sundry hadn't changed much over the years. Jack shouldn't have been surprised that the antique drugstore soda fountain was still there and in use, but he was. The sight of the stainless-steel-and-marble bar catapulted him back to his childhood. How many times had he hopped up on one of these padded red stools and spun himself dizzy? How many chocolate and cherry Cokes had he consumed? For a quarter, no less. Now the flavored sodas were a buck fifty, and the server was no longer referred to as a soda jerk, but the experience was the same. A glass tumbler filled with crushed ice. Cola out of the soda fountain. Flavor of choice added, then topped off with a striped straw.

"Am I going to get fat?" Maddie asked as she watched "Nora" pour Hershey's chocolate syrup into her Coke.

Jack suppressed his anger. Somehow, some way, he'd break this five-year-old of her weight worries. "No, sweet pea. You're going to get a treat."

"Treats are usually fattening," she said, her big brown eyes still glued on Nora, or rather the beverage Nora was now stirring.

"Not if you don't have them all the time. Once in a while," he said, "treats are special."

"Mommy says I'm special."

But her daddy rarely gave her the time of day. The more Jack spoke with Maddie, the more he realized how disconnected she was from the man who fathered her. In light of the divorce and the fact that Frank was a cheating, heart-less bastard, maybe that was a good thing. Fuck Frank. Maddie had Jessie, Jack and, as of this morning, Mrs. Car-michael. Smiling, Jack smoothed his niece's messy hair from her sprite face. "Your mommy's a smart lady."

Hoping to deter the Priss-Butt comments, Jessie had allowed Maddie to dress herself this morning. To his sister's credit, she hadn't crumbled when the kid came down to breakfast wearing jeans and sneakers, layered T-shirts in clashing colors and a Dora the Explorer zippered hoodie sweatshirt. Nor had she balked when Maddie had refused her efforts to comb her hair or to tame it with a sparkly headband. Jack knew Jessie's patience would be short-lived, at least with the hair combing, but at least she was *trying* to lighten up.

Maddie wrapped her little hands around the large chilled glass. "She says I'm going to be Miss America."

"Do you want to be Miss America?"

She scraped her tiny teeth over her lower lip. "I'd rather be a dog doctor." She glanced sideways. "Don't tell Mommy."

Jack just smiled. He also resigned himself, then and there, to ripping that "free to a good home" flyer off the vet's bulletin board. If Jessie couldn't or wouldn't allow Maddie to adopt Shy as her own, Jack would. His niece wasn't the only one who'd grown fond of that quirky mutt. Even Ziffel had crumbled. Now Jack had to caution his deputy *not* to feed Shy people food. If only Dorothy would warm up to the dog. What was he saying? She'd yet to warm to *him*.

"Found it. Got it," said Mrs. Carmichael, showing off a DVD of the latest version of *Lassie* as she waddled toward them. "I just knew I'd seen this at Mac's Video Circus. We'll watch it when you come over on Monday, dear."

Maddie screwed up her face. "Do you think Shy will like it?"

"Shy will love it." Mrs. Carmichael's smile was as bright as her silver-blue hair. "I'll have a root beer float," she said to Nora, then looked to Maddie. "How's that chocolate Coke?"

Maddie sipped through the straw. Her eyes sparkled. "Yummy. Wanna taste?"

"You bet I do!"

Grinning, Jack stood and assisted the chubby senior as she perched on the empty stool next to Maddie. Just as he'd hoped, Mrs. Carmichael had eagerly agreed to become his niece's new babysitter. Wanting to give Maddie a chance to get to know her, Jack had invited the lonely widow to lunch and a small shopping venture. He'd known in the first five minutes that they were a perfect match. Then again, he'd always been a good judge of character.

He would have tagged the day perfect if he could've touched base with Kylie. On the drive in, he'd noted that all the apples on the water tower were once again red. Considering she'd risked her life to *make a statement,* he imagined she'd be ticked when she learned it had been so quickly erased. Even Spenser's teenage love graffiti had lasted longer. He'd wanted to break the news himself, hoping to ease her disappointment, but she hadn't answered when he'd called her home phone. He didn't have her cell number, so he'd contacted Faye, only to learn Kylie didn't *own* a cell phone. He wasn't happy about that. What if her bike broke down on an isolated stretch of road? What if her landline went down and a crisis flared? He could cite a dozen potential emergencies.

Faye telling him not to worry, that Kylie was probably on her way into work, hadn't eased his mind because she'd made a crack about Kylie *bonding* with Travis before she'd signed off. What the hell did she mean by that?

He'd been obsessing on Kylie's whereabouts for the past twenty minutes. He hoped she'd learned her lesson the night before and wasn't out pulling some new crazy stunt. As for Travis Martin...what was his story? Jack had asked around, but no one knew the man very well, even though he'd lived there for seven years. According to those he'd asked, the Martins had kept to themselves. Nice folks, but reserved. Never a source of gossip. That is, until Travis took vacation time to do renovations on McGraw's. Jack wasn't the only one wondering about the man's motives. Hard work, long hours, little pay. Was he angling for a bonus? Counting on her gratitude? Looking to replace his wife? Had he heard the rumor about Kylie being frigid? Like Ashe, was he thinking he could be the one to get her off? Jack's gut warned Martin was up to something. Or after something. Maybe, possibly, Kylie.

His brain said stop speculating, go fishing.

"I'm going out to check on Shy," Jack said. "You ladies finish your treats. I'll be back."

"Take your time, Chief Reynolds." Mrs. Carmichael offered a spoonful of ice cream to Maddie. "Want to taste my root beer float?"

Jack braced for *"Is it fattening?"* but heard *"You bet I do!"*

He reveled in his niece's *Wow* and *Yummy* as he headed toward the front of the store. A bell tinkled, announcing someone's entrance. He caught a glimpse of Ashe Davis breezing in and making a beeline for an aisle Jack had visited recently himself. Martin would have to wait.

Sure enough, when Jack rounded the corner, he found Ashe trying to decide between *Rough Rider* and *Trojan* condoms. Back in high school, the arrogant SOB used to brag about how he refused to wear a johnnie. Said it cut back on his pleasure. If the girl wasn't on the Pill, he withdrew and jerked off. Back then they weren't worried about AIDS. But then he'd fucked up and knocked up Sissy Barnes. Adding insult to injury, he'd refused to marry the girl. That was the first time Jack kicked Ashe Davis's ass. "At least you're responsible these days."

Ashe didn't flinch. "So many choices. Ultra-ribbed. Extra-sensitive. Twisted-pleasure." His lip twitched as he examined another box. "Thank God for the Magnum."

"Not interested in a dick-measuring contest, Ashe."

"No, you're interested in Kylie McGraw." He faced off,

ramped up the testosterone when he saw Jack was out of uniform. "Heard you practically molested her on the water tower. And tonight you have a date. Given she's been in love with you for years, chances are you'll score." He grinned at the sound of a passing motorcycle. "Good luck with that."

Under different circumstances, Jack would've socked that smirk off of his high school nemesis's face. Instead he held his ground and temper. "Whatever happens between Kylie and me," he said when the man turned to leave, "where you're concerned, she's off limits."

"It's a free world, *Chief* Reynolds."

"In which I'm free to kick your ass."

Ashe gave him the finger, then plucked a carton off the rack and tossed it to Jack. *Trojan Vibrating Ring.* "You're going to need all the help you can get."

KYLIE HUNG HER HELMET over her cycle's handlebars, then glanced over at Jack's SUV. The dog-that-wasn't-his was sitting in the passenger seat, her head sticking out of the rolled-down window. That dog sure was cute. Pointy ears. Freckled muzzle. Loving eyes. Shy watched the passing cars and pedestrians. But mostly, Kylie assumed, she watched for her master.

Jack was probably in J.J.'s. Or maybe he was in McGraw's. Her stomach fluttered at the thought of seeing him. She wasn't sure how she'd react. In reality, she was still Spenser's little sister and Jack was still her big brother's best friend. Only, last night the dynamics had shifted and they were on even ground. Just a four-year difference between them. Woman and man. Kylie and Jack. After all these years of lusting after him, finally, he lusted back.

Before the mortifying dating lecture, she'd been thrilled. Now, thanks to the Busybody Squad, she dreaded her upcoming date with her dream man. *Dream* being the key word. Up until now, her love affair with Jack Reynolds had been a fantasy. Even last night seemed surreal. Now she

was grounded and dealing with a major bout of anxiety. Dang Max for bringing up condoms and shattering her fantasy. Safe sex was a real-life issue. Jack boinking her senseless? What if she wasn't skilled enough to please him? What if she disappointed him in the way she'd disappointed Bobby and the two men before him? Or, here was a twist, what if he wasn't the awesome lover she'd dreamed of? What if he was a selfish lover or, wow, a dud?

She rolled her eyes. "Yeah, right."

Anxious, Kylie chewed her thumbnail and ambled toward McGraw's in her knee-high lace-up boots. She was dying to call Faye. *Guess what?* And, *what should I do?* But Faye wasn't herself and their relationship was strained. Maybe she could ask Travis for advice. Maybe a guy's perspective would be a good thing. She unlocked the door, walked in and froze. "Oh, my God."

"You hate it."

"I love it!"

She gaped at the big sign that usually hung outside over the awning. The "base" was essentially the same—white with a scrolled green trim—but the paint was fresh. He'd fiddled with the store's name—*wow*. Plus, he'd stenciled funky shoes—much like the ones in the Andy Warhol print now hanging on the west wall—here and there, utilizing colors that complemented the interior. Between the retro lettering, the funky shoes and the mix of old and new colors, he'd created a trendy sign that still blended with the traditional look of the historical block. She loved it all, but what she loved the most was the new name and motto.

McGraw's Shoe Shoppe
"Walk in Comfort, Walk in Style"

"I didn't want to hang it," Travis said, "until I knew you approved. Although I did hang the plaque."

She glanced at the cashier counter, at the plaque that had been hanging behind it forever and ages. The plaque that used to read "Practical Shoes for Practical People" now relayed McGraw's new motto, thanks to Travis. "Walk in Comfort, Walk in Style." It wasn't radical. It was perfect.

Overwhelmed, Kylie launched herself at her kindred soul and hugged him tight. "Thank you. Thank you for all your hard work. For your amazing ideas. For embracing my vision and bringing it to life." She continued to gush, conscious that he was hugging her back, aware of an emotional surge that she didn't understand, but didn't fear. She gushed until he cleared his throat and eased her away.

Perplexed by the sudden tension in his body, she turned. *Jack.*

Obviously, he was off duty. Faded jeans. A green-and-brown-paisley oxford shirt—tails hanging out. No cap. No badge. No gun. Yet he was the most imposing man she'd ever encountered. And that included her dad, a man she'd simultaneously resented and loved.

Her cheeks burned. Not because she'd done anything wrong, but because he was looking at her like she'd done something wrong. No, strike that. His accusatory glare was directed at Travis. Did Jack read something into that innocent hug? Was he jealous? Instead of flattered, she felt flustered. She'd instigated the embrace, not Travis.

"I was just… Look," she said to Jack while moving to the sign. "Is this perfect or what?"

He studied the sign, then shifted and took in the entire store. All the changes. The colors of the walls, the framed prints, the shelves and display racks, the throw rugs, the brightly painted chairs… "Reminds me of a boutique in SoHo," he said.

She didn't know SoHo, but she liked the sound of *boutique.*

"Impressive," he added, then zeroed in on Travis.

Kylie stood in awe as Jack asked probing questions about her new friend's background and training without sounding insulting or patronizing or—jeez—direct, while Travis answered without really giving up any worthwhile information. It was sort of like watching two boxers in a ring, dancing, dodging punches.

As quickly as it began it was over. A draw—or whatever referees called it when nobody won.

"After I hang this," Travis said as he hefted the exterior sign, "I'm going to be on my way."

Kylie realized with a start that he was speaking to her. "Oh. Okay. So soon?" She glanced at her watch. "It's not even two." She was used to him working straight through until midnight. Then she noted everything around her.

Oh.

Wow.

"I'm an idiot," she said, feeling more self-conscious by the moment. "You've been working so hard and so efficiently...your work here is done."

"Not quite," Travis said as he toted the sign out the door. "But almost."

"I should pay you—"

"Later."

The door shut behind him, leaving her alone with Jack. *Crap.* He had that look. That half-irritated, half-intrigued expression that made her stomach coil in a delicious knot. She braced herself for a lecture. Was he going to attack the changes she'd made in the store? Or caution her on hugging men she barely knew? Was he going to back her against the wall, pin her between his muscular arms? She flashed on that erotic dream she'd had, wondering what was so darn sexy about being handcuffed, then realized it was more about Jack. About being at his mercy while he did naughty, sexy things to her body.

"Is it hot in here?" she squeaked.

"It's getting there."

He started toward her and her insides went squishy. *Oh, God.* "Do you think Spenser will hate the renovations?"

"I think he'll be annoyed that you made big changes and a substantial investment without discussing it first."

"I didn't touch the business finances," she said as he

advanced. "I used my own savings. So what if it wiped me out? Like you said, it's an investment. In McGraw's future. My future. When you think about it, it was more practical than blowing my money on a dream trip. Which should make my family happy. They have this thing about being sensible and practical and... What are you doing?" she rasped when he grasped her wrist.

"Let's take this somewhere private."

Before she could argue, he tugged her to the back of the store, through the storage room and into her office. Jack had been coming here since he was a kid. He knew the layout of McGraw's as well as she did. It didn't surprise her that he navigated the place with ease. But she was floored when he shut the door and locked it. Was he going to yell at her? Kiss her? The heat rolling off of him was enough to set off the store's smoke alarm.

"I have approximately five minutes before Mrs. Carmichael and my niece come looking for me."

She had no idea what Mrs. Carmichael had to do with anything. Then again, who could think straight when the man of your dreams hauled you into his arms? His mouth was hot and demanding. His roving hands an instant turn-on.

Heart and body on fire, Kylie locked her arms around his neck and kissed him with wild abandon. She'd never dreamed...well, yeah, she had. But this was even better. *Hotter.* When he palmed her butt, she jumped up and wrapped her legs around his waist. Her breath caught when his hand slid beneath her shirt, his strong palm skimming her bare skin, his deft fingers unhooking her bra strap.

Oh, my. Oh, God. Take me now. On the floor. On the desk. On the...

"Uncle Jack!"

He broke the electrified kiss, knocked the back of his head against the door. "My niece."

"Chief Reynolds! Yoo-hoo!"

"And Mrs. Carmichael."

Bark!

"And Shy." Breathless, Kylie untangled herself from the most handsome, most thrilling, most infuriating man in the universe.

He smoothed his shirt while she smoothed her hair. "Do you like Chinese?"

She blinked at the change of subject.

"Food," he clarified.

She nodded because she didn't trust herself to speak. Was that scorching, openmouthed kiss a mere taste of what was to come? She'd ached and tingled in new and exciting places. How would she react when they were naked? How would she feel when he boinked her senseless?

Jack nailed her with his blue-blue eyes. "Second thoughts?"

Yes. "No."

"I'll pick you up at six. And Kylie," he added before leaving, "get a cell phone."

CHAPTER TWENTY-SEVEN

"I'VE BEEN TRYING TO call you for an hour."

"I was otherwise occupied." Carmine zipped his pants, then stepped aside and allowed his nephew to enter the brownstone. Shaken by the latest nightmare and palpitations, not to mention the emergency session with his shrink, Carmine had stolen away from work for an afternoon delight with Dixie. Hard to obsess on his worries with her mouth around his dick.

Mario didn't comment on the obvious. He was all business. "Cyber Sam is a frickin' wonder," he said, while following Carmine to the liquor cabinet. He looked around to make sure they were alone, then continued. "I gave that computer freak what little I had and he pinpointed a location. *He-who-shall-not-be-named* is in Eden, Indiana. Or at least he sent the e-mail from there."

Carmine's heart *tha-dumped,* his voice boomed. "Where the fuck is Eden, Indiana?"

Dixie, who'd been in the kitchen trying to make homemade cannolis, God help him, came running as though her name had been called. "About two hours north of Indianapolis. That's the state capital," she said with a proud smile. "I looked Eden up on a map 'cuz I wanted to know where my very first sale was going."

Surely he'd heard wrong. Carmine willed his hands steady and poured wine.

Mario waved off a glass and gawked at Dixie. "You shipped those sneakers to Eden, Indiana?"

Dixie took her time answering. She sipped merlot, then licked sweet ricotta filling from her fingertips.

Normally, Carmine would've been aroused—he'd been hard as hell when she'd licked that same cream off of his holy poker—but he was too busy fighting off a heart attack.

"That's where my client lives," she said. "Kylie McGraw. Sweet lady. E-mailed me about something called the Apple Festival and the tourists who buy anything and everything that celebrates apples and how the high school's mascot is Johnny Appleseed and…"

Carmine could feel the walls of the brownstone closing in.

"Anyhoo, she wanted me to design something especially for her. That is, for Eden." She tugged at Carmine's shirt collar. "Chickie, baby, you saw me painting all those apples and adding my bling. Didn't you think they was cute?"

"Fucking adorable." He massaged his tight chest.

"Anyhoo," she said with a flip of her blond mane, "she, Kylie, that is, said my shoes would be featured in her new store. Well, not new, but remodeled. Apparently McGraw's Shoe Store has been there since dirt was discovered. Kylie hired this guy who's transforming the entire store single-handedly. Said she thinks he was an interior decorator in another life."

Carmine palmed sweat from his brow. His mama's voice echoed in his ringing ears. *Make it right.*

"I'm thinking she's one of those New Age nuts," Dixie said. "Must believe in rein…rein…"

"Reincarnation," said Mario.

"Yeah, that. All her e-mails end with some spiritual quote. Anyhoo…"

"Make it stop," Mario pleaded.

"Zip it, sweetheart," Carmine said.

"But—"

"Zip. It."

Dixie sighed, then mimicked a lip zip.

Mario jerked a thumb, ordering her to beat it.

She knew "the Turk" well enough not to argue.

Dixie left with her wine and Carmine gathered his wits in a rare moment of silence. This was too whacked to be a coincidence. This was a sign.

"*Bada Bling,* Bada Bing. What were the fuckin' chances?" Mario hitched back his leather jacket, giving Carmine a glimpse of his holstered semiautomatic. "Want me to handle it, Chickie?"

Intent on maintaining control, Carmine feigned calm and sipped merlot. He hadn't seen his little brother in seven years. The kid with the soft heart and quick brain. The brother he'd loved. No matter how you sliced it, this was gonna hurt. He had two choices. Honor the family or honor his conscience.

"Make things right."

Carmine met his nephew's anxious gaze. "Book two tickets for the next flight to Eden."

AT 4:30 P.M. TRAVIS WAS midway to Chicago. Risky business driving into the Windy City. Ten years ago, he'd met a few of the boys from the Chicago Outfit. He didn't keep tabs. They could be dead or incarcerated for all he knew. But they could also be alive and thriving. If anyone recognized him, he was screwed. Not that he thought it likely. Thanks to Dutch and Joey, he didn't look exactly as he did before. They'd mangled his face good. The plastic surgeon had done amazing work on his cheekbones and jaw, although he hadn't perfected the broken nose. A small price in Travis's mind. He assured himself that he looked just different enough, especially with the dyed hair. He tried not to think about what a wiseguy would do to a family member who'd broken *omertà*. He'd been through that once and barely survived.

Siding with caution, he'd asked his contact—a friend of a friend of an ex-friend—to meet him in Gary, Indiana, just a few miles south of East Chicago. He'd offered a thousand dollar bonus to seal the deal. He was already paying Slick

Smitty a small fortune for a phony passport, two credit cards and two airline tickets. But he could afford it.

Gripping the wheel tight and easing back from fifty-eight to fifty-five—he'd be damned if he'd risk a speeding ticket—Travis eyed the duffel stuffed with a third of the money he'd stolen from his brother's secret stash just before his run-in with Dutch and Joey. He'd stolen out of spite, and a sense of betrayal. It didn't make it right, but he didn't feel guilty. He'd given up his passion for the family and then the family had cut him loose. He figured Carmine owed him. That stash had been a nest egg for him and Mona, only they'd rarely dipped into what she'd called blood money. Now it would fund two dream trips.

Travis thought about Kylie. A man could choke on all that goodness, or be inspired by it. He'd failed his wife, but he could do right by that girl. It meant heading back to Eden and making his getaway tomorrow instead of tonight, but what was one night after seven years of hell?

The more he thought about escape, the more his juices simmered. On the drive back from Gary to Eden, he'd ditch his old pickup in favor of a rental car. Late tonight he'd drive Mona's hatchback into town and leave Kylie's present in her office. He couldn't risk seeing her again. She'd want to pay for his services. He didn't want her money. He also didn't want to risk another run-in with Jack. The fact that the new chief was digging into Travis's past meant he still hadn't come across the secret file WITSEC had given to the former chief. Maybe Chief Curtis had burned it. It would be in keeping with his turning a blind eye to certain seedy aspects of Eden.

Like the semisecret back room in Mac's Video Circus that featured porno flicks and mags. It wasn't advertised or talked about, but more then a few of the men in town frequented the red-light salon on occasion. A month after Mona's death, Travis had been lonely and desperate enough to sneak in. He'd thought he was alone back there, so he'd peeked at a magazine featuring men-on-men. It had been so long....

He didn't sense Frank Cortez sneaking up on him and looking over his shoulder. But he'd sure as hell been aware of the man's hard-on when he'd pressed up against Travis. It had been unexpected and...exciting. Unbelievably tempting. So much so, Travis hadn't jerked away as quickly as he should have. A straight man would have punched Frank. Travis had savored the moment.

Two seconds later Frank was gone, but he'd shown up later that night, knocking on Travis's door with a bottle of booze and a salacious offer. Lonely and horny, Travis had crumbled, thinking Frank was a closeted, kindred soul. They'd gotten drunk together and Travis had slipped, offering to loan Frank some cash when the man had bitched about a gambling debt called in by a bad-tempered loan-shark. Given his family's business, Travis knew what happened to men who didn't make good on debts.

Frank had thanked him, sexually, and then...he'd crushed Travis's kindred-soul theory. The man wasn't gay. He was a sex addict who swung both ways. He was into some serious kink.

Not Travis's thing. He'd tried to play the moment as a straight man who'd been curious. He'd made it clear he wasn't interested in a second tryst.

Frank didn't argue, but after that night, every time Travis saw that SOB, the lawyer smiled one of those I-know-your-secret smiles. A couple of weeks later, Frank hit Travis up for another *loan*. And then another. The message was clear: *Pay up or I'll leak your secret.* Never mind that Frank had secrets, too. Travis had more at stake. He'd been damned relieved when that prick had left town. Now Travis would be leaving Eden, and the life that wasn't his, behind, too.

Tomorrow morning, he'd trade red hair for black, and bargain jeans and shirts for designer suits and shoes.

Goodbye hardware expert, Travis Martin. Hello, Reggie Smith, interior designer.

As for his former self, as far as he was concerned, Tom "the Artful Dodger" Mancini was dead.

CHAPTER TWENTY-EIGHT

KYLIE WAS DESPERATE. She'd ransacked her wardrobe. She'd tried on six outfits. None of them were right. She should have gone shopping, bought something special. Something that showed cleavage. Something that made her look like a demure sex kitten.

Kim Novak.

Why, oh, why did Jack have to plant that image in her head? How would she ever stack up to that stacked bomb-shell?

It's not that Kylie didn't have curves, they were just five times more subtle than Novak's and Charlotte Avery's, and probably Jack's ex-wife. Then there was her hair. Max and gang had said to wear it down, but the too-long, all-one-length style made her look more girlie than womanly. As for makeup, she wasn't sure what shade of lipstick best complemented her new ebony hair color—which, even after washing it three times, had yet to fade.

"I should have asked Travis."

But she really wanted to ask Faye.

She glanced at her disastrous reflection in the bedroom mirror. She marched into the living room. To hell with pride. This was an emergency. This was about a date with the man of her youthful, and not so youthful, dreams. Not sharing this moment with Faye, no matter their recent squabbles, was unthinkable. She dialed her friend's cell phone…and got her voice mail.

"Hey, this is Faye. Leave a message and I'll get back to

you. Unless you're one of those annoying telemarketers. In which case, go to—" *Beeeeeep.*

"Okay," Kylie said. "I know you know it's me, because you're screening. Or maybe not. Maybe you forgot your phone or you're busy with the kids or Stan or both, but…if you get this message, please call me back. Although, if it's not within the next fifteen minutes, never mind. It'll be too late. Jack will be here in an hour and a half. He's taking me out. That's right. I have a date with my dream man, which you'd know if you were speaking to me. But I don't know what to wear or what to do with my hair. And I could…I could really use your help, Faye."

Dang. Had her voice just cracked? "Call me. Bye." She hung up before she started blubbering. She'd never been a crier. First she'd developed vertigo. Now she was an emotional basket case. Jeesh. What was in store for her when she turned thirty-*three?*

She was halfway back to her bedroom when the phone rang. She swiveled and lunged, banged her knee on the end table—"Ow!"—and nabbed the receiver. "Hello?"

"A date with Jack, huh?"

Kylie wilted with relief. *Faye.* "Can you believe it?"

"So what have I missed?"

"Two kisses."

"In addition to the dud?"

"Mmm. A humdinger and a wow-zinger."

"Whoa."

"I know."

"Where's he taking you?" Faye asked.

"Wong's. I think. He mentioned Chinese food."

"So he's taking you to dinner in the next town over. Away from Eden's prying eyes and flapping gums. Considerate."

"He wants to fuck me senseless," Kylie blurted.

Faye coughed and choked. "I can't believe he said that. I can't believe *you* said it."

"I'm a little discombobulated."

"Understandable. You've had a thing for Jack since you were fourteen."

"Twelve, actually," said Kylie. "A silent crush that morphed into puppy love."

"And now?"

"I don't know. I just know that I've dreamed of this, ached for this, for so long...I want it to happen and I don't, you know?"

"I think so."

Feeling nauseous, Kylie pushed her glasses up her nose, then looked at her watch. "He'll be here in an hour and fifteen."

"I'll be there in twenty."

FAYE BLEW INTO KYLIE'S trailer three minutes ahead of schedule. Kylie knew for certain since she'd been watching the clock like a hawk. That and painting her toenails candy apple red. "Oh, my God," Kylie said, noting the garment bag draped over her friend's arm. "You even brought me something to wear."

"This," Faye said as she whizzed past, "will be the fastest makeover in history. Meet me in the kitchen."

Kylie hauled butt and plopped on a stool at the mini breakfast bar. She didn't flinch when, seconds later, her friend pulled a blow-dryer, flatiron and a pair of scissors out of her psychedelic cosmetic tote. Kylie started to say *"Just don't cut it above my shoulders,"* and thought better of it. "Work your magic, Faye."

"Are you sure?"

"Can you do sophisticated but flirty?"

Faye smiled. "I know just the style."

For the next twenty minutes, they chatted about everything except the blowup. Kylie wanted to know why Faye was so angry about her postponed dream trip, but she was afraid of stoking her temper. Just now her friend was her old breezy, confident and warm self, and Kylie, feeling fragile and anxious, very much needed the old Faye. So she

asked her about her kids, about Stan and the upgrades to
the Orchard House. Faye talked about the kids and the B
and B, but not much about Stan.

"Are you two okay?" Kylie finally asked.

"We're going through a rough patch."

"Because of what I blabbed at Boone's?"

"Because of a lot of stuff," said Faye. "We've been
married a long time, Kylie. Problems flare."

What kind of problems? Kylie wondered. Money
problems? Fidelity problems? Her heart ached for her
friend. "Want to talk about it?"

After an awkward pause, Faye said, "Not really."

Kylie hoped it wasn't because Faye no longer trusted
her to keep her confidence. "Well, if you ever do—"

"Thanks."

Kylie scrambled for a more cheery subject. "I can't
remember if I told you about the customized sneakers I
ordered."

"I'm all ears," Faye said as she clipped Kylie's bangs.

"Well, when I was surfing the Net for unique merchandise, I came across the Web site for *Bada-Bling!* Thanks
to the popularity of *omertà* everyone's always dropping
mob slang: Bada Bing, Gabagool—"

"Jamook."

"I heard Mr. Keystone use that one last week," Kylie
said. "What's it mean, anyway?"

"Idiot," Faye said. "Lamebrain. Jerk. Stan started using
that one a lot with his road rage. But then Sting started
saying it, so I looked it up. It is now a prohibited word
within the Tyler household."

"Huh. Anyway, between the name and Dixie's cool
creations, it felt like fate. I ordered a supply of customized
sneakers on the spot."

"You mean during your late-night drunken buying binge?"

"Never mind that," Kylie said, cheeks flushing. "These
shoes are not only comfortable, but fun. I was hoping to
use Spice to kick-start a fad."

"My daughter, the shy one?" Faye furrowed her brow. "How so?"

"Remember when we were in middle and high school, how we wore T-shirts, sweatshirts and jackets displaying the school mascot?"

"Ah," Faye said. "You want to start a new trend with the teens. You want to get sneakers into that mix."

"I ordered a few different styles. Slip-ons, high-tops and low-tops. Although they all celebrate Eden—apples, Johnny Appleseed, *Paradise in the Heartland,* blah, blah, blah—no two pair are alike." Kylie struggled not to look over her shoulder, hence causing Faye to burn her with that flatiron. "What do you think?"

"I think Spice is going to adore being your walking billboard. I think you're probably on to something big. Not just with the local kids. The tourists will eat up those blingy apple shoes." She squeezed Kylie's shoulder, then passed her a big handheld mirror. "What do *you* think?"

Kylie stared at her reflection. Talk about shaking things up.

"You love it."

"I love it. Oh, Faye." She'd cut off a good five inches, but Kylie's hair still fell well below her shoulders. Graduated layers now framed her face and she had bangs. She hadn't had bangs since she was in first grade. But instead of looking like a little kid she looked…sophisticated, yet flirty. Smoothing out her natural waves with the flatiron had made her darker color really shine. "I feel like a new woman. I feel…different."

"You look fantabulous, if I do say so myself. Now, go and change into the dress I brought while I clean up this mess. Jack will be here in thirty minutes."

Pulse racing, Kylie scurried into her bedroom. Her hands trembled as she unzipped the garment bag Faye had laid on her bed. She felt like she was prepping for her high school prom. "This is nuts. Get a grip, McGraw."

But then she saw the dress. "Holy smokes." So Faye,

and so not her. A retro number, reminiscent of a sixties glamour girl. A soft pink, form-fitting dress that would accentuate her curves. Far from anything in Kylie's closet. Then again, it *was* sort of Kim Novak-like.

Sold.

She shimmied into the dress and realized that, though the front didn't show much cleavage, the back showed an awful lot of skin. She checked the view via her full-length mirror. "Cripes."

"You hate it," Faye said as she walked in.

"I love it, but don't you think it's a little much for Wong's?"

"Honey, if we're doing this right," Faye said as she searched the bottom of Kylie's closet, "you'll never make it to Wong's. Here." She passed Kylie a pair of black heels she'd bought and never worn. "Try these."

Five-inch stiletto pumps. Pointy toes. Ankle straps. Kylie had purchased these fetishlike shoes more than a year ago. Online, on a whim. She'd been looking for another way to please Bobby, only the moment never seemed right, or maybe she'd lacked the nerve.

"Can you walk in them?" Faye asked.

Kylie nodded. She'd practiced.

"The last time I wore a pair of shoes like this, Stan locked me in the bedroom for two days."

Kylie grabbed the shiny pumps and buckled them on.

Faye grinned. "Sit."

Kylie perched on the end of her bed. She squinted at her bedside clock. Five-forty-five. Fifteen minutes to Jack.

"Forgoing your glasses tonight, huh?"

"I won't be able to read the menu, but that's okay. I have it memorized."

"You order in from them enough." Faye swept another coat of mascara over Kylie's eyelashes and smoothed mauve gloss over her lips. "Normally," she said, "I would've opted for red, but Jack's just going to kiss it off and you really don't want to see his mouth smeared with red lipstick. Sort of ruins the moment. Hold still. Good. There. Stand up. Let me see."

Kylie turned in a circle. "Well?"

"I'd do ya." Faye smiled. "If I were a lesbo, that is."

Overly emotional, Kylie blurted, "About our tiff..."

Faye squeezed her hand. "I'm sorry about that, Kylie. It's just...I've been stressed. This thing with Stan. Then you with your birthday crisis...I gave up on my dream to be a rock star a long time ago, but I never gave up on *your* dream. I've been living vicariously through you, anticipating the thrill of your letters and phone calls. The pictures and stories. The adventure. When it hit me that you'd given up on your dream trip—"

"But I haven't." Kylie bounced between miffed and confused. "It's just postponed."

Faye smiled and squeezed her hand. "It's okay. People change. Dreams change. And like you, I need to take charge of my own happiness."

"I didn't realize you were unhappy."

"It's something I need to work out in my own head, then I'll share it with you."

Kylie didn't know what to say, what to think, what to feel. Not wanting to blow things out of proportion, she decided to shelve her concerns until she knew Faye's exact dilemma. "Promise you'll share?"

Faye crossed her heart, then looked at her watch. "Jack'll be here any minute. I better hit the road."

Feeling emotional on multiple levels now, Kylie followed her friend into the living room. Walking on five-inch stilettos was a challenge, but her balance, thanks to her martial arts training and previous practice, was dead-on. "I don't know how to thank you."

"With details of tonight's escapade. Which reminds me." Faye dipped into her tote and handed Kylie two shiny packets.

Kylie blushed. "Condoms?"

"Ultra-ribbed. Have fun!" She hugged Kylie just as someone knocked. She whispered "You look beautiful," then opened the door. "Hi, Jack. Bye, Jack."

"Nice to see you, Faye."

Jack moved in as Faye moved out and Kylie swore she felt the world tilt. He looked amazing. Actually, he always looked amazing, but tonight, he looked *I-could-lick-you-from-head-to-toe* amazing. What was it about a man in a leather blazer?

"You look incredible."

It took her a second to realize that Jack was speaking to her. She'd been so focused on *him.* "Faye," she croaked. "Her dress. Her hair. I mean she cut my hair." *She also gave you condoms.* Kylie clasped her hands behind her back. How was she going to ditch the packets without Jack seeing them?

His gaze fell to her shoes. "Oh, Christ." He dragged a hand over his buzzed hair.

She inched back.

They spoke at once. "I can't do this."

"I knew it," she blurted. "I knew this was too good to be true. No makeover in the world will help. Whenever you look at me you see Spenser's little sister. The moony-eyed girl who asked you to be her first. This is just...too weird. I get it. I—"

"Actually," Jack interrupted, "I meant I can't wait. I intended to take this slow. To wine and dine you, to seduce you over a few dates. But then I saw you and...it's not just the hair and the dress or the shoes—although those heels are smoking hot—it's you. I can't do slow, Kylie. That's what I meant. Not that it matters since you're backing out."

She blinked. "I'm not...I'm...that is, I meant, I can't sit through dinner wondering if we're going to, you know, do it...tonight. I can't stand worrying that I'm going to disappoint you. I'm wired a little different, Jack. Not that I mind, but the men I've been with do. Not that there have been a lot of men, still." *Don't talk about your past boyfriends. Men hate that.* "This is hopeless," Kylie said, heart sinking. "I'm hopeless."

"I'm a bastard."

She blinked. "What? Why?" He didn't answer, and

she struggled to get a bead on his mind-set. The one thing she knew for certain: this man was a genuine old-fashioned gentleman. "Because you want me for the wrong reasons? Whatever they are. Because you're not husband material? So you said. So I've been warned. Don't insult me, Jack. I'm a big girl. I know what I want. I don't want slow."

"You sure about that?"

"Dead sure."

Jack pulled a cell phone from his inner jacket pocket, flipped it open and dialed. "Evening. Jack Reynolds here. I'd like to cancel my seven o'clock reservation." He raked a smoldering blue gaze over Kylie, setting her body on fire. "We'll be dining in."

Oh, boy. Oh, God. No turning back now, not that she wanted to. Kylie's stomach swirled with nerves and anticipation. If she ate just now, she'd hurl. "I'm not hungry."

"I am." His gaze was hot, his grin sinful, and she realized suddenly that he wasn't talking about food. "I have some wine in the car," he said.

She licked her glossed lips. "I'd rather be clearheaded for this. I think." She clutched the condoms in her balled hands. Maybe she could drop them behind her and kick them under the futon sofa without him noticing. Or maybe she should play naughty, take the initiative and tear open a packet—right here, right now.

She stood frozen. "I've wanted you, this, for what seems like forever. Now that it's here…what if it's not everything I imagined it to be?" She could almost hear Max and gang groan.

"The pressure to perform right now would be crushing if I weren't so damned attracted to you, Tiger." Jack shrugged out of that sexy leather coat and closed the distance between them.

She glanced down and noted the evidence of his attraction straining against his jeans. Her heart skipped when he smoothed her new sleek hair from her face, then brushed a soft kiss over her mouth. "I can't be your first, Kylie, but I'll try my damnedest to be your most memorable."

Holy smoke. She closed her eyes and mentally chanted an affirmation. *"I can handle this. I can handle him. I'm adventurous. I'm flexible."*

He kissed her again, but this time he lingered. A slow kiss, a tender kiss. A kiss so achingly perfect, it brought tears to her eyes. His warm palms slid over her shoulders and down her bare arms, inciting goose bumps and pleasure—until his fingers closed around her fists.

"Faye gave them to me," she said as he claimed and inspected the foiled condoms. "I'm now officially mortified."

Smiling, Jack tossed them on the end table. "What you are, hon, is beautiful inside and out. That's what makes you so irresistible."

Her limbs melted along with her heart. "On second thought, a glass of wine would be nice."

He studied her for a moment, then nipped her lower lip. "You get the glasses. I'll get the bottle."

As soon as he was gone, she skittered to her bedroom and kicked her rejected date-wear under the bed. She spritzed herself and the air with a subtle exotic perfume *(men like exotic)*, smoothed her satin quilt, then skittered back to the living room. She was bent over, turning on her CD player, when she heard the door open and shut.

"Don't move."

Her pulse raced as she felt Jack move in behind her, his erection pressing against her rear, his hand caressing the base of her neck, then smoothing down her bare spine.

"I don't know who scores more points," he said in a rough voice. "Faye for providing this kick-ass dress, or you for looking so sexy in it."

"I vote for me." Kylie pressed Play and sensual strains of Yo-Yo Ma's cello enhanced the charged air. She straightened and turned in Jack's arms.

He searched her eyes. "How bad do you want that glass of wine?"

"Not as bad as I want you."

He dropped his forehead to hers, then pulled her against him, one hand stroking her bare back as they moved in time with the music. Slow. Sensual. "What's the name of this song?" he asked, nuzzling her ear.

"I'm embarrassed to say."

"I'm dying to know."

She swallowed and breathed in his signature scent—a combination of soap and subtle after-shave. Her senses flashed back to one of the times he'd crashed at her childhood home after an all-night study cram with Spenser. She'd run into Jack coming out of their bathroom, freshly showered, dressed only in jeans—no shirt, so shoes. She'd been mortified and mesmerized. He was so handsome, so masculine and smelled so yummy. She'd felt an odd ache in her tummy and private parts. A thirteen-year-old could sure pine hard for an unrequited love. This song summed up how she'd feel about Jack until the day she died.

"Love of My Life," she finally answered. She expected him to tense, but he only tightened his hold. As they danced in silence, Kylie's body grew more pliant, her anxiety melting away. She smoothed her hands over Jack's strong shoulders, grazed her fingers through his short, dark hair. Smitten and seduced, she framed his gorgeous face and poured her heart into a kiss.

Her Yo-Yo Ma mix segued into the musician's passionate unaccompanied rendition of a Bach classic. Kylie's limbs turned liquid when Jack took control, deepening the kiss and easing down the zipper at the base of her back. The fabric slid off her shoulders, then pooled to the floor. The feel of his hands roving over her naked flesh nearly sent her over the moon.

"He's the one," her mind whispered. Between the music, her pent-up longing and Jack's skilled touch, the moment was magic.

"Beautiful," he murmured as he kissed his way down her body.

She moaned when he suckled her nipples. Sighed as he licked and nipped her belly. Her body trembled when he caressed and squeezed her rear—bare because of her thong.

But then he stopped.

She looked down and saw Jack inspecting the massive bruise on her thigh. *Shoot.* "It's nothing. Really," she rasped in a breathless voice. "Go back to what you were doing."

After a moment, he gently kissed her injury, then ridded her of the lacy thong. She trembled with anticipation. Was he going to take her here? On the floor? On the futon? She didn't care so long as he took her now. She pitched a fevered glance at the condoms on the end table. But Jack was focused on *her*. He kissed her...down *there*. She froze. That had never worked for her, but she couldn't breathe, let alone form words.

She felt his tongue flicking, teeth nibbling, fingers probing....

The music swelled and Kylie exploded. "Oh, my God. Oh, my..." Her breath caught when Jack stood and swept her into his arms.

He cranked the music, then carried her into her bedroom. Tears pricked her eyes as he gently laid her on the bed, then not so gently removed his shirt and jeans.

"I'm not broken," she said in a croaky, emotional voice. Such a stupid thing to say!

"Easy, baby." He started to remove her shoes.

"No! Leave them. Please." She felt different in the stilettos. Sexy, not sensible.

"You're killing me," he said, rolling on a condom he must've had stashed in his jeans. Even *that* was sexy. Then suddenly, he was on top of her, inside her. She gasped then clung, writhing beneath his spectacular naked body as he—oh, my—*fucked her senseless.*

It happened so fast, an intense orgasm that rocked Kylie to her soul. She screamed Jack's name and a couple of racy new-to-her-lips expletives.

He kissed her hard, drove deep, then shuddered with his own release.

Kylie couldn't think or see straight. But she could hear the beautiful music, the sound of their heavy breathing. She could feel Jack's heart pounding against her chest. The happiest moment in her life, yet she burst into tears.

Jack rolled off and pulled her into his arms, smoothed a hand over her hair. "Not all you'd hoped for, huh?" he teased softly.

She smacked his muscled arm, throat clogged with stifled sobs, her body trembling in the aftermath of two different, mind-blowing orgasms. When she caught her breath, she rasped, "More than I ever dreamed."

JACK WAS TOUCHED BY Kylie's emotional reaction and stunned by his lack of control. First he'd bailed on the dating process, then he'd rushed making love to her. He'd wanted to take it slow. He'd wanted to make her come a dozen times, a dozen different ways. But her honesty and vulnerability, not to mention her sweet face and beautiful body, had done him in. The backless dress and FMPs had pushed him over the edge. Or maybe it had been her choice of music: "Love of My Life." Normally, the sentiment would've scared the shit out of him. Instead, it touched him in a way he couldn't define.

He was still trying to sort it out when Kylie pushed up on one elbow. "This is weird." She trailed her fingers through his chest hair. "You in my bed. Naked."

"A little."

"Regrets?"

"No." He smoothed a hand down her beautiful back, cupped her tight ass and pulled her closer. "You?"

"Only the crying part." She inched back and wiped away the last of her tears. "I need to explain."

He thought he knew where this was going, but allowed her to lead the way.

"I don't always cry after sex. It's just that this was different. And not because I've been crushing on you since I was twelve."

"You mean fourteen."

She blushed. "Right. Anyway, without going into detail, because generally men don't like to hear about past boyfriends, right?"

"Well—"

"The thing is, I thought I was wired wrong. I couldn't seem to…no matter what the guy did, I couldn't…" She blew out a breath. "I thought I was frigid. At least that's what Red and Jerry said. And I assume Bobby—"

"Red Skyler?" Jack remembered him from high school. "Christ, honey, he was your first?"

She gave his shoulder a playful smack. "Someone had to be."

"Red's an idiot."

"Yes, well—"

"As for those other two…" Damn, had there been only three?

"Would you please let me finish?"

"Sorry."

"Where was I? Oh, right. My inability to have an orgasm without the aid of a shower massage or my own hand. So when you…when I…"

"Shower massage, huh?"

"Jack."

"Sorry." He smiled, adoring the kitten and tiger rolled into one. "Kylie, it's not always the woman's fault. Some men just don't know how to push the right buttons. Other times, it's about chemistry. Sometimes a man and woman click. Sometimes they don't. It's a combination of factors. Emotional, physical."

"We click."

"We click." He interlaced his fingers with hers, then noticed, for the first time, a stuffed animal perched at the edge of her pillow. A giraffe wearing an *Into the Wild* T-shirt. A gift, no doubt from her brother, his best friend. Jack reached over and turned the animal away—prying plastic eyes to the wall. "You know, Spenser's going to kick my ass when he hears about this."

She actually looked worried. "Does he have to know?"

"Are you telling me I'm a one-night stand?"

"Are you saying you'd like to see me again?"

Jack held her gaze and stroked a thumb over her knuckles. He liked that she was comfortable with her body. He'd been with women who'd immediately slid under the covers or pulled on their underwear or a T-shirt after sex. Not Kylie. And the town thought she was frigid. Hell, up until tonight she'd thought she was *wired wrong*. What she was, Jack thought, was complex. "What I want and what's best for you aren't the same."

She bristled. "Who are you to say what's best for me?"

"Point taken, but—"

"Do you like me?"

"Very much."

"Did you enjoy the sex?"

He smiled.

"Do you want to see me again?"

Oh, yeah. She made him feel good, grounded, happy. She was more intoxicating than a bottle of whiskey. "This could get messy, Tiger."

"Nothing ventured, nothing gained."

His lip twitched. "That's Spenser talking."

She coupled an innocent shrug with a not-so-innocent smile. "Speaking of Spenser," she said after a glance at her alarm clock, "*Into the Wild* starts in ten minutes." She gestured to the thirteen-inch television sitting on the opposite nightstand. "Did you want to watch? I guarantee every one else in Eden is tuning in."

What he wanted to watch was Kylie squirming in ecstasy. He skimmed his fingers over her collarbone, the swell of her breast. "Do you really want your brother in the bedroom with us?"

She gasped when he pinched her nipple. "Um. No."

"Tell me what you were dreaming about."

She blinked.

"In the jail cell. When I woke you."

"Oh. It's sort of embarrassing."

"Humor me."

"It's kind of kinky."

Jack twitched back to life. "All the better."

Her mouth curved into a shy smile. "It involved you and me and, well, handcuffs."

He slid his hand between her legs, tested for wetness. "Who was the dominant one?"

She wiggled against his probing fingers, moaned. "You."

Hard as hell, Jack trapped her wrists, hauled her arms over her head and rolled on top in one fluid move. "Say no more."

CHAPTER TWENTY-NINE

Philadelphia, Pennsylvania

"WHAT THE FUCK ARE YOU babbling about, Sal?" Carmine peered up at his doctor through squinted, blurry eyes.

Not one to be intimidated, Dr. Salvatore Aversi leaned closer. "Your cholesterol is through the roof. What the hell have you been eating?"

What the fuck did he think? The normal stuff. Carmine tried to adjust his vision. His limbs felt heavy, his mouth dry. "Where am I?"

"The hospital." Aversi straightened. "You had a heart attack, Carmine."

At first the words didn't register. He'd been in and out of the emergency room three times over the past two weeks. Panic attacks, they'd said. Brought on by stress, Aversi verified. To which Dr. Bennett had added, guilty conscience.

But then he noted the IV sticking in his arm. The monitor to his right blipping with his fucking pulse.

A heart attack.

Instead of scared, he felt vindicated. "Told you I was dying."

"You're not dead yet," Aversi said, "but this is a warning." He folded his arms over his barreled chest. "We were able to nip this one through reperfusion."

"More medical mumbo-jumbo," Carmine complained.

"Reperfusion is the process of opening the blocked artery and restoring blood flow to the heart muscle."

"So I'm fixed for good?"

"Fixed for now. You'll have to go on medication, alter your diet, exercise."

"Fine." Not that he thought it would do any good. Death was knockin' at his door. *"You gotta make things right before it's too late."*

"When can I spring this joint? I've got a flight to catch."

"You missed your flight," said Aversi. "And I'm restricting air travel for at least two weeks."

"Are you fucking *oobatz?*" Carmine struggled to sit up.

Aversi pressed him back against the bed. "Calm down. Stress only—"

"Don't lecture me about stress. This trip is about alleviating goddamned stress."

"You'll have to find another way—"

"Where's the phone? I need to call Buddah."

"Buddah and Turk are waiting in the hall. I had to sedate the young woman."

Dixie.

Carmine remembered now. He'd put his wife and kids on a plane to Florida, promising to join them at Disney at week's end. Then he'd met up with Dixie two terminals down. He'd given last-minute instructions to his nephew and consigliere, cautioning them to handle business as usual without any mention of Carmine's real reason for traveling. *"I'm in Eden because of* Bada-Bling! *That's it, that's all. Capiche?"*

Meanwhile, he'd obsessed on what he'd done to his brother seven years earlier and what he had to do now. He'd clutched his chest.

Heart attack.

"Send them in."

Knowing it was futile to argue, Aversi spun off.

Carmine collected his sluggish thoughts, massaged his tight chest. He focused intently on the worried faces of his two most trusted men as they eased into the hospital room. Time was of the essence. "You gotta make this right."

CHAPTER THIRTY

KYLIE KEPT EXPECTING to wake up from a dream. So far her evening with Jack had been too good, too perfect to be true. He'd even brought one of her fantasies to life. Granted, not in a jail cell, but having her wrists bound and being at Jack's mercy while he did racy things to her body was the part she cared about most. The part that shocked and thrilled. Bonus, he hadn't been quick about it. He'd taken his time, driven her insane, the anticipation making the orgasms so intense, at one point she was certain she'd died and gone to heaven.

Oh, yeah. Jack knew how to push her buttons and then some.

Even showering together had been fun and sensual. Bobby had lived with her for almost a year, that is whenever he wasn't out of town on assignment, and she'd never been tempted to share the bathroom with him in any way. With Jack, it felt natural.

Since he'd informed her he'd be spending the night (Oh, yeah. She was still floating from *that* news), and since it was only 8:00 p.m., they'd opted for comfy clothes, dinner in and a movie from Kylie's DVD collection.

At his request, she'd dressed in her striped boxer shorts (she still couldn't believe he thought they were hot) and, of her own choosing, a baby-doll T-shirt featuring a dragon. As for Jack, it turned out he kept a duffel in the back of his SUV stuffed with various emergency supplies—including spare clothes. He'd changed into sweats and a faded blue

NYPD T-shirt. She'd called him super-sexy, to which he'd replied, "You're nuts." But he'd tempered that observation with a warm smile.

Unlike most of the people in town, when it came to Kylie's likes and dislikes, Jack didn't make her feel like an oddball. He appreciated new world music and martial arts films. He was a big fan of Asian food and even liked green tea. When she'd mentioned that Wong's delivered, he'd placed an order, impressing her when he'd pronounced the entries and appetizers with the ease of someone who knew the language. When she'd asked about that, he'd said he'd spent a lot of time in Chinatown. She'd been full of questions about the people and the culture. His answers had transported her to another world. If she never got to Asia, she'd definitely make it to Chinatown in Manhattan.

That's if she could conquer her new fear of heights enough to get on a plane.

Sigh.

Forty minutes later, they sat on her futon drinking wine and eating Chinese takeout. Her coffee table was lined with several cardboard cartons filled with delicious-smelling Asian cuisine. Some new-to-her dishes, some old favorites. She watched as Jack expertly manipulated shrimp lo mein with chopsticks, marveling how a Midwestern boy had grown into a worldly man. No wonder he and Spenser enjoyed a lifelong friendship. Two adventurous souls with old-fashioned values.

Kylie nibbled at a bamboo shoot. "I bet you'd try *zongzi.* Or *chimaki,* the Japanese version."

"I've had *zongzi* and *chimaki.*"

She furrowed her brow and sampled General Tso's Chicken. "They have Japanese restaurants in Chinatown?"

"There are more than two hundred restaurants in Chinatown, hon. Chinese, Cantonese, Japanese, Thai, Vietnamese, Korean…"

"Wow. So, did you like it?"

"Zongzi?" He shrugged. "Kind of bland."

"Oh." Not exactly what she wanted to hear about one of her dream foods. "So, tell me more about your work with the NYPD. I know you started in the 5th Precinct, which includes Chinatown and Little Italy and SoHo—"

"Bits of SoHo."

Another place she'd like to see, after hearing Jack describe it. A popular artsy neighborhood, populated with trendy boutiques and sidewalk vendors. "But then you said you transferred to a couple of other precincts. Because?"

"Various reasons. Promotions. Opportunities. Challenges."

He'd worked his way up from patrol officer to detective. Homicide detective. When Spenser had first told her she'd been in awe, thinking of all the good he did. Now she could only think about the bad he saw. "I can't imagine the crime you battled. The things you've seen."

"Good."

Kylie heard an awful lot of tension in that one word. She allowed a moment to pass, sipping her wine while she garnered her courage. Something told her this subject was off limits, but she was dying to know. "Faye said that Kerri said that Deputy Ziffel said you burned out on big crime."

"That's the short of it." Jack topped off her wine, then refilled his own glass.

"Want to talk about it?"

"No."

"Why not?"

"Because I don't want that stuff in your head."

"The kind of stuff they show on *CSI* and *Omertà?*"

Jack met her gaze and held it. "There's a big difference between fiction and reality, Kylie."

She fidgeted. "I know that."

"Tell me about your dream trip."

The change of subject jolted her, but she decided to roll with it. She'd get to the bottom of Jack's burnout at some point. As long as she sensed suffering, she'd want to soothe it.

"You're a caretaker, not a risk-taker."

Faye's words still stung. They made Kylie feel bland, like *zongzi*. She shrugged off the hurt and drizzled duck sauce on a spring roll. She broached the cursed trip of her dreams. "Not much to tell. I fell in love with all things Asian—" she gestured to her home decor "—around the time I fell for you."

"So you were twelve," he teased.

"Fourteen," she lied. "One time, okay a few times, I followed you and Spenser to karate class and peeked in."

"Spense and I were in and out of martial arts when we were sixteen. A brief fascination with Bruce Lee." His lip twitched. "You would've been twelve."

She blushed. "The point is, I got sucked in by the grace and discipline of the art." *And the way Jack had looked kicking butt.* "I started reading everything I could find on the Orient. Something about their culture, their spiritualism, called to me. I decided I was going to experience it for myself. I wanted to spend a month or two backpacking through Japan and China. Somewhere along the way, I started thinking of it as my dream trip. It wasn't until this past week that I realized it truly is a dream."

"Why's that?"

"It's a long story."

"We've got all night." Jack set aside his food and leaned back against the futon. His earnest gaze was unnerving.

She abandoned her spring roll and sipped more wine. "All right. Here's the short of it."

Jack smiled and her insides fluttered.

Dang.

She cleared her throat. "I actually had the opportunity to visit Japan as part of an exchange student program my junior year in high school. I was pumped. I had my parents' blessings. Actually, I think Dad was happy to get me out of his hair for several months."

"I don't know about that, Tiger."

"I do." She'd been a nuisance, always hanging around

the store. Always trying to impress him with her shoe smarts. "Anyway, I bailed."

"Why?"

"That's the year Grandpa McGraw was diagnosed with cancer. I couldn't go. I just...I couldn't."

Jack nodded. "Okay. I've got the time reference now. Couldn't have been easy to watch Wilbur fade like that."

"It wasn't. But, I loved him and my family was hurting, so...I needed to be here, not there."

Jack reached over and squeezed her hand.

Kylie soaked in his kindness and shut out the past. "Fast-forward to several years later. I was determined to take my dream trip. It was a personal goal, something I kept close to my heart and under my hat. I guess I thought blabbing about it would somehow make it less special. Or maybe I thought people would laugh and chalk it up to another one of my eccentricities. I don't know. Anyway, I worked hard, skimped and saved and was just a few hundred shy of my goal fund when I learned Grandma McGraw was close to financial ruin. Strike that. She'd hit the skids."

Jack frowned. "Spenser didn't say anything about that. He's never said anything about your dream trip, either. I understand about not sharing your plans with all of Eden, Kylie, but why not your brother?"

"It would have meant him coming home for two months to run McGraw's. I didn't want to interfere with his career. First, he was up-and-coming, then he was the star of a hit cable show. The timing never seemed right. Although I admit, I thought he'd burn out at some point and come home to rejuvenate. Then I'd go." She snorted. "Spenser's proving himself tireless."

"You could always hire someone to run the store in your absence. I can't see Spense having a problem with that."

"*I* have a problem with that."

"Ah."

"As for Grandma's crisis, Spenser doesn't know about

that, either. And you can't tell him." Kylie held out her little finger. "Pinkie swear."

Jack rolled his eyes, but he crooked his pinkie around hers and shook.

Kylie spilled the beans about her grandma's depression and her lethal addiction to the shopping network.

"Christ."

"Her pride was at stake, Jack. I couldn't go to Mom or Spenser. I promised her I wouldn't."

"You used your dream trip fund to pay off her debts."

She shrugged. "It's only money."

"But you still wanted to tour Asia. So you started from scratch. Saved again."

"It's not that hard. You just have to be frugal."

"Hence the thrifty trailer in the middle of nowhere, the sparse furnishings. You're the most unmaterialistic woman I've ever known."

Kylie shrugged. "It's the quality of life that matters. A fancy home and lots of stuff won't make you happy if you're not happy on the inside."

"Are you happy?"

"Right now?" She grinned up at him. "I'm delirious."

He smoothed a thumb over her cheek. "I meant in general."

She glanced away. "I'm restless. I don't know what it is, Jack. But ever since my birthday…I guess I'm not where I wanted to be at thirty-two."

"Asia?"

That. And married with children. The former seemed the safer subject. She quirked a self-conscious smile. "I almost had enough for the trip, but I splurged on the renovations to McGraw's. Faye said it's because my priorities have shifted. She said deep down, the trip's lost its appeal. She intimated I've lost my nerve. Said I'd rather run the store and look after Grandma and Mom. She said I'm a caretaker, not a risk-taker. Which really bugs me. If embracing the new means being a bossy Mother Hen obsessed with all work and no play and ending up an old maid, then I'm totally against it."

"You won't end up an old maid, Kylie."

"But I won't end up with you or at least not married to you because you're not husband material. So you say." She slapped her palm to her forehead. "I can't believe I said that. Too much wine." She set aside the glass. "I should stick to beer. I never speak out of turn when I drink beer."

He just smiled and squeezed her hand. "I'd rather know your mind than have to guess."

"Yeah?"

"Yeah."

"Okay. Well, I'm thinking I really enjoyed this night."

"Me, too."

"And that, since we click, maybe we should click a little more. No promises. No expectations. Just live for now and see where it takes us."

"Faye was wrong," he said with a raised brow. "You're a risk-taker."

She started to smile, then worried he might follow up with a brush-off.

Jack hugged her close and kissed the top of her head. They both held silent for a while, assessing, she assumed, how this potential relationship fit into their shaky lives. It was the most awkward moment in the evening.

Jack spoke first. "There's this game," he said, plucking two fortune cookies from the coffee table. "You read your fortune and end it with—"

"I know the game." Heart lighter, Kylie snitched a cookie and cracked it open. She pulled out her fortune and read. "There is a true and sincere friendship between you—in bed."

"Nice." Jack cracked his cookie, grinned. "You shall seek out new adventures—in bed."

She rolled her eyes. "You made that up."

He showed her the fortune.

"Wow."

"Who are we to fight destiny?"

Kylie shifted and straddled Jack's lap. She wiggled against his erection and quirked a wicked smile. "This time I get to be the dominant one."

CHAPTER THIRTY-ONE

JACK WAS ASLEEP WHEN his cell phone rang. He hadn't slept this soundly in years. It took a few seconds to shake off the haze. He disentangled himself from Kylie, smiling when she groaned and rolled back into him, still very much asleep. He nabbed his cell from the nightstand and answered softly.

"It's Jessica," the voice on the other end responded. "I'm sorry to bother you. I know you're...well, busy, but, this is an emergency. I think. Maybe. I'm not sure. But...I need you."

Words he never thought he'd hear from his sister chilled him to the bone.

"Talk to me." Jack rolled out of bed, ignored his sweats and tugged on his dress jeans.

Kylie stirred and pinned him with dazed, worried eyes.

He shushed her with a raised hand and focused on his sister's shaky words.

"I needed some things from the house, my...Frank's house," she clarified. "I loaded Madeline and Shy into the SUV. We drove over and, like always, I parked in back. Told Madeline to stay in the car while I ran inside only...the back door was ajar. I'm sure it was locked when I left. I think...I think someone broke in."

"Tell me you're not inside."

"Give me some credit. What if they're still in there?"

"Where are you now?"

"Driving Madeline and Shy over to Mrs. Carmichael's."

"Good. Stay with them." He sat on the bed and jammed his feet into his shoes. What the fuck?

Kylie moved against him, massaged his shoulders.

He reached up and squeezed her hand, noting her calm and kindness. "I'm on my way," he told Jessie. "But I'm calling Officer Anderson. He's ten minutes closer."

"No. No cops. I mean, other than you. Please," she pleaded. "I don't want people snooping in the house."

"Jessie—"

"I mean it, Jack. Please."

Her pleading got to him. Tore at him. "All right. But stay at Mrs. Carmichael's until I call you."

"Thank you, Jack."

She hung up and Jack clipped his cell to his belt.

"What is it?" Kylie asked. "What's wrong?"

"I have to go." He brushed a quick kiss across her mouth. "I'll call you later. Lock the door behind me."

He was buckled inside the Aspen before he realized he'd probably worried Kylie more by shutting her out. He'd done the same thing with his ex. Shut her out. It was preferable to subjecting her to his seedy, dangerous world. It had also pushed her away.

"Damn."

Old habits die hard. Although he wasn't sure this was a habit he could or even wanted to break. Protecting the people he cared about came naturally. He cared about Kylie. He wouldn't go so far as to say he was in love, but he was sure as hell infatuated.

Intoxicated.

Jack shook off the lingering effects of the night before. He focused on his sister's potential crisis and stepped on the gas.

It was a beautiful September morning, sunny with mild temps in the low sixties, yet Jack's mood turned more grim with each passing mile. Something had driven Jessie out of that house and now someone had broken in? He suspected Frank was at the bottom of this. He mulled over the possibilities, cursed as he neared the Cortez's upscale home. The Escalade parked across the street belonged to Jessie. What the hell?

He parked a few feet behind, relaxed a little when he saw her sitting in the driver's seat. At least she wasn't inside. Jaw clenched, he approached and knocked.

She yelped, then lowered the window. "You scared the pee out of me."

"I told you to stay at Mrs. Carmichael's."

"Waiting for a phone call from Deputy Ziffel informing me you'd been shot or stabbed or bludgeoned, and bled to death because no one was there to help you?" She frowned. "No, thank you."

"I'm touched you care."

"Of course I care." She blew out an anxious breath. "After dropping off Madeline and the dog, I doubled back. I couldn't bear the thought of you going in alone without some sort of backup. At least I can call for help if you get into trouble. At least… Would you please stop smiling?"

"First you ask for my help. Now you're actually worried about me. Does my heart good, little sister."

She glowered. "How can you be so calm?"

"Comes with the job. Besides, I don't think I'm going to find anyone in there. If someone did break in, probably happened in the middle of the night." He glanced over his shoulder at the two-story, fourteen-room house—a small mansion by most of Eden's standards. "Anything of particular value in there?"

"Try everything. We only bought the best."

"Frank keep money in the house?"

"There's a safe in his office, but I assume he cleared it out when he left."

Jack nodded. "Stay in the car. I mean it."

"Wait! Do you have a gun?"

He hitched back his leather jacket to give her a glimpse of his holstered piece.

"That's something, I guess."

"Stay here," he repeated, then angled toward the house.

Following standard procedure, he entered the premises, then swept the entire house, upstairs and down. Certain he was alone, he dialed Jessie.

She answered midring. "Are you okay?" she asked in a hushed voice.

"Whoever was here is gone. Come in through the back. I'll meet you in the kitchen."

In the ten seconds it took her to comply, he pondered the situation. "I need to protect and preserve the scene," he said when she crept over the threshold. "Don't touch anything."

"The *scene?* As in crime scene? What am I in for, Jack?" Hands balled, she hugged herself, then followed him through the kitchen and dining area. When they passed the recreation room stuffed with a myriad of electronics, she spoke. "It doesn't look like anything's missing."

"I don't think we're dealing with a straight-ahead burglary," Jack said, tugging a pair of latex gloves from his pocket. "I think it was personal and directed at Frank. Brace yourself."

He stepped into Frank's home office, grasping Jessie's elbow as she moved in alongside. He wasn't surprised when she swayed. The devastation was extensive. Bookcases overturned, stuffing ripped from the leather sofa. It looked like someone had taken a baseball bat to Frank's computer monitor and hard-drive tower.

"My God, Jack."

"Someone was pissed and they were looking for something. Where's the safe?"

"In that closet, behind the stack of file boxes."

Not wanting his own fingerprints in the mix, Jack pulled on the thin gloves. He stepped over strewn books and broken knick-knacks and opened the door. "The safe's locked," he called out. "Maybe they cracked it then tidied up. Do you know the combination?"

"No. I'm sorry. I never asked. It was Frank's private safe. He said it was for sensitive case files. Now I'm wondering…"

Jack stepped out and noted his sister's crimson face. "What?"

She averted her gaze. "Never mind."

"Any idea what they were looking for?"

She shook her head.

"Frank make any enemies of late that you know of?" he persisted.

She massaged her temples. "I don't suppose he's popular with the husbands of the wives he had affairs with. That's if the husbands found out. Frank was amazingly discreet. He fooled me for years." She met his gaze. "But not you. You never liked Frank to begin with."

"The man was *too* likable," he said. "I didn't trust that. Plus, I had a gut feeling."

"You tried to warn me."

"I tried to bully you into not marrying him. I handled the situation badly, Jessie. I wish I'd had a better perspective."

"Why did you punch Frank on my wedding day?" she blurted.

"Why don't we hold off on that?" She had enough to deal with, and he needed to grab his latent-print kit and camera from the back of the Aspen.

"I'd been mingling with our guests, wondering about Frank. He'd been gone quite a while. I was worried, so I went looking," she said, intent on reliving that moment. "I found him in the garden nursing a bloody nose. He said you punched him. Said you were an interfering asshole. When I confronted you, you dodged the issue. Because of that moment, Jack, because I was blinded by love, I cut you out of my life." Her eyes filled with tears. "Please. I have to know."

"I caught him making out with Jenny Franklin in the wine cellar."

"During our wedding reception?" she squeaked.

Uncomfortable, Jack eased his sister back into the hall, toward the spacious, immaculate living room. "It was pretty hot and heavy. Jenny was obviously drunk and ran off in tears. I rammed my fist into Frank's face before he got a word out. Though after, he claimed that he, too, was drunk. Said it had never happened before and never would again. I didn't believe him, but I wanted to. For your sake."

"The man I loved to distraction for thirteen years cheated on me on our wedding day. Our *wedding day*." The first tear fell. "Why didn't you tell me?"

"Would you have believed me?"

She closed her eyes, sighed. "No."

Jack touched her arm. "Jessie, I need to call this in."

"No! Please. Can't we just, I don't know, look into this privately or maybe ignore it?"

"A crime's been committed. Let me do my job, Jess."

"But I don't want people snooping around here. I don't want them to know..." She broke off, swiped away tears.

"Why did you show up at my house in the middle of the night?" Jack asked in a tender voice. "What spooked you?"

"It's awful, Jack. Dark and ugly and..."

"Tell me."

"I can't. I can't talk about it. But, I'll show you. Just... promise you won't make this public."

How could he promise without knowing what he was dealing with? "I need you to trust me, Jess. Trust that I'll do the right thing."

She quirked a shaky smile. "You always do the right thing. I used to resent you for that." Stiff-backed, she climbed the stairs.

Jack stayed close behind.

She visibly trembled as she entered her bedroom. She looked everywhere but at the bed. The bed she'd shared with Frank. "Our whole marriage was a lie," she rasped. "There was a side to him I never knew, a side beyond the affairs. A dark side." She pointed to her walk-in closet. "In there, on the floor. They fell out of a suitcase when I accidentally knocked it from the shelf. After that I...I couldn't stay here. I didn't know what else he'd hidden or where. I didn't want Madeline to trip upon...any other evidence."

Jack moved into the closet. He saw several magazines

shoved or kicked into the corner. Intrigued, he kneeled and sorted through the titles. "Shit."

Like most men, he'd grown up admiring *Playboy* centerfolds and indulging in occasional skin flicks with inane titles like *Making Mona Moan.* But he was a Boy Scout compared to Frank. His brother-in-law was obsessed with extreme hardcore porn. Raunchy magazines featuring women on women, men on men, threesomes, underage girls, orgies—all sadistic.

Between this revelation, his multiple affairs and the break-in, no wonder Jessie was a basket case.

"I didn't know about his...obsession. He never hinted or slipped or...I'm not a prude, Jack, but, if I'd known, I'm not sure I could have tolerated it. Those pictures, the stories, they're..."

"Twisted." He skimmed the contents. *Jesus.*

"I'm wondering now...what if he has sex toys or illicit videos locked in that safe," Jessie said in a choked voice. "And what if he hid things throughout the house? I couldn't chance Madeline finding.... We couldn't stay here...I hope you understand," she said on a rush of sobs. "I'm an idiot. A fool. Please don't tell."

Heartbroken and furious, Jack removed the latex gloves, left the closet and pulled his sister into his arms. "Listen to me, Jess. Trust me. It'll be all right," he said in a gentle voice. "I promise."

CHAPTER THIRTY-TWO

KYLIE SIPPED HOT GREEN TEA and willed her leg to stop
bouncing. Even a short session of meditation in her Zen
Garden hadn't helped. The morning hadn't gone exactly
as planned. After a late and exhausting night, they'd been
jarred awake by Jack's ringing cell. Kylie had sensed an
emergency right away. She told herself not to take offense
because Jack had taken off like a blur—no explanation.
Obviously, his sister was in trouble. God knew she'd go
running if Spenser ever needed her, not that that was
likely, still...

Whatever the trouble, she hoped it wasn't serious. She
hoped the woman was exaggerating her situation as she
was prone to do. Jessica Lynn had a way of stealing, no,
demanding the spotlight. On the other hand, it was hard to
think ungracious thoughts about a person who'd saved her
from an uncomfortable discussion with Max and gang. A
person who'd tried to make up for past bad behavior.

Kylie sipped tea, ate granola cereal and thought positive.
Whatever the problem, Jack would solve it. She had
complete faith in the man's abilities to save the day. She'd
witnessed many incidents, heard many stories. The more
she reflected on his stellar character and impressive accomplishments, the more she wondered what he saw in her. She
wasn't worldly or exciting or jaw-droppingly gorgeous.
She was Kylie McGraw, manager of a shoe store. A woman
whose ambition stopped at carrying on her family's legacy.
Fitting the needs of those in need of shoes.

"No promises. No expectations. Just live for now and see where it takes us."

Right.

She repeated that notion three times, declaring it today's affirmation. No matter what, she'd always have last night. But she sure as heck wanted more.

If it weren't for the leftover Chinese takeout in her fridge and her achy muscles, she would have chalked up the evening to a fantastic dream. She'd known Jack all her life, but as her brother's best friend and the hunky fantasy man she lusted after. Last night she'd gotten to know him as a real person and a lover. Their dynamics had shifted, and even though she was thrilled, she wasn't secure in her new reality. She kept thinking about how everything she'd "changed" of late had gone wrong. Except for the renovations to the store. Thanks to Travis, those had turned out better than she'd hoped. Of course, that could still bomb, too. What if she ran off McGraw's regulars because they thought the store was too trendy? What if she couldn't woo the Garden Club elite with the designer heels she'd ordered? What if the kids and tourists snubbed her *Bada-Bling!* imports?

Travis would tell her to relax and have faith. She was really looking forward to seeing him this afternoon. She knew his work was pretty much done, but she still needed to write him a check and she'd bought a special thank-you card. She hoped their new friendship wouldn't fizzle when he went back to work at Hank's Hardware. Even though she knew so little about Travis, she knew enough to peg him as a good soul. A hurting soul. Maybe she could help him through the pain of losing his wife and chase away whatever demons haunted him. She suspected he'd do the same for her. Now, if only Jack and Faye would warm to him. She'd have to work on that.

Kylie glanced at the phone, sighed. "As if staring will make that thing ring." Jack had promised to call. She was on pins and needles. Was he all right? Was Jessica all right?

Needing a distraction, she fired up her laptop. She sipped tea, willed her bouncing leg still...again. She weeded out junk mail, checked the status of orders. Mostly everything was in. The *Bada-Bling!* sneakers would arrive tomorrow. The designer heels had arrived yesterday, just before she'd locked up to prepare for her date with Jack. She'd spend today hauling out the previous stock she'd stashed in the storeroom and arranging it on her new shelves alongside special displays for the new shipment of quirky shoes and sophisticated heels. But she didn't want to leave until Jack called.

She could hear him now. *"If you had a cell phone you wouldn't be stuck at home at the mercy of your landline."* Last night they'd gone a round about that. He'd stated several reasons why she needed one, sounding very much like her brother. She'd always considered cell phones a luxury. She still wasn't sure it was a necessity, but she'd *"yessed"* Jack just so they could move on to something else, like kissing each other into a blissful coma.

Again, she glanced at the phone. She'd call Faye, since she owed her details about the date (not that Kylie would tell *all*), but it was Sunday. Faye was at church with Stan and the kids. Most everyone in Eden was at church. Since discovering Buddhism, Kylie had marched to her own spiritual drum.

She checked more e-mails, drank more tea.

The phone jangled. Kylie tripped in her haste, stubbing her toe. *Ow.* "Hello?"

"Have something you want to tell me, Kitten?"

Spenser.

Surprised and wary, Kylie sat on her futon, wondering how to answer. Was he talking about the store? The water tower? Or the fact that she'd slept with his best friend? "Where are you?"

"Still on Pitcairn, though I'm wondering if I should abandon the shoot and come home."

"Why?"

"Mayor Wilson contacted me through the studio. Said you're having a crisis, stirring up trouble. He's worried you're going to sabotage the Apple Festival."

"What?" Furious, Kylie stood and paced. "That's insane. Why would I... Oh. Because I promised to shake things up. Well, believe it or not, I can add a little zing to this town without sabotaging the blessed Apple Festival."

"Zing, huh? Like painting the front of McGraw's pink?"

"Not *pink*. Moroccan spice. Not that it matters. I'm not altering the storefront. The HPS cited some legal mumbo-jumbo and squashed my plan."

"Except you told the HPS this wasn't over."

Kylie swallowed a squeal of outrage. "I can't believe the mayor tracked you down on a remote island to tattle on me!"

"Neither can I. That's why I called. *Are* you having a crisis, Kylie? If you need me, say the word. I'll drop everything and come home."

Her heart swelled, her eyes stung. Great. Now she was angry *and* weepy. "I appreciate that, Spenser," she said in a calmer tone. "But I'm fine. Honest." A few days earlier she'd been disappointed when he said he was extending his filming schedule. Now she cringed at the thought of him coming home. Spenser would have something to say about her hooking up with Jack. She wasn't sure she wanted to hear it. She needed more time, more freedom to explore this relationship without her brother's interference. "I had the birthday blues, that's all. I was bored. I wanted to make some changes."

"So make changes. The HPS doesn't control what we do with the interior of the store."

She blinked. "Are you telling me to redecorate, because I already sort of did."

"I know. Wilson told me. Am I going to hate it?"

"Probably," she grumbled, wondering what other beans the mayor had spilled.

Spenser just laughed. "It's always the quiet ones. Give 'em hell, Kitten. Just don't scare away the tourists."

"My intention, believe it or not, is to attract more business, not drive it away."

"You always were the sensible one."

It was the exact wrong thing to say. "I have to go, Spenser." Jack could be trying to call, and she didn't have call waiting. "Things to do. People to see."

"A town to shake up. Got it," he said with a smile in his voice. "Hey, how's Jack doing as the new police chief?"

"Great," she said, keeping it short and light. "You know Jack."

"Excels at everything he does."

"Ain't that the truth," Kylie blurted, thinking about Jack's magic touch. Face burning, she cleared her throat. "I really need to go, and this call has to be costing you a fortune."

"Small price to know you're okay."

"I'm better than okay. I'm taking charge of my destiny."

"Let me know if I can help."

"I love you, Spenser."

"Love you, too, Kitten."

They disconnected, and Kylie stood in the center of her living room, feeling dumbstruck. She'd expected Spenser to blast her for renovating without discussing it with him first. Then again, it reaffirmed how little interest he had in McGraw's Shoe Store—make that McGraw's Shoe *Shoppe*.

The phone rang. This time when she lunged, she banged her knee. *Ow.* "Hello?"

"Hey, Kylie. It's me."

"Oh." *Rats.* "Hi, Faye.

"You sound disappointed."

"Sorry. I was just…Jack had to leave in a hurry to investigate something. I've been waiting for a call to let me know he's okay."

"I'm sure he's fine. We're talking about supercop Jack Reynolds. Listen, I only have a second. I snuck out of the sermon because the anticipation was killing me. How did it go last night?"

Kylie smiled and rubbed her bruised knee. "Since you

only have a second, I'll sum it up in one word. *Amazing. Romantic. Exciting—*"

"That's three words and going strong," Faye said. "I take it he slept over. Was it everything you hoped for?"

Kylie's heart bloomed. "More than I dreamed."

Faye sighed. "We *so* have to talk. I need details. Unfortunately, my day is jammed with family matters."

Kylie envied that...except...what if those family matters were at the root of Faye's unhappiness? "This thing with Stan, the issue you're sorting out—"

"Still sorting. I've gotta get back inside, Kylie."

"Okay." *Crud.* "Call me when you can. Bye." No sooner did she hang up than the phone rang again. She half expected Travis or her grandmother, or maybe Mayor Wilson. The obnoxious tattletale. "What?"

"That's some greeting, Tiger."

Jack! "Sorry, I thought you were...never mind. Are you okay?"

"I'm fine."

"What about Jessica and Madeline?"

"Also fine."

"Shy?" Maybe something awful had happened to the dog-that-was-now-his.

"Shy's fine. There was an incident at Jessie's house. I need to clear it up. Between that and last-minute preparations for the Apple Festival, I'm swamped."

Kylie wanted to know specifics about the "incident," but didn't want to snoop. Besides, maybe Jack wasn't free to talk just now. Surely he'd tell her when he could. "That's okay. I'll be busy at the store preparing for the festival."

There was an awkward pause. "Listen, hon. I know we had plans for tonight, but I don't feel good about leaving Jessie alone."

She heard the honest regret in his voice as well as the concern for his sister. It cooled the initial disappointment and warmed her heart. "Why don't you invite Jessica and Madeline to join us for dinner? After, maybe we could rent a movie from Mac's Video Circus. Then we can play it by ear."

"You're a good woman, Kylie McGraw."

"Don't say that. Good girls finish last."

"Not in my book."

Kylie smiled. "I'll see you tonight."

"Be careful on that bike."

Self-conscious, she smoothed a hand down her denim-clad thigh, thinking about the bruise beneath. "Always."

KYLIE SOAKED IN THE FRESH country air and brilliant sunshine as she cruised Route 50 on her Kawasaki sport bike. She was still miffed about the mayor's call to her brother, but her anxiety had eased somewhat after speaking with Jack. He was okay. His family was okay—relatively speaking. Jessica Lynn was going through a rough time. Kylie couldn't imagine being horribly betrayed by your husband. An affair was bad enough, but Frank Cortez had seduced a teenager. The "ick" factor was off the scale.

She thought about how Jessica had come to her rescue yesterday, then apologized for an ancient slight. That alone was amazing, but the fact that she'd taken a job at Boone's was a mindblower. Beauty queen turned beer schlepper. When Kylie had asked Jack about it, all he'd said was that Jessica wanted to earn her own way. You had to sympathize with her plight. Kylie promised herself she'd make an effort to befriend Jack's sister. Having dinner together tonight would be a good start.

The tails of her red trench coat whipping behind her, Kylie smiled as her heart bloomed. Bonding with Jack's family gave her a warm, fuzzy feeling and helped her to feel less insecure about their budding romance.

If only she could channel that optimism into the grand reopening of McGraw's.

On a whim, just past Max's place, Kylie cornered onto a narrow dirt road. Instead of her usual straight shot into town, she'd go the long way round, stopping first for a self-pep talk. She wasn't on a set schedule today, and she wanted to walk into the store filled with confidence, not riddled with self-doubt. Whenever she communed with nature, she always got a positive charge. A stroll along the lake seemed the perfect solution.

She eased off the gas as she spied her destination. Across the way hailed Frances Slocum State Forest and Mississinewa Lake. She rolled across the deserted road and parked her bike near a strategic lookout intended for amateur birdwatchers. Rather than view the beauty from afar, she walked a path that led a short distance through the woods and straight to the lake's edge.

Her silver helmet dangling from her right hand, Kylie breathed in the woodsy scents and serenity as she navigated the unmarked trail. Though she was surrounded by green, she was thinking *caliente* and *starburst*. "Travis struck gold with those chosen shades of paint," she murmured to herself. Thinking positive, she imagined the vintage, funky decor of McGraw's Shoe Shoppe.

Change is exciting. Change is good.

Her blissful musing was shattered at the sound of angry voices followed by a muffled pop. Cheeks burning, she froze in her tracks.

"*Fuck!* What are you, *oobotz?* How are we supposed to get money out of a dead guy?"

"He fuckin' spit on my shoe!"

"You've been spit on before."

"Do you know how much these oxfords cost me?"

"Do you know how many pairs of oxfords you coulda bought with your cut?"

"But they're fuckin' Guccis!"

"Unfuckingbelievable."

Dead guy?

Spine tingling, Kylie's instincts screamed for her to back away.

Leave. *Leave!*

Instead, she scanned the wooded area for two hostile

men with East Coast accents. Surely she'd misheard or misunderstood.

Then it dawned on her.

This had to be a joke.

Two sportsmen affecting accents and *pretending* to be wiseguys. She wouldn't be surprised given the popularity of *Omertà*. Since the DVD release, three-quarters of the people in Eden were working their way through six seasons of the gritty show, compliments of Mac's Video Circus. These two idiots were rehashing a grisly scene.

Yeah. That sounded reasonable. Besides, who in the real world killed over a pair of shoes?

Morbid curiosity propelled Kylie into motion. Following the sounds of the voices, she crept closer, using tree trunks to shield her presence.

"Why did I let you talk me into this? When this gets back to the boss, we're as dead as this fuckin' *finook*."

"Then we'll have to make sure no one finds out. Stop bitching and give me a hand."

"All because of a goddamned pair of shoes."

Kylie froze when she spied her prey. Two broad-shoul-dered men, average height. Black leather jackets, dark trousers, dark hoods. As for the spat-upon-shoes—both men were wearing black oxfords. She couldn't make out the Guccis. However, it was the third pair of shoes that made her heart stop. A silver buckle glinted in the sun. The unique soles rang a bell. Were those Ferragamos? She watched in numb horror as the two beefy goons stuffed a well-dressed body, a man with exquisite taste in shoes, into the trunk of a compact black sedan. "Oh, my, God."

"What the…?" The first bruiser whipped around and spotted her as she stumbled back.

Not a black hood, she thought as panic set in. *Black ski mask.*

"I've got him. You get her," said Bruiser number two. "And, dammit, make it clean!"

Survival instinct gave Kylie's feet wings. She flew

through the thicket, the thick rubber treads of her flower-power boots eating up the rough terrain. She heard Bruiser number one slipping on the dewy grass, heard him curse. Heart pounding, she weaved through the forest, an area she knew like the back of her hand, hoping to lose the killer before reaching her bike. *Make it clean!* What did that mean? No blood? So, maybe instead of shooting or stabbing her, he'd just strangle her and dump her in the lake?

Panic fueled her speed. Kylie used her arms to guard her face from low, spindly branches as she fought her way uphill. Still, she felt the occasional sting of a lash. *Better scratched than dead.*

She thought she was a goner when she tripped on an exposed root. She flew forward. Her glasses flew…somewhere else. Adrenaline packed a hearty punch. In a flash, Kylie was back on her feet and sprinting, although squinting. No time to search for her glasses. She was running for her flipping life!

When she heard a foul curse close on her heels, she turned and winged her helmet, clipping the mystery murderer in his fat masked head. The impact sent him tumbling back down the hill into a massive evergreen.

She booked it and cleared the forest, lungs bursting as she heeled her kickstand and revved the engine. The bike peeled rubber, gravel spitting beneath its tires as she raced toward the dirt road leading home. She'd traveled these roads so many times she could probably do so blindfolded. Good news, since she was now visually impaired.

Damn her and her frugal ways! If only she owned a cell phone. She needed to call the police. She needed Jack. *Don't go home,* she could hear him saying. *What if they follow?*

She squinted in her rearview mirror, spotted a dark car turning onto the road. Was it them? From this distance, she couldn't be sure. If it was, surely they saw the dust kicked up by her bike. *Wave a flag, why don't you, McGraw?*

She leaned low and gunned the throttle and jumped her silver Ninja into a grassy pasture. She zipped toward a copse of trees. Three minutes later she came out on the backside of Max's house. She steered her bike into the listing barn, hid it behind accumulated junk and ran toward his house. She didn't bother to knock. Max never locked his doors. She burst inside, shouting his name. "I need to use your phone. Max! *Max!*"

She glanced at the clock hanging above the kitchen sink. *Oh, no.* About now he was enjoying a post-church breakfast with his cronies. It was a ritual. Same café. Same time.

Every. Stinking. Sunday.

Kylie nabbed a nearby phone, punched 911. Nothing. No ring. No dial tone. *Dammit.* Max had mentioned canceling his landline, cutting costs and relying solely on his cell. Apparently, he'd done just that. If only she'd followed his lead.

Kylie squashed the panic eating at her nerves and brain. "Think, Kylie, think." She needed to get to a phone. Better yet, to Jack. Killers were on the loose in Eden. He had to catch them before they got away or, worse, before they found her. Because, cripes, she'd witnessed a *murder.* Not the actual murder, but close enough. She couldn't risk driving her Ninja into town. They knew her bike, or if they didn't, they'd put two and two together since Bruiser number one had her helmet.

That left one option. Senses buzzing with determination, she nabbed the coveted key hanging above the retired fire chief's coffeemaker and sprinted out the door.

CHAPTER THIRTY-THREE

SHY TROTTED INTO THE chief of police's office ahead of Jack, circled three times, then curled on the doggy cushion Dorothy had placed near his desk in an effort to keep the mutt off the station house's padded chairs.

Jack shoved the box of magazines and videos he'd collected from Jessie's house to the back of the closet and locked the door. He didn't want the department's efficient office administrator tripping across the pornographic evidence during her organizing frenzy. If only he could've spared Jessica the unpleasant discovery.

It had taken Jack several minutes to convince his traumatized sister to trust his process. That included consulting with his second-in-command, who, he'd promised, would be discreet. Bottom line, though Jack was acquainted with many of Eden's citizens, he'd been away and out of touch for years. Where details of daily life were concerned, Deputy Ziffel was better connected.

Meanwhile, Jack promised to handle aspects of his sister's B and E on his own. Patrol cars were typically outfitted with basic crime-scene equipment. Jack's SUV was no different. He had immediate access to a latent-print kit and a camera. He'd photographed the crime scene, lifted fingerprints, collected evidence, documented observations. He was certain he was dealing with an amateur. He wouldn't be surprised if it *was* a cuckolded husband, but what was the man looking for? Evidence of the affair? Lewd photos? Homemade video? For that matter, maybe the suspect was one of the adulterous wives.

Though a small force, the EPD did have access to the Integrated Automated Fingerprint Identification System (IAFIS), a computerized database accessing thousands of fingerprints. Between that and basic detective work, Jack felt confident he'd soon nail the culprit. This was nothing compared to what he'd dealt with in NYC. The difference was, this involved family. His family.

By the same token, while investigating the crime scene, Jack's thoughts kept flashing on Kylie. He'd always thought of her as family, but now the stakes were even higher with friend and lover in the mix. Kylie who lived in the middle of fricking nowhere, in a trailer with no security lighting and basic locks on the doors that any half-witted criminal could break. Luckily, Jessie had been away when her home, or rather Frank's office, had been ransacked. Except for last night, Kylie slept at home, alone, every night. She was a crime statistic waiting to happen. He'd have to do something about that.

Ziffel walked in just as Jack claimed the seat behind his recently organized desk.

"Got here as quick as I could, Chief."

Jack shook off thoughts of Kylie, assuring himself she was fine and en route to McGraw's. He focused on Jessie and Maddie, whom he'd talked into joining Mrs. Carmichael over at the Methodist Church. Along with several other women, they were currently coordinating the booths that would feature and sell homemade crafts over the next few days. He felt better knowing they were surrounded by people. Plus it would help to divert Jessie's dark thoughts.

"Sorry to pull you in on your day off, Ed."

Ziffel smoothed his windblown hair and shrugged off the imposition. "Figured it was important." Though dressed in faded jeans and an *Omertà* T-shirt, he still managed to look official in his EPD nylon jacket.

Jack noted his bright eyes and controlled movements. Though playing it cool, Deputy Ziffel was primed for action. "Shut the door," Jack said, then motioned the man to sit in an opposing chair. "Until otherwise notified, what I'm about to say is off the record."

"Understood."

Ziffel listened intently as Jack informed him of the break-in and the possibly connected sleaze factor.

"I can see why Jessica Lynn insisted on keeping this under wraps," Ziffel said, then shook his head. "Why the heck didn't Frank hide his...er, *private* collection in a better place? I mean, jeez, a suitcase on the shelf of their bedroom closet?"

"I wondered the same thing." Jack wondered about a lot of things. "There were two dozen or so fashion and health magazines in the mix. I assume he buried the fetish mags underneath, still..." He drummed his fingers on his desk, worked the puzzle aloud. "Found a few porn videos stashed in a spare bedroom. According to Jessie, Frank's returning to Eden tomorrow. Two reasons. The divorce settlement and unfinished business."

"Maybe that unfinished business includes packing up the sensitive materials he left behind in a rush."

"Maybe."

"Frank split town the same day he broke off with your sister," Ziffel said. "No one saw it coming. There were rumblings of a high-paying job and a lady lawyer friend with influential ties. You know Eden. Folks speculated plenty. The longer Frank was gone, the more certain they were he wasn't coming back." Ziffel shifted, looked away. "You'd be shocked by the buried secrets that started to see light."

"I'm not easily shocked," Jack said, but he was intrigued. He knew Ziffel would have answers. This was almost too easy. "Let's hear what you've got, Deputy."

Ziffel opened his mouth and a siren wailed.

Shy howled.

Jack and his deputy rose as one, although Ziffel was the first out the door.

They both gravitated to the station house's large front pane, Shy howling on their heels.

"What on earth is Max up to?" Ziffel asked.

Jack raised a brow as the retired fire chief's 1951 Dodge/Van Pelt pumper zoomed up Main Street, then skidded to a stop. One of the most popular events of the Apple Festival was the Antique Car and Truck show. Max's hook-and-ladder fire engine was an annual favorite, but that didn't entitle the man to speed into town, siren blaring. "Never thought I'd see the day when I'd have to lecture Max on safety," said Jack. Only it wasn't Max who jumped down from the driver's throne, but Kylie.

"What the hell?" he thought, followed by *"Christ, she's beautiful."*

The petite woman faltered on the running board, the hem of her red coat caught in the door she'd just slammed.

"Man, oh, man," Ziffel said as she struggled to pull her trench free. "I didn't realize she was this desperate."

Jack moved toward the door. "Meaning?"

"Like I have to tell you?" Ziffel asked, hot on his heels. "Kylie's been trying to set Eden on its ear for days. So far we've rolled with the punches, but *this*? There'll be no living with Max Grogan. Kylie stole his pride and joy."

The siren and Shy continued to wail as Jack pushed outside. "How do you know she stole it?"

Ziffel snorted. "I know you've been away for a while, but surely you haven't forgotten. No one drives Red Rover except Max."

Jack cleared the front steps just as Kylie shrugged out of her trapped coat and the owner of the vehicle poured out of Kerri's Confections, followed by his cronies. Shaking his fist, Max bellowed something, but Kylie paid no mind. She ran hell-bent for the station house. For Jack.

Stuck between curious and worried, he focused on the wide-eyed, dark-haired woman flying toward him. Dirt-stained clothes, rumpled hair, no glasses.

Running full out, she tripped and slammed into Jack. "Murder!"

He gripped her upper arms, steadied her, studied her. Her eyes were wild and glassy. Her face was flushed. She had a twig stuck in her tangled hair and a red welt on her left cheek. He willed his pounding heart steady. "Slow down, hon."

"Murder," she gasped. "Lake. Two men. Mobsters."

Jack's blood cooled the moment she mentioned the mob. What the hell was she playing at? If she was looking specifically to shake *him* up, then she'd scored.

"Hooligan!" Max pressed in, flanked by the mayor, Jay Jarvis and Ray Keystone. "*You* are in big trouble!" Max railed to Kyle. "I tried to play nice. Tried to be understanding. In your defense, *I* spearheaded un-vandalizing the water tower. And for what? You broke into my house and stole my priceless truck! I've never felt so…so… violated!"

"I didn't break into anything!" Kylie shouted back. "You never lock your doors. And I didn't steal your truck, I borrowed it!"

"Without asking!"

"It was an emergency!"

Meanwhile the siren whirred and Shy yowled. Jack snapped. "Would someone shut off that damned cherry top?"

Most of the stores in town were closed, but select shopkeepers were hanging "sale" banners in preparation of the festival, and Front Street, one block down and over, had been closed off for carnival rides and food and game booths. Several people started trickling over, curious about the fuss.

"I'll get it," Max grumbled. "It's my truck. Besides, sometimes the door sticks. Gotta know the trick." He jiggled the knob, then tossed Kylie's freed coat. "Hope it got grease on it," he taunted while climbing into the antique red cab to squelch the noise.

Jack caught the coat midair.

Kylie snatched it away. "Are you going to do your job or not?" she snapped at Jack.

He narrowed his eyes. "Mobsters?"

"Yes, darn it! Stop looking at me like I'm nuts! Mobsters. You know. As in wiseguys. Hit men. Gangsters. Didn't you ever see *The Godfather?*"

"Or *Omertà?*" asked Mayor Wilson. "Although not every member of the mob can be classified as a hit man, Kylie. That's generalizing."

"What's the mob got to do with you stealing my truck?" Max railed as he rejoined the show.

"What's with the pansy combat boots?" asked J.J.

"Last time you wore those flowered boots," said Keystone, "you tried to sabotage the historical block. Now you're trying to wreck a historical truck. I'm thinking those crazy boots make you do crazy things."

"Maybe you should return to more sensible footwear," suggested the mayor. "Seems like you gave up your good sense on your birthday when you gave over your practical shoes to Wanda."

"Would you forget about my shoes?" Kyle shrieked. "There's been a murder and the wiseguys are getting away!"

"Lower your voice," Jack said, worried that she'd alarm the growing audience. Instead, the onlookers snickered.

Kylie flushed a deeper shade of red. "You don't believe me," she said in a choked voice.

"Mobsters?" Deputy Ziffel stepped into the fray, brow creased. "In Eden, Indiana?"

Max snorted. "And she accuses us of being obsessed with *Omertà.*"

"Are you making fun of us now?" J.J. asked, looking hurt.

"Enough with shaking up Eden," Mayor Wilson said. "Shaken, stirred and over it, Kylie."

"Don't you lecture me, you…you tattletale!"

The mayor puffed out his chest. "So, Spenser called you, did he? Gave you an earful, huh?"

"Told you that would backfire," Max said to his friend. "Just made her act out more."

"Hey! Check out the old fire engine," a kid called.

"Cool," another added.

"Look, don't touch!" Max yelled.

Wanting to break up the scene, Jack looked to Ziffel.

Shooing the onlookers away, Deputy Ziffel worked his magic. "Move along, people. Nothing to see. Get back to what you were doing. Move along. Move along."

Being law-abiding citizens, everyone cooperated. Except Max and his cronies.

Mayor Wilson focused on Jack. "The Apple Festival opens tomorrow, Chief Reynolds." He angled his head toward Kylie. "Can we or can we not depend on law and order?"

Kylie blew out a frustrated breath. "What do you think I want?" She tugged at Jack's lapels. "While we're standing here arguing, the trail's going cold."

He felt the same way about the B and E case. Jack traced a thumb over the welt on Kylie's cheek. Her claim was preposterous, but her anxiety seemed genuine and she looked like she'd taken a spill in the woods. Had she wiped out on her bike again? Wrecked it? Why else would she *borrow* Max's fire truck? "Give me the key, Kylie."

She stiffened her spine. "You have to believe me. They were shoving a dead guy in the trunk and—"

"Clichéd," said the mayor.

"Pitiful," said Keystone.

"Now," said Jack.

Jaw clenched, she passed him the key to Red Rover.

Jack passed it to the fuming owner. "Sorry about the inconvenience, Max."

"Want to press charges?" Ziffel asked.

Max considered. "No." He glanced at her flowered combat boots. "Clearly, she's going through a crisis."

Kylie whirled. "I'm not—"

"Cheese and crackers!" Keystone exclaimed. "I get it now. She feels inadequate. Her brother's got a hit television show—fame and fortune, a woman in every port. And what does she have?"

"The responsibility of running a store she doesn't even own," said J.J. "And have you noticed how she's always pinching pennies? Plus, she's thirty-two and single."

"With no prospects," said the mayor. "Unless Jack's stepping up to the plate."

"Maybe her baby clock's ticking."

"You mean biological clock."

"Same difference. Maybe she's hormonal."

"Ease up, gentlemen," Jack warned. Holy shit.

Kylie had frozen with embarrassment.

"Looks like she took our advice," said Max. "She let her hair down."

"Except she forgot to comb it."

"Maybe she's going for tousled," Ziffel said in her defense.

"Is that some sort of newfangled hair accessory," Keystone asked, plucking the twig from her hair.

Kylie snatched it back and flung it to the ground. "Without my helmet, you...you busybodies," she sputtered, "my hair got a little windblown. Now, could we please—"

"A little?" J.J. noted with a snort.

"You rode your bike without your helmet?" Jack asked. Part of him wanted to rescue her from Max and gang. The other half wanted to shake her for being so damned reckless. Riding without a helmet? And where the hell were her glasses?

"Did you wreck your wheels," Max asked. "Is that why you stole my truck?"

"She stole your truck to shake up her boring life," said J.J. "Get with the program, Max."

"I feel for you, Kylie. I do," said Mayor Wilson. "We're always talking about your brother and his adventures. Must get tiresome for the sibling who's stuck in low-key Eden peddling humdrum shoes. Still—"

"That's it," Kylie snapped, nabbing Jack's cell phone from his inner jacket pocket. "I'm calling the county police. Those goons whacked the guy out of your jurisdiction, anyway."

Shy whimpered, sensitive to the woman's anxiety.

Jack pried his phone from Kylie's clammy hand. "Let's take a ride, Tiger." Holding her elbow, he guided her away and toward his Aspen, motioning Ziffel to follow.

Unfortunately Max and gang continued to gossip.

"Maybe she thought she'd make the *Eden Tribune* by stealing Red Rover."

"Or the six o'clock news by reporting a murder."

"Mobsters. Wouldn't that be a hoot?"

"If it were real."

"Which it ain't."

"Speaking of bull-hooey claims, what did you think of that legend Spenser debunked last night?"

Kylie sighed as Jack handed her into the front seat. He opened the back door for Shy, who also sighed. Seems his dog had bonded with yet another female in distress. The doe-eyed mutt had already glommed on to Jessie and Maddie. For a man who'd sworn off drama, Jack's life suddenly resembled a damned soap opera.

Deep in thought, he circled to the tailgate to confer with his second-in-command. "You understand I'm obligated to investigate a reported crime."

"Except she's right. The lake is county turf."

"Yeah, but Kylie's my turf."

"Really." Ziffel scratched his head. "After one date?"

Jack had no intention of sharing details of their evening. Nor would he expand on his feelings for Kylie. Feelings he'd just fully realized when he blurted in essence, *she's mine.* For Christ's sake, he *was* in love. The epiphany packed a lethal punch. In one night, he'd fallen hard for a woman who'd been infatuated with him for years.

Well, hell.

Unbalanced, Jack redirected Ziffel's focus. "I need you to run the prints I told you about with IAFIS. Also, those secrets you mentioned? Make a list. I want to know every thing you've heard about Frank Cortez, whether you think it's true or not."

Ziffel grimaced. "I've heard some doozies."

"Like I said, I'm not easily shocked." He rapped the man on his bony shoulder. "Call me if you need me."

"Ditto." Ziffel gave a mock salute, then trotted toward the station house.

Max peeled Red Rover toward the fire station.

Jack climbed into the Aspen, marveling at the difference a day made. Laid-back Eden was hopping with activity. Not all of it good. He frowned at Kylie's disheveled appearance. "I'm torn between kissing and shaking you."

She crossed her arms over her chest and stared straight ahead. "I'm not partial to either if that helps you out."

He bit back a smile and keyed the ignition. "Relax, Kylie. I'm on your side."

"Could've fooled me."

"You have to admit your story's far-fetched."

She turned and glared. "You think I *want* this to be true?"

Something in her eyes and tone grabbed his gut.

Damn.

He couldn't buy the mobster angle, but something was sure as hell rotten in Paradise. Even Shy sensed trouble. As Jack headed for Route 50, the dog hopped into the front seat with a whimper and laid her head on Kylie's grass-and-dirt-stained lap.

Some women would have shooed the dog away. His ex, for instance. Amanda had never wanted pets. *"They're hairy and smelly, and who has the time to feed or walk them?"* she'd complained when he'd mentioned a fellow detective had found a stray hound in need of a home. Amanda used to cringe when she had to clean out the fridge. Forget scooping poop.

Kylie didn't seem to mind that Shy was shedding all over her clothes. She smoothed a kind hand over the mutt's head and body and Jack's heart did another funny hitch.

Although he didn't think Kylie had had a run-in with mobsters, he did believe she'd witnessed something out of the ordinary. Life crisis aside, deep down, Kylie Ann McGraw was a sensible, grounded soul. He reached over and smoothed her tangled hair from her face. "Okay, Tiger. Tell me about those wiseguys. And don't leave anything out."

CHAPTER THIRTY-FOUR

MOLLIFYING. THAT'S WHAT HE was doing. Grandma McGraw used to accuse Grandpa of trying to mollify her. Kylie had asked once what it meant. *"Means he's trying to calm me down by playing nice,"* Grandma had said. *"Gripes my cookies because it's insincere."* After looking up *insincere* in the dictionary (she'd only been eight at the time), Kylie decided if someone ever mollified her, she'd be just as miffed as Grandma. Just now, Jack was really griping Kylie's cookies.

To think fifteen minutes ago she'd been thrilled to see him. Jack Reynolds. The man of her dreams. *The chief of police.* She'd sprinted toward him thinking, *salvation!* He'd protect her from those wiseguys! He'd track and arrest the goon who'd whacked a man just for spitting on his shoe! What kind of a person did something like that?

But the moment she'd mentioned the mobsters, Jack's expression had morphed from concerned to annoyed. He thought she was *lying*. She'd been shocked and more than a little annoyed herself. Was this the same man who'd shared her bed last night? The man who'd transported her to another universe via multiple orgasms and bone-melting affection? The man who'd said they *clicked?* How could he have so little faith in her word? Granted, her story was wild, but she knew what she saw. And heard.

"This isn't some pathetic cry for attention," she said, still smarting from the Busybody Squad's assumptions. "And I'm *not* jealous of Spenser. Envious, maybe. A little.

Okay, sometimes a lot. But it has nothing to do with fame and fortune. I mean that would be really shallow."

"There isn't a shallow bone in your body, Kylie. I know that and so do Max and the boys. They're just pumped." He reached over and squeezed her fisted hand. "Where am I going, hon?"

She ignored the knee-melting warmth of his touch and shot him a perturbed glare. "Stop patronizing me."

"Do you want me to investigate this alleged murder or not?" he asked calmly while slipping on his sunglasses.

She bristled at the term *alleged,* but bit back a snarky retort. "Frances Slocum State Forest. The birdwatcher's lookout."

"Where's your bike," he asked out of the blue.

"In Max's barn. I ditched it because those goons were chasing me. I think it was them, anyway. It could have been a random black car, but I wasn't about to take chances. I lost them, or whoever, when I jumped the road and cut through the field, but they know my bike. At least, I think they do. I winged my helmet at one of them and…" She trailed off. God, this sounded ridiculous.

"Where are your glasses?"

"I lost them when I tripped and fell. I didn't bother looking for them since I was running for my flipping life."

"Can you *see?*"

It was sort of like looking at the world through a fogged-over windshield. She fidgeted in her seat, shrugged. "Well enough."

"Well enough to risk driving?"

"Did you miss the part where I said I was running for my flipping life?"

He slid her a look over the rims of his Oakleys. "So you got that welt on your cheek when you fell?"

She touched her fingertips to the wound and frowned. "No. I got lashed by a tree branch when I was—"

"Running for your flipping life."

Blowing her top wouldn't be productive, so she focused

on stroking Shy's sleek body. She'd read somewhere that petting animals promotes calm. She'd probably pet the poor dog bald before reaching Zen.

"Listen, Jack. I know I had that big meltdown at Boone's. I swore I was going to shake things up in Eden and I've been trying ever since. But I swear to you, I'd never pretend I witnessed a mob hit just to create a sensation. Although...I didn't witness the actual murder. And, I guess, technically it wasn't a hit. They were after the finook's money."

"The what?"

"Or maybe it was finock. No. Fenick." She rubbed her temples. "Some Italian word."

"You know Italian?"

"Obviously not." She resumed petting the dog and leashed her runaway emotions. Those goons had scared the crap out of her. She'd been high on adrenaline for almost an hour. While racing Red Rover into town, her imagination had spun a dozen awful scenarios, but she hadn't imagined those legs sticking out of a trunk or the ski-masked thugs giving chase. She'd prove it, too. There'd be evidence to back her story. Tire tracks. Signs of a scuffle. Maybe even blood. Soon enough, Jack would be scrambling to apologize.

"I'm sorry for doubting you, Kylie."

"You should be."

"Finook *is slang for gay.*"

Of course, Jack would know Italian. Or at least mob-speak. He'd worked Homicide. He'd worked Little Italy. Kylie glanced sideways. "Gay as in happy-go-lucky?"

"As in homosexual."

"Huh." She mulled over the possible clue. "So that means the stiff wasn't from around here."

"You can't know every citizen's sexual inclinations, Kylie. Some people keep those things private."

"Eden's a straitlaced town filled with straight people who lead Adam and Eve sex lives, Jack. Unless someone was in the closet big-time. Given Eden's gossip mill, I can't imagine how anyone could keep something that juicy a secret."

"Then you're naive."

"Maybe you're just cynical."

"Tell me what you saw," he said, not debating the issue. She collected her thoughts, then spewed the story. To Jack's credit he didn't roll his eyes or interrupt. When she finished, her blood was pumping as though she'd tangled with the goons two minutes earlier instead of two hours.

Jack flexed his hands on the steering wheel. "Just want to make sure I heard right."

Here it comes. "Go on."

"They killed a guy, a guy who owed them money, because he spit on the first goon's shoes?"

"I know it sounds crazy, but Bruiser number one sounded like he had an obsession with expensive shoes. Or at least he paid a fortune for those particular shoes. The dead guy, too. He was wearing Salvatore Ferragamo's. I've only ever seen them in a catalog, but they're distinctive. Anyway, unless he scored them at an outlet, they probably set him back five hundred bucks. I'm all for superior quality, but a shoe like that? It's more of a status thing."

"You couldn't make out the license plate number," Jack said, "yet you noticed the make of a pair of shoes?"

"I always notice shoes. Plus, they were hard to miss, sticking up in the air like that. As for the plate number, I told you, the goons were standing in front of it."

"But they moved when they heard your voice."

"They did. But I was already backing away and my view was obstructed by foliage. Then I lost my glasses and everything got blurry."

"Ski masks, huh?"

"They had accents, if that helps."

"What kind of accents?"

"Kind of like the guys on *Omertà.*"

Jack raised a brow.

She cringed. "Okay. So, I've seen the show. I was

curious. It's the talk of the town—aside from Spenser's show. Although I have to say I don't get the appeal. I couldn't even make it through one episode. It's too violent. Too...disturbing. I don't want to think that people are capable of that kind of barbaric behavior. I don't..."

Kylie trailed off when she caught Jack clenching his jaw. She thought back on something he'd said last night. He wouldn't talk about his work in New York as a homicide detective because he didn't want to put *that stuff* in her head. Well, crap. She'd just confirmed his assumption that she couldn't stomach whatever had contributed to his burnout.

A switch in her brain flipped and suddenly her thoughts centered on helping Jack conquer his demons. Maybe not this minute, but she at least needed him to know she was able.

"Not that I'm a wimp," she said, scrambling to do damage control. "In fact, ask anyone. In a crisis situation, I'm a rock." When Jack didn't comment, she rolled on. "I'm not sure where I get it from, but when I need to be strong for a loved one, I'm flipping Hercules."

Still no response.

"I'm just saying I could be there for you. I mean, if you ever needed me. Needed to talk. About...anything."

Jack focused on the road as they neared the state forest. "Are you saying I'm a loved one?"

A fire ignited in her cheeks and blazed through her body. Why, out of everything she'd said, had he glommed on to that? "Are you making fun of me?"

"Definitely not."

"Teasing me?"

"Trying to understand you. This. Us."

"Oh." She didn't know how to answer. "Why?"

"Because it's complicated and I don't want to fuck it up."

"Oh." Wow. Feeling vulnerable and insecure, Kylie concentrated on the passing scenery instead of the man who made her insides squishy. She'd been *in love* with Jack for what seemed like forever. But did she *love* him? As in reality-based love? As in for-better-for-worse-for-richer-for-poorer-in-sickness-and-health love? Did she even know what that kind of love felt like? Although she'd been ready to marry Bobby, she knew now that she'd fooled herself into thinking they were the real deal. If she couldn't have Jack, Bobby would have to do, because no one else was a contender and she didn't want to be single and child-less forever. Now Bobby was gone and Jack was here. Surely her feelings for Jack weren't motivated by a young girl's fantasy and a grown woman's ticking clock?

Three seconds of intense soul-searching told her, no. *Jack's the one. He's always been the one.*

Even so, she was reluctant to confess undying love. He was right. This was complicated. And she was too prag-matic to throw caution to the wind.

"Here's the thing," she said, growing more uncomfort-able by the moment. "In the light of day, in the frustration of this moment—you doubting me—this thing between us…what happened last night…it's surreal. I crushed on you for so long, Jack…I'm having a hard time reconciling fantasy with reality."

He parked his SUV alongside the bird lookout, took off his sunglasses and tossed them on the dashboard.

Sensing trouble, Shy hopped into the backseat.

Jack released Kylie's seat belt and pulled her into his arms. He kissed her. Sweetly, softly. Then with an intensity that sizzled her brain. His possessive touch burned her skin and branded her heart. When he eased back, she swayed.

Kissed dizzy.

Wow.

Jack quirked a tender smile. "Did that help?"

She had to think about the question, then laughed—an odd combination of nerves and elation. Even though her vision was fuzzy, she could see the caring expression on his gorgeous face. "No, it doesn't *help*. Jeez, Jack. I can't think straight when you kiss me, heck, when you *look* at me like that, like you want me—"

"I do want you." He brushed his thumb over her kiss-swollen lips. "I know this is strange, Kylie. After all these years…" He blew out a breath. "Trust me. This is real."

Her heart danced, but thoughts of a dead man in Italian loafers crashed the party. "If we weren't parked near the spot where some poor man met a hideous end less than a couple of hours ago, I'd jump your bones, Jack Reynolds. Right here, right now. In broad daylight. But…" She glanced nervously about as a new thought occurred. "What if they're still around?"

"Knowing you'd report the crime? Assuming cops would investigate?" Jack told Shy to stay, then nabbed his sunglasses and opened his door.

It occurred to her then. He hadn't broken any speed records getting here. Even now, he was taking his time. "You still don't believe me." She hopped out of the SUV before he could answer. She was a lot hurt and a little mad. She'd show him.

"Skirt your actual path," Jack said as she started down the hill. "If there are footprints—"

"Oh, there'll be footprints," she grumbled, then faltered. "Oh, no." There were footprints, all right. *Dozens* of footprints and…tire tracks. Skinny tires. *Bicycles*. Kylie frowned when she heard delighted shrieks and peels of laughter. *Kids*.

Two boys on mountain bikes whizzed past them, jumping obstacles and weaving through trees. They'd traveled up and down the hill who knows how many times, obliterating any signs of Kylie's flee for her flipping life.

"Okay," she said, swiping her newly cut bangs from her forehead. "Never mind the running-for-my-life part. There'll be plenty of proof of foul play at the actual—"

More laughter. Voices.

Oh, no.

Kylie rushed toward the noise. When she arrived at the actual scene of the crime, her heart officially sank. A pickup truck with a camper was parked almost exactly where the black sedan had been. A van and a car were parked nearby.

Two or three families swarmed the area setting up mobile grills and tables. A picnic? A family reunion?

Just. My. Luck.

She looked at Jack. "This isn't good is it?"

"Nope."

"Contamination of a crime scene?"

"Yup."

"Maybe we'll still be able to find something. Like blood or…a shell casing or…" She grappled for a term Jack could relate to.

He smoothed her hair from her face. "I'll take a look."

He was mollifying her. Again. But instead of getting miffed, she felt unsettled. He had no reason to believe her wild claim, but he was still willing to investigate. She swallowed a sentimental lump and gestured back up the hill. "I'm going to see if I can find my glasses." Given her crummy luck of late, Jack's search would be a bust. No blood. No bullets. If she could just locate some piece of evidence. Anything to support her story.

Just then Shy trotted around the trunk of a tree with something dangling out of her mouth. Had she jumped out of the open window to catch a rodent? *Eww.*

Kylie approached and squinted closer. "My glasses!" Giddy, she stooped and retrieved her black frames. They were bent and dirty but not broken. "Good girl!" she said, ruffling Shy's head. "Not for disobeying Jack," she clarified, "but for being an awesome search dog."

Shy barked, announcing someone's approach.

Kylie turned, relaxing when she saw Jack. "Look!" she said, springing to her feet. "Shy found my glasses. It proves I was here."

"Never doubted you on that score, hon."

She frowned. "You didn't find any evidence of foul play."

He shook his head.

"I knew it. Just my luck those families—"

He cut her off with a raised hand. "I want you to consider something."

She folded her arms. "What?"

"This town is obsessed with *Omertà*. Folks have memorized dialogue, scenes. They spout the slang, read related books. Maybe you walked in on an over-the-top role-playing game."

"Are you *kidding?*"

"Just consider the possibility. Remember the stink over those kids who went overboard with Dungeons & Dragons?"

Who could forget? Five boys from Jack and Spenser's sophomore class. Fantasy role-playing gone amok. A boy had died. One of Eden's biggest scandals. Kylie massaged her temples. "But they threatened to kill me. They chased me. At least one did."

"Maybe they just wanted to scare you. An innocent bystander sucked into their game."

She hated that Jack's scenario sounded more plausible than hers. And in truth, a similar thought had crossed her mind, as well—two obsessed locals *pretending* to be wiseguys. Dang.

"What would two East Coast mobsters be doing in a provincial Midwestern town?" Jack asked reasonably.

Looking to shake down a finook was the obvious answer. It was also far-fetched. The stuff movies and TV shows are made of. She must've looked as miserable as she felt because Jack pulled her into his arms and held her tight. He kissed the top of her head. He stroked her hair. It was an intimate, protective embrace. He didn't believe her, but he was giving her the benefit of the doubt. Genuine kindness, not mollifying.

"Here's something else to consider," he said, still holding her close. "If a wiseguy wanted you dead, you'd be dead. Trust me on this, Kylie."

His somber tone sent a chill down her spine. Clearly his observation was linked to experience. Logic told her he was right. *But it had seemed so real.*

"Come on." He guided her up the hill, whistled for Shy to follow.

Kylie shoved on her bent frames. Even though the world cleared, her brain felt fuzzy. Had she mistaken fantasy for reality? "Where are we going?"

"To buy you a cell phone."

CHAPTER THIRTY-FIVE

Philadelphia, Pennsylvania

"WHAT DO YOU MEAN you can't find him?"

"He wasn't at the hardware store. The shoe store's locked tight and we searched his house. He's not here, Chickie."

Carmine resisted the urge to hurl the phone against the putrid green wall. Seeking calm, he looked past Dixie, who was sitting in a nearby chair tapping away at her laptop, and focused on the white clouds floating outside his private room's window. Aversi had promised to release him from the hospital by day's end given there were no complications. Carmine had things to do, mistakes to rectify. He couldn't afford any cardio flare-ups. "Maybe he's food shopping. Maybe he's visiting his wife's grave. It *is* Sunday."

"Thought about the cemetery," said Mario. "We found the headstone for Mona Martin, but no sign of Uncle Tommy."

"You mean Travis," said Carmine. "You're looking for Travis Martin, you *jamook*. And he doesn't look *exactly* as we remember him." Carmine had never seen the end result of the plastic surgery. None of boys had. But surely family would recognize family. As for Buddah, he'd never met Tommy in person, but he'd seen pictures. "I heard they couldn't fix his nose. You're looking for an olive-skinned man with a crooked nose."

"Yeah. I know."

Carmine heard the heat in his nephew's voice. That kid

had the most unpredictable temper in the family. Carmine was in no mood. "Put Buddah on the horn."

A second later, his even-keeled consigliere spoke. "Yeah, boss."

"Between the e-mail Tommy sent to the Vespas about Olivia's death and the info we got from the e-mails that McGraw broad sent to Dixie, we know my brother has been living in Eden as Travis Martin for the last fucking seven years."

"Rest easy, Chickie. If he's here, we'll find him."

"He's there."

"I don't know how he stood it."

"Stood what?"

"Living in this hayseed town. I tried to buy a cup of espresso. *Forgettaboutit*."

Carmine couldn't imagine being cut off from the food and people he loved. Paradise in the Heartland must have been Hell on Earth for his brother. It was beyond time to end his misery. "Find him. But don't make fuckin' spectacles of yourself while you look. Be discreet. Blend."

"Consider us smoke."

Carmine hung up and glanced over at Dixie. Worried sick, she'd refused to leave him last night, so he'd had one of the boys bring over the computer to keep her occupied. Instead of yapping his ear off, she'd focused on her Web site and played games. Mostly she'd been content. Just now she looked white as a sheet. His heart tha-dumped. "What?"

She licked her glossed lips, looked at the screen, at him. "You ain't gonna believe the e-mail I just got from that shoe store owner in Eden."

KYLIE REGRETTED TYPING the e-mail as soon as she hit Send. Pushing away from her great-grandfather's desk, she stood and paced circles around the tiny office in McGraw's Shoe Shoppe. She had to let this morning's saga go. Jack had her mostly talked into the possibility of the role-playing scenario. She had to admit, it made more

sense than mobsters in Eden. Relatively calm, she'd asked
him to drop her at McGraw's after their shopping excursion. In addition to a cell phone, she'd purchased a new pair
of glasses—trendy black rectangular frames accented with
bright flowers. Jack had called them cute. Kylie thought
them daring. They also cleared up her blurry vision, important when attending to details. She had a lot to accom-
plish before the grand opening. Jack had needed to return
to the station house to follow up on his sister's case.

Their goodbye kiss still sizzled through her body. *"Call
me if you need me,"* he'd said. She'd dialed him on the spot,
only her need was rooted in desire, not an emergency.
After another heated kiss, he'd left, and after locking the
front door, she'd beelined for her office. If she didn't
occupy her mind, she'd obsess on her future with Jack or
her wacky, scary morning.

After firing up her computer, she'd scanned orders. Her
gaze fixed on *Bada-Bling!* and…*bada boom,* all she could
think about was her maybe, crazy run-in with mobsters.

Needing to vent, she'd called Faye on her new cell,
only her friend was in the midst of a personal crisis. Her
dad, a widower who'd relocated to Florida, had been in a
car wreck and was going to be laid up for weeks.

"I'm abandoning Stan at our busiest time," she'd said,
"but he'll survive. Not so sure about Dad. What if it's more
serious than he's letting on? You know him—an independent bastard. I have to fly down to Orlando. I'm making it
as easy as I can on Stan, pulling the kids out of school and
taking them with me—"

"I'm sure Stan understands," Kylie had interrupted,
hoping to calm her frantic friend.

"Actually, it's for the best. I think some time apart might
help. I'm sorry I'm going to miss your grand opening,
Kylie," she said, skating over her husband woes, "but—"

"I love you, Faye. Go. Be safe. Give your dad a hug for
me and call with an update when you can."

"Okay. Thanks. Love you back. Have fun with Jack."

Things were wonky with Stan and Faye, and now Faye's dad was in trouble. Kylie was glad the news of her goon sighting hadn't yet reached her friend. Like Faye needed another worry. Although maybe she'd assume, like everyone else, that it was just another ploy by Kylie to shake things up.

Feeling absurdly isolated, she'd clicked on a new e-mail from Dixie, who mentioned she was making a special pair of shoes just for Kylie as a thank-you for being her first and best customer. Kylie hit Reply, expressing her appreciation, then found herself typing: *You'll never guess what happened to me this morning!*

Now Dixie, along with everyone in Eden, was going to think she was one shoe short of a pair. They were business associates who'd traded a couple of chatty e-mails, not friends. Yet Kylie had relayed her tale as though she'd been talking to Faye. Jeesh. It seemed she really needed someone to believe her. If only Travis had been around.

Instead, she was alone. No one to talk to. No one to rely on if she ran into trouble. Like facing down hooligans intent on robbing the store or fitting her with cement shoes.

Yikes.

Suffering an attack of the heebie-jeebies, Kylie zipped out of the office, checking the locks of the back and front door. No matter who those guys were, they'd still chased her and she was currently vulnerable. It was the first time in her life that she didn't feel safe in Eden. Surely the feeling would pass, but until then she was on pins and needles. *Not* the kind of excitement she'd been looking for. She imagined Jack in New York City, where things like this happened all the time and young women didn't stay alone anywhere without a lock on the door.

She thought about her cozy trailer in the woods, beyond screaming distance from any of her neighbors. No wonder Jack had been so intent on security lighting and double locks. Even if he didn't believe Eden had been invaded by true gangsters, he worried about those prowling the world with bad intent in their hearts.

He didn't want her hurt.

For a moment, Kylie wished back her boring, secure existence, where she'd laughed off such concerns.

Then she circled back to the cluttered, blah-boring office and realized there were some changes she didn't wish back, like Jack in her bed, the renovations to the store and knowing Travis Martin. She should've asked Travis to renovate this part of the store, as well. It would have meant him sticking around a little longer. She'd been disappointed not to find him painting or fiddling with a fixture when she'd entered McGraw's. Except he'd accomplished everything she'd asked for and more. His work was done. As for the grand reopening, all she had to do was haul out her merchandise and arrange new displays. For the first time ever, she wished she had help. It had been more interesting to share the workday with someone else.

She remembered then that Travis still needed to come by to pick up his check. When he did, she could always approach him about additional work. Feeling a little better, Kylie returned to the desk in search of her spare personal checkbook. When she opened the top drawer she spied a bulky envelope marked *Kylie.*

She didn't recognize the writing. Curious, she pulled out the contents and gaped. A bundle of one hundred dollar bills, a handwritten letter and a computer printout for a flight reservation. "What the hey?"

She ruffled through the bills, guesstimating four or five thousand dollars. She glanced at the flight confirmation. A round-trip ticket to Hong Kong! Heart pounding, she read the letter.

Dear Kylie,
By the time you read this, I'll be on a plane, flying toward my own dream destination. You inspired me. I've decided to shake things up by living the life I

was born to lead. It's possible you may hear some ugly truths in the future about my past. Please know, I am a good person at heart, though not nearly as pure as you. I worry that you will never experience your dream trip for varied reasons, always putting business or other people's needs ahead of your own. For that reason I am gifting you with a nonrefundable round-trip ticket to Hong Kong and some spending money to use at will. Trust me, I can afford it.

I know the new and imaginative McGraw's Shoe Shoppe will be a hit, and I suspect you'll find much love and joy with Jack. Embrace your passion, Kylie, your dreams. Life's too short.

Your friend, Travis

Kylie read the letter twice. She stared at the money, at the flight confirmation. Conflicting emotions stormed her heart and mind. Confusion. Curiosity. Elation. Sadness. "Who are you, Travis Martin?"

The phone rang. The landline. Jack would've called her new cell. Switching into business mode, she snatched up the receiver, answering automatically. "McGraw's Shoe Shoppe."

"You mean McGraw's Shoe *Store*. And why are you there on a Sunday? Your grandma and I have been trying to reach you for the past two hours. We told you we'd call you today. Did you forget?"

Kylie cringed at the sound of her mom's hurt tone. "I'm sorry. It's been a crazy day. I lost track of the time. So you're in Anchorage now, right? Is it beautiful? What's the temperature? Are you and Grandma taking any excursions?"

"We missed our excursion. I didn't want to go anywhere until I heard your voice. Your grandma said you hired Travis Martin to do some renovations and now it sounds like you changed the name of the store. You blew off work to get your hair done and now you're working on your day off. What's going on with you, Kylie?"

She wanted to tell her mom about what she'd witnessed this morning, but then the woman would worry.

She wanted to gush that she'd had her first orgasm with a man, but that was too intimate. Sex wasn't something she ever talked about with her mom. Plus, she wasn't ready for Spenser to know about Jack, and surely her mom or grandma would find a way to let him know.

If she went into detail about the extensive renovations, they might freak and return home early, thinking she'd flipped her lid. Besides, maybe they'd love the new look at first sight.

She glanced at the ticket to Hong Kong and the stack of money, and imagined her mom stressing over her only daughter, Kylie, wandering around Asia without a chaperone. Not that Kylie was definitely going. She still couldn't believe Travis's generosity.

"I confess I made a few changes, Mom. Chalk it up to a birthday crisis. But mostly everything's status quo," she lied. "Same ol', same ol'."

JACK WAITED ON THE SIDE of the station house while Shy trotted in circles looking for a prime spot to whiz. "Hurry up, girl." Even though work waited, he refused to go in without her. The way his day was going, someone would steal her away or, worse, she'd run into the street and get hit by a car.

Still dressed in yesterday's clothes, Jack surveyed Main Street and the moderate traffic. Even though the Apple Festival got busier as the week went on, a few early birds were flocking in. By this time Wednesday, he wouldn't recognize half of the people in town. He wouldn't know their backgrounds or personalities or what crimes they were capable of. An ordinary day in NYC on a much smaller scale. In one day, he'd gone from relaxed to alert. He hadn't anticipated reconnecting with his old self this swiftly—a blessing and a curse.

Shy squatted and Jack looked in the direction of

McGraw's Shoe Shoppe. He wasn't crazy about leaving Kylie alone. He wasn't thrilled that his sister and niece were out of his sight. Today all of the women in his life had been threatened in some way. Looking at both incidents logically, through the eyes of a cop, he'd been able to put things in perspective.

The physical evidence combined with his brother-in-law's shady behavior suggested the vandalism at Jessie's house had been directed at Frank.

The lack of evidence and the improbability of a mob hit in Eden, suggested Kylie had been the victim of a prank. She'd been rattling a lot of chains lately. Maybe someone had rattled back.

Regardless, even if neither woman was at honest risk, both had been traumatized. Jack had spent the morning vacillating between pissed and concerned. So much for numb. This is how he should have felt—times ten—when they'd found Connie Valachi with a bullet in the back of her head and her tongue cut out. Instead of taking that mob hit in stride, he should have been furious. When they'd broken the news to her family, he should have empathized. But he'd shut down. His partner had called it a coping mechanism.

Jack didn't want to cope. He wanted to serve and protect. He wanted to feel.

This moment he felt like an exposed wire. Alive and volatile.

He refused to shut down, but he did need to get a handle on his emotions. There was a fine line between worrying and obsessing. If he constantly feared his loved ones were in danger, he'd drive them ape-shit by being overprotective.

Step one: uncover the identity of the person who'd broken into Jessie's home.

Jack whistled for Shy to follow. He sensed tension the moment they entered the station house.

Deputy Ziffel sat at his desk, phone in hand. "I was just about to call you, Chief. Did some investigating on my own. Put two and two together." Looking like the cat that ate the canary, he gestured to a man sitting in the adjacent chair. "This is Pete Unger. He's here to make amends."

AFTER A BLOWOUT WITH Dr. Aversi, Carmine had checked himself out of the hospital. The only way to stave off another attack, he'd told the man, was to take action. Exerting control helped him to keep control.

Wanting this business with his brother under wraps, he'd refrained from calling one of the boys for a ride. Instead, he'd relied on a cab to shuttle him and Dixie to the brownstone where Turk had delivered their previously packed suitcases.

For the sixth time in less than forty minutes, he tried calling his nephew, then Buddah. Again, no answer. *"Fuck!"*

"It's a small town surrounded by cornfields and pig farms," Dixie ventured softly as the cab navigated the traffic on Chestnut Street. "Maybe they ain't getting any cell reception."

Or maybe they were ignoring him. Carmine had read the McGraw broad's e-mail twice. Either Turk and Buddah had taken control of the situation and whacked Tommy for breaking *omertà* or two other wiseguys had beaten them to it. Was it possible that computer geek who'd pinpointed Tommy's location had leaked information to the Gambelli family?"

Tommy.

Carmine hadn't said his brother's name out loud in seven years. Now he'd never say it, because, if Kylie McGraw saw what she said she saw, his brother was dead.

He blew out a breath and massaged his chest.

Dixie reached over and squeezed his thigh. She didn't speak. Sometimes she was smarter than he gave her credit for.

His cell phone chirped. "Where the fuck have you been?"

"Sorry, Chickie," said Buddah. "We ducked into a bar and grill to grab a bite, thinking maybe we'd spy, uh, Travis, or maybe overhear something that would give us a clue. We heard something, all right. People think it's a prank. They even laughed. But Turk and I…" He cleared his throat. "I'm leery to report this given your condition."

"Give me the nut." Carmine wanted to hear it from Buddah. His version.

It was almost identical to Kylie's.

When the man finished, Carmine blew out a breath he didn't know he was holding. "So you didn't do it."

"What?"

Carmine told Buddah about the e-mail to Dixie from Kylie. "I thought maybe you and Turk disagreed with my order to bring my brother home—*alive*. Maybe you thought my judgment wasn't so good given my bad heart and decided to make it easy on me by doing what I couldn't do—for the good of the family."

"You thought we betrayed you." Buddah sounded insulted and hurt at the same time.

"Let's just say I can see Turk losing his temper if someone spit on his shoe," Carmine said. "Where is he now?"

"On his phone, digging. He thinks someone leaked information. Thinks the Gambellis might have sent someone to finish what they started seven years ago."

"I had that thought, too." Carmine passed a fifty to the driver after he pulled up to the curb. "Listen to me, Buddah. I want you to keep an eye on this Kylie McGraw. If they think she can identify them, they might be brazen enough to stick around and silence her. I want her safe. She befriended my brother. I owe her."

"Will do, Chickie. And if we run into the Gambellis?"

"I'll be there tomorrow. If I can't make amends with my brother, I *will* avenge his death. *Capiche?*"

"*Capiche.*"

CHAPTER THIRTY-SIX

"I KNOW IT WAS WRONG to break into your sister's place, Chief Reynolds. But I wasn't thinking straight. You have to understand. Mya's my daughter. My only kid. She's seventeen, for God's sake. Frank's in his thirties. Aside from the fact that he seduced an underage girl, he took pictures." Pete Unger shoved both hands through his hair, then sagged back in the chair. "I didn't know about the…affair. Didn't even suspect. I'm a widower. I do my best, but I guess that's not good enough, otherwise she wouldn't have fallen for that perverted prick, right?"

Jack glanced at his office door, making sure it was closed. He didn't give a flying fuck about Frank's reputation. But he cared how the man's exploits would affect Jessie and Maddie, and Unger's kid, Mya. "Mr. Unger—"

"Mya locked herself in her room for three days. You don't know what I went through to get her to confide in me. She thought he loved her. Thought he'd send for her. But of course he didn't. Then she started fretting about the…" Pete turned away, worked his jaw. "About the compromising photos. She said Frank belonged to a racy social network. Worried that he might post those photos on the Internet now that he was through with her. I was in a red haze when I broke into your sister's house. I wanted those pictures. I wanted to destroy Frank. Since he wasn't there, I destroyed his office."

"Did you find the photos?" Jack asked.

He nodded. "On his hard drive. Along with some other

disgusting shit. I worried that maybe he'd seduced and photographed other teens in town. I extracted all the files."

"You know how to do that?"

"I'm a trouble-shooter for a computer company. Allows me to work at home. After I got what I wanted, I smashed the hard drive and monitor and kept going. Couldn't stop myself."

Jack understood and said so.

Just then his office door swung open and Jessie blew in. Well, hell.

"Someone said they saw Deputy Ziffel escorting you into the station house," she said directly to Pete. "I just...something told me...it was you, wasn't it?"

Pete stood and faced her. "I'm sorry, Jessica Lynn, but Frank, he..."

"I know."

Jack stood as well. "You do?"

"I only recently heard and I...I guess I blocked it out. I didn't want to believe..." She blushed head to toe. "I'm so sorry, Pete."

"Not your fault," he said.

"I'm not pressing charges," she said to Jack.

"Okay." Given the circumstances, he was glad about that. He also didn't feel the need to lecture Pete on right and wrong. "You're free to go, Mr. Unger."

"I appreciate that, Chief Reynolds. About the damages, Jessica Lynn, I'll make good."

"I'd rather you didn't," she said. "I'm glad you destroyed Frank's things. And if you see him, feel free to—"

"Jessie," Jack warned.

Pete turned to shake Jack's hand, pressing a flash drive into his palm. "You need to see this," he said softly, then turned to leave.

Jessie didn't follow him out. She stood rigid.

Jack ached to hug her, but sensed it wasn't the time. Discreetly, he slid the flash drive beneath a magazine on his desk. She knew about Frank's affair with their babysitter, but she didn't know about the salacious photos. From what

Pete had said, Jack assumed he'd found incriminating evidence featuring other Eden teens. He wasn't looking forward to reviewing those files.

"You okay?" Jack asked his sister.

"I will be when this is over. When I'm divorced."

"Tomorrow."

She nodded.

"Still think he'll show?"

"He hasn't called to say otherwise. So, yes. I'm glad, actually. I want a chance to give him hell."

"I'll be there."

"You don't have to."

"I want to."

She licked her lips. "Okay."

"Where's Maddie?" he asked.

"With Mrs. Carmichael. She's going to spend the night."

"Why?"

"Wanda tracked me down and asked if I could work late tonight. I said, yes. I need to keep busy, Jack. And I...I want to shield Madeline from tomorrow. From me. I worry I'll be a basket case tonight."

"I'd be happy to look after Maddie."

"I know, but you should pay attention to your own life, too. Kylie's a nice girl, Jack. Don't blow it."

"Easier said than done."

"Just because your marriage to Amanda failed, that doesn't make you a failure at love, Jack."

"Sounds like something Dad would've said."

Cheeks flushing, she glanced away. "He had such high hopes for me and now look at my life."

This time Jack acted on impulse. He walked over and pulled his sister into his arms. "You've got a sweet, beautiful daughter and you're intent on being financially independent. You're resourceful and strong. He'd be proud, Jessie. I'm proud."

She hugged back. "That means a lot coming from my perfect brother."

Oddly, the lack of sarcasm made him uneasy. "I'm not perfect."

"Yes. You are. I always hated that about you."

"And now?"

She eased out of his arms and quirked a small smile. "I think Dad was right. There's more to you than meets the eye."

Jack laughed, thinking how their dad had used the same observation on each of them. Vic Reynolds had never understood the rivalry between his son and daughter. Jack wished he could see them now.

Jessie tucked her sleek hair behind her ears, then motioned to his snoring dog. "I was wondering if I could borrow Shy. Madeline would feel better if—"

"Sure." He coaxed Shy off her cushion and Jessie coaxed her out the door. He wasn't surprised that the dog so easily abandoned him. She seemed to latch on to those who needed her most.

He started to see Jessie to her car, but midway through the administration area, his administrative assistant blew in.

"I need to talk to you," Dorothy said, hooking his arm.

"Don't wait up for me," Jessie called as she and Shy hurried out.

"I was going through some of the papers I'd boxed up of Chief Burke's," said Dorothy.

"Isn't this your day off?" asked Jack.

"Hope I didn't step on your toes, Chief," interrupted Ziffel. "But I'd heard some rumors and then I read your notes and—"

"You did good, Ed." It was all Jack managed before Dorothy shoved him back in the office and slammed the door shut. "What the hell, Ms. Vine?"

She slapped a manila file folder onto his desk. "It's about Travis Martin."

RATHER THAN OBSESSING ON the characters who'd spooked her this morning or Faye and her injured dad or the where-abouts of Travis and the wonder of his gift, Kylie had plunged into work. No matter what else was going on in her life, she had a family business to run. Tomorrow she'd reopen the store and Eden would get its first peek at the renovations and her new merchandise. She clung to Travis's prediction that McGraw's Shoe Shoppe would be a hit. Increased sales would help to smooth things over with her family for not consulting them about major changes. It would also reinforce her confidence in her professional instincts.

As soon as she started unpacking the best of her previous inventory and the bulk of the new, ideas sparked and burned. Inspired, Kylie arranged cool displays for several different styles. Formal. Casual. Trendy. She was especially pleased that the new McGraw's was so diversified. Practical, comfortable, yet trendy. Trendy, comfortable, but not-so-practical. Designer shoes, quality shoes—at a reasonable price. Shoes for men and women. Young and old. And after her *Bada-Bling!* imports arrived tomorrow—shoes for teens and tourists. Kylie had no idea if her dad would approve. She tried not to care. She focused on the future. On steady sales. Her gut told her quality, versatility and a low price point were key. She considered every factor. At this point, only time would tell. She was arranging a display meant to entice the ladies of the Eden Garden Club when someone banged on her door.

She bit back a yelp and ignored the shivers icing down her spine. Mobsters wouldn't knock.

"We're closed!" she yelled.

"It's Jack. Open up."

She nearly tripped over her feet racing to the door. They'd only been apart a couple of hours. It felt like two days. Plus, no one messed with Jack Reynolds. If those two goons were lurking outside, they'd think twice before trying to shut her up, not that anyone believed her story.

"Hi!" Normally, she wasn't comfortable with public displays of affection. But normal, for Kylie, had flown out the window on her birthday. She launched herself into Jack's arms and kissed him full on the mouth. Since making love, suppressing a lifetime of yearning was more difficult than ever. Fire shot through her system as he suckled her tongue and swept her inside. He kicked the door shut and her stomach fluttered with naughty anticipation. Was he going to ravish her against the wall? On the floor? Crazy thoughts, spurred by her adrenaline-charged day.

She was disappointed and dazed when he eased her away and asked, "Where's Travis?"

"What?"

"You said you expected him later this afternoon. Is he here? Did he show?"

"No, and no." Kylie bristled when Jack moved around the store, looking in the storage room, her office. She followed him, confused and insulted. "You don't believe me?"

"I believe you."

"Then why—"

"Just checking."

"For what?"

Instead of answering directly, he grasped her hand and urged her to sit. Then he pulled up the only extra chair in the room and sat across from her, their knees touching. "I'm going to tell you something," he said, still holding her hand, "and I need you to promise that you'll keep it between us. For now."

The hair on her arms prickled. "Okay. I mean, I promise."

"Travis Martin isn't who you think he is."

"Okay." She'd suspected Travis had led another life before Eden, but Jack, as the chief of police, confirming this didn't bode well. "Who is he?"

"I don't know. Yet. What I know is that he's in the witness protection program. Travis Martin is an assumed identity. WITSEC gave him a new life and planted him in Eden."

Kylie's heart bumped to her throat. This was insane. But even as she questioned Jack's news, she sensed it was true. A new identity would account for Travis's dyed hair and suppressed designer skills. For his and Mona's tendency to keep to themselves. Although Kylie was pleased to

discover the reason for Travis's aloofness, she worried
Jack thought the worst. He'd always had a bug up his butt
about the man.

Kylie scrambled to show her friend in the best light.
"The program is designed to protect people, right? It means
Travis did something good. Testified against bad guys,
right?" She'd watched her share of cop shows and movies.
She had a basic grip on the concept.

"Essentially," Jack said. "Thing is, only forty percent
of those in WITSEC are innocent citizens. The other
sixty percent—"

"Travis is in the lower percentage," Kylie blurted.

"You don't know that."

"Yes, I do."

*You may hear some ugly truths in the future about my
past....*

No, she didn't

"Bottom line," Jack said, "if Travis was in the program,
then he testified against major criminals as in drug traffick-
ers, terrorists or organized crime members."

Kylie noticed the subtle emphasis on the latter. She
flashed back on this morning's scary encounter. *Oh, no.*
Pulse racing, she pulled away from Jack and pushed to her
feet. "It wasn't him. I know what I said I saw, and maybe
you believe me now, which is great, but the stiff in the trunk
was *not* Travis. First, he doesn't wear Italian loafers."
Although, she supposed he could afford them. He'd gifted
her with an expensive plane ticket and oodles of cash, plus
he apparently had reserves.

"What did you used to do?"

"You don't want to know."

She shoved away nefarious thoughts and focused on:
I'm a good man at heart.

"Second?" Jack prodded.

She started to say he's not even here. He's out of the
country. But she didn't know specific regulations pertaining to the witness protection program. Was he allowed to

travel? Had he obtained permission? If not, had he broken a rule that would land him in hot water? If whoever he'd testified against learned he was out and about would his life be at risk? "It wasn't him," she repeated, glad she'd locked away his letter and money in the office safe. She didn't like keeping secrets from Jack, but at the same time she felt compelled to protect a friend. It really bugged her that Jack wasn't willing to give Travis the benefit of the doubt. Did his cynicism extend to believing the worst in anyone he didn't know?

Jack moved in behind her and wrapped her in his arms. "I contacted County. I don't have the resources to adequately investigate a compromised crime scene. Also, as you know, the forest and lake are in their jurisdiction."

"Maybe it isn't a crime scene at all." Suddenly, she didn't want to believe what she thought she'd seen. "Maybe you were right. A role-playing game. Two guys obsessed with *Omertà*." It was possible. Probable, even. Just a bunch of crazy coincidences.

"Maybe," Jack said.

Mollifying, Kylie thought.

"Regardless, I called the U.S. Marshals Service, left a message for the inspector assigned to Martin. Dorothy found a document buried in Chief Burke's possessions. Dates back seven years. Notification alerting the local law of a witness's presence. No mention of a criminal history or specific circumstances. Secrecy as a precautionary measure is common, but given recent developments, I need to know what I'm dealing with."

Recent developments meaning her run in with the goons.

Jack tightened his hold, kissed the top of her head, then nuzzled her ear. "I want you safe, Kylie. I want my sister and niece safe. Along with every other citizen in Eden. It's not just my job, it's personal. It's like breathing, this need to protect. Do or die."

"An admirable quality," Kylie said. Attractive, too. When she was eleven, she'd watched him take on three teens who were shooting BBs at a dog. It had been the first of many times she'd thought, *"My hero."* Yet here she was withholding information that might make his job easier.

"This morning when you mentioned the mob, I wrote off what you thought you saw because I didn't want it to be true. My last case involved a young woman, a victim of a mob hit. If there's any chance…"

He trailed off, causing Kylie to turn in his arms. She looked up and met his intense blue gaze. "Nothing bad is going to happen to me, Jack." She didn't want him to worry, and she didn't want him to think she couldn't handle his past demons or future nemeses. She did what she was best at, shoved down her own needs and worries and focused on someone else's.

Jack's.

"Even if what I saw was the real deal, surely those wiseguys are long gone. They'd dispose of the body and hit the road. Or maybe they took the body with them and disposed of it over state lines. Like you said earlier, why would they stick around, knowing I'd report a crime? Surely not to silence the witness," she noted for herself as much as him. "Especially one who's sleeping with a cop. Why risk getting caught?"

Jack brushed a thumb over her cheek and quirked a tender smile. "Nice try, Tiger. But until this thing shakes out, we'll proceed on the side of caution. Between myself, Deputy Ziffel and Officers Hooper and Anderson, you'll be protected 24/7."

She started to argue, but deep down she felt relieved. Having someone watch her back for a day or two, just until the county police solved or discounted the alleged murder, would ease her worries so that she could concentrate on the store. Then again, she felt bad hogging the attention of the local law. There'd be an influx of people with the opening of the Apple Festival. Not that there was ever any real trouble. But there had been some minor accidents and altercations, instances where the EPD intervened. She also felt bad about wasting Jack's time. He'd no doubt launch an intensive search for Travis, wanting to talk to him about his involvement in WITSEC or, when he didn't find him, concluding he was the stiff in the trunk. By looking out for her friend, she was also obstructing an investigation.

"One thing's for certain," Jack said, "you're not sleeping in the middle of nowhere tonight. You can stay with me, at your mom's or at the Orchard House, but that secluded trailer is out."

Kylie worried her lower lip. If she was in trouble, she didn't want that trouble anywhere near Jessica Lynn or Madeline. As for the Orchard House. "Faye's dad was in an accident. She's on her way to Orlando with the kids for a couple of weeks."

"Sorry to hear that. Is Mr. Collins okay?"

"I think so. I hope so. Anyway, I don't want to impose on Stan. I'll stay at Mom's." The house was currently un-occupied but smack in the middle of a crowded block in town. She kept some clothes and toiletries in her old bedroom. She'd be set.

"Fine," said Jack. "Listen, Jessie's working a night shift, so for dinner, it'll be you and me, Maddie and Mrs. Car-michael. Sound good?"

"Sounds great." Moving along with previous plans, acting normal, helped to temper Kylie's nerves.

"Hooper's sitting in a squad car outside. Don't hesitate to call him or me for any reason. I programmed the numbers in your cell."

"Where are you going?" Kylie asked, cursing the nervous flutter in her voice.

"I need to make a run to Travis's place."

Kylie was torn between doing the right thing—clueing Jack in on Travis's trip overseas—and the right thing—pro-tecting a friend whose life was in danger. She couldn't silence Travis's voice. *"I know about trying to live up to family expectations. I know about not being appreciated for who you are."*

He'd given up his identity. He'd lost his wife. Surely he deserved a slice of happiness. She couldn't betray him. Not yet. Not until he'd safely reached his destination. Once he was out of the country, he'd be out of reach. Distanced from both the bad and good guys, right? The neutral zone? She just needed to buy him some time, a day at most. In the meantime, maybe it wasn't a bad thing if people thought he was dead. Six feet under and forgotten.

Kylie hugged Jack tight. She couldn't look him in the eye and lie, so she looked away. "Be careful."

"Always."

CHAPTER THIRTY-SEVEN

JACK DIDN'T CALL FOR THE REST of the day. No news on Travis. No updates on Jessica. Kylie was dying of curiosity and a little peeved that he'd left her in the dark on both counts. Then again, he'd warned her that he was swamped and that was *before* he'd learned about Travis's involvement with the witness protection program.

Still, she wondered what Jack had discovered while searching Travis's house. Did he glean clues about his real identity? Did he suspect Travis had skipped the country? Had he heard back from the U.S. Marshals Service?

And what about Jessica? Why was Jack being so secretive about whatever happened at her house? Why was he leery of her being alone?

On top of all that, even though she *really* wanted to believe the role-playing scenario, Kylie had to contend with the knowledge that she'd possibly witnessed a real murder. Had the county police turned up any evidence to support what she thought she'd seen? Had they found a body? If so, who was it?

It was enough to drive a girl crazy.

Instead of obsessing on what she had no control over, Kylie concentrated on McGraw's. She worked her tail off preparing for the grand reopening. Luckily, the afternoon passed without drama. No goons. No crisis.

Before she knew it, it was time to leave the store and change for dinner. Officer Hooper gave her a lift to her mom's house.

"I'll wait out here until Chief Reynolds shows," he said after walking Kylie to the front door. "Don't worry. No one will mess with you on my watch."

Kylie was touched by Hooper's diligence, but she felt a little silly. Maybe she was being overly optimistic, but she wasn't anticipating a visit from Bruiser number one and two. Either they were long gone or they weren't the real deal. Still, she could hear Spenser saying, *"Better safe than sorry."*

"Thanks, Hooper. I appreciate it." She jammed the key she'd had since she was a kid into the lock and hurried inside. She smelled Lemon Pledge and green apple carpet deodorizer. The house was clean, as always, but cluttered with framed photos, collectibles, mementos and too much furniture. Her grandma had refused to give up her belongings when she'd moved in, and her mom had refused to scale back. So they ended up with two *homes* jammed into one house. Kylie liked it. Every item reminded her of various moments in her life. Even though her mom and grandma weren't here, she could feel them. She also felt the presence of the male McGraws.

Feeling nostalgic and safe, she raced up the stairs and ransacked her old bedroom closet. She found the red dress she thought she'd remembered stashing there. Not too casual. Not too dressy. A perfect match to the red pumps she'd snagged from the store. The perfect ensemble for dinner at Wong's.

She showered and dressed in thirty minutes, ten minutes before she heard Jack knocking. She opened the door and suddenly all the worries she'd spent so much energy fending off slammed into her with blinding force.

Even though Jack was dressed in civilian clothing, there was nothing casual about his demeanor. Was he in bodyguard mode? The bearer of bad news? Or just in a cranky mood?

"You look beautiful," he said.

He sounded sincere, but she was distracted by his uptight aura. "I'm overdressed."

"Not for Wong's, but—"

"We're not going to Wong's?" Was he blowing her off for work? Had he learned something about Travis? Heard something from County?

"Mrs. Carmichael called me last minute, said her arthritis has flared up. She's not up for a night out so I offered to bring over pizza. And, I promised Maddie we'd watch a movie with them. I should've called you, but—"

"You were swamped and rushed. It's okay." She blew out a relieved breath. Not Wong's, but not work. "Sounds like fun. I'll just change into something more casual."

"I wish you wouldn't." He swept an appreciative gaze over her body, the dress, the shoes. "You're a pleasant distraction from an unpleasant day."

"What a nice thing to say." Blushing, she broached the safest subject regarding his day. "This thing with your sister, do you want to talk about it?"

"I can't."

"Oh." She waited for him to elaborate. He didn't.

He nodded toward his SUV. "Ready?"

Flustered, she abandoned talk of his sister and noted his faded jeans and pullover. She glanced down at her spiky red heels. "All right. But if Shy wants to play fetch, these shoes are coming off."

"Bare feet. Red toenails," he said as she nabbed her purse and locked the door. "Sexy."

Even though he was preoccupied, his attraction to her was fierce. She felt it with every fiber of her being as he wrapped an arm around her waist and escorted her to his Aspen. Her own body tingled in response, but, although she felt connected physically, an emotional chasm stretched between them. He had secrets. *She* had secrets.

Jack dismissed Officer Hooper with a nod. The squad car drove off, and Kylie wrestled with guilt as Jack helped her into the passenger seat of his SUV. He wouldn't be happy when she confessed she'd withheld information. The longer she put off telling him Travis had skipped the country, the angrier he'd be. She thought about the plane ticket and wad of cash locked in the store's safe and the guilt intensified.

Hands trembling, Kylie fumbled with her seat belt as Jack rounded the vehicle.

He slid her a glance as he slid behind the wheel. "Hear from Travis today?"

Was she that transparent? "No." It wasn't a lie, exactly. He hadn't called so she hadn't actually *heard* from him. Her cheeks flushed all the same. She fished in her purse for a mint, lipstick, anything to avoid making eye contact. "Did you hear from County Police?"

"They haven't found any evidence to suggest foul play."

Kylie suppressed a gleeful squeal. "Why don't you sound happy about that? It's good news, right? Means I witnessed a hoax, right?"

"Maybe. They're still investigating."

"Oh." Clearly he wasn't in a talkative mood. Regardless, she needed more clarity. "Did you hear from U.S. Marshal Service?"

"No."

He keyed the ignition and backed out of the drive.

She swished red gloss over her lips. "Would you tell me if you did?"

"Yes."

"Would you tell me what they said?"

After a weighty pause, she looked over and caught his enigmatic gaze. "Depends."

"On?"

"Whether I want that stuff in your head."

She knew his intentions were good, but unlike the last time he'd uttered that phrase, she didn't feel protected as much as manipulated. "Anyone ever told you you're a control freak?"

"Takes one to know one," he said, eyes back on the road.

She grunted. "Sounds like something Spenser would say."

"Speaking of Spense…"

Uh-oh.

"He called me today."

Crap. Kylie clasped her hands in her lap so as not to wring them. She, too, focused on the road. "Did you tell him about the water tower?"

"No."

"My run-in with the goons?"

"Why worry him when it could be nothing? I'll wait till County weighs in."

"Did you tell him about...us?"

"Not the right time."

That was a relief, except she realized suddenly that he'd not only kept her in the dark about certain things, but he'd also danced around the truth with his best friend. "Even though you're an honest man, you're not always honest—in a full disclosure kind of way."

"No, I'm not." He cast her a look. "That a problem?"

She didn't know. Her fantasy man was becoming more real by the day. Her stomach fluttered, and not in a good way. "Maybe."

Jack didn't comment.

Kylie wrestled with the concept of loving a man who kept secrets. "So what *did* you and Spenser talk about?"

"He mentioned his conversation with the mayor. He wanted to know if you were all right. I told him you were a pain in the ass, but nothing I couldn't handle."

Kylie snorted.

Jack cracked his first smile of the evening. "It was that or the truth."

"Which is?"

"You're a pain in the ass and I'm scared to death of you."

Kylie's jaw dropped.

"Scratch that," he said as he pulled into Mrs. Carmichael's driveway. "I'm scared of loving you."

His words slammed into her, seizing her breath, boggling her mind. Was he speaking literally or hypothetically? She couldn't suppress the question. "Do you?" she squeaked as Madeline and Shy came racing across the lawn. "Love me?"

He caught her gaze just as kid and dog bopped in front of the driver's window, demanding his attention. "Maybe."

JACK SPENT THE MAJORITY of the evening questioning his sanity. Knowing how he felt about Kylie and admitting it aloud were two different beasts. Only he hadn't admitted the truth. He'd just blurted *"Maybe."* A dumb-ass thing to say, but he didn't want to lie and he didn't want to commit, so he'd straddled the fence.

Dumb-ass.

Why the hell had he brought up love to begin with? Except, she *was* a pleasant distraction from an unpleasant day. She'd stolen his breath when she'd opened the door. So pretty, so sweet. So damned fascinating.

Even though he suspected she was holding something back about Travis Martin, he was more intrigued than pissed. He liked that she fiercely defended someone she considered a friend, even though he questioned her judgment. He admired her inclination to trust, even though he thought it made her vulnerable. She possessed a curious mix of strength and sensitivity.

Yes, she'd been a pain in the ass the past few days, but she'd also befriended Shy and defended his sister. In the past, she'd forfeited a dream trip to be with her ailing grandpa and she'd depleted her savings to bail her grandma out of debt.

Kylie was kind. Good. And yes, he loved her. Problem was, he didn't trust that love. So he'd held back. He knew she wouldn't leave it at *maybe.* She'd want an explanation. He didn't blame her. That conversation lurked in the background for the next few hours.

Amazing that he was still able to enjoy himself. But he did. They all did.

Even though the mystery of Travis Martin dogged him, even though he worried that an element of the mob had infiltrated Eden, and even though he was worried about Kylie's safety and his sister's emotional well-being...this evening had been an unexpected delight.

Sheer joy had pumped through his blood as he'd watched Kylie and his niece playing a canine version of tag with Shy. Just as promised, Kylie had kicked off her shoes. She'd also kicked up a lot of fun and lively conversation, connecting as keenly with Maddie as Mrs. Carmichael.

Jack had soaked in the sounds of laughter, the feeling of family as they'd gobbled pizza and watched a flick featuring a superhero dog. The only thing missing was Jessie.

Jack tucked his niece into Mrs. Carmichael's spare bed. He helped her say her prayers, swallowing a surge of mixed emotions when Maddie blessed her dad—*even though he doesn't love Mommy and me.* Maybe Jessie was right. Maybe he should steer clear of the courthouse tomorrow. Jack wasn't sure if he could see Frank Cortez without inflicting bodily harm.

"Mrs. Carmichael said it's okay if Shy sleeps with me if it's okay with you," Maddie said, rousing Jack from his musings.

"Sure thing, sweet pea." He called the dog, trying to get her to curl at the end of the bed. Instead, Shy curled up in Maddie's arms. "Not sure your mom would approve of that, hon."

"Maybe you could square it with her."

"Hmm." He bit back a grin. He'd have to remember to watch his phrasing with this kid. She remembered everything.

Maddie smiled and yawned. "Good night, Uncle Jack."

"Good night, baby." He kissed her on the forehead, then left.

Kylie was waiting just outside the door. She had that dreamy look women get when they're charmed by an endearing sight. On the one hand, it made him uncomfortable. On the other...it made him want to kiss her senseless.

She hooked his arm and drew him down the hall. "You're great with her, Jack."

"So are you. I can't believe how many times you made her laugh," he said softly. "You teased her out of her shell."

Kylie shrugged off the compliment. "I do okay with kids."

"You do okay with lonely widows, too." Mrs. Carmichael craved attention and was prone to overdramatize. Kylie just rolled with the punches.

"I've had a lot of practice with Grandma."

They reached the bottom of the stairs and Kylie touched his arm. "I came up to tell you I promised to roll curlers into Mrs. Carmichael's hair. She said her fingers are too stiff."

Jack raised a brow, lowered his voice. "They didn't look stiff when she was dealing the deck for that game of Old Maid."

"I think she just wants some girl time. I'll be fifteen minutes tops."

"I'll wait outside. I need to check in with Jessie."

"Then we'll go," she said.

"Then we'll talk," he said.

"Maybe we should sleep on it."

"Maybe."

The word hung in the air as she left to tend to Mrs. Carmichael.

Jack moved outside, clueless as to what he was going to say to Kylie whether they spoke tonight, tomorrow, or next week. How the hell do you say, *"I love you, but I'm not right for you."*

"Dammit."

Frustrated, he dialed his sister's cell.

"Hi, Jack. Everything okay?"

"Everything's great. I—"

"Hold on," she shouted over the background noise. "I can't hear you. Let me step outside."

"It's late," Jack said, raising his voice to be heard. "Just move to a quieter part of the bar." The last thing he wanted was for Jessie, or any woman for that matter, to be loitering in the dark, alone.

"Okay, okay, Mr. Worrywart. I'll move away from the TVs. Hold on. There. That's better. How did it go with Madeline?"

"Just tucked her in. Her tummy's full of pizza and hopefully she's having sweet dreams about a superhero dog."

"Is Shy sleeping with her?"

"It's only for one night."

"She said that last night when the dog snuck into our room."

Jack gazed up at the quarter moon, smiled.

"It's fine. Really. Shy makes her happy. I want Madeline to be happy, Jack."

"She's doing okay. It's you I'm worried about."

"Starting tomorrow, I'll have a new life. I just have to get through the divorce proceeding. Maybe it's a good thing you're coming. You can restrain me if I go for Frank's jugular."

Jack chuckled. "I was counting on you to restrain me."

"Are you kidding? I'd cheer you on." She lowered her voice and vented. "With each passing minute, with every scandalous image that permeates my brain, I despise that son of a bitch even more."

"I don't blame you."

"Part of me wants to blot him from my mind forever, never see him or speak to him again. But the other part, the part that has to live with the betrayal and the fact that word is spreading through Eden regarding his indiscretions…that part wants revenge. Almost makes me wish one of these mobster wannabes was for real."

A muscle twitched in Jack's tense jaw. "What mobster wannabes?"

"Hey, sweetheart!" he heard someone shout in a lame Italian accent. "How about some *gabagool?*"

"I'm on break!" she shouted back. "So annoying," she said to Jack. "What is *gabagool,* anyway? Customers have been spouting slang from *Omertà* all night. A few even dressed the part. Baggy trousers and boxy, short-sleeved shirts. Gaudy gold chain necklaces and pinkie rings."

Jack's past and present collided. His gut kicked. "What the hell?"

"It all stemmed from Kylie's claim that she witnessed a mob hit in the park," Jessie said. "The story spread like wildfire. No one believes it, but they're sure having fun with it. Especially Max, J.J. and Mr. Keystone. Even Boone got into the spirit. He's showing back-to-back episodes of *Omertà* on the two mounted televisions. Grown men playing mobsters," she said in a disgusted voice. "Nothing like putting thugs on a pedestal. All I can say is if even half of what's on that show reflects reality, I don't know how you lasted so long in New York City."

Jack massaged his temples as a dozen gruesome memories attacked his brain.

"Are you still there?"

"Yeah. Just trying to wrap my mind around Max and the boys dressed like gangsters." A partial truth.

"They're not alone. Fifteen or so other dimwits dressed the part. The place is packed. Everyone's not in mobster garb, but everyone is watching the show and spewing mobster slang. I don't even know some of these people. Wanda pointed out that a few folks always trickle in early for the festival."

"Especially the men driving in the collectible wheels for the car and truck show," Jack said. "Happens every year." He imagined them easily falling into the mobster fan-fest. Even Ziffel glorified that damned show.

"I never paid attention. I guess I was too absorbed in my own life. Anyway, any two of these *wiseguys* could've been the ones who spooked Kylie. For what it's worth, I keep listening for one of them to slip up and brag about it."

"I appreciate that, Jess, but if you do hear something, don't engage, just pass the information on to me."

"You don't think they're actually dangerous?"

"I don't know what to think." The wannabe craze certainly supported his role-playing scenario. Logic, based on the town's obsession with *Omertà*, suggested Kylie had been the victim of a fantasy-game-gone-wrong. End of story. Maybe Travis Martin and the WITSEC angle were totally unconnected. It would sure as hell be a welcome coincidence.

Jessie sighed. "I'm sorry I rambled. It's just…I'm over the mob thing."

"You and me both."

"At least it's distracting me from the divorce. And at least they're not gossiping about *me*. Not tonight anyway. I have to get back to work, Jack."

"You get off at one, right?"

"Right."

"I'm going to ask Officer Hooper to follow you home."

"That's silly."

"Indulge me."

"Do I have a choice?"

"No."

"Didn't think so. Have a good night with Kylie, Mr. Worrywart."

In spite of his wary mood, Jack smiled. "I think this was the most you've ever talked to me in one session."

"I know. Weird."

"Nice. Good night, sis."

"Good night."

Jack disconnected, called Hooper, then signed off just as Kylie moved out of the shadows. "Everything good?" she asked.

"As good as can be expected." He thought about sharing Jessie's description of the mobster wannabes, but he didn't want Kylie thinking the town was making fun of her. His inclination was to shield her from hurt—whether she liked it or not.

"Ready to go?" she asked softly.

"Sure." He grasped her elbow and guided her through the moonlit yard.

"The 24/7 protection thing. I guess that means you're staying over."

"Have a problem with that?"

"Sort of."

Jack backed her against the passenger door of his SUV. "Talk to me."

"It's just...that love thing. I'm confused, too. I mean, I have some concerns. About me and my illusions. About you and your...mind set. But that doesn't stop me from wanting to tackle you and have wild sex. Because I really liked it. The sex, that is. I don't want you to think I'm using you, just because, you know, it was great, but I want more. With you. Sex," she clarified. "If we sleep in the same house I'm not sure I'll be able to control myself. Truthfully, I don't *want* to control myself. I'm sick to death of suppressing my feelings and urges. Right now, this moment, I want sex. Specifically with you. And if that makes me a slut, so be it."

Heart pounding, Jack squinted down at her. "Are you for real?"

She shut her eyes, frowned. "I'm hopeless."

"Get in the car."

"What?"

He pulled her aside, opened the door and lifted her in. "Buckle up."

She was lucky he didn't take her right there—in the grass, against a tree, in the car. Sex wasn't a cure-all, but it was sure as hell a Band-aid. "If you're hopeless, I'm pathetic. What fired you up?" he asked, as he keyed the ignition.

"Seeing you interact with a lonely widow, your bashful niece and a needy dog. You?"

"Seeing you interact with a lonely widow, my bashful niece and a needy dog."

They reached across the seat at the same time, fingers brushing. Jack clasped her palm, experienced a rush of affection and lust. "Damn."

"Yeah," she said.

"About that talk—"
"Later."
"Yeah."

CHAPTER THIRTY-EIGHT

AFFECTION AND PASSION proved a powerful mix, clouding the guilt Kylie felt for withholding information about Travis. Jack hadn't said anything about visiting the man's house other than—he wasn't there. He wasn't telling her everything, but she wasn't being forthright, either. If she pried, he'd pry. The more she avoided conversation about Travis Martin, the less she had to dance around the truth. She *really* hated lying to Jack and had to keep reminding herself why she'd chosen to do so in the first place.

To give an injured soul a fighting chance at life, at happiness.

Yeah, that was it.

Hopefully, Jack would understand her motivation when she showed him the letter. She wasn't sure how he would feel about the money and the ticket. She wasn't sure how *she* felt about the money and the ticket. Every time she thought about it, her stomach cramped. Not a good sign.

Kylie squeezed Jack's hand, focused on his strength and compassion. His tolerance. She pushed aside unsettling thoughts in order to embrace warm ones. Thoughts of her and Jack, together and in love.

Maybe.

Before she knew it, Jack pulled into the driveway of 146 Newberry Street, the house she'd grown up in. The house now occupied by her mom and grandma, only they weren't here. They were in Alaska. Miles away, like Spenser. Thank goodness. Not that they'd mind her spending the night, she was always welcome, but they'd sure as heck mind that she planned on getting naked and messing up her little-girl sheets with a man.

The McGraws were an old-fashioned lot. Even her globe-trotting brother. What was good for him wasn't specifically good for his baby sister. Just because he'd sneaked a girl into his old bedroom and had premarital sex, that didn't mean he'd approve of her doing the same. For some reason, every time she crossed the threshold of their childhood home, she regressed fifteen years in her brother's eyes.

Yeah, well. He wasn't here to see this. So there.

Thanks to her security-minded mom and a nifty auto-timer, light shone through the living room window. She'd have to douse that lamp the moment they entered, otherwise a neighbor might catch a glimpse of her and Jack ripping off each other's clothes. Talk about fuel for gossip.

Her pulse skipped and skittered. Maybe it was the bizarre day. Maybe she needed to blow off anxious energy. Maybe it was the realization of how short life can be and needing desperately to feel alive.

Kylie couldn't wait to get Jack naked. She couldn't wait to touch and kiss every exquisite part of him, to experience another earth-rocking orgasm. She wanted to lose herself, to forget the bad and to feel the good.

Even with the porch light on, she had a hard time getting the key in the lock, probably because her hands were trembling so badly. A heady combination of nerves and anticipation. She breathed a sigh of relief when Jack took over.

As soon as the door swung open, she yanked him inside and slammed it shut.

He turned the dead bolt.

She killed the light.

They collided in an explosion of lust.

Clothes flew and limbs tangled. Tongues dueled as Jack swept her into his arms and carried her up the pitch-black stairway. He knew this house as well as she did. A thousand memories assailed Kylie as he bumped open her bedroom door. Kid memories. Teenage memories. Suddenly, she was half her age and her dad and mom were only one room away. When Jack laid her on the double bed adorned with a pink bedspread and herd of stuffed animals, she bolted upright. "Can't do this. Not here. Too weird."

He whisked her away and into the hall. "Spenser's room."

"Is now Grandma's room. Ick. And don't even think about Mom's room." But even as she protested, she unbuckled his belt and unsnapped his jeans.

Jack backed her against the hall wall, kissed her deep and long. *Okay,* she thought hazily as his tongue swept over hers and suckled, *I can do this standing up.* She even fumbled with the zipper of her jeans as his hands caressed her bare breasts. But then he hauled her up and over his shoulder, much as he'd done on her drunken birthday. Had that only been a few days earlier?

"Jack—"

"Trust me."

The air crackled with anticipation as he descended the stairs. All she could think about was getting down and dirty. She ached to know that the intense orgasm she'd experienced wasn't a one-time thing. That he'd rock her world just as he had the night before. That he wasn't a fantasy quenched, but a fantasy realized. The lover who'd satisfy her sweet and lustful yearnings again and again. The intensity of her desire nearly split her apart.

She needed Jack.

Inside her.

Now.

Draped over his broad shoulder, she slid her hand beneath the waistband of his jeans and cotton briefs and palmed his butt. Taut. Sexy. Oh, the things she ached to do to him. The things she prayed he'd do to her.

At this point Kylie didn't care if Jack bent her over the living room sofa.

She breathed deep, willing her erratic pulse steady, and caught a whiff of apple cobbler and pumpkin pie. The fragrant mixed potpourri her mom used to keep the recreation room smelling fresh. Mostly this room had been a male hang—her dad and grandpa, Spenser and Jack and their friends—although, when she was younger, Kylie used to horn in on the fun. A pool table that doubled as a Ping-Pong table. A pinball machine and an old foosball table.

Oh, yeah. And a pullout sofa.

Kylie anticipated the feel of worn, soft cushions and instead felt the erotic bite of a harder surface. The felt-covered pool table. Holy cripes.

"Just so I'm clear," Jack said. "This. Tonight. It's just about sex."

"This is as close to *just sex* as I'll ever get," Kylie said.

He grasped her chin and nipped her lower lip. "Understand you're forfeiting flowery words of endearment."

"In exchange for down-and-dirty, earth-rocking sex? Understood."

"No pressure there."

She smiled her naughtiest smile.

"Don't move," Jack said.

Move? She was paralyzed with anticipation!

He flicked on a small table lamp, filling the room with soft amber lighting and sexy shadows. Next she heard music. *Journey*—Spenser's favorite eighties rock band. The cassette had probably been in the old player since the last time her brother was home. *Escape* was one of his favorite albums. "Don't Stop Believing" was one of Kylie's favorite songs. The raw energy of the rhythm and melody transported her to another world as Jack's hands roved and caressed her naked torso. Or maybe it was his hot, possessive kisses that shot her over the moon.

She was delirious with need by the time he peeled off her dress and satin panties. Oh, my, God. Was she *panting?*

"Flexible, huh?"

"Let's just say I'm capable of most of the positions featured in the *Kama Sutra*," she rasped as he smoothed strong hands down her thighs and calves.

"You've read the *Kama Sutra?*"

"Mostly I looked at the pictures," she teased, heady with naughty anticipation as he clasped her ankles. Truthfully, she'd explored the book in a quest to link pleasure and spirituality. But the picture thing sounded sexier.

Jack's grin was downright wicked as he urged her legs up and open. Suddenly, he hovered over her, his hands braced on the table, her ankles resting on his shoulders, his rock-hard shaft brushing her wetness.

She'd read about this position—the Deep One. Total penetration. *Oh, yeah.*

"You game, Tiger?"

Hopped up on an erotic rush of adrenaline, Kylie reached down and urged him inside. "Slide home, Jack."

MOONBEAMS SLICED THROUGH the edges of curtains. Silence filled the apple-and-sex-scented air. Body and mind limp from an energy-charged day and sexually charged night, Kylie snuggled with Jack on the sleeper sofa. The pool table had been exciting, but the mattress was much more comfortable. Besides, now all she wanted to do was sleep. "Just sex is pretty awesome," she whispered, overly exhausted.

"Just with me," he said, close to her ear.

"Bossy *and* arrogant," she teased.

He smiled and smoothed a hand over her bare hip, inciting a rush of goose pimples. "Kylie."

"Hmm?"

"I'm having a hard time thinking about you with anyone else."

"Me, too." She couldn't imagine anyone setting her body and soul on fire the way Jack did. "You've ruined me for other men."

"I'm serious."

"Me, too." Eyes closed, she snuggled deeper into his strong arms. She didn't want to think about yesterday or tomorrow. She wanted this moment to stretch on and on. She wished Jack would shut up, because she was pretty certain he was going to say something she didn't want to hear.

"I'm a protective bastard."

"I know."

"And selfish."

She managed to lift her head from his shoulder and regarded him through bleary eyes. "How so?"

"I want you even though I'm not right for you."

Suddenly she was wide awake...or at least more alert. "Who says you're not right for me?"

"I suck at marriage. I'm too committed to my work. Too set in my ways."

"Your protective ways," she ventured.

"Mmm."

"Well, guess what? I suck at marriage, too."

"You've never been married, Tiger."

"That's what I mean. I'm thirty-two and I've never even been engaged. Just almost engaged. And it's not for lack of wanting a husband and family."

"That's another thing. Children. You want them."

"Sure. Don't you?"

"I'm not comfortable with the notion."

Her stomach flopped. "But you'd make a wonderful dad. You're so loving with Madeline."

"She stole my heart the moment she first spoke to me. I can't imagine how I'd feel if something bad happened to her."

Kylie processed that comment and caressed Jack's face. "And, by nature, if something bad happened to one of your own children, you'd be even more devastated. An understandable fear, but isn't the potential joy worth the risk?"

He clasped her hand, gazed into her eyes. "Maybe. I'm not sure."

Kylie grappled to make sense of this unexpected news. She put herself in Jack's shoes, in the shoes of a homicide cop, and it clicked. "Is it because of your job? Because of the things you've seen?"

"Yes."

"Do you want to talk about it?"

"No."

"Because you don't want that stuff in my head?"

"Damned right."

She wasn't surprised and she even understood. Still... "Maybe you should talk to someone else. Someone neutral, subjective."

"Like a shrink?"

"Well...yeah."

"Saw a marriage counselor a few times. That was as close to a head doctor as I want to get."

She wanted to shake him. "How can you keep all that *stuff* bottled up?"

"It's my way."

"Well, your way stinks. Maybe it's time to step out of your comfort zone."

"I already did. Numb was my comfort zone. Now I'm feeling again and it's an adjustment, goddammit."

Kylie fell back on her pillow with a groan. "Why did you have to bring this up tonight?"

"Because I know marriage and children are important to you and I don't want to mislead you."

"Noble," she grumbled, "but annoying. Whatever happened to taking this slow?"

"I've never fallen for anyone so fast and certainly not as hard."

Kylie's heart bumped against her ribs. "Just when I was good and mad, you had to say something romantic."

Jack pulled her into his arms. "Let's not go to sleep angry, Tiger. You never know what tomorrow will bring."

"Wise and cynical at the same time."

"Something tells me I slipped off my pedestal tonight."

She didn't comment. As exhausted as she was, her mind was spinning like a tornado.

"What are you thinking?" Jack finally asked.

"That you're trying to sabotage our relationship before it barely gets off the ground. What are you thinking?"

He kissed her forehead. "That I've finally met my match."

CHAPTER THIRTY-NINE

THE FIRST STREAKS OF DAWN peeked through the partially opened curtains of the McGraws' recreation room. Kylie stirred in Jack's arms, but she was still fast asleep. He'd been awake for hours. The sleeper sofa was comfortable enough, and having Kylie safe in his arms was a blessing, but his mind and conscience wouldn't shut down.

Growing up, Jack had spent a lot of hours in this room. He'd had a lot of laughs, played a lot of games. Last night, he'd played dirty and played for keeps.

He'd never felt guilty about having sex, but he was feeling a little uneasy about what could only be equated to calculated manipulation. He knew Kylie hadn't experienced ultimate satisfaction in lovemaking until their first time together. He knew she was adventurous and hungry for more. He'd used that knowledge to his advantage, pleasuring her in countless ways, in countless positions, making it impossible for any other man to compete. He hoped.

Fundamentally, he'd been motivated by lust and honest affection. But there'd been a troubling dose of jealousy and insecurity in the mix.

In the heat of the moment, Travis Martin had invaded Jack's mind. It's not that he thought anything sexual was going on between Kylie and Martin, but there was a bond. A *deep connection,* something Jack avoided, according to that quack he'd agreed to visit in a failed attempt to salvage his marriage. Only now, Jack realized that counselor had been dead-on in his assessment. Jack *had* been a guarded coward. It pissed him off that Martin had more "emotional" guts than he did. Worse, he was certain the man had a tarnished past. He felt it in his bones. It chafed that he couldn't prove it. It made him seem overly suspicious and petty in Kylie's eyes.

If only he'd found incriminating evidence against Martin when he'd searched his sequestered farmhouse. But there'd been nothing suspicious. No hint of a former life. No hint of being dragged out against his will. Just verification that he was widowed and, after speaking with his boss, probably on a much-needed vacation.

Or…he was swimming with the fishes.

Kylie rolled over and rested her cheek against Jack's chest. She flung a leg over him and slipped her arm around his waist. Snuggling closer, she made a sleepy, satisfied sound that warmed his blood.

Jack clung to her goodness, her optimism. It had taken him seventeen years to discover the power and beauty of Kylie Ann McGraw. He didn't want to lose her to another man. Although if he didn't change his views on marriage and children, he certainly stood that risk. Unless *her* views changed. Or, hell, maybe they'd both mellow and find a happy medium. Who knew what would happen in time? He told himself to take a breath. *Slow down.* Maybe Kylie was right, maybe he was trying to sabotage their relationship. If he committed heart and soul at the deepest level, he'd be doomed if he ever lost her. He thought about all the atrocities he'd seen. The accidents and homicides. Imagining Kylie suffering any one of those fates turned his insides to stone.

No, he cautioned himself. *Don't shut down. Fire up.*

Mind racing, he pressed a kiss to Kylie's temple, then gently untangled himself from her gloriously flexible limbs. She snuggled deeper beneath the covers while he quietly dressed, then stole away into the kitchen. He placed a call to Officer Anderson, asking him to drive over and to keep tabs on Kylie until further notice. While waiting, he made a cup of instant coffee and ticked off a mental check-list, duties he could delegate to his officers regarding the Apple Festival, facts he wanted from WITSEC. He also intended to push County to step up their investigation. He wanted to know what he was dealing with. He wanted this over. He wanted Paradise in the Heartland and a shot at happiness with Kylie McGraw.

KYLIE RELEASED A PENT-UP BREATH when she heard the front door open and shut. Jack was gone.

It had taken him a good fifteen minutes to leave. Pretending to be asleep while he'd dressed had been hard, but certainly easier than addressing the bigger lie—Travis's whereabouts. Yes, she was unsettled about Jack's hang-ups about marriage and kids, but that was way down the pike and this snafu with Travis was right in her face. She'd wrestled with the dilemma in her dreams. It's not that she didn't trust Jack. She didn't trust the situation. What if she shared the information with him and then he shared it with WITSEC and then somehow news leaked? What if, for the sake of easing her conscience, she put a man's life at risk?

Somewhere in the middle of her exhausted sleep, she'd decided to keep quiet awhile longer. Maybe County's investigation would show that she had indeed been the victim of a hoax. Or maybe they'd find the actual body and the authorities would focus on that poor soul rather than Travis.

The trick was to put it out of her mind, otherwise she'd fret herself sick. She was already worried about Faye. Even though her friend had called last night to say she and the kids had arrived in Florida safely and that her dad was doing great for a man who'd broken both legs, she'd still sounded stressed to the max. Kylie had volunteered to drop everything and fly down to help, but Faye had insisted they were fine. "*Besides,*" she'd said, "*you need to focus on McGraw's grand reopening.*"

No one could argue with Faye and, besides, she was right. UPS had promised an early delivery. With luck, Kylie

would have the *Bada-Bling!* imports on display before she
opened the doors for business. Those customized sneakers
were the last slice of the renovation pie. Today, Eden would
get a peek at the new and vastly different McGraw's Shoe
Shoppe. How sad that Travis wasn't here to see people *ooh*
and *aah* over his creative masterpiece.

Don't think about Travis!

Right.

Instead, she thought about Jack. Kylie stretched her
normally limber muscles, aching in new and wondrous
places. With anyone else, some of the sexual intimacies and
positions she'd engaged in last night might have felt weird
or wrong, but with Jack they were just wildly exciting. She
was in touch with her spiritual side enough to know it was
because she was deeply, madly in love with the man. Real
love. True love.

She wanted to believe they could work out their issues.
She wanted to believe they stood a chance. That he was *the
one* and she was *the one* and that they'd be together just as
she'd always dreamed.

Channeling positive thoughts, Kylie swung out of bed
and made a beeline down the hall and up the stairs. She
showered and dressed, focusing on the good things in life.
She counted her blessings. She chanted positive affirmations. She envisioned McGraw's Shoe Shoppe being the
talk of the town, of increased traffic and mega sales. She
envisioned more erotic sex with Jack, more snuggle time
with Jack, walks in the woods, dancing under the stars and
dining on pizza and chop suey with Jack.

She worked herself up from worrywart to happy
camper—a delicious state of oblivion.

She was actually humming when she padded down the
stairs, dressed to impress for the grand reopening of
McGraw's. Craving a cup of hot tea, she headed toward the
kitchen, freezing in her cushy, soft, patent-leather, apple-
red loafers at the sound of footsteps. Someone was in the
house, in the kitchen!

That *someone* was coming her way.

Burglar? Mobster?

"Jack?" she choked out.

Her cell phone was in the recreation room.

The landline was upstairs and in the kitchen.

She could bolt for the front door, but then the intruder might shoot her in the back. Too late, anyway. The wood floor creaked louder and Kylie adopted a fighting stance. The element of surprise was on her side. She hadn't attended a martial arts class in quite a while, but basics were ingrained in her brain. A series of defense moves and body-target areas flashed in her head. *Courage and commitment,* she thought just as the intruder rounded the corner.

Aiming at her opponent's temple, she launched a round-house kick, pulling short when she noticed the uniform. Regardless, she clipped Officer Andy Anderson in the shoulder, sending him flying back, two cups of brew in hand. Or rather, on his uniform.

"Jesus!" he hissed. "Are you nuts?"

"I'm sorry!" Kyle rushed forward and stifled a nervous laugh. The man was sitting on his butt, his EPD uniform soaked with hot beverages. It wasn't funny. But she was just so dang relieved he wasn't some goon. "What are you doing here?" she snapped as she relieved him of the china cups. At least he hadn't dropped and broken them. Grandma would have freaked.

"Protecting you." He pushed to his feet, looking equally embarrassed and mad. "Chief Reynolds assigned me to drive you to work, to watch over you. You've got him spooked with that mobster talk, Kylie. You should be ashamed. Haven't you heard about his burnout on big crime in the Big Apple?"

She'd heard. "Know any details on that?"

"No. You?"

"No."

"Shoot," they complained in unison.

She rushed into the kitchen, placed the cups in the sink

and soaked a sponge with cool water. "How long have you been here?"

"The chief let me in on his way out," Andy said, coming up behind her. "I thought you were sleeping so I stayed in the living room, read a magazine. When I heard you come out...I started to say good morning but you raced right up the stairs and you were..."

Naked as a jaybird.

"I thought I was alone," she squeaked, turning to dab at his stained shirt and pants.

"Obviously." He nabbed the sponge and attacked the mess himself. "Anyway, I wanted some coffee, but settled for tea since there was a box of Lipton right there on the counter. I thought you might like a cup, too."

"That was nice."

He grunted. "Please don't tell Chief Reynolds I saw you in the buff."

"Please don't tell *anyone* you saw me in the buff."

"Deal. Nice body, by the way."

"Thanks."

Even though he was concentrating on his stained shirt, she could see he was blushing. That made two of them. The trick would be *not* to blush every time she ran into Andy from here on out. "Why are you here again?"

"To protect you from phantom mobsters and to drive you to work."

"Oh, right." She pushed aside her mortification and focused, once again, on McGraw's. "Gotta grab my purse. Meet you at the front door."

"No wonder Ashe is bent," Andy muttered as she headed for the recreation room.

Kylie froze in her tracks. "What?"

"What?"

"You said something about Ashe Davis."

Andy, who was two years Kylie's junior, placed the sponge in the sink and brushed past her. "I was just thinking about your body and... Never mind."

"I'd appreciate it if you'd blot the image of me in my birthday suit from your brain."

"Right. Sorry."

"But that other thing…" She followed him into the living room. "What's Ashe got to do with me?"

"Nothing. That's why he's bent."

Kylie shifted her weight while Andy fanned the wet spot on his pants with a magazine. "Are you saying Ashe is angry because I, um, hooked up with Jack instead of him?"

"Sort of. Let's just say his pride and pocket are bruised. Ask Faye. Stan knows about the betting pool. I'm sure he told her."

Kylie's face grew hotter. *Betting pool?* "Faye's not here. You're here. And if you don't spill the beans, I'm going to swipe that magazine out of your hand and whack you with it!"

Andy glanced up. "Never knew you were so violent."

"I'm not. Usually. Then again, I haven't been myself lately."

"I've heard the stories."

She took a menacing step forward. "Andy—"

"Oh, all right." He slapped the magazine down on her mom's coffee table, then adopted an official stance— shoulders back, hands braced above his leather holster. "Ashe and Chief Reynolds faced off the other day in J.J.'s Pharmacy and Sundry. They were buying—" he cleared his throat "—condoms and arguing about who would…well, ring your bell."

She blinked.

"Sure you don't want to ask Faye about—"

"Go on," Kylie grit out. She would *not* die of mortification. At least not before she got the whole story.

"All right. But don't hit me. I'm just the messenger."

"Noted."

"Ever since that journalist dude you were sleeping with

split town, Ashe has been bragging that he'd be the first man to…uh…"

"Ring my bell."

"You know Ashe. He's an…"

"Arrogant dog."

"When Jack showed on the scene, some of the guys started ribbing Ashe about losing his chance to be your…um…"

"Bell ringer?"

"Ashe reacted by placing his money where his…well…"

"I get the picture." Kylie wanted to hit something, or more pointedly, someone. She balled her fists at her sides, breathed deep.

Andy took a step back. "Everyone knows Jack and you…that he…well, hell, Kylie. There's a bounce in your step that wasn't there a few days ago. Some of the guys are nudging Ashe to pay up. He's bent. About losing the money and, mostly, losing out to Jack. Way I hear it, their rivalry goes way back."

Kylie spun off to get her purse. She'd heard all she needed to hear. Now someone else was going to get an earful.

A minute later, she was buckled into Officer Andy Anderson's squad car. Wisely, he didn't speak during the two-minute drive into the center of town. Nor did he complain when she asked him to stop at Kerri's Confections instead of driving her straight to McGraw's. He did however, reach for his cell phone.

"Don't you dare call Jack," Kylie warned as she shoved open the passenger door.

"But—"

"This is between Ashe and me."

"You're not going to cause him bodily harm, are you?"

She didn't answer. She didn't know. But she did know that Ashe Davis stopped at Kerri's every morning to grab breakfast and to flirt with the waitresses before heading to his car dealership. She knew that he always sat at the counter. She spied his smarmy self the moment she breached the café's door. Her ears and blood burned with gossipy whispers from the other diners as she marched in his direction. She wanted to blast him. She wanted to slap him.

He pivoted on his red stool, saw her and actually had the gall to *smile*.

At that same moment Kerri hustled out of the kitchen to place a fresh frothy meringue pie on a dessert platter.

On instinct, Kylie relieved her of the pie and smashed it in Ashe's arrogant face.

The café exploded in laughter and applause.

Ashe sputtered and wiped lemon goo and white froth from his eyes.

Kylie calmly turned to the café's owner and chief baker. "How much for the pie?"

"I heard about the bet." Kerri's lip twitched as Ashe groped for a napkin. She winked at Kylie. "On the house."

"Thanks." Head held high, Kylie swiveled and faced the teeming café. "All right. How many of you knew about the bet regarding who would ring my bell?"

Three-quarters of the diners raised their hands, including Max, J.J., Mr. Keystone and Mayor Wilson. *Great*. No doubt they'd have some sage advice on attaining orgasms.

Prebirthday meltdown, she would've crawled under the nearest booth and stayed there forever, wishing it were a six-foot hole. For someone who'd always strived to keep her private life private, this was the height of tabloid hell. But that was the old Kylie. The new Kylie intended to live life to the fullest, and if it meant making a spectacle of herself, so be it.

"Right, then. Just so everyone's clear on this, Jack rang my bell. Not once. Not twice, but several times. For those of you who placed bets accordingly—" she jerked a thumb at the jerk behind her "—see that man for your money."

Once the chuckles and murmurs subsided, Kylie made one more announcement. "On another note, McGraw's is typically closed on Mondays, but as you know, I have a sudden gripe with routine."

Several people snickered.

Kylie bolstered her spine. "In honor of the Apple

Festival, I'll open my doors today, this Monday only, from 12:00 p.m. until 6:00 p.m., giving Eden's own a sneak peek at the new-and-improved McGraw's Shoe Shoppe. *Walk in Comfort, Walk in Style.* Shake up your lives and treat yourself to a pair of quality shoes. Affordable, stylish, fun, functional and comfortable. I guarantee McGraw's has something for everyone. And if we don't have it, we'll get it!" she added on a whim. "Plus, this week only, enjoy twenty-percent off customized sneakers made especially, *exclusively* for Eden." She clasped her heart. "Paradise in the Heartland."

Everyone, with the exception of Ashe, cheered.

"That's our girl," said Mr. Keystone.

"Nice speech," said the mayor.

"For what it's worth," J.J. said as she walked by, "we weren't in on the pool."

"For what it's worth," Kylie said, "Thank you." Blood pumping, she exited Kerri's Confections alongside Officer Anderson.

"Man, oh, man," he said. "You sure gave Ashe what-for. Remind me never to get on your bad side."

"Just don't tell anyone about the birthday suit thing and we're good."

His lip twitched. "What birthday suit thing?"

She patted his arm. "Good man."

"*Now* can I escort you to work?" he asked.

"One more thing." Kylie whipped out her new cell phone and dialed Jack.

He answered midring. "You okay?"

"Depends. Where are you?"

"In my office. Where are you?"

"Across the street. Be right there."

Andy sighed and followed her. "Even though the chief argued with Ashe, I don't think he knew about the bet. I mean, he didn't say anything. I heard it from Hooper who heard it from Boone who heard it from—"

"Save it," Kylie said as they breached the station house.

Jack met her midway across the reception area. Anderson hovered behind.

"Tell me it wasn't just about being the first to push my buttons," she blurted in a hushed whisper.

"What?" Jack grasped her forearms. "Let's take this—"

"Tell me you didn't know about the bet."

"What bet?"

"Last night was so... You were so..." Kylie spied Deputy Ziffel and Mrs. Vine out of the corner of her eye. She knew Andy was nearby, too. She veered from sex talk but couldn't drop the subject. Her head and heart were pounding. "Is that why you brought up marriage and kids? To scare me off? You had your fun, cinched the bet, and then panicked because you actually fell for me?"

"What freaking bet?"

Ziffel groaned.

Kylie lost it. "Did you or did you not argue with Ashe about condoms and...and...*doing me?*"

Someone cleared their throat. "Don't mean to interrupt, but I'm looking for Chief Reynolds."

Red-faced, Kylie turned and spied a good-looking man, dressed in jeans, an open-collared shirt and a brown blazer.

"That would be me," Jack said.

The stranger moved forward, hand extended in greeting. "U.S. Marshal Noah Skully."

CHAPTER FORTY

"IS THIS PLACE FOR REAL?"

"I like it, Chickie."

"I'm not surprised." Carmine pulled their rental car to a stop a few feet shy of the Orchard House. A brown-and-pink Victorian monstrosity set on vivid green manicured grounds and surrounded by frickin' apple trees. According to Buddah it was either this or a cheap roadside motel.

Carmine didn't do cheap.

He looked across the seat at Dixie.

Not most of the time, anyway.

He'd told her to dress like a professional. He should have been more specific. Her banana-yellow skirt was too short, her red leather jacket too tight, and her blingy opened-toed heels too high. She might not have raised eyebrows in Brooklyn, but in Hayseed, Indiana, she was a walkin' billboard for *bimbo*. Maybe he could get her to tone it down before they actually went into town.

That's if they made it into town.

Carmine's ticker felt like the fuckin' clock of doom. He kept waiting for it to stop. He was certain it would stop. And all because he was late. Too late.

He had every reason to believe his brother was dead. In many ways, it was for the best, but he couldn't let. He couldn't move on. He had to make it right. And Kylie McGraw was the key.

"I know we've been over it," he said to Dixie. "But you know how to play this, right, baby?"

She fluffed her blond hair and beamed a thousand-watt smile. "No worries, Chickie."

From her luscious mouth to the Almighty's ears.

Carmine eyed the bed-and-breakfast, craving a hot bath and a long nap, knowing he'd get only one. He palmed his cell phone and called his nephew, praying for a connection. Reception had been damned spotty since landing in Indiana. How did anyone correspond out here?

"Yo, Chickie," Mario said. "Are you close?"

"I'm here. Need to check in, wash up, then we'll be payin' a visit to Miss McGraw. Any action on that end?"

"Zip. I'm thinking the Gambellis are long gone."

"Put Buddah on."

After a grunt and some jostling, he heard, "Yeah, boss?" to which he responded, "Give me the nut."

"Like Turk said, no Gambellis, no action. Like you asked, we've been laying low, keeping watch. Not that Miss McGraw needs our protection. The woman's been with one or another cop 24/7."

"I thought you said no one believed her claim."

"No one does. But she seems to be tight with the town's chief of police. He's either humoring her or being cautious. Either way, I'm with Turk. I think the Gambellis are dust. Thinkin' we should be the same, boss."

"Not until I get some closure."

"Some what?"

A term he'd picked from Dr. Bennett. "The Gambellis ain't ones to leave loose ends. Keep watch on the McGraw woman. Keep her safe. I'll be in touch."

Carmine disconnected, put the car in gear and nosed into the gravel driveway of the Orchard House.

Dixie bounced in her seat. "I can't wait to see my shoes in Kylie's store!"

Carmine couldn't wait to see Kylie.

KYLIE ALMOST KISSED the UPS guy. Not only because he'd delivered four cases from *Bada-Bling!* but also because he'd provided her with a distraction. She'd been mortified when U.S. Marshal Skully had walked in on her condom tirade. Worse, Jack hadn't included her when he'd invited Skully into his office. Even though he knew she was dying to hear the report on Travis. Nope. He'd promised to call her later, then he'd shut her out. He probably thought he was protecting her from whatever ugly news Skully had to share, which meant he still believed the worst of Travis. It griped Kylie's buns. At the same time, the moment she'd met the U.S. marshal her stomach had flopped. What did he know about Travis? What was he telling Jack?

She wanted Travis to be an interior decorator who'd renovated a mobster's mansion and unwittingly witnessed or overheard something that helped to put a criminal behind bars.

She wanted him to be a good guy who'd done a great thing.

She hated that she had a bad feeling.

Focusing on the *Bada-Bling!* sneakers derailed negative thoughts. The actual product exceeded her expectations. Good quality, fun and unique, no two pairs of shoes were exactly alike. Everything apple—apple pie, appletinis, apple trees, apple bushels, Johnny Appleseed and Eden's apple water tower—airbrushed in the style of a funky graffiti artist and decorated with assorted bling.

Kylie shucked her loafers and slipped on the pair of high-top sneakers featuring the water tower and *Paradise in the Heartland* spelled out in rhinestones. Inspired, she started arranging a display in the front window. "These are going to sell like hotcakes!"

A few seconds later, someone knocked on the door.

Engrossed in her display Kylie shouted, "Not open until twelve!"

Another, more insistent knock. "It's Jessica Lynn. Jessie. Jack's sister."

Kylie sprung into action and unlocked the door. The vulnerability in the woman's voice shook her. The sight of her was nearly as troubling. She looked like a living China doll.

Beautiful, but fragile. When had she gotten so thin? She was wearing a periwinkle-blue pencil skirt and matching cropped jacket. She'd brushed her straight black hair to a high gloss, and her makeup was celebrity perfect. Still, for all she appeared put together, Kylie sensed the woman was ten seconds from falling apart. "What's wrong?"

"My heel broke."

Looking down, Kylie saw the woman balancing on her right pointy-toed Jimmy Choo. The left was indeed minus a heel. She also saw Shy sitting on the sidewalk, just a few inches from Jessica. That dog sure seemed to have a thing for women in distress. "Uh. So, where's the heel?"

Jessica held out her hand, displaying the detached three-inch spike. "I dropped Madeline off at school," she said in a brittle voice. "Shy jumped out the open window and tried to follow her inside. I chased after the dog and...I'm not sure what I did, but my heel broke. I can't go into court like this. I need to look my best when I face Frank. I need to feel confident when I..." Her pale skin flushed. "I know you're not open yet, but..."

Kylie gently gripped the bright-eyed woman's bony elbow and urged her and the sad-eyed dog inside. She noted the squad car parked across the street. Blushed when Andy waved. She just knew he was thinking about her in her birthday suit.

Dang.

"I'm not sure if I can fix your heel, Jessica Lynn," Kylie said as she closed the door and turned. "Shoe repair isn't my strong point."

"Can you sell me a new pair?"

So her first customer was going to be the snappiest dresser in town? *Great.* "Uh. Sure."

Shy curled up on one of Kylie's new shaggy throw rugs.

Jessica kicked off her broken heels and padded straight to the new display of designer shoes intended to seduce the wealthy ladies of the Garden Club circle. She picked up a classy pair of sleek Prada pumps. "These are ideal. Do you have a similar style in a more conservative price range?"

Kylie blinked. A woman who favored top-shelf shoes searching for rock-bottom prices? Then she remembered the former pageant queen had taken a job as a waitress and, according to Jack, was determined to make her own way financially. Naturally, she couldn't afford to blow three hundred bucks on one pair of shoes. Still, there was Jessica's designer taste to consider. "I have a killer pair of Steve Maddens. Moderately priced."

"How moderate?"

Well, jeez. Was she seriously that strapped? Concerned about Jessica's pride, Kylie considered an alternative. "It just occurred to me that you must have dozens of awesome shoes in your closest. Are you worried that you don't have time to run home before your court hearing? If you loan me your house key, maybe I could zip over and—"

"That's sweet, but…" Jessica stiffened and gestured to her broken Jimmy Choos. "I won those as part of a clothing package in one of the pageants. The shoes in my closet were bought with Frank's money. I'd rather not."

Kylie started to say she understood, but she wasn't sure she did. "I'll get the Steve Maddens." She hurried into the storage room and nabbed the appropriate shoe box, heart aching for Jessica Lynn. Suddenly, Kylie's own life seemed like a veritable party. Her best friend was dealing with a troubled marriage and a seriously injured parent. Her new friend was apparently running for his life. And this woman had been raked over the emotional coals by her sleazebag husband.

Instead of resenting all the things she'd never experienced, Kylie counted her blessings. When she returned to the main room, Jack's sister was padding around in her bare feet, eyeing all the changes. The vibrant walls and ceiling. The hip lighting and vintage shelving, the eclectic mix of shoes. Knowing Jessica Lynn Cortez was a woman with exquisite taste, Kylie had to ask. "What do you think?"

"I think it's…unique. An impressive blend of old and new. Stylish *and* practical. I think you reinvented the family business."

Kylie nearly wilted with relief. "You know my brother. Think he'll kick my ass?"

"If he's smart, he'll kiss it."

Kylie smiled. "Coming from you that means a lot, Jessica Lynn."

"Please call me Jessie. The apple sneakers are cute," she said as she sat in a zebra-painted chair and allowed Kylie to fit her with a new shoe.

"Custom-made by a woman named Dixie," Kylie said. "She runs a Web-based store called *Bada-Bling!*"

"A one-woman show?"

"As far as I know."

"Like you." She sighed. "I really admire you for running your family's business, Kylie."

Embarrassed, she shrugged off the compliment. "It's easy when you love what you do."

"I've never had to work before, and though serving beer and wings is honest work, I don't plan to do it forever. Unfortunately, I can't think beyond today. I just have to get through this morning and then…" She trailed off as if realizing suddenly that she was rambling on about herself and her life—sort of like the old Jessica. She cleared her throat, flexed her foot and admired the pointy-toed black pumps. "Perfect, Kylie. Thank you." She glanced at her watch, then, hands trembling, opened her small designer handbag. "How much do I owe you?"

The woman was on her way to get divorced from a jerk who'd repeatedly cheated on her. A man who'd deserted her *and* their daughter. Kylie felt guilty about taking money from someone whose life was falling apart, especially the sister of the man she loved. "You know what's even better than moderately priced? Free. Which is what these heels would be if you were an employee of McGraw's Shoe Shoppe."

Jessica licked her pink-glossed lips. "I don't understand."

Kylie stood and pushed her new flower-power glasses up her nose. "You know that thing about me being a one-woman show? Well, I'm sort of over that. I want a life. I mean, more of a life. Outside of work, that is. Your brother and I, well, we clash a little but mostly we click."

Jessica quirked her first smile. "I think you're a good match."

"You do? Well, that's good. Great, actually. Hopefully, Spenser will feel the same. Anyway, I'm hoping the renovations and new stock will boost business. I need help and you know shoes."

Jessica stood, her fingers gripped tight on her handbag. "You're offering me a job?"

"It doesn't pay much. Actually, I don't know what it pays. I need to figure that out. Hopefully, I can make it worth your while. I think you're a perfect fit, pardon the pun."

Shy barked, startling both women. The door creaked open and Kylie's heart raced. She'd forgotten to lock it!

Get a grip, McGraw. Andy's just outside.

Then she saw it was Jack and her pulse fluttered. *Yay!* Except Skully was with him. *Dang.*

"Three out of four of my favorite ladies." Jack bent over to pat the eager dog's head as she leaned into him. "The blonde here is Shy. You met Kylie," he said with a warm look in her direction. "And this is my sister, Jessica Lynn Cortez. Ladies, this is U.S. Marshal Noah Skully."

"Pleasure," Skully said, looking directly at Jessica.

Kylie didn't mind being invisible where that man was concerned.

Jessica looked mortified by his regard. Was it because she was self-conscious about her frail state, Kylie wondered, or because she hated all men just now? Frank, the bastard, had really done a number on her head.

"I need to go," Jessica blurted. She looked at her new shoes, at Kylie. "I…"

"Catch up with me later. You know, after. We'll grab a drink, chat."

Jack looked at his watch. "The hearing's in a half hour, right?" he asked as Jessica bolted for the door in her shiny new heels.

She nodded. "But I'm meeting with my lawyer beforehand. If you've got business with Marshal Skully..."

Jack nabbed his sister's hand and squeezed. "I'll be there. Just need to speak with Kylie first."

Jessica split and both men turned their attention to Kylie. *Dang.*

CHAPTER FORTY-ONE

KYLIE'S OFFICE SUDDENLY seemed the size of a toddler's oxford heel. Partly because Jack and Skully were so dang imposing. Partly because an ugly truth was closing in.

After urging her to sit, Jack crossed his arms and leaned back against the file cabinet. Noah Skully perched on the corner of her desk. Shy hid under it. Apparently the dog sensed trouble. Smart dog. Kylie felt trapped, smothered, and as the U.S. marshal shared a sordid, albeit sketchy, tale about Travis's background and the events leading up to his entering the program, her lungs squeezed tighter and tighter.

"Poor Travis," she rasped. "And all because he's gay?" She was incensed, *stunned*. How could his brother disown him just because he was...different? And because the judgmental bastard had vented and outed Travis, a pair of homophobe past associates had beaten him within an inch of his *life?* Her stomach turned at the thought.

Jack frowned. "Did you miss the part about Travis being the lawyer for a major mob family? An organization run by his *brother?*"

Needled by his sarcasm, Kylie leaned back in her chair and crossed her arms over her churning stomach. "No, I didn't miss that part. It's shocking and disappointing, but not nearly as shocking as what happened to him all because he didn't live up to other people's expectations. It's not like he wanted to be a lawyer. He wanted to be an interior decorator. And so what if he preferred men? So what if he was different? That didn't make him bad."

"No," Jack said. "Manipulating officials, bending the law so his family could get away with an array of crimes made him bad."

"But he didn't kill anyone," she blurted. "Not even the man he stabbed in self-defense. Marshal Skully said that goon got away and that someone else killed him later."

"We're pretty sure it was Travis's brother or someone designated by his brother," said Skully. "Retaliation."

"Which doesn't make sense," Kylie said, "since his brother disowned him."

"It doesn't have to make sense," Jack said. "We're talking about the mob and you're missing the point."

"Criminal behavior is not exclusive to homicide, Miss McGraw," said Skully. "The man you're defending may not have participated in acts of violence, but he enabled them to happen."

Kylie resisted the urge to cover her ears. She didn't want to hear this. She didn't want to taint the memory of the man who'd boosted her confidence and encouraged her to trust her instincts. The man whose artistic spirit soared throughout the new and improved McGraw's. Her gut cried that Travis had sacrificed his own dreams for the sake of family, and boy, could she empathize with that. Granted, *his* family was shady and dangerous, but it's not as if you get to pick your parents. Or your brother. The way she saw it, between sacrificing his passions, being beaten so badly that he had to get a new face, giving up his identity and then losing his wife to cancer, Travis Martin had paid for his sins. And for some reason, Kylie needed Jack to believe that, too.

"Travis associated with bad men," she said evenly. "Was…*is*…related to bad men. But he also did a good thing. He cooperated with the feds to protect his wife. He testified against that rival mob family. Because he had all that inside information, the government was able to incarcerate seven mobsters. Seven dangerous criminals. Five of them guilty of murder!"

She felt as if she was talking in code. A code she didn't have the key to. Marshal Skully had revealed a portion of Travis's past without revealing his true identity or the identity of his brother or his attackers. He'd said it was to protect her as well as Travis—if he was still alive. Which he was, not that she was inclined to share that knowledge at this moment. Would the long arm of the law stretch all the way across the Atlantic Ocean to drag Travis back? And to what end?

Jack rubbed a hand over his face, clearly struggling for patience. "Looking at this through your eyes," he said to Kylie, "yes, Martin was a stand-up guy for the reasons you stated. But his actions weren't selfless. By ratting on made men he broke *omertà,* an offense punishable by death."

"By testifying, Martin not only protected his wife, but himself," said Skully. "And as a bonus, he got revenge on the family who disfigured him."

Kylie stood to pace off her mounting anxiety. Too much information. *I don't want this stuff in my head,* she wanted to say. But then Jack would think she was a wimp, and he'd go out of his way to shield her from the bad stuff in his life, his work, even at the expense of bottling up his own angst. She wanted to break that habit, not encourage it.

Her caretaker instincts kicked in. Forget sticking her head in a hole. She'd suck it up, get the facts and deal—a skill she had down to an art.

"Why are you telling me this?" she asked Skully. "Especially when you specified up front that this was against policy and that I couldn't repeat a word of this conversation to anyone."

"Because I asked him to," Jack said. He caught Kylie as she paced past and pulled her into his arms. "Because I know you consider Martin a friend. I thought you'd grieve his death less if I shattered your illusion of the man."

Kylie felt her calm slipping. Guilt stabbed at her conscience. Jack was trying to protect her, to comfort her, but because she'd been secretive, his efforts were misguided. "It's not an illusion," she said in a small voice. "He's a good man who did bad things, but he's changed."

"You keep referring to Martin in the present tense," Skully said from behind. "Based on his history, the crime you reported, and the fact that he's missing—"

"I'm sorry I doubted you, Tiger," said Jack, his gaze full of remorse. "If I hadn't dragged my feet because of my own issues, the trail wouldn't have grown this cold. But with the help of County and now the Marshal's Service—"

"Stop." The reality of the situation was crushing. By buying Travis some time, she'd caused countless others, including Jack, precious effort and frustration. She placed a trembling hand to Jack's chest. "I don't exactly regret withholding pertinent information, because I didn't know it would cause so much trouble. Plus, I didn't know about the mob stuff. I just thought...I thought Travis was a good guy who'd been at the wrong place at the wrong time. He seemed so sad and I thought he deserved a shot at happiness, so I didn't tell you about the letter, although I had every intention to today. At some point. When the time was right, which doesn't feel like now, but the longer I wait the madder you'll be, right?"

Jack didn't answer, but his eyes said, *What fucking letter?* If Skully hadn't been there, he'd probably have backed her against the wall and lectured her on the perils of withholding evidence. Then he'd have made it personal. *Why did you lie to me?*

"I'm sorry." Throat tight, Kylie backed away from Jack's tense body and hurried toward the store's safe. Her brain buzzed as she dialed the combo. She'd been on a roller coaster the past few days experiencing multitudes of emotional highs and lows. Just now she felt as though she was hurtling through space in a downward spiral. Falling off the water tower would have been less painful. Splat, you're dead. Instead, she could feel the heart-wrenching demise of Jack's trust.

"I know what I said I saw," she rambled as she grasped the bulky envelope, "and I wasn't lying, but I'm thinking, hoping, it was that role-playing thing, and whoever they were stuffing in the trunk wasn't really dead, just playing dead. All I know," she said as she straightened and faced the two somber lawmen, "is that it wasn't Travis. It couldn't be. He was already long gone." And with that she plucked the handwritten letter from the envelope and passed it to Jack.

He read the note, then passed it to Skully, who read it, then glanced at Kylie. "Mind if I hang on to this?"

What was she supposed to say? No doubt he considered it evidence. "I guess you'll want the ticket and money, too," she said, handing the U.S. marshal the rest of the goods.

"You sound disappointed," Jack said. "Were you planning on using them?"

His flat tone and expression broke Kylie's heart. She knew he could be cynical, but this was cold. What had he said last night? *Numb was my comfort zone.* Was he in the zone now? It was…disconcerting.

"He wouldn't have flown under Travis Martin," Skully said, breaking the tense silence. "Nor under his real name. If anyone knew how to get around legalities, it was the Artful Dodger. He'd purchase a false passport, credit cards. According to that letter," Skully said to Jack, "he could afford it. Like I said before, I was only recently assigned to T.M., but I read his files and poked around. There were rumors he'd stolen a hefty amount of cash from his brother."

"Dirty money," Jack said, still staring down Kylie.

I get it, she fired back with a hot gaze.

"Wonder why he didn't use it to take off before now?" Skully mused.

"Maybe he was worried about putting his wife at risk," said Kylie. "No matter his sexual inclinations, it's obvious he loved her. Now Mona's gone and…" She trailed off, realizing she was once again defending Travis and that her efforts weren't appreciated, especially by Jack.

"Think he made the flight?" he asked Skully.

"I think they intercepted him before he even made it out of town."

"That's my guess, too. How did they know he was here, dammit?"

"There's only one explanation," said Skully. "He broke the number one rule of the program by contacting a former associate or unprotected family member."

Kylie snorted at the marshal's arrogance. "How do you know one of *your* people didn't screw up?"

"Because, Miss McGraw," the man said, "no witness who followed the rules of the program has ever been killed."

Someone's phone rang—Jack's—saving Skully from Kylie's sharp tongue. She couldn't remember the last time she'd felt this anxious, this frustrated.

Oh, yeah.

Her birthday.

To think she'd bemoaned her boring life. If she hadn't shaken things up, if she hadn't strode into the hardware store intent on renovating McGraw's, she never would have disrupted Travis's routine.

You inspired me.

Kylie swayed. Had she unwittingly stirred the hornets' nest? Had she inspired Travis to break the program's number one rule in order to arrange for a false passport?

"Are you all right?" Skully asked her.

She didn't answer. She wasn't sure.

Jack snapped his phone shut. "They found a body."

That clinched it. She was not all right. Although he'd said *a* body, not *the* body.

"ID?" asked Skully.

"Unclear," Jack answered without looking at Kylie. "Let's roll."

That command prodded Shy from beneath the desk. The dog trotted out when Jack opened the office door.

Skully started to leave, then glanced at his watch. "Your sister's hearing," he reminded Jack.

"Shit."

"I'll go." Kylie nabbed her purse from her desk and shimmied past Jack. Jessica needed someone and Kylie was more than willing to be that person. It was better than hanging around here wondering about the identity of the dead guy. Wondering if Jack was ever going to forgive her for keeping secrets, and wondering if she could get past the cynical, cold side of him. He must've developed that tough edge in New York City. A survival skill. She got that. Big city, big crime, big emotional and physical stakes. But this was Eden.

A small, quiet town, she thought. *Until you shook things up.*

Kylie locked the door behind them, noted the mounting activity on the street. "Folks are gearing up for tonight's festivities. The car and truck show always pulls in a big crowd. The carnival rides will be in full swing. Not that there's ever been any major trouble, but the EPD has always been visible, especially on opening day." She gestured to Andy, still sitting in the squad car across the street. "You can probably release Officer Anderson from his watchdog duties," she said to Jack. "Seeing that you're tied up—"

"I put Deputy Ziffel in charge of patrolling the festival. He's got Hooper and Mrs. Vine on board. They can handle it. Anderson stays with you. He'll escort you to the courthouse. I'll instruct him to be discreet, but he stays." Jack glanced at the store, at Kylie. "What about your grand opening?"

She shrugged. "It'll wait. Friends and family before business."

"You mean before you. Always putting others' needs ahead of your own," Jack said. "I used to admire that quality."

Kylie's stomach constricted. "And now?"

"I'm worried it'll be your downfall."

CHAPTER FORTY-TWO

"IT'S LOCKED."

"That would account for the sign that reads Closed." Carmine shot Dixie an annoyed look as she continued to jiggle the doorknob, then quickly bit back a curse. He wasn't angry at her. He was angry at life. It kept kicking him in the *coglioni*. All he wanted was some kind of closure. A discussion with Kylie McGraw. A look at the work his brother had done on her store. He couldn't even peek inside because the fucking window was draped with fucking black canvas. What the hell?

Dixie knocked, but no one answered. "She must be in the back or something. Turk said she's been here all morning, right?"

"Last I spoke to him." Carmine's cell reception was spotty at best. Being out of immediate touch with his boys made him antsy. He peered up and down the two-lane street. What if the Gambellis were watching the store? Watching him? He patted the revolver holstered underneath his lightweight jacket. Acquiring the gun at a local sporting goods store had been laughingly simple. "Come on," he said. "Let's mosey, as they say in these parts, around to the back entrance."

Dixie strode beside him in a pair of her sparkly *Bada-Bling!* sneakers. She'd also changed into skinny jeans and a dark blue blazer. Although tight on her curvaceous figure, at least they didn't scream *puttana*. "I'm thinking the alley is for deliveries only, Chickie."

He pointed to the box in her arms, a gift box containing a pair of shoes she'd made specifically for Kylie. "You're makin' a delivery, aren't you?"

She giggled. "Oh, yeah."

Not for the first time Carmine marveled at the hick town, wondering how Tommy had managed all these years. His little brother had expensive taste in clothing and cars. In Philly, he'd kept a fancy home. In Eden, he'd lived in a run-down farmhouse, driven a beat-up truck, worked in a hardware store and dressed in flannel and jeans. Buddah had given Carmine a full report after they'd searched Tommy, or rather, Travis's home. "Unfuckingbelievable," he muttered as he and Dixie turned down the pristine alley of a historical block.

A minute later they were knocking on the back door of McGraw's Shoe Shoppe.

No answer.

"Fuck!"

"Honestly, Chickie," Dixie complained. "You told me to tone it down. Said we needed to blend. I don't think they say that word around here. Not in front of ladies, anyway."

Carmine swallowed a rude observation and massaged his chest.

"You feelin' okay, honey?"

He shot her a look, then turned at the sound of tires crunching on gravel. He had a story. Husband of the woman who'd created special shoes for McGraw's. Here to surprise Kylie. Yada, yada. Only he didn't need a story. The dark car rolled up and Mario rolled down the window.

"Where's Buddah?" Carmine asked.

"Keeping tabs on the McGraw broad. She's at the courthouse. He went in. I stayed in the car. Saw you drive by. Knew you'd have a wait, so I slipped into that bakery place and grabbed you some coffee." He passed Carmine a steaming cardboard cup. "Figured you could use some caffeine."

"Didn't the doctor tell you to lay off that stuff?" Dixie asked.

"A cup of coffee isn't going to kill him," said Mario. "Stop being a nag."

A habitual coffee drinker, Carmine drank deeply, grateful for the jolt. He grimaced at the sickenly sweet taste.

"I loaded it with sugar, Chickie. Trust me. It's the only way to drink the beans they brew out here."

"What about me?" Dixie pouted.

Mario passed her a bottle of diet cola.

"Aw," she cooed. "You remembered. Thanks, Turk."

"Sure."

Carmine drank coffee and eyed both ends of the alley. No action coming their way. Everyone was busy window-shopping or setting up food booths and carnival games. A frickin' Apple Festival. Who the hell celebrated apples? Dixie was eager to try the apple chips their B and B host had bragged about and to attend the car and truck show later today. Carmine was eager for answers. Now. He eyed the store. "How long you think Kylie's going to be away?"

"No idea," said Mario. "You wanna wait inside, Chickie?"

He was anxious to see his brother's handiwork. He still couldn't believe he was dead, but if he was, at least the renovations would be a reflection of him. "Yeah," Carmine said, knowing his nephew could crack the lock. "I want in."

When Kylie returned, he'd say the door was unlocked and they took it as an invitation. Then Dixie would distract her with shoe talk, ask her about her scare in the woods. He wanted details, and then somehow, some way he'd swing the discussion around to the guy who'd renovated the store.

"Gee, Turk, I've never seen you so dressed down. You almost look like one of the locals."

"Don't insult me."

Carmine fought a bout of anxiety when Mario popped the lock and creaked open the back door. He kept envisioning his brother hard at work, coordinating colors and fabrics, arranging furniture, painting, draping—doing all the things he'd loved to do as a kid.

The three of them weaved their way through a cramped

storage room, then into the main salon or whatever the hell you called it.

Dixie squealed when she saw the window display dedicated to *Bada-Bling!* Carmine drank coffee and admired his brother's work. His chest tightened as he took in the impressive sight. The colorful walls and polished floors. The antique cashier counter.

He could *feel* Tommy.

His throat grew tight and dry.

More coffee.

His heart tha-dumped.

Suddenly he was no longer in McGraw's. He was in his childhood home. Hundreds of memories flashed through his mind. Memories of two brothers. Happy memories that clouded, then clashed with painful visions.

His arm tingled, his chest hurt.

His mamma yelled, *"Make it right!"*

Carmine's knees buckled. He didn't remember falling, but he heard Dixie scream, felt her rolling him onto his back. He blinked up, saw his nephew backing away.

"You stay here," Mario told Dixie. "I'll get an ambulance." Then he was gone.

Carmine saw Dixie crying. He couldn't hear her sobs, just the loud, slow, sparse beat of his own defective heart. "Get…help," he croaked.

Her mouth moved. He read those luscious lips. "Turk—"

"No. You. Get…help." He didn't trust his nephew. Dixie, the bighearted bimbo, he trusted.

Sobbing, she scampered away.

Heart thudding slower…and slower, Carmine stared up and through the ceiling. He saw the stars, heaven. And just before the world went black, he swore he saw Tommy.

"Sorry," Carmine mouthed.

His brother gave him hell but all Carmine could think was, *closure.*

"I CAN'T BELIEVE HE didn't show up."

Kylie gripped Jessica's elbow as they exited the courtroom. The woman was in a daze. The judge had given Frank more than ample time to arrive. He had other cases to hear. The divorce was uncontested and only one party needed to sign the papers for the divorce to be legal and final, so…

Minutes later, Jessica Lynn was a single woman.

Kylie had been shocked and frankly a little saddened by how easy it was to end a marriage. Although, in Jessica's case… "Maybe it's for the best," she said as she led the woman into the bustling hall. "I mean, did you really want to see that cheating bastard?"

Jessica looked away. "You don't know the worst of it."

"Something worse than engaging in multiple affairs?" Kylie whispered.

"I can't talk about it. And you're right. I didn't really want to see him, but I did want, I was hoping for…"

"Closure?"

"Yes." Jessica sank onto a wooden bench. "I need to catch my breath."

Kylie sat next to her. "I have to say it was weird and uncomfortable, but it's done. You're divorced. Free to pursue a new and exciting life with Madeline."

"We won't be staying with Jack forever," she said with a quick glance at Kylie. "Just for a while."

"Don't hurry on my behalf. It's not like I'll be moving in anytime soon."

"No?"

"We had a fight. Sort of. I don't know Jack like I thought I did."

"I'm sure there's a lot you don't know about Jack and vice versa, Kylie. He's been away a long time and you two hooked up, what, a week ago?"

Kylie tapped the toes of her blingy sneakers against the marble tile. "When you put it like that…"

"Jack's worth fighting for."

"Frank wasn't," Kylie said, hoping to ease Jessie's mind.

The woman bolstered her bony shoulders. "If I never see that sick, cheating bastard again, it'll be too soon."

"That's the spirit."

Jessica quirked a faint smile. "Thanks for being here, Kylie."

"It's the least I could do for a new friend."

The woman's pale cheeks flushed red. "I don't know what to say."

"Say you'll work with me at the store or at least give it a whirl."

Jessica blew out a breath, nodded. "I'll give it a whirl."

Kylie was trying to decide whether to hug the woman or shake her hand when she heard her purse ring. Well, not her purse, but her new cell phone. Had to be Jack. Kylie motioned to Jessica to give her a second, then she walked a short distance for some privacy. "Hi, I—"

"Don't speak. Listen."

The hairs on Kylie's arms stood on end, her heart raced. She didn't recognize the voice, but she sensed urgency. *Danger.*

"I'm with a friend of yours. An old guy. Max? Fucking pain in the ass. It'll be a pleasure to pop this *cafone* and that's exactly what I'll do if you aren't here within forty-five minutes."

Kylie tried to swallow past the lump in her throat. *The goons.* They were still in Eden and they had Max. How? Why? "Where?" she whispered.

"His place. And Kylie," the mysterious voice added, "come alone. If we see anyone, any of your cop friends, the old guy gets it."

It sounded like dialogue from a B movie. Still… "Why should I—"

"Call anyone and we'll know. We're listening…and watching."

"I don't—"

"Get the skinny bitch to loan you her car."

They knew she didn't have her bike, that her car was in

the shop. They knew she was with Jessica. Kylie tried to search the hall without moving her head. Were there more than two of them? Was one of them here? Or outside with binoculars? How would they know if she phoned Jack? Or alerted Andy?

"Forty-four minutes," the ominous voice said. "Tick. Tock."

He disconnected and Kylie flew into action. "Come to the bathroom with me," she said to Jessica just as Officer Anderson rounded the corner with a cup of coffee. Forcing a smile, she whisked the woman down the hall. "Gotta go," she said to Andy, squeezing her legs together for effect as she steered her companion into the ladies' room.

Andy rolled his eyes, blushed. He was probably thinking about her in the stall—bottom half naked.

The main door shut and Jessica whirled. "What's wrong?"

"I need to borrow your car. It's an emergency."

The woman dug in her purse and handed Kylie her keys.

"Thank you." Kylie willed her trembling hands and galloping heart steady. "I also need you to distract Andy. Jack told him to stick to me like glue."

"What's going on, Kylie?"

"Please, just—"

"Okay. No problem," Jessica said. "I'll distract Andy."

"Give me a ten-minute start, then tell Andy to call Jack. They're going to pop Max if I don't show. Tell him I had no choice, to hurry, but to be discreet."

Jessica wet her lips. "I don't know what you're talking about."

"Jack will. Tell him Max's house." She nudged Jessica toward the door. "Now, go do your thing with Andy."

"Anything for a friend," Jessica said as she took a breath and eased out the door. "Be careful, Kylie."

"Always." The minute the door shut, Kylie sprinted for the window, grateful they were on the first floor and that she was wearing sneakers. She squeezed through the open pane and race-walked for the parking lot. She hoped

Jessica's fancy SUV was fast. She was down to forty-one minutes and she couldn't speed until she got out of town.

"Hang on, Max. And whatever you do, don't spit on his shoes." She hopped into her borrowed wheels and revved the engine. She knew it was crazy, walking into the hornets' nest, but those goons wouldn't be in Eden if she hadn't stirred things up. No way was she going to let Max Grogan pay for her restless, reckless actions. On the other hand, she knew she was no match for a couple of gun-toting wiseguys. Hence ignoring their warning and alerting Jack. He'd know what to do. He was used to dealing with mobsters. She just needed to keep her and Max alive until he got there. She could do that. Get them talking, keep them talking. Shoes. One of them had a thing for shoes. She could talk about shoes until the cows came home.

Travis popped into her head. He'd had a way with words, a gift for distracting her from her worries. For the first time since she'd learned about his mob ties, Kylie reflected on what he really used to do. She thought about the episode she'd watched of *Omertà*, remembered how she'd told Jack she couldn't stomach the violence and how he noted that it didn't compare to the real thing.

For the first time and to her dismay, Kylie had unkind thoughts about Travis Martin.

CHAPTER FORTY-THREE

THEY FISHED THE CAR OUT of the lake. A rental car. They pried the guy out of the trunk. It wasn't pretty. But Jack had seen worse. Still, he couldn't feign calm when they uncovered the bloated corpse for inspection. "Jesus."

"You know him," Skully said.

Bullet to the head. Expensive suit. "Show me his shoes."

The medical examiner complied.

Italian loafers with a silver buckle. "Exactly as Kylie described him, from the knees down."

"Dresses and looks a little like Tommy Mancini before the reconstructive surgery." Skully waved away a pesky fly. "Dark hair, swarthy complexion. The nose is right. Crooked."

"I did that." He'd thought about doing worse. Someone else had actually followed through. "My brother-in-law," said Jack.

"Fuck."

"Yeah."

Skully took a long look. "Sure? He looks pretty bad."

"Positive."

"What the hell, Jack?"

"Give me a minute." He rose and turned away. "Shit." Jack absorbed the clusterfuck while Skully traded words with the county sheriff and M.E. He worked the sordid puzzle, flexing muscles he hadn't used since he'd left the NYPD. He hated that it felt good. Something he'd think about later. He had a lot to think about later.

Was he willing to risk his heart to a woman who'd

crushed him with one relatively benign secret? To a woman who saw gray in a black-and-white situation?

How was he going to tell his sister that her husband had been murdered and dumped in the lake?

How was he going to break it to his niece that her daddy was in hell?

One thing he knew for sure. Frank Cortez hadn't earned a place in heaven.

Skully came up behind him and peeled off his latex gloves. "Thoughts?"

"Lots of them."

"I'm interested in the ones pertaining to your brother-in-law."

"Thought you were interested in Tommy Mancini."

"What if they're connected?"

He thought about Frank's porn collection. "They had a couple of things in common. A background in law. A taste for men."

"Your brother-in-law was gay?"

"He had fetishes. Not for common knowledge," Jack added.

Skully nodded. "So maybe Cortez's return visit was twofold. The divorce and Mancini?"

Jack worked the pieces of the puzzle. "Maybe Frank drove in a day early to visit Travis, but Travis was already gone. Maybe the wiseguys saw him coming out of the house or driving away from the house and snagged him, thinking he was Mancini. A case of mistaken identity."

"That's thin," Skully said. "It would mean the wiseguys didn't know the Artful Dodger that well or refused to believe Frank when they told him they'd pinched the wrong guy."

"Maybe they didn't give him a chance to talk." Jack braced his hands on his hips, stared up at the rain-swollen clouds and indulged in dark thoughts. "Kylie said one bruiser was angry because the other whacked their guy before they got the money. They wanted money."

"Mancini had money," Skully reminded him. "Lots of it."

"And Frank needed money. A shitload." Jack told Skully about the flashdrive he'd been given by Pete Unger, about the accounting files he'd reviewed early this morning. "Frank was in debt up to his eyeballs. Gambling. Prostitution. There were notes, names I didn't recognize. Aliases, probably. What if he owed a shark?"

"Possible. And potentially dangerous." Skully crossed his arms, angled his head. "Maybe he went to Manicini for a loan. Or maybe he was blackmailing him, sex secrets. Cortez split Eden, but Mancini was still trying to keep up the pretense of being the straight, redneck widower."

"Maybe those wiseguys snagged the right man," Jack said. "What if they were after Frank all along? Time to pay up. Not the Mancini or Gambelli family, but an unknown faction."

"Speculation," said Skully.

"A shitload of speculation."

"It'll shake out."

"You sound awfully sure."

"I'm good at my job and so are you." Skully eyed him. "Looked into your history before I got here." He noted the county sheriff and his team. "For a region that hasn't seen a murder in more than a decade, they're doing all right."

Jack didn't comment. His head was jammed.

"Meanwhile," Skully said, "someone needs to break the news to your sister."

Jack ignored his throbbing temples, palmed his cell and autodialed Kylie. He wanted to ask about Jessie's mindset and their exact location.

She didn't answer.

The phone beeped and Jack switched over to call waiting. "Jack Reynolds."

"You're fucking my little sister?"

Spenser. Christ. Jack distanced himself from Skully. "There's more to it than that."

"Spare me the details. We're talking about, Kylie. My *sister*."

"Would it help if I said I'm in love with her?" Jack shifted as the silence stretched on. "Still there, Spense?"

"Yeah."

"And where is that, exactly?"

"Too far away to kick your ass."

Jack's lip twitched in spite of the tension. "Who told you?"

"Ashe Davis. Went out of his way to get me the news. Fucking prick." Spenser paused, blew out a breath. "Love, huh?"

"Still trying to wrap my mind around it."

"Kylie must be thrilled. She's been hot for you since she was fourteen."

"Twelve."

"What?"

"Never mind." Jack glanced at Skully. The man looked deep in thought as he watched Frank's body being loaded into the coroner's van. "I have to go, Spense. How about if we touch base in a couple of days?"

"After *I've* had a chance to wrap my mind around it? Good idea. Oh, and when you see Davis, tell him I said to go screw himself."

"Will do." Jack disconnected, only to get another call. Kylie, he hoped. "Yeah?"

"Chief? It's Ziffel. Big doings here. Some guy suffered a heart attack in Kylie's store. Guess who called the station house? Travis Martin. He wants to talk to you."

Jack dragged a hand over his head. What the fuck?

"Chief Reynolds?"

"Tommy Mancini?

"You know who I am," said the other man.

"I do. Why'd you come back?"

"Because I didn't want to fail Kylie the way I failed my wife. I couldn't shake the fear that I'd put her in harm's way. I came back to admit my past to you and to take charge of my life. *My* life. No more dodging. I came straight to the store and...face-to-face with my past."

Jack started moving toward his vehicle. "Who had the heart attack?"

"My brother. Carmine." He cleared his throat, lowered his voice. "They're loading him into an ambulance. He came here to find me. To make amends. Only, he thought I was dead. I'm having a hard time making sense of it. There's a woman here. My brother's mistress, I think. She's hysterical. Deputy Ziffel said Kylie claimed she saw two goons stuffing a body in a trunk."

"Just found the car and the body," Jack said, against his better judgment. "Frank Cortez."

"Shit."

"You two have a history?"

"We do. Did."

"I need details," Jack said.

"I'll give them to you. Later. I don't think my brother's going to make it. I need to go with the ambulance. Those *goons*," Travis said, "I'm thinking they mistook Frank for me. I don't know who they are, but I know they're associated with the family. If Kylie witnessed…she's not safe. Tell me you've got her under police protection."

"She's protected," Jack said. But he suddenly feared, not well enough. His phone beeped with another incoming call. "Put Deputy Ziffel back on."

"Chief?"

"Don't let Travis out of your sight, Ed. I'll be in touch soon."

"Right-o."

Jack clicked over to the incoming call. "Yeah?"

"It's Andy, Chief. Big trouble."

Jack listened as the officer relayed a message from Kylie. He shelved his chaotic emotions as he whistled Skully over and checked his sidearm. After relaying instructions to Andy, he pocketed his phone and slid behind the wheel. "You armed?" he asked as Skully climbed in the passenger seat.

"Armed and dangerous."

KYLIE HAD THE PEDAL to the metal. She didn't dare glance at the speedometer. Guessing she was going ninety on the narrow back road and knowing it were two different things. However, she did check the rearview mirror. Just to make sure Andy wasn't on her tail, siren whirring. That's when she spied the dark sedan.

Was it them? Or at least one of them, keeping tabs on her while the other guarded Max? Only, they or he wasn't being the least bit discreet. The car was gaining speed, closing in. She squelched her panic and focused on the road, on getting to Max. That's when she spied the farmer's slow-moving monster tractor taking up more than half of the road.

Just. My. Luck.

If she braked, the sedan would slam into her bumper. She veered into the opposite lane, saw another SUV racing toward the intersection. *Jack?* She swerved to avoid a collision, spun around and ended up speeding down the crossroad. The road that led to Francis Slocum State Park.

The scene of the crime, her mind whispered.

After that her thoughts blurred. She needed to turn around, to get Max, to save Max. Although if Jack *had* been driving that SUV she'd almost crashed into, then *he* was speeding toward Max. *It'll be all right,* she told herself.

Unless Jack recognized his sister's car and did a one-eighty.

She felt a hard hit, gritted her teeth and squeezed the steering wheel. The sedan was trying to muscle her off the road. What the hell?

"I've got him. You get her. And, dammit, make it clean!"

Kylie couldn't get the goons' voices out of her head. They hadn't grabbed her after she'd caught them stuffing a body in a trunk, so this was a fresh attempt to eliminate the only witness to their crime. They were trying to kill her, to run her off the road, to flip the car—crash and burn.

Kylie chanced a look in the mirror, saw an arm and a gun. *Crap!* They were going to shoot out her tires or race up and shoot her through the window. Either way, she refused to die at their hands. She gunned the SUV and zoomed toward the bridge that spanned the narrowest part of the lake.

She heard shots.

No shattered glass, no blown tire. *No blood.*

But she did take another hard hit.

Her tail end swung.

Compensating at high speed, Kylie missed the bridge, instead sailing off the edge of the embankment.

The strangest thought slow-moed through her head as she went airborne. She'd always thought if she ever pulled a Thelma and Louise, Faye would be strapped in the seat beside her. Instead, it was a bedraggled teddy bear.

JACK HAD BEEN SPEEDING toward Max's place when another SUV almost broadsided him. Recognizing his sister's car, realizing it was Kylie and seeing that sedan on her tail, he'd joined the chase. Skully took out the rear tires on the wiseguy's car. Still, the bastard managed to ram the Escalade, pushing Kylie off course, before crashing his own car, head on, into a tree.

In the same instant that car exploded into flames, Jack experienced a new brand of numb when he saw Kylie's car disappear over the embankment.

"Shit," Skully said. He called 911, relaying their location as Jack raced the Aspen down a narrow rugged path to the lake's edge.

"Fuck," Jack breathed as he skidded to a stop. The front half of the Escalade was already submerged.

He jumped out of the car and dove into the chilly lake. A gruesome image of Kylie strapped in her seat, unable to open the car door due to the water's pressure, crowded Jack's chaotic thoughts. Fearing the worst, he died a thousand deaths as he pumped his arms and legs in a ferocious effort to get to her. His future flashed before his eyes, a future without Kylie. In that instant he knew he'd risk anything and everything to share a lifetime with the risk-taking caretaker who wore flowered glasses and crazy shoes.

His brain barely registered the sight of that woman's head breaking the surface of the lake. Relief surged through him as he lunged forward and snagged her.

Gasping for air, she clung to him. "Jack," she croaked.

"I've got you, baby."

Skully was there, too, and together they guided a limp Kylie toward shore.

Shy was swimming toward them, and when Kylie saw the dog, she burst into tears. As they neared the shore, Jack hauled Kylie into his arms and carried her to dry land. Shy whimpered and plopped in the grass alongside Jack and Kylie. "There's a blanket in the back of the Aspen," he told Skully.

"Max," Kylie choked out as she shivered uncontrollably.

Always putting other people first, Jack thought as he held her close. "Max was never at risk, hon. It was a ploy to get you away from us and out of town so he could strike."

"He?" she asked, looking dazed. "Only one?"

"Only one in the car, and that guy's dead."

"I should probably feel bad about that, but I don't."

"Good. As for the second guy, we'll track him down."

"What about the other dead guy?" she asked in a weak voice. "The one in the trunk? Was it Travis?"

"No," he said as Skully returned with the blanket. "It was Frank."

"Cortez?" Her shivering continued even after he wrapped her tight. "Why would mobsters kill Frank?"

"We're still piecing that together," said Skully.

Kylie's crying escalated to sobs.

Jack rocked her. "Don't mourn Frank, Tiger."

"Not that," she croaked. "Thought I was going to die before I told you."

"What, baby?"

She looked up at him through dazed tears. "I love you,

Jack," she whispered. "Always have, always will." Then she passed out.

Panicked, Jack checked her pulse. Strong.

"Shock," said Skully. He glanced toward the road. "Ambulance should be here soon."

"Fuck that," Jack said, carrying Kylie toward his SUV. He transferred her to the marshal's arms as Shy leaped into the back seat. "I'll drive. I know a shortcut." His hands trembled as he threw the Aspen in Reverse.

"She'll be okay," Skully said in a calm voice.

"I know," Jack said as he peeled onto the back road. But that didn't stop him from worrying all the way to the hospital.

CHAPTER FORTY-FOUR

KYLIE WOKE UP DISORIENTED. She blinked to clear her vision, reached for her glasses, then remembered they were at the bottom of the lake. She squinted at the man hovering next to her. "Officer Anderson," she croaked.

"If I weren't so happy to see you awake, I'd blast you for giving me the slip, Kylie McGraw. You scared me to death, plus I'm in deep shit with the chief."

She vaguely remembered waking up on a stretcher and seeing Jack hovering over her in wet clothes. He'd kissed her forehead and told her she was okay. He'd told her to get some sleep. "Where is he?"

"In the hospital chapel with Jessica Lynn, breaking some bad news."

Kylie focused on her surroundings. She was in a hospital room, in a hospital bed. She felt okay, except her throat was dry and sore and she felt a little dizzy. The bad news was about Frank Cortez. *Dead.* "Do you know any details about Frank?" she rasped.

"No," he said, moving closer. "You?"

"No."

"Shoot," they said in unison.

"Where's Marshal Skully?" she asked.

"Out tracking some mobster named Turk."

Kylie massaged her pounding temples. "Turk?"

"I don't know details about him, either."

Hearing a familiar whimper, Kylie pushed up to her elbows and saw Shy curled at the bottom of her bed. "Um. I don't think they allow dogs in hospitals," she whispered.

"You're right. But Shy snapped at the attendant who tried to remove her and Chief Reynolds threatened to shoot anyone who called animal control."

In spite of her splitting headache and sore throat, Kylie smiled. Then she thought about the way Jack and the dog had swum to her rescue and tears sprang to her eyes.

"Oh, hell," Andy said. "Should I call the doctor?"

"No, I'm fine. Just emotional. And…thirsty. Could you get me a soda?" She really wanted a minute to herself to collect her thoughts and wits. All she knew was that Frank was dead and Travis wasn't. One goon was dead and the other, Turk, was on the loose. Skully was chasing him and Jack was breaking bad news to his sister. Oh, and she'd confessed her forever and always love to Jack. She was pretty sure he hadn't returned the sentiment. She'd never felt so vulnerable.

"I'm not supposed to leave you alone." He poured her some water from a pitcher. "Here."

"Thanks." She drank, and though the cool water soothed her throat, it didn't stop her tears. "I need some privacy, Andy."

"But—"

"Oh, for heaven's sake, just stand outside my door and don't let any goons in. Five minutes. Please."

He narrowed his eyes. "You won't sneak out the window, will you?"

"I'm not even sure I can get out of bed." A lie, but she was desperate for a private cry.

He sighed. "I'll be right outside the door."

He left and Kylie fell back on the pillow and let the tears flow.

Her brain had done some humdinger buzzing when she'd been swimming for her flipping life, and she'd decided if she got out of that mess alive, she'd go for what she really wanted. That included a long-term relationship with Jack and ownership of McGraw's. She didn't know how she was going to attain those goals exactly, but she was going to give it her full attention. Faye was right. Her priorities and dreams had shifted. Sure, she'd enjoy touring Asia, but she no longer wanted to do it alone. Maybe someday. With Jack. That's if he didn't bail on her.

She'd always thought Jack Reynolds was the most courageous, most amazingly gorgeous man in the universe. She still thought that, with the exception of a few flaws. Yes, he was brave when it came to facing physical danger, but matters of the heart? She was pretty sure if she peeled away his tough-guy, superhero exterior, she'd see a six-foot-two marshmallow.

He was particularly partial to rescuing and protecting women. His sister, his niece, the dog. *Her.* Showing her the orgasmic stars wasn't a traditional rescue, but he had breathed new life into Kylie's sensual being. She'd never felt more alive than she had this past week, even when she was flirting with death. The water tower. The encounter in the woods. The car chase. The plunge into the lake.

Kylie bolted upright. "That's it,' she said to Shy. "Jack's Achilles' heel."

In spite of his strength, physically and emotionally, losing someone he cared about would bring him to his knees, especially a woman. What had he said about his last case, the one that had burned him out on big crime, the one that had spurred his return to Eden? Not much. Just that it had involved a young woman. *A victim of a mob hit.*

"Holy cow."

Whatever had happened to that woman, whatever he'd seen and felt and done, haunted Jack. Until he faced up to the ghosts of his past, he'd never be able to fully commit to a future with her. No wonder he wasn't willing to risk marriage or children. "How am I going to get him to talk about it?"

Shy whimpered.

"Tell me about it."

The door swung open and Officer Anderson peeked in. "She's not a goon, but she's kinda weird," he whispered.

"Says she's a business associate of yours. I told her you weren't up for business and she burst into tears. I—"

A woman squeezed between Andy and the doorjamb. Tight clothes, big hair, sparkly sneakers. "Kylie McGraw?" she asked in a scratchy voice.

Kylie nodded.

The woman moved closer and therefore grew less fuzzy, given Kylie's restricted vision. She could see now that the blonde was not only well endowed, but gorgeous—except for the black mascara streaking down her face—and clutching a metallic shoe box to her Dolly Parton-size breasts.

"Hi," she said, extending a limp hand. "I'm Dixie Darling, owner and creator of *Bada Bling!* shoes." She burst into fresh tears. Loud, heaving, heart-wrenching sobs. "Poor Chickie!" she wailed.

Chickie?

"Criminy," Andy complained.

"Would you please wait outside?" Kylie said, waving him away. He was a good cop, but the man had the sensitivity of a turnip.

The door clicked shut in his wake.

Kylie nabbed a handful of tissues from the box beside her bed and passed them to her blubbering visitor. "I don't understand why you're here, Dixie."

"To see my shoes in your store and to bring you these." She shoved the shoe box into Kylie's hand. "Remember I said I was going to make you something special?"

"Yes, but I thought you'd mail them. Aren't you from Philadelphia?"

The woman nodded, causing her teased hair to bob and sway. "I hope you like 'em."

Dumbfounded, Kylie tore away the metallic pink wrapping paper and plucked off the lid. "I'm speechless."

"Yeah. They kinda have that affect. Beautiful, ain't they?" she said with a watery smile.

"Mmm." Kylie inspected the glittering red stilettos,

wondering where in the world she'd ever wear the whimsical, sexy FMPs. Except maybe in the bedroom.

"You kinda remind me of Dorothy what with you being so sweet and living in the cornfields. There's no place like home, right?"

"Right." Kylie didn't point out that Dorothy was from Kansas and this was Indiana. Dixie didn't seem too bright, but she sure had talent and heart. "Thank you, Dixie, but…I still don't understand why you came all this way."

The woman burst into a fresh wave of tears. "I wanted to see my shoes, I mean people wearing my shoes. I wanted to meet you, my first client, and Chickie wanted to talk to you about Tommy."

"Who?"

"His brother. He was admiring the renovations and it made him sad. Thinking his brother was dead, thinking he couldn't make amends. Between that and the coffee…" She sobbed into the handful of tissues. "Can't see," she said, fanning her dragon nails in front of her face. "Mascara in eyes."

"There's a bathroom," Kylie said. "Right there behind you. Maybe if you splashed your face with cool water…"

Dixie bawled and turned in circles.

"Right. Can't see." Heart pounding, Kylie slid off the bed and guided the woman into the bathroom. "Take your time." She shut the door, then palmed her spinning head. She wasn't sure if she was dizzy because of the accident or because of the blond tornado that had just blown in.

Chickie? Tommy? *Brother?*

What was Dixie talking about?

"He was admiring the renovations and I think it made him sad."

Oh, no. It couldn't be.

Kylie stumbled back to the bed and sat down before she fell down. She mentally sorted through the information she'd gleaned from Travis, Jack, Skully and now Dixie. So, what? Dixie was married to Chickie, who wanted to talk to Kylie about his brother Tommy, who'd renovated McGraw's, meaning Tommy was Travis?

"Thinking his brother was dead, thinking he couldn't make amends."

But the man in the trunk was Frank, not Travis. Travis was on his way to France, wasn't he? Kylie rushed over and spoke through the bathroom door. "Dixie, are you sure Tommy's dead?"

"No. He's with the deputy," she wailed, "and Chi...Chi..."

Chickie. Kylie massaged her throbbing temples and stumbled back to the bed. So Travis...or rather Tommy, was back in Eden? She needed to speak with Jack.

The door creaked open.

Shy jumped off the bed.

Kylie looked over, expecting Andy, hoping for Jack, and instead saw a doctor.

"Afternoon, Miss McGraw. I'm here to administer your sedative."

"I don't need a sedative." Although maybe she did. She felt as if she was on the verge of hyperventilating.

"According to your chart..."

Shy growled, a menacing growl that caused Kylie's skin to prickle.

The doctor looked down. "What the fuck?"

Kylie's heart leaped to her throat. She peered over the edge of the bed. Shy skittered away, leaving a puddle of pee in her wake.

"That fuckin' dog pissed on my fuckin' *shoe!*"

As he shook his leg, the long hem of the man's urine-soaked scrub pants shifted, giving Kylie a glimpse of a shiny black oxford.

Guccis.

She gaped at the rabid man, who kicked at the snarling dog and missed.

"It was you!" she rasped. "You shot a man just for spitting on your shoe. And now... If you touch that dog—"

He lunged.

Kylie rolled off the bed, onto her feet. She screamed for help. "Andy!"

Dixie burst out of the bathroom. "Turk! You...you murdering *bastard!* First you went after Tommy, then Chickie. Your own blood! And for what? So you could take over as fucking *boss?*"

"Carmine was weak, you stupid bitch. In mind and body. I just helped him along."

"I knew it. You put something in his coffee, something that messed with his bad heart."

"The man was a fucking time bomb. He was going to let Tommy live. Do you know how that would have made the Mancini Family look? Tommy broke *omertà*. He got what he fuckin' deserved."

But he didn't kill Travis, Kylie rationalized. He killed Frank. How could he confuse the two? And where the hell were Andy and Jack?

Dixie curled her dragon nails into her palms. "What did you put in Chickie's coffee?"

"Don't worry your fluffy head about it, Dix. Shut your trap, play your cards right and maybe you can be my *goomah.*"

Kylie didn't know what that was, but it made Dixie's face burn.

Someone knocked on the door. "What's going on in there?"

Kylie saw the door handle jiggle. Oh, God. He'd locked it from the inside.

Turk eyed the open window next to Kylie. An escape route.

"Over my dead body," Kylie said.

"Exactly what I had in mind." Turk lunged, and wrapped both hands around Kylie's neck.

Don't panic.

Hands cupped, she swung out and in, smacking her attacker's ears simultaneously.

"Imagine clapping two cymbals together," she heard her martial arts instructor say.

Turk screamed and backed away, blood trickling from his ears.

Shy attacked his leg.

Kylie launched a roundhouse kick, connecting with his bloody ear and knocking the dazed goon to the floor.

Dixie grabbed a ruby stiletto and started whacking away. "You bastard! You fucking bastard!"

Someone pounded on the door.

Kylie lunged for the lock, but Turk grabbed her ankle.

She was pretty sure she screamed Jack's name before her head smacked the floor.

CHAPTER FORTY-FIVE

BREAKING THE NEWS to his sister about the death of her husband had been tough. It got worse when, in obvious shock, Jessica sank onto a pew and asked Jack to leave. He preferred to stay, to offer comfort, but then she whispered, "Please."

That one word tore at his heart, rang in his ears as he stepped outside the small chapel. But then it got worse. Ziffel showed up with Travis, aka Tommy Mancini, in tow. The man was devastated by his brother's death and needed a place to grieve.

Travis took one look at Jessie and backed out. "I can't invade her space. Not knowing what I know about Frank. Not after what we..." He shook off his words, then locked gazes with Jack. "Can I see Kylie?"

"No."

"I just want know she's okay."

"No thanks to you," Jack said. "You brought the fucking mob into this town."

"I know. I'm sorry. Turk's the only one left and I'll do whatever I can to help you catch him. He threatened Kylie and killed my brother. I want—"

"Revenge?" Jack raised a brow. "After what your brother did to you?"

"Carmine apologized. I accepted."

"All's forgiven just like that?" Jack asked.

Travis didn't flinch. "In my heart, he'll always be the big brother who allowed me to decorate our tree house."

Jack studied the man in his designer suit and shoes, thought about the time and imagination he'd poured in

McGraw's, and the dream trip he'd tried to bestow upon Kylie. He thought about the respect he'd just afforded his sister. Maybe Kylie was right. Maybe Travis Martin/Tony Mancini wasn't *all* bad.

Just then his cell rang. "Yeah?"

"Jack. It's Skully. Turk's in the building."

In a heartbeat, Jack slapped a pair of cuffs on Travis. The last thing he needed was for the former mob lawyer to go postal on the man who'd killed his brother. "Take him to the station house and lock him up," he said to Ziffel. "Now. And take Jessie with you."

Seconds later Jack hit Kylie's floor. He saw Skully coming from the opposite direction.

Kylie screamed Jack's name and they both broke into a run.

Jack had ordered Anderson to stay with Kylie, but now the young officer was slumped in a chair in the hall.

"Drugged," said a nurse, while a doctor continued to pound on the door.

An attendant rounded the corner in a red-faced frenzy, stabbed a key in the lock.

Skully flashed his badge. "Stand clear. And stay out until we say it's safe." He turned the key a split second before Jack kicked open the door.

They entered, guns drawn, and assessed the situation.

Skully pulled the shoe-wielding banshee off of the groaning doctor. "Let me guess," he said. "Mario 'Turk' Mancini."

The man took a wild swipe at the dog gnawing at his shoe, then fell back with a groan. "What about Wolverine?"

Jack called off Shy—when had she gotten so brave?— and knelt beside Kylie, who was sprawled flat on her back.

She blinked up at him. "We've got to stop meeting like this."

A reference to that first night at Boone's. Her birthday spill. Jack didn't see the humor. He couldn't. Kylie was covered in blood.

They were all smeared with blood.

Jack looked down. He smoothed his hands over Kylie's trembling body. "Where do you hurt, baby?"

"I think…I'm just a little stunned. When he yanked me to the floor, I hit my head. It's okay. I'm okay."

"Your neck is bruised."

"He tried to strangle me."

"Your hands are bloody."

"I broke his ear drums."

Jesus.

Jack tried to take it all in. Tried to be objective. His gun burned against his hip. The urge to shoot the bastard who'd hurt Kylie was fierce.

"She smacked Turk hard, then kicked him in the head," said the other woman. "I wish I could fight like that. I just beat him with my shoes."

"You did some damage," Skully said, eyeing the five-inch spiked heel, then the man's bloody chest.

"I was trying to pierce his heart," she said. "Heel for a heel. He killed Chickie."

"Carmine Mancini," Jack clarified while helping Kylie to sit up. "Boss of the Mancini crime family. Travis's brother," he whispered in her ear.

"Is Travis dead?" she whispered back.

He shook his head.

Kylie sagged against Jack while Skully flipped Turk and cuffed his wrists. "Clipped your uncle," the marshal said to the mobster. "Don't imagine that'll go over well with the Administration."

"Buddah will smooth things over," said Turk

"Buddah smashed his car into a tree," said Skully. "Dead."

"Good," said the blond woman.

"Turk's the goon who killed a man for spitting on his shoe," Kylie said. "He tried to inject me with something, but Shy peed on his shoe and he freaked."

Jack ruffled the dog's head. "Good girl."

"I've been mauled, stabbed and beaten," Turk complained. "Can I get some fuckin' medical attention?"

The lawmen answered as one. "No."

"What about you, miss?" Skully asked. "Are you okay?"

The buxom blonde burst into tears.

"Her name's Dixie," said Kylie.

Skully squeezed the sobbing woman's shoulder. "Dixie, what's wrong?"

She spilled her guts.

Kylie chimed in, squeezing Jack's hand as she repeated some of the things Mario had said in between trying to drug and choke her.

Jack absorbed the women's words. In the back of his mind he calculated ways to shield Kylie from having to testify.

"You and your friend should think twice before repeating any of that, Dix," Turk said. "You know what happens to rats."

The threat burned through Jack's body and ignited images. Suddenly he was back in Manhattan, seeing Connie Valachi's tortured body. All the disgust and fury he should have felt then, he felt now. He pinned Mario "Turk" Mancini against the wall, one hand around the bastard's throat, the other on the trigger of his Glock.

Turk wheezed. "Yo. Cocksucker, I—"

"Shut up." Jack pressed the nose of his revolver against the man's forehead.

The door swung open and Jessie pushed in. "What's going on? Oh, my God. Kylie, you're *bleeding.*"

"I'm fine," Kylie called.

Jack didn't take his eyes off Mancini. He didn't ease up on the pressure. "Get out of here, Jess."

"Jack." Jessie's voice was fragile, almost childlike. "Who is this man? Is he the one—"

"Goddammit, Skully," Jack said. "Get the women out."

"And miss Turk getting his due?" Dixie shrieked. "Forgettaboutit."

"Time to go, Sunshine." Skully hustled Dixie from the

room. Jessie wouldn't budge, so he physically removed her, then returned.

Jack tightened his hold on Mancini. "You, too, Kylie."

"No."

"That's right, sweetheart," wheezed Turk. "Stay right where you are." He smiled at Jack. "You're not gonna pop me. It would traumatize your girlfriend. Besides, that would be murder. Got murder in your soul, Chief Reynolds?"

When he thought about how this man had tried to kill Kylie? And what he'd try to do to her if she testified against him? "I'm thinking of it as a preemptive strike."

"Crank it down a notch, Reynolds." Skully said close to his ear.

Jack's temples throbbed. Skully knew his history. He knew about Connie Valachi.

"Let it go," the marshal added.

Jack knew he was right. He couldn't save a dead woman. Or the world. And he couldn't protect Kylie, or anyone else, if his ass was in prison. Still, Mario "Turk" Mancini represented what Jack hated most. Corruption. Immorality.

The mob.

"Don't do it, Jack." Kylie moved in and wrapped her arms around him, her front flush to his back. "I need you. Jessie and Maddie need you."

He heard Shy whimper, felt the wonder-dog leaning against his leg.

"Remember the water tower? You asked me to trust you. You told me to let go." Kylie tightened her hold. "Whatever this man represents, whatever ghosts he conjured, we'll conquer those demons together. Trust me, Jack."

He'd come back to Eden to reconnect with his soul. He thought about his family. He absorbed the strength and love emanating from Kylie.

Jack holstered his gun and passed Mancini off to Skully.

He let go, and when he and Kylie were alone, he turned around and held on.

To Kylie. To life. To love.

Kylie melded into him, sighed.

"What are you thinking, Tiger?"

"I'm thinking I've had enough excitement for a lifetime."

"It's not over yet, hon. There'll be an investigation. A trial. A shitload of gossip."

She looked up at him with a watery smile. "That's nothing compared to the thought of losing you."

He thought about her nosedive into the lake. "Funny. I had a similar thought today." Jack cradled Kylie's sweet face and poured his heart into the kiss.

When he eased away, she smiled. "What are *you* thinking, Jack?"

"I'm thinking there's no *maybe* about it. I love you, Kylie. With an intensity and depth I can't describe. It's..."

"Scary?"

He smiled. "Wonderful."

"That does it," she said, her eyes shining with tears. "You're stuck with me for life."

He moved in for another kiss. "Paradise."

CHAPTER FORTY-SIX

"GRANDMA, HOW ARE WE going to make a profit if you keep hoarding the stock?"

"But I love these."

Kylie watched the seventy-year-old woman lace up a pair of high-top sneakers. Part of Dixie's new animal line—cheetah print with metallic black laces. "But don't you think they're a little young for you?"

"Young schmung."

Kylie's mom, who'd been restocking the gum ball machine, chimed in. "Consider it an investment in advertising, Kylie. Every time your grandma leaves the store in a new pair of shoes, at least two people come in asking for something similar. Must be the spring in her step."

Kylie frowned. "Yeah, but, is the spring because of the shoes or because she's suddenly dating two men?" Kylie still couldn't believe it. Then again, it had been one surprise after another for the past three weeks.

Her grandma shrugged. "I'm exploring my options."

"With Max *and* Mr. Keystone?"

"Who knew they could be so charming?" she said as she two-stepped in her Cheetahs. "Although, Max is the better kisser."

Kylie grimaced. "Too much information."

Oblivious, the silver-haired woman glanced at her rhinestone watch. "Dance lessons at the firehall in twenty minutes. Thanks for the shoes!" she called as she shuffled out the door.

"Send some customers our way," shouted Kylie's mom.

"Ever since you two returned from the cruise, you've been getting along," Kylie said. "It's weird."

"After learning about what happened while we were gone, we decided life's too short."

Her mom and grandma weren't privy to *everything* that had happened, only the things Marshal Skully and Jack had deemed necessary. They'd branded details regarding Travis's past and other mob-related issues as classified. Which was fine with Kylie. She didn't want that stuff in her mom and grandma's head. Not that they hadn't gotten an earful. There'd been plenty of buzz about Frank Cortez and his multiple affairs, not to mention his death, which the locals attributed to his monstrous gambling debts.

Meanwhile, Jessica had started working at the store and she and Maddie were on the mend emotionally.

Faye had returned from Florida and she and Stan were on the mend, too.

Turk was looking at life in prison and Travis was looking forward to a new life in France, thanks to some fancy footwork by Noah Skully.

Dixie was currently in protective custody, though she'd nixed WITSEC, deciding instead to take her chances and relocate on her own when the trial was over. Kylie couldn't decide if that was brave or stupid, but she'd promised to keep McGraw's stocked with *Bada-Bling!*

The only fly in the ointment was Spenser, who'd been threatening to return home ever since he'd heard rumors about Kylie's run-in with mobsters. He'd given her hell. He'd given Jack hell. She was *still* waiting for Spenser's blessing regarding their relationship.

"Earth to Kylie."

Kylie blinked out of her musings and saw her mom snagging her purse from under the cashier counter. "Sorry, Mom. What?"

"I said I'm going to run next door to J.J.'s for a chocolate Coke. Would you like one?"

The woman had been hooked on chocolate Coke since

as long as Kylie could remember. Same ol', same ol'. Kylie smiled. "Sounds great."

Her mom left and Kylie busied herself rearranging the designer shoe display. As she'd hoped, the high-end merchandise had been a hit with the ladies of the Garden Club, teenagers and tourists had glommed on to the sneakers by *Bada-Bling!* and she'd even managed to entice more conservative shoppers with a line of quality but affordable work boots. Variety in pricing and stock had been key. She'd trusted her gut and her instincts had paid off.

Business during the week of the Apple Festival had tripled, keeping Kylie busy and distracted from the fallout of the Mancini mess. Her mom and grandma had returned from the cruise that weekend, and seeing Kylie and Jessie were overwhelmed, pitched in. She hadn't been able to get rid of her mom yet, but honestly, she was a surprisingly decent saleswoman.

As for the renovations, the McGraw women as well as everyone else in Eden had been impressed. They all applauded Travis's creativity, which made Kylie happy—knowing it had been a labor of passion for the man—but it made her sad because she couldn't pass on the compliments. During their face-to-face goodbye, Travis had said that this time he wouldn't come back, nor would he keep in touch. She'd been hurt, but then Jack had said, *"Travis is a smart man. He knows the only way to protect his new life is by cutting all ties. Plus, he considers you a friend. He's not going to risk reintroducing danger into your life. He'd want you to move on and engage in new adventures, like him."*

Logically, she knew Jack and Travis were right, but that didn't stop her from sending positive thoughts her friend's way. Other than that, she didn't make waves. She'd sworn off shaking things up...for a while, anyway.

Once she had enough money saved up to buy out Spenser, she'd go another bout with breaking tradition. Until then, she'd sworn Jack to secrecy.

Jack didn't see things her way—the man had a hard time

separating family from business—but he'd agreed to respect her wishes. She liked that about him. The fact that they could agree to disagree and still be madly in love. Mostly because they seemed to disagree a lot.

The bell over the door tinkled and Kylie turned, expecting her mom with two chocolate Cokes. Instead, she saw Jack with one chocolate Coke. Shy trotted in and curled up on a pink shaggy rug.

"Ran into your mom in J.J.'s," he said, passing Kylie the red-and-white-striped soda cup.

She sipped and smiled. Partially because the cola tasted so good. Partially because Jack looked so good. The most handsome man in the universe. *Ever.* Still in uniform, still on duty. "What were you doing in J.J.'s?"

He massaged the back of his neck and turned a little red.

"Oh, no," she squeaked, lowering her voice to a whisper. "Don't tell me you were buying condoms."

"We've been a little active, Tiger. I needed a new box." He rolled back his shoulders. "It gets worse. I ran into your grandma."

"In J.J.'s?"

He nodded.

"What? Was she buying more lipstick?" She'd already been through four new shades since she started dating Max.

"Not exactly."

She blanched. "Condoms?"

"She referred to them as *love gloves.*"

Kylie covered her ears. "La, la, la."

Jack smiled. "Hey. I hope I can still get it up when I'm in my seventies."

So did she, but that wasn't the point. "We're talking about my *grandma.* And Max. Or maybe Mr. Keystone." Or maybe both. "Oh, God."

"I know," he said, still smiling. "Weird. But kind of sweet, too."

"I knew it. A big marshmallow."

"What?"

"Never mind." She sipped more cola, then stashed the cup on a coaster under the counter. "Speaking of folks hooking up, I've been thinking about Noah Skully."

"What about him?"

"He's been dropping by Eden quite a bit."

"Following up on Travis's case," Jack said.

"He's bought three pairs of shoes in here over the past three weeks. From Jessie," she said, then waggled her brows.

"Don't go there, Tiger."

"I know it's too soon for her, but I think he's interested and patient and...I'm just saying. I think he'd be good for her and she deserves a good man. Don't you think?"

Jack bit back a smile and readjusted her new metallic red glasses. "You've got a heart of gold, Kylie McGraw."

She quirked a cheeky grin. "Yes, I do. And you're lucky to have me."

"Smartass."

"Someone's got to keep you on your toes," she teased.

"You do that and them some, Tiger." He backed her against the wall, in between the counter and the gum ball stand. He kissed her dizzy, filled her head with erotic thoughts.

The bell above the door tinkled.

Jack eased back.

"We're closed!" they called in tandem.

The door shut and Jack reached over and locked it.

Her body tingled with anticipation. "Are you going to take me here against the wall? Or carry me into my office and ravish me on the desk?"

His blue eyes glittered. "Are those my only choices?"

Her pulse skipped. "You have a better idea?"

He reached into the inner pocket of his EPD jacket.

She expected a condom. She got a ticket. No, two tickets. To Tokyo.

"We leave in two weeks. We'll be gone for three."

"But—"

"Jessie and your mom can run the store. They don't mind. I already asked."

"But—"

"Mayor Wilson was more than happy to give me the time off, and Deputy Ziffel is more than capable of leading the squad."

"I—"

"Your savings are designated to the store. Mine are designated to family. That includes you."

Tears burned her eyes. "You've thought of everything."

He pulled her into his arms. "One more thing. Spenser will be filming at Mount Fuji. We'll be meeting up with him."

She wasn't sure which shook her more. Anticipating the thrill of seeing Mount Fuji? Or the dread of her and Jack facing her brother for the first time as a couple. "Spenser hasn't quite adjusted to the thought of you and me. I think he's uncomfortable with the sex part."

"Well, he's about to get more uncomfortable."

"Why?"

"I asked your mom and she told me to ask Spenser."

"For what?"

"For your hand in marriage."

Shy's tail thumped wildly against the hardwood floor.

Kylie smiled down at the dog. "I…I guess she approves," she rasped, her heart thumping as wildly as Shy's tail.

Jack raised a brow. "Don't you?"

She clutched the tickets to her fluttering chest. "I don't know what to say."

"Say you love me."

She beamed. "I love you, Jack. Always have, always will."

Jack kissed her sweetly, then deeply. "I love you, Kylie. Madly. Deeply. As for kids…definitely worth the risk."

Overwhelmed, Kylie jumped up and wrapped her arms and legs around Eden's chief of police, the boss of her heart. "I would have married you even if you hadn't said that," she said honestly.

Jack kissed her, then whisked her to the back of the shoe shop, away from Shy's happy dog eyes. "*Now* I'm going to ravish you."

EPILOGUE

Two and a half weeks later

JAPAN WAS MORE BEAUTIFUL than Kylie had ever dreamed. But she couldn't imagine being here without Jack. Not just because they were madly, deeply in love, but because he appreciated the culture as much as she did. Because he wanted to sample new experiences and wasn't afraid to take chances.

Jack was a fantastic travel buddy and an imaginative, attentive lover. It occurred to her that she would've been just as pleased if they'd taken a week's vacation to Manhattan's China Town. Out of Eden was out of Eden, and paradise was anywhere with Jack. But they were here, because Jack wanted her to have her dream trip. And today they were specifically at a small town near Mount Fuji because he wanted to ask Spenser for her hand in marriage.

Kylie hugged herself against the frigid air. Jack was right. She should've worn more layers under her parka. It was flipping freezing. "What if he punches you?"

"He won't."

"What if he says no?"

"He won't."

Kylie squinted at Jack through her prescription sunglasses. "How can you be so sure?"

"Because Spenser knows me."

"Better than me?"

His sexy mouth twisted into an ornery smile. "Only in

certain matters." He gestured to the quaint bar where they were supposed to meet her brother. "Can we go inside now, Tiger? It's fricking freezing."

She peered up the snow-covered volcano. "That's what we get for coming in the off season."

"Are you complaining?"

"Are you kidding? It's not like I wanted to climb Mount Fuji. I'm not crazy like Spenser. I just wanted to see it."

"I bet it's just as breathtaking when you're looking at it through a window with a cup of hot chocolate in your hands."

Kylie rolled her eyes. "All right. Let's go inside."

As soon as they entered the cozy establishment, Kylie started peeling off her parka. She had one arm out of her sleeve when she spied Spenser. Her heart raced and her stomach pitched. She'd never been so excited and scared to see him. She tried to remember where she was, to respect the more reserved culture of Japan, but when her big brother pulled her into his arms, she hugged him as tight and long as she could. It had been months. Way too long. She eased back and slapped his chest. "That's from Grandma. She says it would be nice if you remembered where home is." She stood on her tiptoes and kissed his cheek. "That's from Mom. Same message."

Spenser chuckled. "Duly chastised." He smiled down at Kylie. "You look good, kitten. Considering you were nearly killed a half dozen different times last month."

She rolled her eyes. "You're exaggerating."

"Not by much." He frowned at Jack. "I hope you're taking better care of her these days."

"Good to see you, Spense." They shook hands, then hugged.

No thrown punches, Kylie thought. So far, so good.

Jack helped Kylie out of her parka, then put his arm around her waist. Kylie noticed Spenser noticing and felt his unease. "This is weird," she said.

"You have no idea," Spenser said.

Uh-oh.

"I told myself to get over it, but I can't," he said to Jack. "I'm not comfortable with you and Kylie sleeping together, as in having sex. Out of wedlock," he clarified.

"That was direct," Jack said. "And old-fashioned."

"And embarrassing," Kylie whispered. "Jeez, Spenser."

"Are you going to marry her?" Spenser asked Jack.

"Yes."

"When?"

"We haven't set a date. I haven't even asked her yet," Jack said. "Not officially. I wanted to ask you first."

Spenser grunted. "What? You think I'd say, no?"

"No. But I wanted to do the right thing. Ask you face-to-face, and since you had no plans to come home anytime soon," Jack said, "here I am."

Kylie squirmed in the awkward silence that followed. "O-o-o-kay. Great!" she said a little too brightly. "So we're all on the same page. Jack asked for your blessing, sort of, and you gave it—sort of. We're getting married. Woo-hoo!" she whooped, hoping to break the tension. "All that's left are the details."

"Like setting the date," said Spenser.

"The sooner the better," said Jack.

"What about now?" Spenser raised a challenging brow. "I know this man."

"What kind of man?"

"A spiritual man. There's a temple not far from here."

"Would it be legal?"

"It would be spiritual."

Kylie gawked at the men. "What is this? Some bizarre game of chicken?"

"You could have a big church wedding later," Spenser added. "Back in the States."

Jack glanced at Kylie. She noted the twinkle in his blue eyes. He wasn't opposed to the idea of a spontaneous wedding. Not one iota. "Because it would make my brother feel better about us sleeping together?" she asked.

He noted the breathtaking vista then, smiling, grasped her hand and kissed her palm. "Because it feels right."

"Romantic." She basked in the warmth of his loving gaze, reveled in his adventurous spirit. "Let's do it."

Spenser blinked. "Really?"

"Your sister the caretaker is also a risk taker," Jack said.

"No risk in marrying the man I love."

"Don't get sappy on me," Spenser said. "And no tongue kissing until after the ceremony."

Kylie was basically tuning her brother out at this point. She was thinking about marrying Jack in a temple in Japan—a spiritual union. She could scarcely breathe.

Jack squeezed her hand and winked. "Let's do it."

Heart full, she leaned in for a kiss.

Spenser interceded, handing her and Jack cups of sake. "Here's to a long and happy life together."

They toasted and drank.

Kylie shuddered as the strong alcohol burned a path down her throat. At least it wasn't a Cosmo.

"One last thing before we go," Spenser said. He shoved an envelope across the table. "Your wedding present."

Intrigued, Kylie opened the envelope and unfolded a long document. She read and frowned. "You signed the store over to me."

"Should've done it a long time ago," Spenser said as he refilled their glasses. "You love shoes. I don't. You live in Eden. I don't. I can go on," he said when she continued to stare.

Kylie switched her focus to Jack.

"I didn't say a word."

She looked back to her brother. "I wanted to buy you out."

"What? After all the sweat and blood you've put into McGraw's over the years? And besides, you're family, Kylie. I won't take money from you."

"But you expect me to take the store from you?"

"It's a gift. A wedding gift. For you and Jack and your children."

"What about your children?" Kylie asked. "What about tradition?"

"Time to shake things up, little sister. I recently invested in The Explorer Channel. That's what I'll pass on to my children. If I ever have any."

"A wife would help," Jack teased.

"Let's not make this about me." Spenser offered more sake and another toast. He uttered two clichés back to back and Kylie burst into tears.

"I'm sorry," she blubbered. "It's just that that's so you, Spenser. So wonderful."

Jack snatched the cup from her hand. "No more sake for you," he said with a genuine smile. "Or you," he said to Spenser. "Until after the spiritual event. Then we'll get drunk and do something crazy together."

More tears flowed—not because she was tipsy, but because she was with the two men who meant the most to her in the whole world. And because they both loved her so much "This is the best dream trip ever."

"It's been your only dream trip," Jack teased.

"But the best." She cradled Jack's handsome face. "Look away Spenser."

"Why?"

"I'm going to tongue kiss my almost husband."

"Oh, hell."

"Do it."

"I'm going to the men's room."

"Even better," Kylie whispered as her mouth met Jack's. It meant a longer kiss.

* * * * *

*September 2010 will mark the release of
Beth Ciotta's thrilling new adventure-filled
contemporary romance from HQN Books,
INTO THE WILD!
Read on for an exciting sneak peek!*

"What do you mean they canceled the shoot?"

"An executive decision." Spenser McGraw thumbed his cell to vibrate and placed it beside his empty beer bottle as Gordo Fish, his friend and professional sidekick, dropped into an opposing chair. The popular café buzzed with good cheer, offsetting the men's grim expressions.

They'd flown from the Scottish Highlands to South America to film an episode for the popular cable show *Into the Wild*. Spenser was the talent. Gordo was the one-man camera/audio crew. He met his friend's baffled stare. "They want to introduce an element of danger into the show."

Gordo frowned. "You're kidding."

"Nope."

"Something tells me Necktie Nate is behind this."

The nickname they'd given to Nathan Crup, their new Armani-suited producer. "Probably."

"Has that asshole watched even one show over the past five seasons?" Gordo complained. "We've battled extreme elements and hostile people. We've survived mud slides, cave-ins, avalanches and assorted injuries."

"None of them life-threatening."

"Like hell. What about the time I got food poisoning in Cairo?"

Spenser found it amusing that a man who'd endured extreme temperatures, snake bites and altitude sickness would label the time he'd hugged the porcelain throne in a ritzy hotel room as a near-death experience. "You weren't even close to dying."

"I ended up in the hospital."

"Because you called an ambulance."

Copyright © 2010 by Beth Ciotta

HQN™

We *are* romance™

New York Times and **USA TODAY** bestselling author

LORI FOSTER

returns with three steamy classics in one tantalizing new volume.

No one ever said seduction was easy....

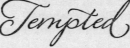

featuring *Little Miss Innocent?*, *Annie, Get Your Guy* and *Messing Around with Max*.

"Lori Foster delivers the goods."
—*Publishers Weekly*

www.HQNBooks.com

PHLF-444

She may resist his bite,
but she can't resist his charms...

MICHELE HAUF

Werewolf princess
Blu Masterson refuses to
let her seductive vampire
husband consummate their
arranged marriage with
his bite. But when she
uncovers her pack's secret
plot to destroy the vampire
nation, she struggles to
choose between the only
life she's ever known and
the sexy vampire she might
just be falling in love with....

HER VAMPIRE HUSBAND

Available now!

"Dark, delicious and sexy."
—*New York Times* bestselling author Susan Sizemore

HQN™
We *are* romance™

www.HQNBooks.com

PHMH499

REQUEST YOUR
FREE BOOKS!

2 FREE NOVELS
FROM THE ROMANCE COLLECTION
PLUS 2 FREE GIFTS!

YES! Please send me 2 FREE novels from the Romance Collection and my 2 FREE gifts (gifts are worth about $10). After receiving them, if I don't wish to receive any more books, I can return the shipping statement marked "cancel." If I don't cancel, I will receive 4 brand-new novels every month and be billed just $5.74 per book in the U.S. or $6.24 per book in Canada. That's a saving of at least 28% off the cover price. It's quite a bargain! Shipping and handling is just 50¢ per book in the U.S. and 75¢ per book in Canada.* I understand that accepting the 2 free books and gifts places me under no obligation to buy anything. I can always return a shipment and cancel at any time. Even if I never buy another book, the two free books and gifts are mine to keep forever.

194 MDN E4LY   394 MDN E4MC

Name	(PLEASE PRINT)

Address	Apt. #

City	State/Prov.	Zip/Postal Code

Signature (if under 18, a parent or guardian must sign)

Mail to **The Reader Service:**
IN U.S.A.: P.O. Box 1867, Buffalo, NY 14240-1867
IN CANADA: P.O. Box 609, Fort Erie, Ontario L2A 5X3

Not valid for current subscribers to the Romance Collection
or the Romance/Suspense Collection.

Want to try two free books from another line?
Call 1-800-873-8635 or visit www.morefreebooks.com.

* Terms and prices subject to change without notice. Prices do not include applicable taxes. N.Y. residents add applicable sales tax. Canadian residents will be charged applicable provincial taxes and GST. Offer not valid in Quebec. This offer is limited to one order per household. All orders subject to approval. Credit or debit balances in a customer's account(s) may be offset by any other outstanding balance owed by or to the customer. Please allow 4 to 6 weeks for delivery. Offer available while quantities last.

Your Privacy: Harlequin Books is committed to protecting your privacy. Our Privacy Policy is available online at www.eHarlequin.com or upon request from the Reader Service. From time to time we make our lists of customers available to reputable third parties who may have a product or service of interest to you. If you would prefer we not share your name and address, please check here. ☐

Help us get it right—We strive for accurate, respectful and relevant communications. To clarify or modify your communication preferences, visit us at www.ReaderService.com/consumerschoice.

MROM10

PRESENTING THE SIXTH ANNUAL
MORE THAN WORDS™ COLLECTION

Five bestselling authors
Five real-life heroines

Little by little, one person at a time, we can make our world a better place. The five dedicated women selected as this year's recipients of Harlequin's More Than Words™ Award have done just that, by discovering a seed of compassion and nurturing it to effect real change in their communities. To celebrate their accomplishments, five bestselling authors have honored the winners by writing short stories inspired by these real-life heroines.

Visit

www.HarlequinMoreThanWords.com
to find out more or to nominate a real-life heroine in your life.

Proceeds from the sale of this book will be reinvested in Harlequin's charitable initiatives.

Available now wherever books are sold!

PHMTHV6744

Beth Ciotta

77360	EVIE EVER AFTER	___ $6.99 U.S. ___	$6.99 CAN.
77298	EVERYBODY LOVES EVIE	___ $6.99 U.S. ___	$8.50 CAN.
77207	ALL ABOUT EVIE	___ $6.99 U.S. ___	$8.50 CAN.

(limited quantities available)

TOTAL AMOUNT	$ _____
POSTAGE & HANDLING	$ _____
($1.00 FOR 1 BOOK, 50¢ for each additional)	
APPLICABLE TAXES*	$ _____
TOTAL PAYABLE	$ _____

(check or money order—please do not send cash)

To order, complete this form and send it, along with a check or money order for the total above, payable to HQN Books, to: **In the U.S.:** 3010 Walden Avenue, P.O. Box 9077, Buffalo, NY 14269-9077; **In Canada:** P.O. Box 636, Fort Erie, Ontario, L2A 5X3.

Name: _____
Address: _____ City: _____
State/Prov.: _____ Zip/Postal Code: _____
Account Number (if applicable): _____

075 CSAS

*New York residents remit applicable sales taxes.
*Canadian residents remit applicable GST and provincial taxes.

HQN™

We *are* romance™

www.HQNBooks.com

PHBC0410BL